Frederick Temple

ARCHBISHOP OF CANTERBURY

This book is for
the Right Reverend Frederick Stephen Temple,
sometime Bishop of Malmesbury,
in gratitude for much help and encouragement

Frederick Temple

ARCHBISHOP OF CANTERBURY

A Life

PETER HINCHLIFF

CLARENDON PRESS · OXFORD
1998

Oxford University Press, Great Clarendon Street, Oxford OX2 6DP

Oxford New York

Athens Auckland Bangkok Bogota Bombay
Buenos Aires Calcutta Cape Town Dar es Salaam
Delhi Florence Hong Kong Istanbul Karachi
Kuala Lumpur Madras Madrid Melbourne
Mexico City Nairobi Paris Singapore
Taipei Tokyo Toronto Warsaw

and associated companies in
Berlin Ibadan

Oxford is a trade mark of Oxford University Press

Published in the United States
by Oxford University Press Inc., New York

British Library Cataloguing in Publication Data
Data available

Library of Congress Cataloging in Publication Data
Frederick Temple, Archbishop of Canterbury: a life
Peter Hinchliff
Includes bibliographical references
1. Temple, Frederick, 1821–1902.   2. Church of England—Bishops—Biography.
3. Anglican Communion—Bishops—Biography.   I. Title.
BX5199.T4H54   1997   283'.092—dc21   97–38247
ISBN 0–19–826386–4

1 3 5 7 9 10 8 6 4 2

Typeset by Pure Tech India Ltd, Pondicherry
Printed in Great Britain on acid-free paper by
Biddles Ltd., Guildford and King's Lynn

FOREWORD

by the Right Reverend Lord Runcie

It is a privilege inevitably tinged with sadness to commend this last substantial fruit of Peter Hinchliff's scholarly career. His sudden death, only a year before retirement from one of Oxford University's most distinguished chairs, came as a grievous shock to his many friends, depriving the Anglican Communion of an historian who could speak from within the tradition, who was both wise and candid. Yet it is a blessing for us that in his last months he was able to bring this book so near completion. We owe a debt of gratitude to his former student, Dr Grayson Carter, for the tactful way in which he has overseen the text, and tied up the loose ends which remained in it.

Frederick Temple is in many ways an appropriate subject for Peter Hinchliff to have chosen. There is, of course, their common experience of Balliol, the college which Peter served so faithfully, and which he loved until the end of his life. But beyond that is a deep interest in the education of the young; a common heritage of liberal Catholicism in an Anglican context; an undemonstrative faith that put the sacramental life at its heart, but which additionally was not prepared to avoid the tussles of the intellect experienced by those of mature belief. Appropriate too is the work of rediscovering and doing justice to a neglected predecessor of mine. In 1900 Frederick Temple revived archiepiscopal residence in the city. It had been neglected for centuries. The move played no small part in giving 'Cantuar' world-wide visibility.

Peter Hinchliff was never afraid to champion unfashionable causes. He lacked the brusqueness of manner which led one of Temple's former pupils ruefully to describe the former Headmaster of Rugby as 'a beast, but a just beast'. Nevertheless, Peter could speak his mind with courage in the face of injustice, most especially as he contemplated the tragedies of apartheid and the eventual triumph of freedom in his own native South Africa. This book is a fitting memorial for a man of integrity and quiet courage.

September 1997
St Albans

ACKNOWLEDGEMENTS

I have received a great deal of help in locating and using the archival source material for this book. Bishop F. S. and Mrs Temple have been welcoming and encouraging in allowing me access to family papers. I have received particularly generous help from Miss Melanie Barber, the deputy librarian at Lambeth Palace Library and herself the original cataloguer of Archbishop Temple's papers, who has drawn my attention on a number of occasions to items which I might otherwise not have come across. All the staff at Lambeth Palace Library have been unfailingly patient and helpful as, indeed, have the staff of every library or archive I have needed to visit. The librarian and voluntary staff of the Devon and Exeter Institution were particularly anxious to find out-of-the-way material for me. I must also record my gratitude to my colleagues in Oxford for their willingness to allow me a sabbatical term for the writing up of the book.

P. H.

Following Peter Hinchliff's death in 1995, the publication of this work has been facilitated by the kind and dedicated assistance of Dr Grayson Carter, whose additional comments appear within square brackets in the text.

CONTENTS

1. Formative Years   1

2. Educating England   25

3. Rugby and Religious Controversy   52

4. The School and the Schools Commissions   90

5. Yet More Controversy   119

6. Bishop, Husband, Father   136

7. Religion and Science   166

8. The Ecclesiastical Edifice   194

9. Ceremonial, Schools, and Sweated Labour   214

10. The Rest Cure   254

11. A Crowning Achievement   281

    Index   297

1

Formative Years

There has never been a full biography of Frederick Temple. Soon after he died W. Francis Aitken published a short popular life of the archbishop, and in 1906 seven of his friends co-operated in producing a two-volume work entitled *Memoirs of Archbishop Temple*, to which each of them contributed a memoir of one period of his life. The whole was edited by Ernest Sandford,[1] who had been a boy at Rugby during Temple's headmastership, his domestic chaplain and archdeacon when he was Bishop of Exeter, and a lifelong friend and admirer. Sandford also contributed a supplement, which occupies about half of the second volume and was subsequently published separately. This is really an attempt at assessing the personality and achievements of the archbishop and is unashamedly partisan. The whole work, produced with the active co-operation of the archbishop's widow, is what its title implies—a very personal account of how Temple's friends remembered him. It is a rich collection of anecdotes, for the friends wrote and asked other friends to contribute *their* memories, too. But it is not a biography. The archbishop hated the making public of what he considered private—and he was a very private person. He once said, 'I hope no one will write my life', which probably explains why there never was a biography of the kind that were written about other Victorian bishops. But because there has been no biography, Temple has been somewhat underestimated and neglected. An attempt to write an account of his life after nearly a hundred years can hardly be regarded as an invasion of his privacy and he is well worth writing about. He lived through an interesting period of English history and was involved in some of its most significant events. He died at the very end of the Victorian era, the age of Oscar Wilde. One of the last things he did was to crown Edward VII. But he had been born in 1821, the age of Jane Austen and the

---

[1] E. G. Sandford (ed.), *Memoirs of Archbishop Temple by Seven Friends*, 2 vols. (London, 1906), ii. 252. The work is referred to in the text below as 'the Sandford Memoir'.

aftermath of the Napoleonic wars. England had changed beyond belief.

The decade between 1820 and 1830 was itself a period of rapid and radical change, in spite of the fact that the wars with France between 1793 and 1815 had ended in the restoration of the ancient French monarchy. British politics and British society were subject to all sorts of radical developments though, because there was no written constitution, the changes were not obvious to the naked eye. Parties had become very different from the personal cliques and factions which they had once been and by 1830 the monarchy itself was less politically significant than before the war. Moreover, war itself had changed in style and objective. In the eighteenth century the consequence, and often the cause, of European war had been the acquisition of territory; and peace had been made by its formal redistribution. By the nineteenth century the permanent territorial gains and losses were less often on mainland Europe itself; more often on off-shore islands or in colonial dependencies. Older beliefs—that colonies were necessary for the maintenance of a mutually reinforcing system of both strategic strongholds and trading monopolies—were beginning to give way to the view that they were expensive to run. But rapidly growing manufacturing industry at home needed new sources of raw material and outlets for its finished products. A new orthodoxy was developing—provided one's goods were better than those of one's rivals, all that was needed was a free market. Nevertheless, maintaining an international network of trade involved Britain, sometimes very unwillingly, in what has sometimes been described as a 'creeping' imperialism.

In 1820 men in their thirties, who were just establishing themselves in their careers, would not remember a time before the wars. Many of them, indeed, would have found the wartime army a natural place in which to look for employment. In the aftermath of the war the army, as a fighting organization, had less need of officers. For those of them who belonged to the 'middle' classes, between the landowners on the one hand, and the labouring classes on the other, the colonial acquisitions—old and new, creeping and otherwise—provided useful, if not very lucrative, scope for continued employment. The middle classes, even those who were 'profession' rather than 'trade', were dependent on finding for themselves some source of income. What marked them off from those above them, was the fact that they possessed no solid, land-based wealth. And they were often acutely aware of the difference.

When Frederick Temple had become Bishop of Exeter, and might be thought to have arrived safely among the superior classes, he wrote to the young woman to whom he was engaged (Beatrice Lascelles, grand-daughter of two earls) about

...the totally different view of life taken by your class, the propertied class, and my class, the wage-earning class. Of these two classes, the former is at the upper end of the social scale; the latter of the lower. But they overlap. For the proper-tied class includes families with small properties. And the wage-earning class includes judges, bishops, the learned professions, and the merchants, as well as the labourers in the field. And besides overlapping, members of one class are perpetually passing over to the other in each direction. So that the views of life taken by each class may easily be compared.

And as I say they are very different. For the social duties, the duties of maintaining kindly intercourse by the aid of joint pleasures are held far higher by one than by the other. To me and my class such duties hardly present themselves as duties at all, but as refreshments: and whenever they put them-selves into a higher place we resent it and push them back. We assign to them very little time. We take very little trouble about them.[2]

Certainly, there was very little time or room for social entertainments in the life of the young Frederick Temple. His father, Major Octavius Temple, had been commissioned in the army in 1799 and promoted to the rank of brevet-major in 1814. Stationed with his battalion at Mar-seilles during the Waterloo campaign, Major Temple served out the rest of his military career in the Mediterranean, in Malta and then, from 1819, in the Ionian Islands where he was first sub-inspector of militia and then, a year later, resident in Santa Maura (Levkas) for the lord high commissioner. Finally, Temple became, in 1828 when he was forty-four, administrator of the ecclesiastical and municipal revenues of the island of Corfu.

These were not very important appointments, though they may indicate that the major was regarded as a relatively able administrator. They also reflected, very neatly, the post-Napoleonic character of the Europe of that time. In a brief intermission in the wars between Britain and France, the Treaty of Amiens of 1802 had required the former to abandon all her colonial conquests of earlier years. In most cases this involved handing over the territory to a French satellite, so that the Cape of Good Hope, for instance, had to be surrendered to the Batavian Republic rather than to the Prince of Orange.

[2] Family papers in the possession of the Right Revd F. S. Temple: Frederick Temple to Beatrice Lascelles, 28 June 1876.

France did, however, recognize an independent republic of the Ionian Islands, once Venetian territory, under the protection of Russia and Turkey. The islands again fell under French control by the Peace of Tilsit of 1807 but, by the final rearrangement of Europe of 1815, they became once more an 'independent' republic, this time under the protection of Great Britain. The British crown was represented by a lord high commissioner on Corfu who was assisted by 'residents' on the other islands. Although there was an Ionian civil and ecclesiastical establishment, the effective administration of the islands was in the hands of British officials backed by a detachment of some 3,000 regular soldiers at a time when the total population of the islands may not have been larger than 200,000.[3] This curious, quasi-colonial arrangement lasted a surprisingly long time despite the existence of a popular movement for a genuine independence. Major Temple's position was that of a smallish cog in the administrative machine.

Information about Frederick Temple's early life is limited. There are some valuable letters, written to his mother from school and university. The most important of these are printed in the Sandford *Memoir*, which also contains some of his siblings' recollections of their childhood.[4] There is, in addition, a curious work entitled *The Early Associations of Archbishop Temple.*[5] This was published not long after Temple died and is a mixture of bad local, school, and family 'history', all very sentimental and often far from reliable. The author thought, for instance, that Major Temple had a good claim to be regarded as one of the 'heroes of Waterloo'.[6] Much of it is the kind of speculation which guide books peddle as history. And it has the hagiographer's delight in discovering events which appear to cast long shadows. Describing, for instance, the way in which Temple, as Bishop of Exeter, used to attend many of the annual meetings of the old boys of his Devonshire school, the author says:

On one occasion as the picture [a group photograph] was about to be 'snapped' the Bishop observed to the Old Boy next him (Mr A. R. Payne, of Milverton) that the scene had been changed, for instead of standing, as in former years, in

---

[3] Sandford (ed.), i. 5.

[4] The letters are in the possession of the Right Revd F. S. Temple, grandson of the archbishop.

[5] F. J. Snell, *The Early Associations of Archbishop Temple: A Record of Blundell's School and its Neighbourhood* (London, 1904).

[6] Ibid. 80.

front of the main building, they were gathered under an arch. 'Ah!' replied Mr Payne quickly, 'that is to indicate your future position, my lord. You are to be *Arch*bishop.' This remark, read in the light of Temple's translation to Canterbury, deserves to rank as a prophecy.[7]

Most of the book may, in fact, be safely disregarded.

Frederick Temple was born in 1821, during the time when his father was the resident in Santa Maura, and until he was nine he lived in the Ionian Islands. The family appears, in what would have been the usual contemporary way of dealing with colonial situations, to have had very little to do with the locals though the children enjoyed life on the islands. They seem not to have worshipped in the local churches (in spite of the fact that part of the major's job was the administration of ecclesiastical revenues) for Mrs Temple used every day to read the psalms and lessons from the Book of Common Prayer with her children to make up for the absence of regular English services.[8] Nor do they seem to have learned much of the language. It is true that the Sandford *Memoir* speaks of the Temple children 'mixing so freely with servants or others as to acquire, without labour, some fluency in Italian and modern Greek' and says that Frederick was able to write letters to his sisters in Italian.[9] But it is extremely difficult to reconcile this with the way in which Frederick was made to learn classical Greek and Latin.[10] And the Temples lived their own English life and appear not to have acquired Mediterranean habits.

The home seems quite unaffected by the accident that it was not in England. The religion of the mother was eminently practical, unspeculative, unquestioning. So strong was this influence on the children that the superstitions of nurses and servants and other foreign modes of thought among which they were brought up made no impression upon them.... his mother took Cornwall with her to the Ionian Islands, and it was in a Cornish home that the child grew up to boyhood.[11]

The one thing that seems really to have impressed itself on the children's memories was an earthquake on Santa Maura in 1825.

When the family returned to England in 1830 Major Temple bought a farm called 'Axon', near Culmstock in Devon, which was to be their home for some years. Octavius himself did not occupy it for long for in

---

[7] Ibid. 322.   [8] Sandford (ed.), i. 18.   [9] Ibid. i. 21, and ii. 402.
[10] See below, 8.   [11] Sandford (ed.), i. 22.

1833 he was offered an appointment as lieutenant-governor of Sierra Leone. The colony had been founded in 1787, in the same year as the creation of the Society for the Abolition of the Slave Trade, by an alliance between missionary, commercial, humanitarian, and political interests. It was intended to be a free settlement for slaves, but its constitution was too utopian and its climate too inhospitable: it had very soon almost collapsed.[12] It was refounded in 1790 and soon afterwards was reinforced both by some white settlers and by a large body of freed slaves from North America. Since Britain was by then embroiled in the wars with France the government began to take some interest in the settlement and it may have hoped to use it as a naval base for the protection of the sea route to India.[13]

Zachary Macaulay, a dour, devoted Evangelical and a bitter opponent of slavery, was governor from 1793, acting for the St George's Bay Company, which had been formed by William Wilberforce, Granville Sharp, and other Evangelicals in a bid to enlist some commercial support and to rescue the settlement. He imposed a savage discipline upon the settlers and made them more self-sufficient but he could not prevent the settlement being pillaged by the French. His own health was ruined by the unhealthy climate. Nor were relations with the surrounding people very easy. It seems to have occurred to no one that the liberated slaves, in spite of the colour of their skin, would be as alien in West Africa as any white. It was with considerable relief that the company handed the settlement over to the British government. In 1808 Sierra Leone became a crown colony and in 1821 it was joined with Gambia and the Gold Coast, whose origins had been commercial rather than abolitionist, to form British West Africa with a governor in Freetown. This amalgamated territory had a hardly less troublesome history than the original Sierra Leone. Its governor committed suicide after suffering a disastrous defeat at the hands of a powerful and disciplined Ashanti army, the colony was the cause of continuous and acrimonious quarrelling between abolitionist and commercial interests at home, and it was the subject of a parliamentary commission of enquiry. Moreover its constitutional and administrative position was always changing and its stability was further undermined in the 1830s by the rapidity with which

[12] Robin Furneaux, *William Wilberforce* (London, 1974), 124.
[13] R. Hyam and G. Martin, *Reappraisals in British Imperial History* (London, 1975), 48.

administrators followed one another in Sierra Leone. Major Temple himself died in August 1834, less than a year after accepting the appointment.

It is not easy to discover anything at all about his brief period of office. The family remained at Axon, so its opinion of the major as a colonial administrator is not worth a great deal and must be based on his work in the Ionian Islands rather than on anything that happened in West Africa. His children remembered him as a hot-tempered but painfully just and honest man, of whom they were proud.[14] But their pride has an overtone of pathos because his departure and early death meant that several of them would hardly remember him at all. He evidently displayed some sympathy for the condition of the agricultural labourers in England during the short time that he lived in Devon, though it seems that he may have had a reputation for wanting to make the Poor Laws tougher.[15] He may also have been in favour of the repeal of the Corn Laws and is said to have been the only man in the parish who supported 'the radical candidate' (presumably in the election of 1830).[16]

Very shortly after his appointment as lieutenant-governor, Major Temple was also made superintendent of the Liberated Africans Department.[17] This office, which recalled the original purpose for which the first settlement had been founded, was maintained at considerable expense and was much resented by those who represented the commercial interests. It would have identified the lieutenant-governor with the abolitionist lobby and it is worth remembering that the year of his appointment was also the year in which slavery was legally abolished throughout British territory. In the Sandford *Memoir* the major is described as 'a man of unusual force of character, original, impulsive, resolute; an ardent reformer in matters of Colonial administration; and for a time regarded by the authorities with no great favour'.[18] There is, however, no way of discovering what that assessment was based on.

From the time that the family returned to England from the Mediterranean, Frederick lived at home in the West Country until he was sent to Blundell's School in Tiverton not long after he turned twelve. His early education, whether in the Islands or in England, had been

---

[14] Sandford (ed.), i. 5. [15] Ibid. i. 6, but cf. Snell, 73 ff. [16] Snell, 75.
[17] Sandford (ed.), i. 6. [18] Ibid.

almost entirely directed by his mother. What it consisted of was graph-
ically described by his older sister in these terms:

She taught us to read and write; she taught arithmetic, with very little
knowledge of arithmetic herself, by steady repetition. She had a key to the
sums in the arithmetic book, giving the answers. If a sum was brought to
her and the answer was wrong, she drew her pencil through it and made no
further remark. It had to be done again until it was done right. When it was
time for my brothers to begin Latin the same system was adopted. She could
not pronounce it, but Frederick had to learn a few lines each day, always
repeating the old until seven or ten pages had been learnt. Then the first
four or five pages would be left, and a further advance made. That went on
day by day and year by year until he was twelve years old, and he went to
school knowing his grammar perfectly, as no other boy knew it. He was unable
to pronounce it, and was therefore put to the bottom of the school but he
soon picked up the pronunciation and rose rapidly. Euclid was the same. She
did not understand a word. He began to do so as he advanced in the subject and
could substitute one expression for another, or change the order of the letters.
She interposed . . . 'Say it', she ordered, 'precisely as it is here,' touching the
book.[19]

And it seems that, if the young Temple had any ideas of his own,
his mother would say, 'Freddy, don't argue; do your work.'[20] He
was plainly a devoted son but he was later to express a vigorous
disapproval of the kind of teaching which contented itself with conveying information.[21]

   Life would have been difficult in other ways, too. Frederick was the
thirteenth child of a family of fifteen, only eight of whom survived
beyond childhood. His mother, Dorcas, was a daughter of Richard
Carveth of Probus near Truro in Cornwall. There is some suggestion
that neither family approved very much of her marriage to Octavius
Temple[22] but it seems to have been a happy one. By the time Dorcas
settled at Axon one of her sons and one (or possibly two) of her
daughters had married and set up their own homes: one son had
been drowned at sea. But even four children, two of them late teenage
girls, were hard for the major's widow to maintain on not very generous
resources. She received a pension of £100 a year from the government[23]
and the farmland was let so that she retained only the house in which
the family lived. They had never been rich enough to afford any

---

[19] Sandford (ed.), i. 17 ff.   [20] Ibid. i. 20.   [21] See below, 149, 239.
[22] Sandford (ed.), i. 4 and 13 f.   [23] Ibid. i. 24.

luxuries: they now became actually poor, sometimes unable even to afford fuel for a fire in the winter.

Her husband had believed that no small boy should spend more than two hours a day on his lessons[24] and Mrs Temple—for all her determination to make her sons acquire knowledge even if they did not understand it—was also a devoted and obedient wife. The young Frederick was allowed to spend a good deal of his time out of doors working on other people's farms or running messages for his mother. The 'work' was often as trivial as weeding or picking stones out of fields but it earned a little money and, after he had become archbishop, Frederick claimed that he had learned as a boy to 'plough as straight a furrow as any man in the parish'.[25] [He also became accomplished at covering great distances on foot, one account claiming that as a youthful Devonian Temple could walk up to fifty miles a day and up to six miles an hour.[26]]

The flavour of those years is marvellously conveyed by a story told by his older sister. Axon was in a very lonely place and there were no shops near at hand.

My mother wanted some nails; she told Frederick that he was to walk to Wellington, five miles off; she gave him a bag and some money. She had not the least idea of the price of nails; but he thought he was to bring back as many nails as his money would pay for. Time went on, he was expected home. My mother began to walk anxiously about, looking up the road, hour after hour. At last was seen the little boy with his bag of nails, so heavy that he could not carry it; he could only just give it a little swing along the road. And when she saw what she had done she burst into tears, very unusually for her, and petted and comforted her poor little exhausted boy.[27]

It is an evocative picture of a very obedient and over-conscientious small boy trying, in the conventions of the day, to be the man of the house; and his mother preserving an austere, determined self-discipline which would allow her love for her children to manifest itself only on very rare occasions.

It would seem to have been typical of Dorcas Temple that she should have refused more than one offer from Blundell's School to take her sons without a fee: she would not send the boys till she could pay for them. But Blundell's was where their father had wanted them to go so, when it was possible, that was where they went. But they had to go on

[24] Ibid.   [25] Ibid. i. 26.   [26] Snell, 255.   [27] Sandford (ed.), i. 25.

the most economical terms possible.[28] The school seems to have catered largely for the sons of moderately well-to-do land-owning families most of whom lived not very far away. Boys could, therefore, get home quite often in term. The education provided was typical of the grammar school of the time, concentrating on mathematics and the classics and probably not making over many demands of an academic kind. 'I have sometimes thought', Temple said when he had become a bishop, 'that we might have been taught to learn a little more than we did, and have wished that the course had been a little wider than it was; yet I have never been able to get rid of the feeling that if you have few lessons and a great deal of time, to those who, like myself, took a great interest in the work, you found an incentive in the freedom you were left.'[29] Even as a boy, however, he had been ready to pass judgement on the quality of the teaching he received. 'I do not think Mr Mills a very good mathematician...' he had told his mother bluntly when he was thirteen.

He wrote frequently and regularly to her and the letters[30] provide an often naïvely frank but rather charming picture of a somewhat priggish but clever boy, not entirely at home in what was plainly a rough environment. He told his mother on 1 February 1834, not long after arriving at the school, 'I now learn Ovid's *Metamorphoses* and *Old Testament* in Latin. I can assure [you] I find it rather hard but all the boys of my class come to me for an explanation of any difficulty that may chance to arise.' When he had first arrived at Blundell's, at the age of twelve, he was put in a class of seven-year-olds, because of the eccentricity of his early education.[31] But he was soon able to tell his mother that he was head of his class and likely to get a prize. The humiliation of being put with boys half his age drove him to fight his way up the forms so that in little more than twelve months he had passed through the junior school. He was still reporting to his mother that he was head of his class when he had but a year to go and was already in the top form in the whole school.[32]

He seems always to have been short of paper to write on. In what must have been a very unsatisfactory arrangement for an intelligent and

---

[28] Sandford (ed.), i. 29.   [29] Ibid. i. 34 f.

[30] Family papers in the possession of the Right Revd F. S. Temple: 'Schoolboy letters from Blundells'. There are several original letters in this file, some of which are printed in Sandford (ed.), i. 29–38.

[31] Temple's own account of his schooldays in Sandford (ed.), i. 32.

[32] Family papers: Letters to his mother; letter dated 22 Mar. 1838.

hard-working pupil, the boys were not provided with paper nor were they permitted to go and buy it in the town. The man who sold it only came to the school on certain days, so poor Dorcas was always being asked to send him further supplies. Nor was this the only problem that worried him. The boys swore in a fashion he found offensive and some of them became drunk from time to time. He was laughed at for his rustic and home-made clothes and he was teased and bullied a good deal. There were savage fights of which he won some and lost some and remembered both all his life. [Much later, Temple admitted to a group of schoolboys that 'a great deal of fighting' had occurred at Blundell's:

We used to fight each other on rather small provocation *con amore*, and, as a general rule, if two fellows fought they became intimate friends before they left the school, and dated their friendship from the time they used their fists on each other's faces.[33]

Temple's overall assessment of his standing at Blundell's at the time was characteristically concise:] 'The boys like me very much in the school, but not much out of it.'[34]

[Young Frederick's relationships with the other boys may have suffered by his boarding, at least for a portion of his schooling, 'outside the gates'; that is, with a Mrs Folland in nearby Cop's Court (later renamed the Retreat) on Gold Street.[35] In the eyes of many young Blundellians 'boarding out' was regarded as a mark of social inferiority.] Yet Temple seems not to have been unpopular since he often reported to his mother that he had been invited to visit other boys, or to accept a lift home from them. And he and his brother regularly spent Sunday evenings and the weekly half-holiday with the family of a friend in Tiverton.[36] His company seems always to have been in demand but he made no show of his popularity, such as it was. The only reason why there was any mention of the invitations he received was that he was always careful to obtain his mother's approval before accepting them and, indeed, never went home to Axon on the briefest visit without first getting permission to do so. Regularly sending the boys off home seems to have been a part of the Blundell's regime and the Temples, who lived eight miles away, seem not to have found it very easy to make the journey.

---

[33] Snell, 192 f.   [34] Sandford (ed.), i. 33.   [35] Snell, 166.
[36] Sandford (ed.), i. 33.

There had been one period when even Dorcas was willing to encourage visits home. Frederick was confirmed during his first year at Blundell's, when he was not yet thirteen which was then thought very early. The clergyman responsible for preparing the boys did no more than gather them together and make them recite the catechism. Dorcas's children had all been required to get the catechism off by heart by the time they were six years old and it may have been for this reason that she decided that the preparation at Tiverton was insufficient. For the last few weeks before the confirmation Frederick was required to return home each weekend by coach so that she could prepare him herself. He would arrive at Axon at about noon, would be presented with a list of specially prepared questions, spend the afternoon answering them and then be sent back to school in the evening.

Dorcas had made the children learn the catechism in the same way in which they had learned everything else. It was taught, Frederick's sister was later to recall, 'systematically, but not a word was said about it'.[37] So little explanation was ever offered to the children that the girl had imagined that Jesus had been crucified *four* times because she assumed that each gospel was describing a different event. Frederick's confirmation classes seem to have been some improvement on this: he was to maintain that no one was ever better prepared than he. Though this recollection dates from the last few months of his life,[38] there is no reason to suppose that it was inaccurate. And he demanded books which would enable him to find out more. When he was sixteen he asked for his mother's Bible which had cross-references: there would be no misapprehension in *his* mind about the significance of parallel passages in the gospels. Another book for which he asked at this time was Robert Nelson's *Companion for the Festivals and Fasts of the Church of England* and this may provide a rare clue to the kind of Christianity in which the boy was being brought up.

Nelson was a seventeenth-century non-juring layman educated by George Bull whose *Defensio Fidei Nicaenae* was much admired by the High Churchmen and even, in the second half of the nineteenth century, by Dr Pusey and his party in Oxford. Bishop Bull's very celebrated treatise had maintained that the Patristic writing on the Trinity before Nicea had been entirely consonant with Nicene and post-Nicene orthodoxy. It was thus much read and used by those of the High Church

---

[37] Sandford (ed.), i. 18.   [38] Ibid. i. 19 and 30 f.

party who wished to uphold the idea that Christian truth, once committed to the saints, had been entirely unchanging thereafter. Nelson, who was Bull's biographer, belonged very firmly in this tradition of what were usually called 'Church principles'. It seems, therefore, that it was in the pre-Tractarian High Church tradition in which Frederick Temple was being educated by his mother. This school of thought, with a 'high' doctrine of Church, Sacraments and episcopal ministry; earnest, disciplined, and sincere, was not much different from the Tractarians in theology but had none of the interest in ceremonial or elaborate vestments of the later Anglo-Catholics. It was, however, a sincerely devout Christianity; not at all the 'high and dry', indolent formalism which was how it was represented in Tractarian historiography.[39]

Frederick was evidently encouraged to observe the Church's calendar. Both brothers were made to promise that they would continue at Blundell's the practice that their mother had taught them of reading the psalms and lessons when they were not able to attend service at church. And they seem to have kept their promise.[40] Frederick was confirmed young and encouraged to receive the Sacrament more frequently than was usual at the school. He was taught that religion was serious and required obedient discipline. There was nothing fussy or superficially emotional about his religion but being a churchman was the important thing.

It is said of almost all the leading figures in English religious history of the middle and later nineteenth century, whether they turned out to be radical theologians or Roman Catholic cardinals, that they had been Evangelicals in early life. It is true that on closer examination, such a statement often turns out to be somewhat misleading or to signify little more than that the person concerned came from a family which had Evangelical connections. In Temple's case there is not the slightest suggestion that there was any Evangelical influence in his early years. Dorcas was no 'enthusiast'. When her Methodist sister used to ask her when she had been converted, her reply was the crushing, 'I don't know what you mean. I have tried to please God all the days of my life.'[41] And

---

[39] Scholarship in the last fifteen years has radically revised the view of the old-fashioned High Churchmen as 'high and dry'. One of the best accounts of their tradition and influence is in F. C. Mather, *High Church Prophet: Bishop Samuel Horsley (1733–1806) and the Caroline Tradition in the Later Georgian Church* (Oxford, 1992), particularly the first chapter.

[40] Sandford (ed.), i. 33.

[41] Ibid. i. 18.

it was so clearly Dorcas who was the dominant influence on the young Frederick that it is difficult to believe that a piety alien to her under-standing of Christianity would be allowed to affect him.

His father was remembered as saying, 'I don't *care* about the mir-acles.'[42] But the context and therefore the significance of the remark has not survived. Frederick's paternal grandfather had been a clergyman and a close friend of Dr Johnson's Boswell. The indirect connection with Johnson would tend to confirm that the Temple family were High Church in the old-fashioned sense though they remembered Boswell's influence on his friend as 'mischievous'.[43] At all events, the Revd Wil-liam Temple had died a quarter of a century before Frederick was born and can have had no direct influence, for good or ill, on his upbringing. The clergymen who looked after the parish in which Axon fell seem to have been worthy and conscientious but not very memorable. And the story of Frederick's confirmation suggests that those in Tiverton, even Mr Sanders his headmaster whom he was later to make archdeacon of Exeter, did not quite measure up to the standard of 'Church principles' observed by the boy and his mother.

Perhaps the most important consequence of Frederick's education at Blundell's was that it led directly to his admission to Balliol College, Oxford. Dorcas Temple could certainly never have afforded to send him to a university; and scholarships, particularly at Oxford, tended to be available only to persons from a specified family, area, or school. It happened that one Peter Blundell, an earnest Puritan merchant of the sixteenth century (who had begun life as a poor boy in Tiverton and ended it a very wealthy bachelor) had founded the school and directed his executor to set up scholarships at either Oxford or Cambridge. The complicated scheme which resulted gave the school a privileged rela-tionship with Balliol. By the nineteenth century, there were always two Tivertonian scholars and two Tivertonian fellows; the scholars succeed-ing more or less automatically to the fellowships on their becoming vacant.[44]

It appears that Frederick at first thought in terms of Cambridge rather than Oxford (partly for fear 'of getting among the Puseyites'[45]) and of Wadham rather than Balliol; but the scholarship at Wadham was

[42] Sandford (ed.), i. 33
[43] Ibid. i. 4 and 8 f.
[44] John Jones, *Balliol College: A History 1263–1939* (Oxford, 1988), 84 f.
[45] Sandford (ed.), ii. 435.

limited to 'natives' of Great Britain. 'Of course I cannot try; Balliol now is the only thing I can look to. This makes me feel a still greater preference for Cambridge as there almost everything is open. But if I can get to Balliol that would be the best.'[46] Even the Blundell scholarship, however, was hedged about. Candidates whose fathers were not resident in the borough had to find ten householders willing to consent to their candidature. This done, Frederick was admitted to the examination. Two candidates survived that hurdle and the final decision between them was taken by the governors of the school. There was, apparently, a good deal of canvassing and one of the governors who was persuaded of Temple's merits and who continued thereafter to be his friend and patron, was Sir Thomas Dyke Acland, a member of a prominent Devon family. But while the headmaster, Dyke Acland and other governors, and some local notables congratulated the boy—he was still only sixteen and a half—not everyone was pleased. At least one person complained 'that an interloper and foreigner had no right to benefit from the scholarship'.[47]

Nor, when he arrived at Balliol in April 1839 did Temple find that Blundell scholars were wholly welcome in the college. By this time, the connection, which had originally been enormously to the financial benefit of the college, had come to be thought of as an academic *dis*advantage. The Blundell fellowships were the only ones in the college for which there was not an open election.[48] Richard Jenkyns, the Master of Balliol, was a determined (though very conservative) campaigner for raising academic standards. He did not, therefore, much approve of the Blundell's connection. It seemed to him merely to preserve two fellowships in the college (which only possessed a total of ten or eleven) for bucolic and not very brilliant Devonians. Even after Temple had got a double first (in classics and mathematics) before he was twenty-one, Jenkyns said to him, 'You *Blundell* scholars have certainly very great advantages; coming up as you do very *inferior* men into the society of very *superior* men; some of you are improved by it, and some are not.'[49]

---

[46] Ibid. i. 36.

[47] Family papers in the possession of the Right Revd F. S. Temple: file marked 'Letters from school and university' (though it contains papers from other periods in the archbishop's life as well), Henry Sanders to Frederick Temple letter marked 'Received 28 December 1838'.

[48] John Jones, 'Sound Religion and Useful learning: The Rise of Balliol Under John Parsons and Richard Jenkyns, 1798–1854', in John Prest (ed.), *Balliol Studies*, (Oxford, 1982), 95.

[49] Sandford (ed.), i. 48.

Much of Temple's path through the university was characterized by a slightly shamefaced acceptance of the advantages of this system, and there were always those at hand to remind him just how lucky he had been. But his good fortune had not made him wealthy. His time at Balliol was one of poverty, of cold, of no luxuries, and of very hard work.

The 1830s were not a peaceful time in the university. If Keble's assize sermon of 1833 had marked, as Newman thought, the start of the Oxford Movement, by the time Temple arrived at Balliol in 1839 Newman himself had delivered his *Lectures on the Prophetical Office of the Church* and his *Lecture on Justification*. He had, in other words, begun to wrestle with the issues which disturbed his Anglicanism, raised doubts about ecclesiastical authority, and began to break the Movement into its component parts. Two years later came the publication of *Tract XC* which alienated those sympathizers with the original aims of the Movement whose convictions were really those of the older High Churchmen. And the questions about authority were beginning to be asked in a much more radical sense. The Noetics of Oriel had been asking them for almost two decades, though at first in a muted form. This brilliant group of fellows who found themselves associated with that college were at first characterized by a concern to develop a natural theology in which reason would be called in aid of revelation. With such a concern John Keble and even Newman himself could live without too much discomfort. But when the debate turned upon such issues as the nature of religious truth and its relation to scientific truth and, the fundamental question of all, how one determines the truth of religious belief, it was not just the future Tractarians who became uneasy.

The more radical Noetics, like Baden Powell and Thomas Arnold, believed that science and theology were independent spheres of enquiry, though not sealed off from one another. One should not limit scientific enquiry by dogmatic preconditions but theological discussion should be open to be influenced by secular truth. More conservative Noetics like Whately thought that such a view gave science and secular knowledge far too final an authority and allowed no place for revelation.[50] For the Tractarians the important thing was to maintain an integrated view of the world in which the Church, the nation, and the university would all have their place and reason would be subject to revelation and

[50] Pietro Corsi, *Science and Religion: Baden Powell and the Anglican Debate, 1800–1860* (Cambridge, 1988), 83–142.

tradition. It was a world view which, for its proper realization required that there should be a close and natural relationship between the Church and the nation, and between the Church and the university. Because such relationships had come closest to existing in the Middle Ages, Tractarian hopes for their return seemed, in one sense, reactionary. Yet the fact that the longed-for relationships were ideal, meant that they had never really existed. Therefore to hope for them was radical and innovative. The formal religious character of much of the university's life—assent to the *XXXIX Articles of Religion*; regular attendance at chapel; ordination as a requirement for holding a fellowship; even the quasi-liturgical form of the degree ceremony—needed to become real, *ex animo*, an expression of a devoted life.

Their opponents were no less critical of the empty formalities of university religion. When Arnold asked for an openness towards the life and thought of the world, he was not intending that there should be a wholly secular university devoid of religion. What he wanted was a religion which would be real if undogmatic; which would allow one freedom to think; which did not continually force one to choose between tradition and reason. This, after all, had been the ideal which he had set himself to create at Rugby when he had been appointed headmaster in 1828. In 1833 his *Principles of Church Reform* had been published in which he had argued forcefully along Lockian lines, that theological differences were inevitable because there could be no demonstration of doctrinal correctness. Two years later he had attacked the ecclesiasticism of the Tractarians, whom he designated the 'Oxford Malignants', in the *Edinburgh Review*. When Temple arrived at Balliol a new generation of liberals, influenced by Arnold, was just beginning to open up a debate which would become more vigorous in the 1840s. It was at first somewhat disguised by the controversy over the Oxford Movement and its revival of 'Catholicism' in the Church of England but it gradually became more openly concerned with the nature of a university and the nature of all knowledge. Did one know things to be true because authority—one's teacher, the university, tradition, revelation, the Church, God—told one so or because one had investigated the matter critically for oneself, reasoned it out logically on the basis of the evidence available and reached a rational conclusion? So the debate was not about abstract or general questions of politics or religion but about the actual shape of Oxford itself. As pressure for the reform of the university built up and the theological liberals argued for the second approach, it became apparent that the issues were not separate from one another. However hard one might try to remain uncommitted it would be almost impossible not to take sides. Having done so, one would be labelled as belonging to that side in every remaining battle of the war.

While Temple was an undergraduate and the university was convulsed by all these questions, the senior common-room at Balliol was itself something of a battlefield. It contained W. G. Ward, an ardent Newmanite who took all Newman's ideas to an extreme with an immense enjoyment of his own brilliantly logical mind. Stripped of his degrees in 1845 on an occasion when Newman was saved from the same fate by the interposition of the proctors' veto, he was to become a Roman Catholic. The college chaplain, Frederic Oakeley, belonged to the same school of thought, though he left the college in the year in which Temple started his studies there. But not all the fellows were Tractarians. Archibald Campbell Tait was a Broad Churchman, a Scot who retained much of the character of a Scottish Moderate and a firm believer in the importance of a National Church. He was to be one of the 'four tutors' who delivered the famous public attack on *Tract XC* in 1841. Master Jenkyns was a conservative who mistrusted Tractarians and radicals alike. And in the same year in which Temple was elected into his Balliol scholarship there was elected into a fellowship of the college, though he had not yet taken his degree, Benjamin Jowett who was to become the centre of a Balliol/Rugby group of young liberals.[51]

It was probably not an easy time in which to be an undergraduate. One gets the impression that Frederick Temple tried very hard, through the turmoil and excitement into which the university and the college were thrown by all this controversy, to keep his head and keep it down. He got on with his work but could not avoid thinking about theological issues or the personalities who expounded them. He continued to write regular letters to his mother from which glimpses of these events, ideas and people emerge.[52] The young man who wrote these letters had changed little from the boy who had written to his mother from

---

[51] Peter Hinchliff, *Benjamin Jowett and the Christian Religion* (Oxford, 1987), 17–25, 35 f. and 69–72.

[52] Family papers in the possession of the Right Revd F. S. Temple: 'Oxford letters to Mother 1839–42'. These are copies (all except one are typed copies), almost certainly typed by Beatrice Temple herself, who learned to type in order to help her husband when he was archbishop. The fact that one of the letters has been wrongly dated '1903' suggests that the copies were made in that year. The likelihood is that they were copies made by Beatrice in the year after the archbishop died and probably for the *Memoirs* edited by E. G. Sandford. Most of the letters appear in whole or in part in the supplement to the memoirs (Sandford (ed.), ii. 408–62).

Blundell's. He worked enormously hard, enjoying theology and mathematics (for which he had a particular ability and flair) and reading prodigiously in, for instance, Herodotus and Cyril of Jerusalem, admiring the ideas of Carlyle, the romantic poetry of Wordsworth, and the thought as well as the poetry of Samuel Taylor Coleridge. He was still anxious to have his mother's approval, telling her those anecdotes of his week which he thought would please her. He found most undergraduates superficial because they lived according to artificial rules of good manners rather than Christian morality or even sincerity. He could not afford to drink wine (and later became a teetotaller on principle) so he was only able to entertain friends to breakfast, in any case the cheapest meal of the day. He was uneasy with the kind of undergraduate who was more interested in dogs and horses than in work and found it difficult to think of anything to talk to them about. He was deeply shocked by the casual dishonesty of the college servants, almost as if he had never encountered petty thieving before.

Most of his friends were other scholars and it is interesting (because it reflects a surprisingly romantic, almost mystical streak in this otherwise very practical and down to earth young man) that two of his closest friends were Arthur Hugh Clough and Matthew Arnold. He greatly admired some of the ideas of Matthew's father, professor of Modern History in the university as well as headmaster of Rugby, liked his 'manly' style but wished that he was not quite so much of a Whig (for Temple regarded himself throughout his undergraduate years to be a thoroughgoing Tory: it went with his Church Principles and the enjoyment he derived from the daily chapel service of the Book of Common Prayer).

In spite of his earlier fears of getting among the Puseyites he seems to have been fascinated by many of the ideas of the Oxford Movement. He told his sister, soon after he arrived in Oxford, that

The Pusey party are the quietest, most unobtrusive set you can imagine; they have been much misrepresented, and that of course helps rather than injures them; they are exceeding clever men, and decidedly, as far as man can judge, they embody the chief part of the religious portion of Oxford. After this you will easily imagine how they can get on; while their most pernicious doctrines are defended from their character of religion and talent, or concealed beneath this external plausibility, it must be extremely difficult to check them. Besides this their opponents, by confounding themselves with the Low Church party, have ranged against them those who would be their most useful assistants.[53]

[53] Sandford (ed.), ii. 438.

But within six months he was telling her that he had been reading several of the *Tracts for the Times* and thought 'they have done incalculable mischief by working their opinions so incautiously and so strongly that the natural sense of their writings is very different from what they meant to express'.[54] He then proceeded to analyse the argument of Isaac Williams's tract on 'Reserve in Communicating Religious Knowledge'. There is actually a hint in his letter that Temple thought Newman had written the tract— 'this very man is noted for bringing forward the Atonement in his parish Sermons at every opportunity....'[55] Again, he defended the tract on the ground that it has been misunderstood and added 'it is a great pity that leading men who can write so beautifully as they do should not be more careful not to mislead others'.

Allowing for the fact that his letters of the period were all written to his family at Axon and that he would have had to explain to his mother, and justify, any opinion he expressed, it appears that Frederick remained essentially loyal to the 'Church principles' which he had been taught. He was as scathing about 'the free and easy religion of the Wesleyans, who generally think religion to consist in rapturous emotions' as his mother had been about her sister's enthusiasm for conversion. What first attracted him about the 'Newmanites' was their 'severe, stern self-watching and self-denial'.[56] And Pusey's sermons which he thought were marvellous—immensely long but seeming to pass in a flash—moved him to even greater efforts of discipline so that he debated with himself the advisability of giving up his breakfast parties during Lent. Newman he found less attractive:

He has a very musical voice and a great command over it, but I confess I do not like his tone; he *whines* so very much. His manner of reading is, however, generally admired. He is an exceedingly ugly man, and his features are the hardest I ever saw; his face looks as if it was made of board, and he has the appearance of great austerity.[57]

Of his tutors at Balliol only Ward, who taught him mathematics, was a 'Newmanite'. He invited Frederick to dinner and gave him volumes of Newman's sermons. The undergraduate found him intellectually quite brilliant, fascinating, full of ideas—some quaint, some extreme, some compelling. Robert Scott, conservative High Churchman, he took longer to get to know. He had assumed at first that he also was a 'Newmanite' and then was surprised to discover that Scott was actually

[54] Sandford (ed.), ii. 439.   [55] Ibid.   [56] Ibid. ii. 441.   [57] Ibid. ii. 444.

very critical of the way that Tractarian ideas were developing. Many High Churchmen, who had originally sympathized with the tracts, became alienated in the years between the publication of Hurrell Froude's *Remains* and the appearance of *Tract XC*. But, having got to know him, Temple came to be on easy terms with Scott, whose Churchmanship was most like that which his mother had inculcated in him. After Scott was married and went to be incumbent of the college living of Duloe in Cornwall, Frederick went to visit him there and sympathized with his exertions over the *Lexicon*, particularly because Liddell—when only the last and most difficult of the entries remained to be done—took himself off and claimed to be unwell.[58] Scott plainly liked and felt sorry for the very poor, slightly awkward Blundell's scholar and tried to get help for him to make his life a little easier.[59]

Frederick heard that Oakeley had said that Froude's *Remains* had 'done more good than any [book] yet published' but only partly agreed with Tait's riposte that 'Froude was the only [Tractarian] person who had yet given his real opinions'.[60] It is, in fact, Tait's influence on the young Temple which is most difficult to assess. Their close relationship was to last for the rest of Tait's life, though it went through some very difficult periods particularly just after the publication of *Essays and Reviews*.[61] And it was Tait whose protégé Temple really became. The older man always held the younger in very high regard, strove to promote his interests and continued to press his claims on every possible person of influence.

Temple's 'Church principles' did not prevent his liking and associating with those of a very different outlook. He much admired Thomas Arnold who had made of Rugby a citadel of Broad Church opinion. He had liked his strong personality, his common sense and his championing of justice and fairness. Nor did theological differences prevent his admiring Tait for much the same reasons—his kindness and common sense, his open-mindedness, his honest and forthright expression of opinion.

The fact that in the late 1830s Tait tended to gather round himself the very clever young men,[62] the scholars of the college who were Temple's

---

[58] Henry George Liddell and Robert Scott collaborated in the compilation of the *Greek–English Lexicon* published in 1843.

[59] Sandford (ed.), i. 46 f.

[60] Ibid. ii. 445.

[61] See below, 73–4, 76–81.

[62] See R. T. Davidson and W. Benham, *Life of Archibald Campbell Tait, Archbishop of Canterbury*, 2 vols. (London, 1891), i. 107.

natural friends, may explain something of his influence on Temple. The Tractarians and anti-Tractarians were, in a very real sense, fighting for the souls of the undergraduates. Tait was one of those who was most determined and most effective. Long afterwards, Benjamin Jowett was to say to Tait: 'Supposing that the Tutors of Balliol had been all like Ward, where should I have been? [I] remember with gratitude that at the time of my election to the fellowship you helped keep up some light of common sense in me.'[63] People like Jowett and A. P. Stanley (whom Temple admired enormously) had ceased to be undergraduates at the moment at which Temple became one, but Tait continued to gather round himself intelligent, broad-minded undergraduates and to introduce them to the slightly older people of Jowett's generation. And, indeed, Temple and Jowett became friends even before the former also became a fellow of the college. As colleagues, they became very close friends and associates. And a great many of the closest friendships Temple made between going up to Balliol and himself becoming headmaster of Rugby in 1858 were with people who also belonged to this particular circle.[64] While the members of the circle differed in their beliefs and opinions, for they were too young for their views to have hardened, they were all interested in new ideas and willing to argue and to think about them. It is clear, too, that they were thought of as a group and that Tait was regarded, even by more senior people, as the centre of the circle. Tait was tolerant, determined not to be controlled by any Church party, and he had his feet very firmly on the ground of the wider world. He was, in that sense, the obvious person for critical and enquiring young men to attach themselves to.

The dons of the day did not much interest themselves in the doings of undergraduates. Most of them were under no obligation to teach. A very few fellows were appointed as tutors by the head of each college and they alone had any real responsibility for undergraduates. In Oriel in the early 1830s tutors had first begun to develop closer relationships with the young in what eventually came to be thought of as the typical Oxford pattern.[65] Tait is usually given the credit for introducing this much more personal style of tutorial relationship into Balliol,[66] though

[63] Lambeth Palace Library: Tait Papers Personal Letters: vol. 78, fos. 268–71.

[64] See below, 35–6.

[65] S. Rothblatt, 'The Student Sub-culture and the Examination System in Early Nineteenth Century Oxbridge', in L. Stone (ed.), *The University and Society*, (Princeton, 1974), 264.

[66] Jones, *Balliol College*, 190 f.

it is clear that Temple himself was on terms of friendship with all the tutors with whom he had dealings. It is not surprising that his tutors thought well of him. He was one of the cleverer undergraduates of his generation and one of the hardest working. A whole network of prize exercises, essays, and examinations, had been set up in the university in the hope of raising standards.[67] Temple went in for a number of them and did well enough for even Master Jenkyns to think well of him in spite of his Blundell's background.[68]

A Blundell fellowship fell vacant at about the time when he completed his undergraduate career but Temple could not be elected into it because he was not yet twenty-one. Arnold's death in 1843 meant that the headmastership of Rugby was vacant and Tait was appointed there. He was anxious that Temple should go with him as assistant master, the first time he was able to offer him some direct patronage. But Jenkyns also offered him the position of lecturer in mathematics at Balliol in the place of Ward who had just been forced to resign. Temple declined to go to Rugby because it was too much identified with undogmatic Christianity. He told his mother:

When I first came to Oxford I came with a strong feeling against Puseyism, and naturally was thrown very much into the society of Tait and those men who oppose Pusey most strongly. At the same time, I felt somehow that what I now saw and heard was not what I had been taught from childhood; that though the Doctrines were nominally the same, yet they were understood in a very different sense...that in fact I had thought I was believing one thing when I was really believing another. I began to find that the principle of obedience, which you know was made the keystone of our education, was professed by Pusey and his friends and was acted upon, but was really, though not nominally, rejected by the others. You must have seen that I was changing, but I do really think that it was merely my head that was changing and not my heart, and that what appeared inconsistent was really the truest consistency. My mind is now, I believe, made up as to the *line* of doctrines I should accept, though I should not pretend to say that it is on particular points. And now I am thinking of going to Rugby, the place of all others from which the most violent opposition to such doctrines has proceeded...[69]

In the end he decided that he was still too much of a churchman for Rugby. He stayed at Balliol and was subsequently made a fellow of the college.

---

[67] Rothblatt, 288.   [68] Sandford (ed.), i. 48 f.   [69] Ibid. ii. 463.

At this stage of his life Temple was a tall, rather raw-boned young man; serious, very strong physically, with an abrupt but diffident manner. His face was bony, with prominent nose and jaw, very dark hair and strongly marked eyebrows; not really a handsome face but certainly not a bland one. His voice was harsh and he spoke with a marked Devonian accent which was not in those days necessarily a social disadvantage[70] but, when allied with other signs of awkwardness, might mark him as unused to polite society. He, however, made no attempt to disguise his poverty or the fact that he was decidedly provincial and lacked polish. [At the same time, it must be acknowledged that at Blundell's, and more especially through Tait's influence at Oxford, Temple had been transformed, socially and intellectually. Though traces of his provincial accent, youthful brusqueness, and congenital austerity remained to the end of his days, these proved no disadvantage in his rise through the various layers of social and clerical respectability. Temple's considerable intellectual attainments, his remarkable capacity for hard work, and his important Balliol connections (which would serve him well, particularly at critical moments), all combined to overcome numerous obstacles and ease his elevation through the ranks of the educational and religious establishments. The foundation had been laid.]

[70] J. R. de S. Honey, *Tom Brown's Universe: The Development of the Victorian Public School* (London, 1977), 231.

2

*Educating England**

Temple was not one of the tutors of Balliol. He taught mathematics in the college (but only the very brightest of undergraduates—potential 'double firsts'—would take mathematics) [and lectured in classics and logic. He had no personal or pastoral responsibilities for a group of undergraduates as the tutors did. While not exercising the kind of lasting influence which Tait or Scott had upon him, Temple did manage to make an abiding impression on a number of Balliol undergraduates. James John Hornby, who later became Provost of Eton, retained a vivid recollection of Temple's kindness and buoyant personality, as well as his college lectures. Together with most first-year undergraduates, upon coming up to Balliol Hornby was placed in the large Euclid lectures in the college hall, presided over by Temple. Although the subject matter was rather dull, Temple's animated style brought the whole exercise to life:

Temple kept us alert, walking briskly about the Hall, talking very loud, turning suddenly upon us with questions, and greeting blunders with boisterous laughter. He seemed to be always in high spirits, as though the whole thing were very enjoyable. At the same time he exacted work, showing marked displeasure at any neglect or idleness, and using great plainness of speech.[1]

During the following Term, Hornby was placed in Temple's lectures on Lucretius. This was prior to the publication of the important critical editions of Lucretius by Lachmann (1850) and Monro (1860), and so the undergraduates were required to make do with whatever notes they could obtain informally, which were often of poor quality. Nor did Temple exhibit much enthusiasm for the subject, and so the majority of the lectures passed uneventfully. When, however, from time to time,

---

*The substance of this chapter was originally published as 'Archbishop Frederick Temple and the Reform of Education', in *Anglican and Episcopal History*, 63: 315 ff. and is reproduced here by kind permission of the editor.

[1] E. G. Sandford (ed.), *Memoirs of Archbishop Temple by several friends*, 2 vols. (London, 1906), i. 87.

Temple stopped the construing to gather up the argument and to talk about the Philosophy, he was quite in his element, and very interesting and instructive.[2] More effective were Temple's lectures on logic. As Hornby later recalled, these exhibited the imprint of his industrious— and slightly eccentric—personality:

There was a noticeable peculiarity in his delivery. After going on rather rapidly for five or ten minutes, he would pause and reflect a moment, and then say, as if to himself, but quite aloud, 'Yes' seeming to mean 'that is what I meant to say,' 'All right so far.' Then he would start afresh. The lectures had been prepared with great care. I believe that he had given much work in term time, and several vacations, to making a full study of the subject, after taking his degree. He had the Aristotelian Logic at his finger-ends, and he seemed to have read a great deal of the Scholastic Logic at first hand. Certainly, he criticised and corrected the ordinary manuals with great vigour and clearness, making havoc of Aldrich and Whateley, and showing how their interpretations of many common scholastic terms were mere guesses, more or less ingenious, but not true historically to the usage of the schoolmen, and thus involving, not unfrequently, absurdities and contradictions. He introduced us to Kant; and, going beyond the borders of Logic, he gave some very interesting lectures on Comte and the *Positive Philosophy*. He did not meddle with Hegel, whose time at Oxford had not yet come.[3]

Although he lacked the responsibilities of a college tutor, Temple nevertheless became involved in the pastoral and spiritual development of junior members. On the evenings prior to the monthly administration of communion in the college chapel, for example, he would invite undergraduates to his rooms to hear brief devotional addresses. These were 'simple, earnest, affectionate' homilies, 'full of sympathy with young men in their trials and difficulties', and sometimes delivered 'with marked emotion'. They proved particularly popular, Temple's rooms often becoming crowded to excess. Having entirely overcome the disadvantages of his provincial upbringing and the limitations of his early education, Temple quickly turned into a popular and respected fellow of Balliol; here he secured the affection and sustained loyalty of senior and junior members, avoided partisan conflicts, and (unlike a number of his contemporaries) remained almost entirely free from the theological extremes of both Tractarian enthusiasm and Jowett-inspired liberalism.[4]

Temple also became interested in educational issues outside the college and university.] The diocese of Oxford had very early taken up

---

[2] Sandford (ed.), i. 88.
[3] Ibid.   [4] Ibid. i. 89.

parliamentary grants made available for funding teacher-training colleges in 1838. A Board of Education had been founded in the same year and Edmund Hobhouse, one of its most enthusiastic members, was a friend of Temple's and interested him in its work. A diocesan training college was opened in Summertown two years later and again Hobhouse was the moving spirit behind it. When Hobhouse became vicar of an Oxford parish in 1843 he asked Temple to give tuition to some of those preparing for admission to the college. Temple's experience with a particular young orphan and the fact that he had recently been reading a paper which argued that pauperism in England was virtually hereditary, seem to have given him an interest in the education of the working classes.[5]

It may also be that his own perpetual poverty and the desperate business of getting himself educated caused him to think more seriously than most young men about the social aspects of education. As early as 1843 he had begun to exhibit unease about wealth and poverty in British society. Initially this appeared in a form which suggests Tractarian influence. He told his mother that he had begun to wonder whether the Church were not 'at present the Church of the rich and not of the poor?' and then went on to say, 'I cannot help feeling doubts whether in the Reformation much was not cast away which was intended for, and suited, the poor; and there has been little in its place. I confess I think the abolition of the compulsory confessional was a most hazardous experiment.'[6] By 1848 he was writing to a friend in much sharper, less romantic terms, about the dangerous effects of industrial poverty in the north of England, the possibility of its breeding a revolutionary violence, and the complacency of the political parties:

For nowadays institutions are no longer habits as they once were, but ideas. Men will not yield them obedience from the mere force of long usage; but they must be believed in and bear to be reflected on, and a terrible judgement awaits them if they will not bear it. All this education, which we are driving along as fast as we can, adds to the necessity. To educate without reforming is sure to produce revolution, as sunshine without rain is sure to injure the crops. To teach people how to criticize institutions, and not to enable the institutions to bear the criticism, is the maddest of follies.[7]

'All this education' referred, in part, to proposals emanating from Lord Ashley (afterwards the seventh Earl of Shaftesbury). There was to

[5] Ibid. i. 74 f.   [6] Ibid. i. 70.   [7] Ibid. i. 72.

be compulsory schooling of workhouse children and that meant that teachers would have to be provided for the task, and that, in turn, meant that someone would have to train the teachers.

The 1840s and 1850s were a period when the whole question of a national policy on education was high on the political agenda and when the existing provision of education, from elementary school to university, was subject to scrutiny and reform. Government was compelled to concern itself with the provision of schooling. Policy was in the hands of a Committee of the Privy Council, an embryo department of education, and its staff was expanding and becoming, in a very real sense, more professional. Temple joined the staff of the Committee of Council in 1848 as an 'examiner' of schools and by the end of 1849 had been appointed principal of Kneller Hall a new institution for training men to teach pauper children in poorhouses.

It has been suggested that Temple's move to the Committee of Council was arranged by Benjamin Jowett as part of a design to use the Civil Service as a place in which able young men from Balliol could make a worthy and influential career.[8] In one sense, this suggestion has a certain plausibility. Jowett certainly took an interest in the Civil Service, at home and in India, in the early 1850s.[9] Choosing and placing young men in positions of power and influence was what he was famous for when he had become Master of Balliol in 1870.[10] Robert Lingen, a close friend of Jowett's, was already established as an examiner (in effect an assistant secretary with special responsibility for maintaining a uniformity of standards in schools) and was becoming an important figure in the department. And it is quite clear that Lingen wanted Temple to join him there.[11] Nevertheless 1848 seems too early for Jowett to have developed such imperial ambitions. He was then only thirty years old; a young and obscure college tutor who, though he had been among Temple's tutors, was only by four years the older man. It seems too soon for him to be securing patronage for Temple. Nor would Temple have needed to have a place found for him. He had his fellowship and he was not planning marriage (the usual reason why fellows resigned). He might simply have stayed at Balliol, as indeed Jowett himself did.

---

[8] Richard Johnson, 'Administrators in Education Before 1870: Patronage, Social Position and Role', in Gillian Sutherland (ed.), *Growth of Government* (London, 1972), 118 f.

[9] Peter Hinchliff, *Benjamin Jowett and the Christian Religion* (Oxford, 1987), 36.

[10] Ibid. 100 f.

[11] Johnson, 119.

Much more plausible is the suggestion that Temple's appointment was really a ploy in a long-standing battle between the Tractarian sympathizer, Archdeacon Denison of Taunton, (determined to prevent governmental interference in Church schools) and James Kay-Shuttleworth (effectively head of the embryo education department and determined to break the Established Church's monopoly of education).[12] Kneller Hall was to admit persons of any religious persuasion and was not to examine its students in any religious teaching other than biblical knowledge. Having won these two points, Kay-Shuttleworth—himself the son of a Nonconformist minister—made two concessions. He agreed that the principal of the institution should be required to profess the doctrine of the Trinity, and he sought a suitable clergyman of the Church of England to fill the office.

Temple seems, in fact, to have gone to the department from a real sense of vocation. Samuel Wilberforce, Bishop of Oxford, had ordained him deacon in 1846 and priest in 1847. A bald statement of the fact appears in the Sandford *Memoir*[13] but we know nothing of the state of mind in which he approached ordination. The reports which the bishop received from his examining chaplain exist and are both enthusiastic about Temple's intellectual ability—'most original mind'; 'looks like Gladstone'; 'far the best'—and satisfied with the orthodoxy of his thinking.[14] And while it may seem odd that he should decide to enter the Civil Service so soon after ordination, there were several other clergymen employed by the Committee of Council. The two things were not thought to be incompatible.

The poorhouse children whom Temple's students were being trained to teach were regarded as little better than the offscourings of society. Therefore the students themselves were hardly likely to be, in any sense, star quality. They seem to have been rather simple young men, with very little education, and often immature. It must have been perfectly clear that the job would bring few material advantages. Though the new principal was to receive a salary of £1,000 a year such a salary was not precisely lavish. It was a little less than two thirds of what a senior

---

[12] Owen Chadwick, *The Victorian Church*, 2 vols. (London, 1966 and 1970), i. 345. Chadwick, however, described Kneller Hall as 'a normal or model school for teachers', without mentioning that it was meant to train men to work in poorhouses.

[13] Sandford (ed.), i. 63.

[14] Lambeth Palace Library: Manuscript Series 3219, fo. 83.

master at Rugby would get when he was headmaster there a decade later.[15]

As it happened, Temple's commitment to Kneller Hall was severely tested soon after his appointment. Before the year was out he had received a letter from Tait, who was about to become Dean of Carlisle, asking whether he would like his name to be considered for Rugby. Temple's reply was clear and decisive:

Educating the people is something very much more than educating boys at Rugby. With the latter you cannot but feel that what you give is but a small part of their life. They have an education at home, they have an education from society, they have resources independent of all education whatever.

The education of the poor is to them everything. The children in the workhouses, which are my particular care, must from the school derive their characters, their habits, their powers, their hopes, and even the child of the cottage labourer derives an immeasurably large proportion of his inner life from the village school than a gentleman's son from Rugby....

Simply to spread knowledge among them would be but a small thing, and yet even bare knowledge to such men is as bread from Heaven in most instances. But may I not hope in forming the characters of so many who are to go out as Teachers, to give something more than knowledge?

If I could be the means of diffusing among the poor a religious consciousness of their own value and of the value of the lives they lead, some sense of the work they have to do in the world 'as unto the Lord and not unto men' I would not change my day's labour at the end for any other that I know.[16]

It is one thing, of course, to claim—even to possess—high ideals and quite another to put them into practice. But in so far as it is possible to discover what Temple was like at Kneller Hall, he seems to have been a good and understanding principal. The estate had belonged to the family of the painter Godfrey Kneller and was near Twickenham. The Committee of Council spent £40,000 in purchasing, rebuilding, and fitting the house;[17] and there were 30 acres of land, of which 25 acres were available for farming and most of the rest formed the garden of the house itself.[18] The first impression of lavish provision which this

---

[15] *Report of Her Majesty's Commissioners Appointed to Inquire into the Revenues and Management of Certain Colleges and Schools and the Studies Pursued and Instructed Therein*, (1864), iv. 251, para. 323.

[16] Lambeth Palace Library: Tait Papers, vol. 78, fos. 76–9, letter from Temple to Tait, 13 Nov. 1849.

[17] Sandford (ed.), i. 100.

[18] Lambeth Palace Library: Manuscript Series 1798, fos. 14/15, letter to [the Revd H.] Moseley dated 16 Jan. 1851.

suggests did not extend to every aspect of the institution. In his second year Temple complained that he could have admitted ninety-one students, rather than merely eighty, if the committee had not insisted that the servants must occupy one of the students' dormitories.[19] Nevertheless, though the fees were £30 per annum, exhibitions were awarded to students which covered almost the whole of that sum and there were also grants available, of £30, £25, and £20 to cover residence and board. And these bursaries were available, not only to the most able students but to all who reached a certain, not very demanding standard.[20]

The appointment of the staff also suggests an erratic generosity. The vice-principal was Francis Turner Palgrave (to become famous as the editor of the *Golden Treasury*), who had been a pupil of Temple's at Balliol and was a fellow of Exeter College, Oxford. But there were only two other members of staff and they were required to teach a wide range of subjects. Thomas Tate taught mathematics and physics, and James Tilliard taught languages, geography, and music.[21] Industrial training was supervised by the gardener.[22] A drill sergeant was appointed a little later.[23] The principal himself acted as chaplain, took services, and gave instruction on the Bible and, in spite of the regulations, on Church history, and 'the Church formularies and Catechism'.[24] There seems to have been no one to assist him with the details of administration, however small. He had, of course, to submit his annual accounts to the secretary of the Committee of Council and he had to wrestle with demands from the Commissioners of Inland Revenue over unpaid taxes on the Hall.[25] But he had also to be able to turn his hand to cleaning out a pigsty and to arrange for a young Radnor sow to be sent to a boar.[26] He had to send in regular orders for pens and exercise books for the students.[27] And he wrote despairingly to a local handyman, 'We are

---

[19] Ibid., fo. 4.
[20] Ibid., fos. 12 f., letter to the Hon. and Revd G. Wellesley, dated 16 Jan. 1851. (There are some discrepancies between the figures in Temple's letter-book (fos. 12–15) relating to salaries, fees, bursaries, and other matters and those contained in Sandford (ed.), i. 99 f.)
[21] Ibid., fos. 14 f.; letter to Moseley.
[22] Sandford (ed.), i. 101.
[23] Lambeth Palace Library: Manuscript Series 1798, fos. 25 and letter to Secretary of the Committee of Council dated 24 Jan. [1851].
[24] Sandford (ed.), i. 101.
[25] Lambeth Palace Library: Manuscript Series 1798, fos. 5 and 41.
[26] Sandford (ed.), i. 101 n. and Lambeth Palace Library: Manuscript Series 1798, fo. 57.
[27] Ibid., e.g. fo. 6.

really put to great straits from the condition of our mangle. I wish you would be so good as to see to it at once'.[28]

In the press of so much business his efficiency sometimes suffered. On 18 March 1851 he wrote to Lord Lansdowne, who as Lord President of the Council was the minister responsible for the embryo department of education:

In accordance with instructions communicated to me through your Lordship's secretary I wrote to Mr N. F. Zaba and requested him to give me an opportunity of examining his system of mnemonics. Mr Zaba came to Kneller Hall and explained his system very fully.... Historical events or facts or statistics are represented by compartments, the number of dates associated with them by the position occupied by the Beads on the sheet; and their character by the colour of the Beads. In this way the impression on the eye is made to assist that made on the mind.

The system appears to me in some respects superior to any other with which I am acquainted and I have no doubt could be found useful in studies in which it is desired to employ the aid of an Artificial Memory.[29]

A week later he was writing to his old Balliol friend Matthew Arnold, who was Lansdowne's private secretary, to complain that 'Zaba plagues me to death' with demands for a favourable judgement on his system. As his letter to Lord Lansdowne had included a statement of his opinion he wondered whether a copy of it could be sent to Zaba.[30] Unfortunately he wrote to Zaba on the same day and put the two letters in the wrong envelopes. When Zaba wrote to complain about what Temple had said to Matthew Arnold, Temple's apology was hardly abject.

It would be unfeeling of me not to regret that any act of mine should have annoyed one from whom I certainly had received no injury whatever. I am really sorry that the accident should have happened. But I confess I cannot but feel a good deal surprised that you should not at once have understood how it occurred.

I will thank you to return the letter which was intended for Mr Arnold.[31]

In dealing with students, however, Temple was almost always pastorally sensitive and a good first principal for a new and experimental

---

[28] Sandford (ed.), i. 101 n. and Lambeth Palace Library: Manuscript Series 1798, fo. 33.

[29] Ibid., fo. 64.

[30] Ibid., fo. 70.

[31] Ibid., fo. 72, letter to Zaba dated 1 April.

training institution. He was plainly tough and demanding in the matter of academic standards. He would not recommend students until he was sure that they had been adequately trained.[32] At first there were very few books and the students were almost entirely dependent on what was told them in class. When Temple received an application from a candidate who was very deaf, his reply to the candidate's sponsoring clergyman was both clear and kind.[33] Similarly, when a candidate failed to get an exhibition, Temple took the trouble to explain that the real reason was that his earlier studies had not prepared him properly—'a man can hardly know what he has not learnt'.[34]

Temple was capable of being both firm *and* understanding, as in a letter which he wrote to Gerald Wellesley, nephew of the Duke of Wellington and rector of Strathfieldsaye. Wellesley, who was to become Dean of Windsor in 1854, had taken an interest in Kneller Hall from the start and had sent a young parishioner to be trained there. The lad, however, had run away. Temple wrote:

You must have heard before this time of the strange conduct of young Graffham. I was not able to find out from him why he thought fit to take such a sudden flight but from the character given of him by his Father I presume the other students must have made him uncomfortable by laughing at him.

Of course after he has shown himself so silly it is a question whether he is fit for our purposes but it seems hard to be very severe on a piece of boyish folly and if he will come back before Sunday I shall put no obstacle in the way of his readmission.

I will add that the other students have never shown the least want of kindness in their intercourse with one another and I feel convinced that nothing unkind was done to Graffham.

From practical jokes I could pretty well guarantee any student. From jokes which do not go beyond words I should not desire nor profess to do so.[35]

Kneller Hall seems to have become a gathering place for Temple's friends—mainly those (including Robert Lingen) who had been undergraduates with him and his former tutors from Balliol. Since most of the group were professionally involved in education, their conversation was quite often about radical reforming ideas. For this was a time when the campaign for the reform of the university in the 1840s had revealed a convergence between theological, political, and educational liberalism.

[32] Ibid., e.g. fos. 1 f.
[33] Sandford (ed.), i. 100, and Lambeth Palace Library: Manuscript Series 1798, fo. 83.
[34] Ibid., fo. 10, letter to C. J. Vinall dated 14 Jan. 1851.
[35] Ibid., fos. 29 f.

And Gladstone's political shifts—in just this period—served to focus that convergence. His writings on Church and State of 1838 and 1840 had been a High Churchman's defence, both political and religious, of the ecclesiastical establishment. As President of the Board of Trade in Sir Robert Peel's administration from 1843 Gladstone had begun tortuously to evolve towards greater political and religious liberalism. In 1845 he resigned from the cabinet because it decided to make grants to the Roman Catholic college at Maynooth. He believed that giving financial support to denominations other than the Established Church was a policy inappropriate for a Tory administration. Once he had resigned, however, he did not oppose the grants in parliament and later in the same year he spoke vigorously in favour of the Dissenters' Chapels Bill which rescued Unitarians from a potentially disastrous loss of property.[36] He had already, of course, become a supporter of free trade and was soon to move (through Aberdeen's coalition government from December 1852 to February 1855) into prominence among the political Liberals of the mid-1850s.

Temple seems also to have evolved, at the same time though in a less public fashion and on a more modest scale. As an undergraduate he had thought of himself as an old-fashioned Tory High Churchman. He had been at one time attracted to the Tractarians but even before he had left Oxford he had begun to adopt more liberal ideas, theological as well as political, [supporting, for instance, Renn Dixon Hampden, the liberal Regius Professor of Divinity, who in 1847 was offered the vacant see of Hereford by Lord John Russell, provoking a vehement High Church and Evangelical protest].[37] And at Kneller Hall he had become someone who was widely believed to be in every way in the liberal camp. His friendship with Jowett was influential in the change, though Temple seems to have regarded Jowett with a certain ironical detachment. In 1847 he told his mother

Meanwhile Jowett . . . proposes various undertakings with magnificent names . . . I always feel that it is especially incumbent on those who take the safe side, as I have done now, not to make it the lazy side.[38]

He was a member of the committee which campaigned for Gladstone's election as one of the Members of Parliament for Oxford University in

[36] H. C. G. Matthew, *Gladstone, 1809–1874*, (Oxford, 1986), 68–9.
[37] Sandford (ed.), ii. 532.
[38] Ibid. i. 71.

the Election of 1847.[39] Gladstone's victory in a constituency where the majority of the voters were clergymen was due to an unusual coalition of High Churchmen with theological liberals. The High Churchmen were able to support him because he was known to be sympathetic to the Tractarians. Liberals, no doubt, approved of his support for liberal causes, religious as well as political. His election has been described as showing 'that [university] reform was essential. Gladstone's member-ship for Oxford thus represented . . . a desire for change, and in a Liberal direction'.[40]

Jowett, with Arthur Stanley, was very much in the forefront of the campaign for university reform and he seems to have enlisted Temple's support also. He was actually staying with Temple at Kneller Hall when he wrote to Gladstone in 1853 enclosing what was virtually a draft reforming bill.[41] Some of Jowett's ideas were embodied in the act which was passed by the Commons in 1854. And this was also just the period when Jowett and Stanley were producing their commentaries on the Pauline Epistles. Jowett's volumes, at least, were controversial works, widely suspected of being heterodox, and he dedicated them to Temple in fulsome terms. When the act had been passed and the royal commis-sion was being appointed to carry out the detailed reforms, both Jowett and Temple were possible candidates for the job of secretary. Gladstone then thought that there was very little to choose between the two men: their views were as alike as it was possible for the views of any two powerful and independent personalities to be.[42] In the end Stanley was offered the appointment.

Temple and Jowett did not hold quite such identical views as Glad-stone supposed though it is clear that during these years, Temple became part of a liberal circle at least in so far as ideas about education were concerned. Many of the Balliol friends who visited him were leading liberals but Temple's niece, who lived in his household at Kneller Hall for two years and to whom we are indebted for a vivid picture of visitors from the outside world, mentions that Robert Scott was also among them.[43] In 1854 Scott and Jowett became rivals for the mastership of Balliol. Jowett was anxious to make the college what

[39] W. R. Ward, *Victorian Oxford* (London, 1965), 142.
[40] Matthew, 71.
[41] Hinchliff, 36 f.
[42] British Library; add. MS 44.291, fos. 186 f., Gladstone to Lord John Russell, 26 May 1854.
[43] Sandford (ed.), i. 113.

Arnold had made Rugby—a bastion of real but undogmatic Christianity. Scott was the conservative candidate, regarded by Jowett as a man brought back from his living in the country to frustrate the forces of reform. Precisely why and how Scott came to be elected is not easy to determine.[44] The Greek lexicon ensured that he was the better-known scholar: Jowett's writings were only just beginning to appear but he had not yet acquired any great notoriety as a liberal theologian. Scott had once been one of Jowett's tutors and the two had been good friends rather as Temple and Scott were friends. Friendship did not, however, easily survive the election. Scott became master: Jowett, in what looks like a protracted sulk, set himself to oppose virtually everything the new master wished to achieve. For fifteen years he was virtually the leader of a far from loyal opposition within the college.[45]

It is the fact that the battle over the mastership took place within such a close circle that makes it peculiarly difficult to disentangle. Of the friends listed by Temple's niece as those who used to come calling on Saturdays, three were fellows of Balliol at the time of the election and therefore entitled to vote in it.[46] They were Jowett himself, W. C. Lake, and Theodore Walrond. Neither Scott nor Temple, as former fellows, were electors; though Temple appears also to have been a candidate in the very early stages. Both Lake and Walrond appear to have voted for Scott[47] so the group of friends was not uniformly liberal in opinion or else their liberalism did not determine how they voted. Some of Lake's ideas were liberal as regards education though probably not in matters of theology.[48]

There was, in fact, a wide variety of opinion within the circle and many degrees of liberalism even among the liberals. Gladstone's assessment of Jowett and Temple suggests that the latter was identified in his own day with the more radical wing. More recently he has been described as 'a radical reformer like Jowett', a 'heterodox Anglican' and 'a dedicated Broad Churchman'[49] but there is actually very little

[44] John Jones, *Balliol College: A History 1263–1939* (Oxford, 1988), 202 f.; and Hinchliff, 39 ff.

[45] Hinchliff, 39 ff.

[46] It may be significant that Temple's niece ceased to live at the Hall in 1854, the very year of the election, Sandford (ed.), i. 112 f.

[47] Jones, 203.

[48] Hinchliff, 41.

[49] Jones 202; and Simon Green, 'Archbishop Frederick Temple on Meritocracy, Liberal Education and the Idea of a Clerisy', in Michael Bentley (ed.), *Public and Private Doctrine: Essays in British History Presented to Maurice Cowling* (Cambridge, 1993), 150.

evidence to support these assertions. Such evidence as there is, in fact, suggests a rather different picture. Temple's friendship with Robert Scott continued throughout the period. His letters to his former tutor indicate that he thought of himself as standing between Scott's conservat-ism, on the one hand, and the radicalism of Jowett and Stanley on the other.[50] The choice seemed to him, when he put it bluntly, to be between 'petrifaction' (a closed mind) and 'putrefaction' (heterodoxy). 'Putrefaction is offensive,' he told Scott, 'but petrifaction is hopeless.'[51] If he had to choose, he would choose putrefaction. Therefore he leant towards Jowett rather than Scott although it is obvious that he was never entirely easy about Jowett's position. If, therefore, he had become part of the liberal, reforming group, he was not one of the more radical members of it. But he was developing clear ideas about the nature of education and about the educational needs of the country and, as his ideas became known, they came to be thought of as important by many of his contemporaries. It has even been held that he was the most influential of the educational theorists of the nineteenth century.[52]

Temple made his first very public venture into the educational debate with a contribution on 'National Education' to the volume of *Oxford Essays* of 1856.[53] The question addressed by the essay was how to establish a system of schools throughout England, at least partly funded by the State and open to everyone regardless of religious allegiance. A good deal of the essay was devoted to a very careful analysis of the situation as it then was. The problem was that the Established Church had a virtual monopoly of existing schools which it would not willingly relinquish while Nonconformists could neither finance their own alternatives nor swallow their resentment at their children being instructed in Church teaching along with elementary education. Temple argued that there were, in effect, three possible solutions; the 'denominational', which sought to have separate schools for each denomination; the 'comprehensive', which would only allow such religion to be taught as was not objectionable to anyone; and the 'combined', which really desired a purely secular education. He set out the problems inherent in each of the policies and in the legislative proposals then being

---

[50] Sandford (ed.), ii. 499–517.
[51] Ibid. 504.
[52] Simon Green, 'Archbishop Frederick Temple on Meritocracy', in Michael Bentley (ed.), *Public and Private Doctrine: Essays in British History Presented to Maurice Cowling* (Cambridge, 1993), 150.
[53] *Oxford Essays Contributed by Members of the University* (London, 1856), 218 ff.

canvassed, noting that the purely secular option was not any longer attracting much support. He did not mention that there were many Nonconformists who were vigorous in their determination that all education should be a matter for voluntary effort rather than for State provision.[54]

It was the Tractarians who were Temple's particular target in the essay. Perhaps it was inevitable that he should write as the spokesman and apologist for the Committee of Council as Oxford High Church ecclesiasticism was the *bête noire* of Robert Lingen who had, by this time, succeeded James Kay-Shuttleworth as its effective head.[55] But, whatever the reason, Temple's distancing himself from those whom he had formerly admired is significant. He also enunciated, and defended, the fundamental principle which underlay the practical policies of the committee and its staff. They did not exist to undertake the work of education themselves. What they did—providing inspectors to report on schools, for instance—was designed to improve the education that already existed.[56] Public aid was only provided where the result would be an increase in the amount of financial support from the local community. The aim was 'not only to get the children taught what children ought to know, but to get the local authorities taught how to manage the schools which they erected'.[57] But the existing system had become overloaded and was in danger of breaking down altogether. A new system was desperately needed to take its place.

One of Temple's own contributions to the debate was an interesting distinction between religious freedom for denominations and religious freedom for individuals. Religious freedom was the battle cry of the 'denominational' group, whether High Churchmen or voluntaries. But freedom for a denomination might be simply a licence for its leaders to impose extremely tough regulations upon the ordinary members. 'The smaller and busier section ... look on themselves, and are looked upon by a sort of tacit consent of the rest, as the truly religious.'[58] But the majority of members really want to be left alone. 'They want to take as much of the religious system in which they find themselves, or which they have joined, as suits their religious need, and no more.'[59] It was,

---

[54] David Bebbington, *Victorian Nonconformity* (Bangor, 1992), 60 f.

[55] Johnson, 135.

[56] *Oxford Essays*, 229.

[57] Ibid.

[58] Ibid. 240 f.

[59] Ibid. 241.

therefore, nonsense to argue that religious liberty demanded a denominational system. A system of national education needed some basis other than ruthless denominational autonomy.

Temple's developing notion of what education ought to be seems partly to have been influenced by the experimental school at King's Somborne in Hampshire set up by the local incumbent, Richard Dawes. Dawes had intended the school to provide an economical education, of a good standard but of a practical kind, for the children of both tenant farmers and agricultural labourers. He had plainly hoped that his school would help to overcome differences of social class and religious intolerance, alike[60] and his *Hints on an Improved and Self-supporting System of National Education, Suggested from the Working of a Village School in Hampshire*, of which a second edition had appeared in 1847, contained a description of the school as well as the thinking behind it. Dawes had been rewarded for his efforts by being made Dean of Hereford, on Lord John Russell's recommendation, in 1850.

Temple's first, fairly sketchy attempt to set out his idea of the nature of education was contained in a letter, written in 1851, to a colleague in the department. It is specifically about the school at King's Somborne. It shows how his ideas were forming five years before his essay.

I was in King's Somborne (now in your District) the other day and was much struck with the difference between my notion of it as obtained from Moseley's report and the reality.[61] Moseley, following his own bent therein, has given the world the notion that the characteristic feature of the School was the amount of physical science taught and of information of that kind. To my eye the characteristic was the degree of cultivation (as distinct from mere information) and the thorough appreciation of the beauties of style and language shown throughout the School.

I think you would do a real service if you would bring forward more prominently this excellence of the School now that Moseley has called attention to the other.

Cook, I remember, after first reading Moseley's Report, spoke of it as an evil rather than a good inasmuch as it would encourage physical science to the exclusion of literature. Had he seen the School he would have thought differently: for physical science is, in reality, only Dawes's means not his end. If you

---

[60] On Dawes's views see W. A. C.. Stewart and W. P. McCann, *The Educational Innovators, 1750–1880* (London and New York, 1967), 124 ff.

[61] The Revd H. Mosely was one of H. M. Inspectors under the Committee of Council, whose report on the school was well known, see D. I. Allsobrook, *Schools for the Shires: The Reform of Middle-Class Education in Mid-Victorian England* (Manchester, 1986), 82.

could disabuse the minds of the world on this I think it would be a great gain. I had no idea before I went that I should hear poetry read and quoted as it is there.[62]

By the time Temple came to write his essay on National Education, King's Somborne had become an established success. Indeed, Temple actually referred to the school at one point,[63] though chiefly to stress one marked difference between Dawes's ideas and his own. It was the conventional orthodoxy of the day that parents who were of even the most modestly independent means would refuse to send their children to the same school as those of the labouring classes. Dawes's experiment claimed to disprove the truth of this belief. Temple's essay vigorously maintained that social and economic divisions were more important and intractable in matters of education than religious divisions. What he took from Dawes was the conviction that it would be perfectly feasible to create an economically viable school for working-class children which would educate them to what even the middle classes would recognize as a good standard: where he differed from Dawes was his insistence that the classes would need to be educated separately.

Temple pointed out that the upper classes had already separated themselves and devised their own educational system in the public schools and that the middle classes now desired to do something similar. The reasonably well endowed grammar schools might make ideal institutions for them, provided some places were reserved, and open to competition, for lower-class boys.[64] Elementary education on a national basis was, therefore, primarily a necessity for the labouring classes. But Temple always had, since his own experiences when looking for a place at university,[65] a horror of scholarships restricted to certain families or localities. This seemed to him to be wasteful of endowments. Equally wasteful, he thought, was indiscriminate free education provided for scholar and idiot alike. And in this he would have received support from Dawes for in the same year in which Temple's essay on national education appeared, Dawes published a sermon on a related question.[66] Dawes was no advocate of indiscriminate charity and the

---

[62] Lambeth Palace Library: Manuscript Series 1798, fos. 16 f.

[63] *Oxford Essays*, 238.

[64] Ibid. 262 ff.

[65] See above, 14–16.

[66] R. Dawes, *The Evils of Indiscriminate Charity and of a Careless Administration of Funds Left for Charitable Purposes; With Remarks on the Dwellings and Social Habits of the Labouring Classes* (London, 1856).

King's Somborne experiment, which 'taught all the children alike, but called upon the parents to pay according to their means', tried to avoid that 'evil'. Temple was not convinced that this was the answer. The scheme had worked as a temporary and local expedient. 'But, considered as a national plan, it will not bear five minutes' examination.'[67]

This is not to say that Temple thought that each working-class parent should be solely responsible for financing the education of his own children. With a very Victorian confidence in market forces, he argued vigorously for elementary schools to be funded by a local rate locally administered. 'People who are administering a rate from a [national] tax know that a hundred pounds wasted will not make a difference of half a farthing in their individual taxation.'[68] He was, however, willing to admit that there might be injustice in any very localized system: a poor parish might not be able to provide as good an education as a rich one. Therefore a unit larger than the parish would be necessary and subsidies would have to be provided for very poor districts.[69] Local rating was the urgent necessity and a bill, however imperfect, was needed to create a system which would absorb existing schools, provide new ones where there were none, prevent the overloading of the Committee of Council and limit the total cost of national education to what was reasonable.[70] It must also allow parents the right to withdraw their children from whatever religious instruction was given in the local school. This device was several times referred to in the essay and was plainly rather more than a means of getting some sort of bill through parliament. Temple seems, throughout his life, to have favoured the principle of a parental right to opt out.

The other matter which made his name familiar to a wider public during his years at Kneller Hall was a proposal, put forward in the following year, concerning the provision of a standardized examination for grammar schools.[71] The idea seems to have been first mooted, anonymously, by T. D. Acland, son of his old benefactor from Blundells.[72] The proposal was that the University of Oxford should validate

[67] *Oxford Essays*, 238.
[68] Ibid. 248.
[69] Ibid. 254 and 249.
[70] Ibid. 268.
[71] Lambeth Palace Library: Manuscript Series 3219, fos. 57–64, document headed 'Appendix B to Report of Rev H. W. Bellairs for the Board of Education sent by the Rev F. Temple', and dated 11 Apr. 1857.
[72] Sandford (ed.), ii. 553.

the examinations and appoint a board to set them. There should be, taken at fifteen, a preliminary examination in elementary subjects including religious knowledge if the parents did not object. One would then enter one of four 'schools'—modern languages, English (including English history and geography), mathematics, and a school of physics (teaching the elements of mechanical, chemical, and physiological sciences). The examination in these schools, taken at seventeen and held primarily in Oxford, could also be taken in any place where the local authorities and gentry wanted it and were willing to meet the extra cost. It would be open 'to all boys from whatever rank and however educated' on payment of some such sum as five shillings.

The proposal was put to a meeting of the Birmingham Education Association, which sent a delegation of three (Temple himself, Acland, and a colleague called Bellairs) armed with memorials from other parts of the country also, to visit Oxford. There the 'governing body' (presumably Hebdomadal Board) 'received it with favour' and Cambridge was next approached. It was unable to 'refuse that boon to the country at large which the sister university has so handsomely professed' and so there was established the Oxford and Cambridge Local Examination Board.

The premiss upon which Temple's argument was constructed was, once again, coloured by free-market assumptions which were characteristic of nineteenth-century liberals, not yet disillusioned by the cruelty implicit in it. Temple maintained that the education of the middle classes in England suffered from two chief defects. The teachers had no means of knowing what subjects to teach or what standards to aim at. The parents had nothing to guide their choice of a school for their children:

Everyone who knows anything of education knows how fatal the former deficiency must be. Without any means of testing his own methods of attaining it, the schoolmaster flounders from one mistake into another or persists year after year in a false system, depending for his bread not on hard work and honest endeavour after excellence, but on plausible appearance and skilful puffing. The parents, meanwhile, though they know certainly enough about (if not of) Education to desire it for their children, are constantly misled into preferring showy useless accomplishments to solid knowledge and real cultivation.[73]

The final word in that paragraph was Temple's favourite term, already used in his letter about King's Somborne, for describing what education

[73] Lambeth Palace Library: Manuscript Series 3219, fos. 57 f.

was all about and it is, therefore, of some importance to understand what he meant by it. 'Cultivation' stood for a kind of teaching which was less concerned to communicate facts than to immerse pupils in a culture. And Temple, like any other Englishman of his generation and class, assumed that there was only one culture—that which was enshrined in Christian, classical, and English literature.

Other liberals in the educational field also favoured much the same ideals about teachers and teaching, so it is not surprising to discover that Jowett once wrote in terms not unlike those which Temple himself used.

Some persons may never have understood that teaching has anything to do with sympathy. The gifts which they look for in the teacher, are knowledge of the subject, clearness in the arrangement of materials, power of illustration, accuracy, diligence, nor can anyone be a good teacher in whom these qualities are wanting. And yet much more than this is required, for the young have to be educated through the heart as well as the head; the subtle influence of the teacher's character, his love of truth, his disinterestedness, his zeal for knowledge, should imperceptibly act upon them. Dry light, without any tincture of the affections, may truly under a figure describe science. Of teaching it would be truer to say that it must be clothed in the language of affection and enthusiasm, that it must be warm as well as light.[74]

It is possible that Temple owed something to the ideas of von Humboldt in his developing concept of education as 'cultivation'. The first volumes of von Humboldt's encyclopaedic *Kosmos* appeared in the late 1840s and he had managed to combine an enthusiasm for traditional culture with a precise and detailed knowledge of the new sciences, to some of which he had made an original and seminal contribution. Since von Humboldt had been involved in the reconstruction of education in Germany after Jena, in establishing proper training and qualifications for teachers, in raising the standards in secondary education, and a thorough overhaul of elementary schools, it is tempting to wonder whether Temple might even have thought of himself as a lesser English version of the Prussian savant.

Unfortunately, there is no clear evidence that he had read anything of von Humboldt's. It is not even certain how much German Temple knew, though he seems to have intended at one time to co-operate with Jowett in making a translation of some of the works of Hegel.

[74] B. Jowett (ed. W. H. Fremantle), *College Sermons* (London 1895), 157 f.

(Jowett himself was no fluent writer of German.[75]) A more likely influence on Temple's ideas about education was the personal relationship with one's tutor which had been a feature of his own undergraduate life. One of his friends described Temple's style as principal of Kneller Hall as follows:

What such students required more than knowledge was refinement and strength of character, next to religious temper and moral principles, and this could be produced only by contact with a cultivated mind, superior not so much in knowledge as in moral qualities and mental discipline.[76]

And that description makes it quite clear that a principal function of the teacher was to provide a role model for his pupils. There was an immense difference between his own upbringing and that of his students, of course, but Temple had been conscious of having gone to Oxford without much polish. What Tait had given him then, Temple himself was now trying to provide at Kneller Hall. It was natural for him to hope to impart a little polish to those whom he taught at Kneller Hall though there was much, no doubt, that was patronizing in the way the hope was expressed. 'Cultivation' meant a very personal kind of education indeed.

It has been argued that Temple's plans for education were really a more practicable, more realizable, version of some of Samuel Taylor Coleridge's ideas and that all his life he strove for an educational system that would produce a meritocracy, a 'clerisy' in Coleridge's sense.[77] There are really several quite different points here. Very few educational systems have been egalitarian,[78] for it is quite undeniable that human beings vary in academic ability. Temple was certainly anxious that those who *could* be well educated *should* be well educated: but 'meritocracy' is about who should govern rather than about who should be educated. It would be difficult to demonstrate conclusively that Temple aimed to put in place an educational system for the training, in a Platonic sense, of a new governing class. Thomas Arnold and Benjamin Jowett both had ideas about how to educate those who would become the country's administrators and Jowett attempted to create in Balliol an institution, modelled on Arnold's Rugby, which would do precisely that. Moreover

[75] Hinchliff, 80.

[76] Sandford (ed.), i. 103.

[77] Green, 152 and 166.

[78] Some of Green's remarks (149 f.) suggest that he is anxious to prove that Temple was not a trendy twentieth-century 'liberal'.

in a very broad and general way almost everyone believed that the extension of the franchise was a reason for extending education, too. Since Temple belonged for a time to the Rugby/Balliol circle it is just possible that he *may* have had ideas about educating the nation's rulers but there does not seem to be much evidence that he ever consciously played the game which Jowett was so good at, of picking, training, and placing his 'old boys' in key administrative positions. At Kneller Hall he simply did not have potential material to hand.

Temple *may* have been influenced by Coleridge, for he had admired Coleridge's religious thought as well as his poetry from the time when he was an undergraduate. The Sandford *Memoir* claims at several points that Temple was influenced by Coleridge's ideas. The problem is that no evidence for this influence was ever provided nor does the *Memoir* ever become specific about the precise points at which Coleridgean concepts are to be found in Temple's writings.[79] It is also very clear that Temple's ideas about education changed and developed throughout his life.[80] Whatever he may have said later, many of his letters *of the 1840s*, quoted and referred to earlier in this chapter, express an uneasiness about inequalities in society. There is absolutely no doubt that, even if he subscribed to some kind of 'elitism' in this period, it was not one which prevented his being determined to secure better opportunities for the underprivileged.

It is also clear that his concept of education as 'cultivation' possessed a strong moral and religious dimension. By the late 1840s this might even have seemed a little old-fashioned as the new sciences inculcated a more value-free approach, a more 'cold' light, in education. But a good many people would have been relieved to find that Temple advocated values with which they were at home. 'Cultivation' stood for more, even, than the Platonic educational ideal of bringing one's pupils to know themselves and of making them recognize their own mistakes and their own innate knowledge. It meant acquiring an appreciation of literature (though nothing is said of art or music). It included not merely the liberal education based on the Greek and Latin classics, which a public-school boy would have received at Rugby, but also something of that wider education by experience which a gentleman's son would acquire naturally. Above all, it meant having a teacher who was himself 'cultivated', who would be a pattern on which his pupils would model themselves, who would demonstrate how a disciplined

[79] See below, 181–2.   [80] See below, 257.

Christian gentleman ought to behave and spur them on to imitate him by establishing a kindly relationship with them.

What is surprising, perhaps, is that Temple with his dislike of 'information' did not share the somewhat disparaging view of science which other liberals, like Jowett for instance, often expressed. Jowett was always anxious that clever young men from the middle classes should receive an Oxford education. Because it was social mobility rather than radical political change which he favoured, he feared that too much natural science might mean that they failed to acquire the polish which a proper education ought to provide. Science did not broaden the mind and even mathematics, though it might need considerable intellectual brilliance, was not the same thing as scholarship (the knowledge of the literature and thought of civilized man).[81]

Temple, for all his impatience with information, was never—least in these years—anything but enthusiastic about mathematics and the sciences. One can find him actually complaining that science was given an insufficiently important place in some schools. In his essay on 'National Education' he had said:

Since the Grammar Schools were founded, there has grown up an English Literature, equal in many of its qualities to Greek and Latin, several foreign literatures of not less extent and value, and a whole army of physics and practical mathematics. If refinement be the object of education, and if education cannot be continued beyond school to college, there can be no comparison between the youth who, at the age of seventeen, had to commence his apprenticeship to the world with a taste for the great English, and some knowledge of the great foreign classics, and one who can just construe Horace and Euripedes... The discipline of Greek and Latin is valuable; but... the discipline of learning physics and practical mathematics, English history and political economy, French and German, is, or may be made, equally valuable.[82]

Jowett never could have said that the learning of natural science contributed to 'refinement': Temple plainly thought that it did. If his own early education was at least partly responsible for making him dislike the teaching of mere information, perhaps it was the necessity of being practical and down to earth in his years at Kneller Hall which made him less narrowly classical and conservative than some of his contemporaries.

It also seems that Temple acquired some expertise in the more unusual aspects of education. It was not simply a matter of waiting

---

[81] Hinchliff, 24 f.   [82] *Oxford Essays*, 265 f.

for new educational schemes, such as the device invented by the unfortunate Zaba, to be referred to him. He actively set himself to discover
what was happening at other experimental institutions, such as the
agricultural college at Cirencester.[83] And he clearly came to be thought
of as someone who understood the education of the awkward and
difficult. In 1854 Robert Lingen, for instance, asked him to comment
on a proposed scheme for teaching young criminals. The plan was to
divide the boys into groups of forty or fifty with a schoolmaster and two
or three warders for each group. The burden of watching the boys
would chiefly fall on the warders who were never to leave them entirely
alone and were to be capable of providing some elementary instruction.
The schoolmaster would have to be qualified to teach the boys in the
more advanced subjects and might also have to train the warders to do
the elementary instruction.

Temple's reply is an extraordinary document.[84] He approached the
task with apparent relish and an air of great command, generalizing
authoritatively about the juvenile criminal mind. He was prepared to
admit that there were good points about the proposed scheme. Separating juveniles from adult criminals would be an obvious advantage.
Another would be the proposed uniformity of the curriculum so that
instructors would know exactly what they ought to be teaching in
whatever reformatory they might find themselves. A surprising note
was that his approval extended to what he called 'mechanical regularity'
in the new system. It looked like a reversal of everything he had ever
said about cultivation as opposed to information but, 'crime was so
much a matter of habit: that inculcating good habits, even if only learnt
mechanically, must act as a corrective'.

When, however, he came to spell out the things that worried him
about the proposals his older ideas reasserted themselves. He feared that
a merely punitive system would be too negative and that, unless the
warders were men of quite exceptionally attractive moral character,
clever juvenile offenders would soon realize that they were able to run
rings round them. 'You cannot cure a taste for evil except by evoking a
taste for good, and mere custom will not do that.' And he feared that:

The little instruction given by half taught instructors would seem very dull and
poor in comparison with the more brilliant teaching of the indecent play or the
conversation of his companions. The imagination of this class is often very

---

[83] Lambeth Palace Library: Manuscript Series 1798, fo. 19.
[84] Ibid., Manuscript Series 2961, fo. 109, letter dated 22 May 1854.

active; but confined as their memory is within the range of vice, the pictures created by their fancy are ever those of sensual pleasure or triumphant crime. It has often been found that men kept in solitary confinement for months have gone forth with the most vivid relish for their old pleasures, having kept their desires perpetually heated by dreaming over in new combinations the scenes of past wickedness. You cannot meet this evil by a few uninteresting lessons in the most uninteresting, namely the mechanical, part of education. The lad would come out with his understanding and taste still enlisted on the side of vice, only bent in future to be more careful in avoiding detection.

What he thought *should* be attempted was almost an exact mirror image of what had been proposed.

A steady Warder at the head and schoolmasters under him; the Warder to be of 40 or thereabouts, capable by rank and character of easy control over his subordinates; the schoolmasters of various ages from the well-tried and skilled manager of such children to the young student from a Training School who has still much to learn in his business; but in all cases selected primarily for character and tact and *secondarily* for attainments; such a system would seem to me to promise better results than the other.

The Schoolmaster ought to be with the Boys always, and should have charge of the work in the Field as well as of the instruction in the School. But there is no labour in the world equal to that of superintendence such as this, and care should be taken to provide such a number of Schoolmasters as would render it possible for them to relieve one another.

Temple had not, in fact, abandoned his favourite notions about education at all. The really good teacher was still someone who could provide a role model for his pupils, not just by being himself a moral and an educated man, but by being an attractive character of the kind whom the young would wish to imitate. And that meant that Temple's variant on the original scheme would be expensive because instructors in reformatories were paid half or less than half of the £100 *per annum* which was the salary of a 'national schoolmaster' (that is a schoolmaster employed by the National Society for the Education of the Poor in the Principles of the Established Church, usually simply called the 'National Society'.

What I am proposing is expensive. But it may as well be stated at once that Reformatory education is the most expensive of all: just as Medicine is more expensive than food, and you pay the Physician more than you do the Baker. The money now spent on adult crime and on well-constructed cells and other precautions against escape in juvenile prisons would be more wisely laid out in providing a proper number of able teachers.

There is an extraordinary note of self-confidence in all this as if the job at Kneller Hall had unlocked an unexpected reservoir of ability. Even more important, other people were beginning to think of Temple, too, in spite of his comparative youth, as someone who had sound ideas about improving education. He may have liked to think of himself as an authority on working-class, disadvantaged, and even criminal children but the truth probably was that he was better at understanding middle-class needs and how to meet them. He was more middle class than, perhaps, he knew and for all the novelty of some of his ideas he inevitably shared many of the unquestioned assumptions of his class. Tait had always regarded him as, by nature and temperament, a potential public-school master. Paradoxically, the years at Kneller Hall had given Temple the experience and the reputation to provide him with an opportunity to realize that potential.

Unfortunately the Kneller Hall experiment did not last long. For a number of reasons it was closed at the end of 1855. It was expensive to run. The Great Exhibition, which in 1851 had seemed to promise so much in the way of peace and co-operation among the industrialized nations, failed to inaugurate an era of plenty. The Derby administration which took office in 1852 had no interest at all in maintaining so Whiggish an institution as Kneller Hall. The Aberdeen coalition—which allowed itself to drift, under the pressure of popular patriotic fervour, into the Crimean war—had neither energy nor money to spare for experimental projects. In spite of Gladstone's presence as Chancellor of the Exchequer, Temple failed to convince the government that his work was important. They talked about his resigning and then refused to accept his resignation. Lord Granville, Lord President of the Council and therefore in charge of the department, was friendly but achieved nothing very much. Lord John Russell, who succeeded Granville was, said Temple, only concerned 'to control the Orders in Council, not to govern the education; so that he will do me no good' though 'for form's sake he issues the usual orders for returns, reports, etc., which belong to a new Lord President; and so he gives me much work'.[85] Palmerston, taking office for the first time as Prime Minister in February 1855, had to devote himself to bringing the war to an end. Temple found that he talked encouragingly but complained that there was no money to spare.

There were also religious issues involved. The Hall was regarded with some jealousy by Nonconformist training colleges because it had

[85] Sandford (ed.), ii. 579.

government backing. But Churchmen were no happier about it. The Tories did not like educating paupers and were also highly critical of the fact that Nonconformists might be trained at the college. That only four had been admitted and that they had all left as members of the Church of England ('not High Churchmen but still Churchmen' was Temple's sardonic comment[86]) did not mollify the critics. No ecclesiastical party was positively in favour of the place; none would fight for its survival. When the decision was finally taken to close it, the immediate thought in the principal's mind was 'What a triumph for Denison and Co.! Down goes the godless College! Harrah for the true Church!'[87]

Above all, perhaps, the real reason for closing the college was that the policy which it had been intended to underpin—of establishing schools in poorhouses—had never become effective. Temple had been the one and only principal. He went back to being a Civil Servant in the department and was made an inspector of 'Church of England Male Training Colleges'. This he did not enjoy, for it seemed to him to be no job for a clergyman.[88] After about a year of it he wrote to Tait, who had just been appointed Bishop of London:

I am not at all in love with my present position and in fact only took it because when I resigned Kneller Hall I had no other opening. It is not sufficiently the proper work of a clergyman to suit me. At Kneller Hall I had my chapel and had also the spiritual supervision and instruction of the students. Here, except that the clergy prefer to deal with a clergyman in regard to their [schools] I might just as well be a layman. So that I should be very glad if I could find any reasonable opening for getting to more clerical work.[89]

There is one small but possibly significant point to note about Temple's reaction to the closing of Kneller Hall. He wrote a long and emotional letter to one of his very close friends. It was obviously one of a series of similar outpourings, in which he had admitted to ambition and eagerness for success and yet despised himself for such feelings. He had obviously talked wildly at some time of becoming a Roman Catholic or marrying a rich widow; but now told his friend that he was not insane enough to do either. He found it difficult to pray privately[90] but

[86] Sandford (ed.), ii. 577.
[87] Ibid. ii. 580.
[88] Ibid. ii. 113.
[89] Lambeth Palace Library: Tait Papers, vol. 78 fos. 85 f., letter dated 20 Oct. 1856. The word rendered 'schools' in the text is actually illegible in the original.
[90] Sandford (ed.), ii. 582.

found some solace in praying in church with a congregation. It was all very overwrought, emotional, and deeply angry; and he wished that he were sufficiently sure of himself to react differently. What is significant is that Sandford's *Memoir*, before quoting the letter, says, 'Times of anxiety affected Temple's health...'[91] He was always thought of by others as robust and tough and it seems likely that it was a nervous rather than a physical illness from which he was suffering. [In any case, this anxiety seems to have had little or no serious effect upon Temple's health. Despite his reluctance to return to the department, there is no evidence to suggest that he was anything but a conscientious and effective Civil Servant. Nor did the closure of Kneller Hall damage his emerging reputation as an educational reformer. Though Temple might have been criticized (perhaps justifiably) for failing to secure a coalition of liberal-minded religious and political figures to support the school, this proved unimportant: as long as he retained the confidence of Tait (and a few others) his future was unaffected by the school's demise. As it turned out, Temple's return to the civil service was to be short-lived; he would soon be offered preferment within an environment more suited to a clergyman with a bent for educational reform.]

[91] Ibid. ii. 580.

3

Rugby and Religious Controversy

Tait had tried twice before to lure Temple to Rugby. In 1843 he had offered him an appointment as an assistant master and in 1849 had hoped to persuade him to be a candidate for the headmastership. In 1857 Rugby was vacant again and again it was Tait who canvassed Temple's name. Temple's educational theories were well enough known by this time to make him a strong candidate and his beliefs had changed sufficiently for him to be attracted to the school. He had become identified with the Rugby/Balliol circle among whom radical ideas for the reform of theology and education were commonplace and, though he was one of the more moderate members of the group, he no longer thought of Thomas Arnold's Rugby as the home of a Broad Church-manship which he did not share. Arthur Stanley, who was almost the embodiment of the Arnold tradition—Arnold's favourite pupil at Rugby and the author of Arnold's biography[1]—was by this time Regius Professor of Ecclesiastical History at Oxford. He wrote several times to Tait[2] about the vacancy. His letters claimed for himself the title of one who 'loved Rugby' and who was qualified to know what would be best for the school. And he hoped that Temple would go there.

Temple's supporters did not think of themselves as extreme men. Stanley was the ultimate liberal; not always agreeing with the sentiments voiced by his more radical friends but determined to defend their right to express them. His share in the commentaries on the Pauline Epistles had been historical rather than theological—and Stanley always thought of history as an exciting tale which was made boring and repulsive by theology.[3] He had never, for this reason, aroused the violent controversy occasioned by the theological opinions in Jowett's

---

[1] A. P. Stanley, *The Life and Correspondence of Thomas Arnold*, 2 vols. (London, 1844).

[2] Lambeth Palace Library: Tait Papers, vol. 78, contains several letters or fragments of letters from Stanley on the subject.

[3] Peter Hinchliff, *History, Tradition and Change: Church History and the Development of Doctrine* (Inaugural Lecture) (London, 1993), 3.

commentaries.[4] Nor was Tait a radical though he was decidedly a Broad Churchman. In the religious crises in Oxford in the first half of the 1840s he had been willing to approve Ward's degradation, even though Ward had been his friend, but he would not vote for the imposition of a stricter religious test upon members of the university. This was the position he continued to hold as a bishop and, eventually, as archbishop. He was determined to preserve the comprehensive character of the Established Church so he wanted no narrow definition of doctrinal orthodoxy. But he also insisted that clergymen should stay within the limits of the range of opinion which was permitted in the Church of England.

Moderate as Stanley and Tait were, they were both undoubtedly 'Arnoldite'. The Rugby tradition had sometimes been suspect in certain quarters. It had been attacked by *The Guardian* during Tait's headmastership, which had claimed that 'the tendency of a system of education conducted by either [Arnold or Tait] is to a false and irreligious liberality'.[5] E. M. Goulburn, Tait's successor as headmaster, was widely regarded as having been appointed to counteract that liberalism. Goulburn was a Balliol man and had been a fellow there from 1841 to 1846, more or less a contemporary of Temple's at the college. But he had also, and more recently, been chaplain to Samuel Wilberforce, the High Church Bishop of Oxford. When the trustees had chosen Goulburn, the other candidate had been W. C. Lake, yet another Balliol man and a moderate within the liberal circle but regarded as 'a confessed disciple of Arnold'.[6] It is entirely understandable that nervous trustees might prefer someone less likely to be accused of 'a false and irreligious liberality'. At the same time they could not afford to allow potential customers to think that the school no longer pursued the great educational ideals acquired under Arnold's headmastership. So a history of the school, produced in Goulburn's time, appears to have been designed to make Arnold's Broad Churchmanship appear as harmless as possible.[7] For Rugby was, in any case, no longer quite what it once had been. The effect of the Crimean War upon the school seems to have been

---

[4] Peter Hinchliff, *Benjamin Jowett and the Christian Religion* (Oxford, 1987), 45 ff.

[5] R. T. Davidson and W. Benham, *Life of Archibald Campbell Tait, Archbishop of Canterbury*, 2 vols. (London, 1891), i. 152.

[6] J. B. Hope Simpson, *Rugby Since Arnold* (London, 1967), 23.

[7] In *The Book of Rugby School: Its History and its Daily Life*, publ. 1856–7, Arnold is said to have introduced special services on All Saints' Day and Maundy Thursday, the 'Chanting of the Nicene Creed', and the holding of school confirmations in the chapel.

disastrous. The number of boys fell sharply and Goulburn seems to have been blamed (and to blame himself) for the decline. This must have been unjust: the war seems to have affected other public schools in much the same way but Goulburn admitted that he did not understand boys, expecting 'too much advance in holiness' and had been disappointed in them.[8]

Temple and his friends seem to have been equally anxious to adopt an eirenical position. Temple himself was inclined to exonerate 'poor Goulburn' from blame for falling numbers in the school, arguing that Goulburn was not to blame, that the war had created a situation for which he could not be held responsible. And one of Temple's great admirers thought that 'The years of the Crimean War and the Indian mutiny, with dear bread, the income-tax at 13d., and the rush of youngsters to the army, were not a favourable period for any Head Master.'[9] The Sandford *Memoir*'s account of the condition of the school when Temple arrived there was also anxious to explain that Goulburn had not undermined any of the good things achieved by Arnold and Tait but had, possibly, eliminated some of the 'peculiarities' of the place.

The inner condition of the school was healthy; it was sufficiently staffed by masters of high character and exceptional ability; the boys at the head of the school...were of a kind that keeps a school steady, and maintains and raises moral standards.[10]

In actual fact Goulburn seems not to have been a total disaster as a headmaster. In 1857, which was during his rule, the school experienced what has been called its *annus mirabilis*, for in that year almost all the open awards at Oxford and Cambridge were won by Rugbeians. He appointed the first regular science teacher in the school (a personal friend, a clergyman called Beardmore Compton) and persuaded the trustees to vote money for, and himself contributed to, the building of a special room for the teaching of science. (He also appointed E. W. Benson to the staff and was, therefore, in a sense, responsible for an important friendship between Benson and Temple.) He was undoubtedly conservative in both religion and politics. He is said, as a young clergyman, to have been a decided Evangelical but, perhaps because of

---

[8] Simpson, 25.

[9] 'Our Public Schools: vol. iv, Rugby', *the New Quarterly Magazine*, NS, 2 (Oct. 1879), 262.

[10] E. G. Sandford (ed.), *Memoirs of Archbishop Temple by Seven Friends*, 2 vols. (London, 1906), ii. 588 f.

his time as Wilberforce's chaplain, he became more High Church and was responsible for some modest 'ritualism' in the school chapel.[11]

This tension between liberalism and conservatism at Rugby (carefully muffled though it was) appears to have had its part to play in Temple's appointment. The very trustees who had been so anxious to avoid a third 'Arnoldite' in 1849 seem to have been ready for it by 1857. And it is understandable that, at a time when it was essential to recruit more entrants, the trustees should have felt that a man in the tradition of Tait and Arnold might serve them well. It is also understandable that Tait, regarding the appointment of Goulburn as something of a rebuff to himself and an implied criticism of his work as headmaster, should have chosen to put forward Temple's name indirectly. He wrote, not to any of the trustees in the first instance, but to Lord Granville—the minister formally responsible for the education department. Granville's reply, indicating that he did not know many of the trustees but would do everything he could with those he did know, drew attention to his own disinterestedness in campaigning on Temple's behalf. 'Mr Temple will be almost an irreplaceable loss to us at the Council Office.'[12] In spite of choosing a roundabout approach, Tait was himself convinced that he had been largely responsible in securing Temple's appointment. Long afterwards Randall Davidson (who had been Tait's chaplain for the last four years of his life and had married Tait's daughter) told the editor of the Sandford *Memoir*, 'It is absolutely true to say that Temple's appointment to Rugby was due to Tait, who frequently told me so himself and rejoiced in the fact.'[13]

That Temple was Tait's preferred candidate, and that Tait made no attempt to hide the fact, meant that his candidacy would be seen from the very start as that of an 'Arnoldite' with the disadvantages as well as the advantages that that implied among the trustees. No doubt the collection of testimonials, which Temple had to assemble in accordance with contemporary custom, had something of the same effect. Walrond acted as campaign manager and collected the testimonials. He, Lingen, and Francis Sandford,[14] all colleagues in the education office, were among those who supported Temple. So, too, were all three Lords President under whom he had served, Lansdowne, Granville, and

---

[11] Simpson, 24.
[12] Lambeth Palace Library: Tait Papers, vol. 78, fo. 149, letter dated 4 Sept. 1859.
[13] Ibid., Davidson Papers, vol. 109, fo. 325, Davidson to E. G. Sandford, 18 Nov. 1905.
[14] The future Lord Sandford, not Archdeacon Sandford who edited the *Memoirs*.

Russell, and, as if this was not enough, so was Matthew Arnold, the legendary doctor's son. The only conservative to import a note of ambiguity into this collection of political Whigs and faintly anti-clerical civil servants, was Robert Scott, as master of Temple's old college and his former tutor. (Temple told him that he did not intend to read the testimonials though, as they were to be printed by Spottiswoode, he can hardly have avoided knowing what was in them.[15])

His candidacy was not without opposition. He was told of the objections that were being made against him 'in the ears of the Rugby Trustees' and listed them sardonically, for there was the same note of slight ambiguity there, too:

1. I am a Puseyite
2. I am a Rationalist
3. I know no Greek
4. I have no experience in teaching
5. I am not a gentleman
6. I failed at Kneller Hall[16]

Though some of the accusations were patently untrue and some contradicted others they might, nevertheless, have been dangerous to his cause. But in the end, he was elected. Tait was plainly delighted that his candidate had been elected and sent a message to Temple's mother so that he should receive the news as soon as he got home. He was elected by the trustees on 12 November 1857 and seems to have begun work early in 1858 after the Christmas holidays.[17]

In its origins Rugby was probably not much different from Blundells, a local school, founded by a local boy made good, intended to provide more or less free education for other local boys. Lawrence Sheriffe, the founder of Rugby, was a cut above Peter Blundell, having been one of the Princess Elizabeth's gentlemen during the reign of Mary I and afterwards Second Warden of the Grocers' Company. Like Blundell he left provision for the establishment of a school after his death and provided the endowment for its maintenance. The transformation of this very local institution into a nineteenth-century public school, drawing its clientele from all over the country, was not solely the

---

[15] Sandford (ed.), ii. 584 ff.

[16] Ibid. ii. 588.

[17] Ibid. i. 151. That he started at the school in the following January seems to be the implication of the reminiscences in Sandford (ed.), i. 158.

achievement of Thomas Arnold. After a somewhat shaky early history, when its endowments were misappropriated, its first trustees proved inefficient, and one of its headmasters apparently died of starvation, things had begun to improve by the eighteenth century. There were good and effective headmasters, numbers rose to about 250, there was some considerable new building, and an Act of Parliament of 1717 set the financial affairs of the school on a better footing just at a time when there was an increased income from the rents of the London property which constituted a large part of its endowment. As a result, and well before Arnold's time, Rugby had become much more than a local grammar school: 'it was one of those which Dr. Johnson called "the Great Schools"... drawing its pupils from all over the country and distinguished for the quality of its scholarship.'[18]

Arnold's personal achievement had been to impose a different kind of educational goal upon the school. Without in any way diminishing the academic standards which some of his predecessors had set, his priorities were, in his own words, 'first religious and moral principle; secondly gentlemanly conduct; and thirdly intellectual ability'.[19] Arnold was the supreme believer in the moral purpose of education and was convinced that moral and intellectual excellence were inextricably intertwined. Since immorality tended to spread by example, it was important to eliminate it from the school. 'Evil being unavoidable,' he said, 'we are not a jail to keep it in, but a place of education where we must cast it out to prevent the taint from spreading.' Hence his early reputation as a disciplinarian. He set himself to try and ensure that only those who were 'worthy' entered the VI form. For them the birch was discontinued. And they were given authority over other boys in order that they should regard themselves as at least partly responsible for the moral tone of the school.

In Arnold's Rugby the chapel was an important focal point. It was not a particularly beautiful building, being in a style called 'Georgian Gothick', with immensely heavy buttresses to avoid its having any trace of the classical.[20] But Arnold tried to make it more attractive and in 1831 he persuaded the trustees to appoint himself as chaplain and thereafter

---

[18] Simpson, 5. Most of this brief account of the early history of Rugby is based on the opening pages of Simpson. Some of the basic facts about the school and its history are contained in the 'List' which the school published at the start of each term.

[19] Ibid. 5 f.

[20] There is a rather wry description, possibly written by Goulburn himself, in *The Book of Rugby School*, 68 ff.

regularly preached twice weekly. He also created proper boarding-houses and put masters in charge of them. As a result of all these reforms the school became extremely popular, particularly among 'the liberal portion of the educated population'.[21] By the time Arnold died the numbers had risen to well above 350 and continued to increase during Tait's period as headmaster until they reached almost 500.

Temple's arrival at Rugby seems to have caused something of a stir. The boys were fascinated by a rumour which quickly spread, that one of his first actions had been to climb the old elm trees in the school close— perhaps to see if they were safe for the boys but more likely because he simply had an irresistible urge to do so.[22] The respectable citizens of the town were scandalized by the new headmaster's first arrival, walking from the station, dressed in a swallow tail coat, and carrying his own bag.[23] Temple also abandoned a good deal of the pomp with which his predecessors had gone about their daily business as headmaster. He did not find it necessary always to be preceded by his butler, to be dressed in full canonicals, or to be treated with ceremonial deference. This was almost certainly not eccentricity: it was Temple's natural behaviour. The manners of the establishment did not come easily. At Kneller Hall he had, after all, had to clean the pigsty.

School histories are given to the mild exaggerations which turn headmasters into heroic figures. Nevertheless Temple's impact on Rugby does seem to have been impressive. The Sandford *Memoir* provides a wealth of anecdotes about the way in which both masters and boys reacted to the enthusiasm, physical energy, and sheer hard work which he brought to the job. It appears to have been, quite literally, captivating.

So complete was Temple's mastery that at the height of the storm over *Essays and Reviews*, a boy wrote home to a worried parent: 'Temple's all right, but if he turns Mahomedan, the whole School will turn Mahomedan too.'[24]

And there lay the snag. The new headmaster had brought with him a time bomb which was quietly ticking away. It would be no comfort to that worried parent to be told how much the boys admired Temple, for this was precisely why his contribution to *Essays and Reviews* caused such a stir and why the controversy hung over the whole of his time at

---

[21] Simpson, 8.   [22] Sandford (ed.), i. 159.   [23] Simpson, 42.   [24] Ibid. 43 f.

Rugby. If the overpoweringly impressive headmaster were to turn unbeliever, the whole school might turn unbelieving, too?

The *Essays and Reviews* project is said to have been born at a meeting
on 26 March 1858 between H. B. Wilson (like Tait one of the 'four
tutors' who had protested against *Tract XC* in 1841 but by this time a
parish priest), Rowland Williams (professor of Hebrew at St David's
College, Lampeter, and already under attack for his rationalist views),
and Mark Pattison (fellow of Lincoln and, like Jowett, at this time
embittered by his failure to be elected head of his college).[25] After the
meeting either Pattison or Wilson recruited Jowett, who agreed to
become a contributor because he had already begun work on an essay
which had been intended for his commentary on Romans but had not
been ready in time. Jowett recruited Temple.

There is some confusion about the precise chronology of events.
Temple was later to tell the boys at Rugby that he had already agreed
to allow his essay to be published *before he came to the school* and that it
simply never occurred to him to revoke it.[26] If nothing at all had been
said about such a volume of essays before the meeting of March 1858
that statement was simply untrue. But there is some evidence that he
knew himself to be involved in a risky enterprise at the time of his
appointment. He told a close friend on the eve of the election that he
would not purchase Rugby at the cost of his right to think for himself.[27]
That suggests that the project had been in the air earlier than November
1857 and it is clear that, in fact, Wilson had been talking for some time
about the possibility of a quarterly journal or an annual volume of
essays.

On the other hand the suggestion that the process of recruitment
worked in a snowball fashion, with new contributors enlisting yet
further possibles—though it would have had to start earlier than the
meeting of March 1858—is plausible. It would explain both the somewhat haphazard character of the contributions and why the sources
differ about the identity of the person responsible for organizing the
volume. Each contributor thought that the person who approached him
was the moving force behind the whole scheme. It would also explain
why different contributors had different notions about what the

[25] Josef L. Altholz, *Anatomy of a Controversy: The Debate Over Essays and Reviews*
(Aldershot and Vermont, 1994), 11.
[26] See below, 75–6.
[27] Sandford (ed.), i. 220 and ii. 611.

character and purpose of the volume was. Jowett, for instance, said it was to be a blow for freedom:

...we are determined not to submit to this abominable system of terrorism, which prevents the statement of the plainest facts, and makes true theology or theological education impossible.[28]

Stanley, that 'light horseman' who took 'an active part in many a hot battle' but managed never to make any real enemies,[29] may have been frightened off by this account of the project. After toying with the idea of an anonymous essay, which Jowett rejected, Stanley concluded that the whole scheme was ill-considered. By the time Jowett came to present the proposal to Temple, he was—at least in Temple's own account of the matter—putting it in a rather different light.

Temple's account ran:

There was a series of essays published in several successive years called the *Oxford Essays.* In that series I wrote [the essay on National Education], and so did Max Müller, Maine, etc. It came to an end simply because it was intended as a vent for what several of us wanted to say, and we had not more to say.

It was then suggested that it should be followed by a series (not a volume only) on religious subjects. I liked the idea, and I liked particularly the opportunity that it would give for speaking out. It appeared to me that at that time there was prevalent amongst the clergy a most unwholesome reticence. I believed that startling things would be said; but I believed that it would be worth while that they should be said. I asked, before I agreed to write, what the probable line would be. I was told that it would be in the Liberal direction, but strictly within the limits allowed by the Church of England. I did not even ask who was to be the editor; and did not know till he wrote to ask me for my paper. There was neither plan nor organization. The *Oxford Essays* had suggested the publication. And these new essays were supposed to be, and as regards composition actually were, as independent of each other as the different papers in the *Oxford Essays.*

Now, no one supposed that these papers would live. They were not of that texture. I wrote my essay in less than ten hours: a man who was taking part in a serious organized attack on existing opinions would have never dreamt of effecting anything by a ten hour's production.[30]

---

[28] Ieuan Ellis, *Seven Against Christ: A Study of Essays and Reviews* (Leiden, 1980), 49.
[29] 'Mr Jowett and Oxford Liberalism', *Blackwood's Edinburgh Magazine*, 161 (1897), 723.
[30] Sandford (ed.), ii. 605.

It is possible, of course, that because he had been fiercely attacked, Temple had told and retold the story of 'what really happened' to himself and to others until the awkward edges had been smoothed away and the whole episode had begun to appear in the most favourable possible light. But his version of events is not implausible.

When he was actually asked for his contribution, time was running short. What he did was to revise a sermon, 'The Education of the World', which he had already preached twice—in the school and before the university (perhaps when the British Association for the Advancement of Science was meeting). Curiously—if this was a sermon for scientists—he implied that the physical universe had originally been created in the form it now has, saying 'The planets, the moon, and the stars, may be unchanged both in appearance and in reality.' Though Darwin had not yet published his theory of evolution, it had already been argued, on the basis of geological evidence and the existence of fossils, that creation had not remained unchanged. But a contrast between a static universe and a developing human race was Temple's main theme—the growth, the progress, and the *education* of the human race.

There was something of a paradox in the way in which he approached this. He insisted, in the first place, that human beings could not be considered as individuals: what made human beings human was their existence in society. Indeed he went so far as to say that a modern child with the same 'faculties' as a child 'born in the days of Noah' would be vastly more developed because of 'the influences exerted by the society in which the child may chance to live'. Yet society, itself, may be regarded, he said, as if it were one human being and the lives of individuals as if they were days in the life of that society. The idea that society or history could be understood by analogy with the individual was commonplace in the mid-nineteenth century but Temple argued for it at greater length and in more detail than was usual. It was plainly a contrivance that was essential to his argument. And, indeed, it enabled him to assert that humanity had passed through phases in its history which amounted to childhood, youth, and 'manhood'. Childhood, he thought, required rules and regulations; youth required an example; adulthood required resources for self-development. So God's religious education of humanity had consisted of the Law, the life of Christ, and the gift of the Spirit.

This part of his argument occupied most of the actual sermon and its clarity was sometimes obscured by an ambiguity about whether he was describing the secular or the religious history of humanity. The essential point, however, was that humanity had developed in its understanding of religion and that it would be inappropriate for it to be instructed in childish ways now that it was fully grown. An adult ought to behave like a responsible, developed adult, not needing the rules of childhood or the role model which youth requires, but capable of thinking for himself. And so, in the last two or three pages of the sermon, Temple came to what he really wished to say—'The immediate work of our day is the study of the Bible.'

Not only in the understanding of religious truth, but in the exercise of the intellectual powers, we have no right to stop short of any limit but that which nature, that is the decree of the Creator, has imposed on us. In fact no knowledge can be without its effect on religious convictions; for if not capable of throwing direct light on some spiritual questions, yet in its acquisition knowledge invariably throws light on the process by which it is to be, or has been acquired, and thus affects all other knowledge of every kind.

And the sermon ended with the words:

For we are now men, governed by principles, if governed at all, and cannot rely any longer on the impulses of youth or the discipline of childhood.

For all that Temple's contribution has usually been regarded as the least offensive of the essays, there are things in it which might have been thought controversial in the 1860s. He was implicitly proclaiming what could be called progress in religious understanding. He was suggesting that religious truth might be enriched by new ideas and new knowledge. Bland though this may seem now, it would not have been universally acceptable then. H. P. Liddon, Pusey's most devoted disciple, would deliver the Bampton Lectures in 1866 and resolutely reject any notion of development in belief which implied 'the positive substantial growth of the belief itself, whether through an enlargement from within... or through an accretion from without of new intellectual matter gathered around it...'.[31] In a footnote he added a specific denial that 'increasing comprehension... involves any addition to or subtraction from that one unchanging body of truth'. For men of Liddon's outlook a growth in scientific knowledge could not develop one's understanding of the doctrine of creation. The only growth of which he could conceive would be some pure reflection upon the revealed truth unaffected by any

[31] H. P. Liddon, *The Divinity of Our Lord and Saviour Jesus Christ: Eight Lectures Preached Before the University of Oxford, 1866*, 8th edn. (London, 1878), 426 f.

extrinsic learning. Liddon was to be one of the first to launch an attack on *Essays and Reviews*.[32]

It has hardly ever been noted, in spite of its title, that Temple's piece was about education—the education of the *world*, no doubt, but his theme was that 'the world' was simply the individual writ large. Therefore it is not surprising that many of the familiar ideas from his time at Kneller Hall reappeared. There was a great deal about 'cultivation'. The word itself appears again and again, particularly in the section of the sermon which deals with the role of ancient Greece in the development of humanity. And there is a passage which clearly evokes the role of the teacher as friend and model.

The youth, when too old for discipline, is not yet strong enough to guide his life by fixed principles.... He admires and loves, he condemns and dislikes, with enthusiasm. And his love and admiration, his disapproval and dislike, are not his own, but borrowed from his society. He can appreciate a character, though he cannot yet appreciate a principle.... He cannot follow what his heart does not love as well as his reason approve; and he cannot love what is presented to him as an abstract rule of life, but requires a living person.

For it is obvious that it is when the world or the individual is youth, rather than child or adult, that education (in the sense of being taught to understand) takes place. In the religious schooling of the world Christ is the beloved tutor whose example cultivates the disciple and moves him to Christian adulthood.

Temple did not ignore the need for education in the other two phases of life and history: childhood and adulthood. (It is almost impossible, in fact, to read his description of a mother's duty towards her child without seeing in it a reference to his own mother.)

When he is to go to bed, when he is to get up, how he is to sit, stand, eat, drink, what answers he is to make when spoken to, what he may touch and what he may not, what prayers he shall say and when, what lessons he is to learn, every detail of manners and of conduct the careful mother teaches her child, and requires implicit obedience.

And he had a good deal to say about the adult's continuing need to be cultivated and developed, to learn and to educate himself. But it is easy to understand why so much of a sermon preached by a professional educator should be devoted to the cultivation of youth. It also provided him with a way of proclaiming his own devotion to the Christ who was

---

[32] See below, 68.

his role model and it is possible to understand why he was so puzzled by the way his essay was attacked for infidelity.

The sermon had attracted no adverse comment when he had preached it before. This may partly be because Temple's debt to Arnold was fairly clear. Arnold had always maintained that the history of a nation was a matter of growing 'from what I may call a state of childhood to manhood'. History was, in short, the biography of a nation and possessed for Arnold a strongly religious dimension.

Whatever there is of variety and intense interest in human nature in its elevation, whether proud as by nature or sanctified as by God's grace; in its suffering, whether blessed or unblessed, a martyrdom or a judgment; in its strange reverses, in its varied adventures, in its yet more varied powers, its courage and its patience, its genius and its wisdom its justice and its love, that also is the measure of the interest and variety of history[33]

Such ideas might be anathema to Liddon but a Rugby congregation, hearing Temple develop the theme that human apprehension of the Christian revelation had grown and matured along with the progress of civilization, might think that it was hearing what Arnold had often said.

Temple spent a few hours revising the text and then sent it direct to the printers. He had not seen the other contributions or known what the overall tendency of the volume would be. And his account of his general state of mind is quite credible.[34] He had contributed his piece on national education to the *Oxford Essays* of 1856. The other pieces in that volume had had no kind of connection with his or with each other, any more than the papers published in the proceedings of a learned society are part of a concerted campaign. The essay had been designed to get certain ideas about the provision of elementary schools off his chest, at a time of heated controversy—and of controversy, moreover, in which religious tempers had run very high. He had attacked the intransigent dogmatism of the Oxford High Churchmen, but he had not then been accused of irreligion nor would anyone have dreamed of holding him responsible for what other contributors had said about their own very varied subjects. That volume had not, moreover, been the first in the series. The 1855 volume had actually carried a disclaimer not unlike that found in *Essays and Reviews*: 'Each writer is responsible for his own opinions and for none but his own; and

---

[33] T. Arnold, *An Inaugural Lecture on the Study of Modern History* (Oxford, 1841), 29.
[34] See above, 60.

no attempt has been made to give a general unity of thought to the publication.'[35]

Temple's own deputy at Kneller Hall had contributed an essay on 'Alfred de Musset' to the 1855 volume. Mark Pattison had written about 'Oxford Studies', reviewing the academic developments in the university over the past century. James Anthony Froude had provided a piece entitled 'Suggestions on the Best Means of Teaching English History'. And the topics contributed to the 1856 volume were quite as varied. If one thought of *Essays and Reviews* as being roughly the same kind of volume then Temple's *apologia* makes perfect sense. Jowett had represented the volume as another opportunity for opposing the dogmatism and obscurantism of the Oxford men. The suggestion had come from the circle of Balliol/Rugby friends—mostly liberals but varying widely in their liberalism—with whom he had often shared exciting conversations without necessarily agreeing with every view expressed. He had been asked by his friends to make use of the vent and had done so. The note 'To The Reader' with which the volume was prefaced, seemed to make it clear that this was a publication to which individuals had happened to send in a number of pieces on a wide variety of unrelated subjects.

It will be readily understood that the Authors of the ensuing Essays are responsible for their respective articles only. They have written in entire independence of each other and without concert or comparison.

The Volume, it is hoped, will be received as an attempt to illustrate the advantage derivable to the cause of religious and moral truth, from a free handling in a becoming spirit, of subjects peculiarly liable to suffer by the repetition of conventional language, and from the traditional methods of treatment.

Yet there is something just a little disingenuous in the suggestion that the whole thing was simply an innocent mistake. Temple must have realized that the volume would appear to be a much more concerted attack upon standard 'orthodox' opinion than the earlier volumes had done. They had contained articles which might deal with classical archaeology, government policy, international affairs. Even though they might all have an academic (and, therefore, inevitably in the nineteenth century, a religious) interest, they would not have appeared to be united in a common purpose in the way the contributors to *Essays*

[35] 'Advertisement' printed immediately after the title page of *Oxford Essays contributed by Members of the University,* 1855.

and Reviews were bound to appear, particularly as so many of them were already well known for their liberal opinions. Jowett, Williams, Wilson, and Baden Powell, at least, were known to be Broad Churchmen or radicals and some of them had already been in rather public trouble for their unconventional theology. Their declared intention to depart from the traditional language of theology sounds like an attempt to offer an excuse in advance. On the other hand Temple *was*, in some ways, naïve and innocent. All the natural ebullience with which he had arrived at Rugby suggests an unaffected simplicity which might very easily be unaware of the possible dangers. His friends were going to have a go at the shibboleths of religion: it would be fun to join in. Since he had not thought of the headmastership as clothed with pompous dignity, he might genuinely not have realized how damaging his promise to contribute to the volume might become when he had taken up a job which put him in the public eye as he had never been before.

As a matter of simple objective fact, the articles *were* very varied. Rowland Williams wrote a review (for in the terminology of the day, some of the contributions were reviews and some were essays) of the biblical scholarship of a former Prussian ambassador at the Court of St James. Bunsen's approach was idiosyncratic and devout as well as critical. Williams, like any reviewer, expressed his own opinions (which were largely favourable) as well as summarizing Bunsen's. Baden Powell wrote an essay which was an attack on the then much admired argument of Paley that miracles provided evidential support for the truth of Christianity. Powell, who believed that 'evidence' was by its very nature something to be assessed juridically, maintained that the new scientific view of nature left little room for miracles and that their evidence could really only weigh with those who had actually witnessed them. Wilson on the National Church was a rambling plea for much greater doctrinal latitude and a glance at a number of different ways in which this might be achieved. Charles Goodwin's 'On the Mosaic Cosmogony' was the work of the only layman among the contributors. He may have felt less constrained by the prevailing orthodoxies than his clerical colleagues for he wrote in a savagely sarcastic style and attacked, with every appearance of relish, those who attempted to harmonize the Genesis accounts of Creation with the discoveries of the geologists. Mark Pattison's essay was historical in form, a survey of 'Tendencies of Religious Thought in England, 1688–1750'. This was an account of the deist controversy and, though its method was strictly historical, it exposed much of the obscurantism and dishonesty of both High Churchmen and Evangelicals. Jowett's contribution, 'On the Interpretation of Scripture', was the last and much the longest. It was, in a sense, a defence of the critical approach to the study of the Bible though it indulged directly in no attempt to make use of critical methods. But it gave great offence by the use of the phrase 'like any other book' to describe the proper way to interpret a biblical text. Very few people, then or since, have noticed that Jowett and Stanley had used the very same phrase when campaigning for the introduction of an undergraduate Theology school and had meant by it the 'common-sense' method of interpretation advocated by Thomas Arnold. Jowett intended only that one should read the text as simply and directly as one would read a passage from a classical author[36] but was taken to imply that scripture had no greater value or authority than any other book.

Temple's contribution was printed first in the book. In places its ideas were so loosely expressed that he would have found it difficult to defend them. Gladstone, who did not much like *Essays and Reviews* and who marked his copy with a good many harshly disapproving comments on Jowett's essay, was more discriminating when he came to Temple's. He gave several of the passages an approving tick but wrote, 'Homer! Dante!' against Temple's assertion that a modern child of twelve stood at the intellectual level once occupied by a grown man.[37] That statement had been in the part of the sermon in which the secular and religious history of humanity had been somewhat confused and it revealed very clearly the occasional carelessness in the essay. (Temple was always inclined to produce good common sense generalizations which were insufficiently finely tuned.) His belief in the progressive development of humanity was flawed but if it contained any obviously heterodox tendency, it was that—like Jowett's essay—it implied that divine revelation was dependent on human intellectual capacity. Unfortunately, perhaps, several of the other essayists made the point that religious beliefs were not static but developed; or pleaded for a Christianity that would be responsive to new knowledge and popular rationalism. This made it easy for readers to assume that there was a purposive structure to the book in which Temple set out the fundamental principle, others provided detailed instances, and Jowett's essay demonstrated how it was to be applied. When Samuel Wilberforce, the Bishop of Oxford, came to review the book he was able to make a reasonable job of showing that

---

[36] Hinchliff, 31 f. and 75 f.
[37] Gladstone's copy is in St Deiniol's library in Hawarden.

there were common themes in the volume and a common purpose and that Temple was as much responsible for the views of the other contributors as they were themselves.[38] One has also to remember that between the conception of the volume and its publication came the appearance of Darwin's *Origin of Species*. While, on the one hand, what Darwin had to say meant that, for instance, Goodwin's essay on Genesis and geology was rendered out of date; it also meant, on the other, that *Essays and Reviews* seemed like part of a growing fury of rationalist attack on the old certainties of authority and faith. And in the case of *Essays and Reviews*, it seemed, faith was being stabbed in the back by those who professed to be its friends. Temple could be represented as the standard-bearer of this dangerous crew.

The dynamics of the controversy have been carefully analysed and there is an immense amount of detail available for charting its course almost blow by blow.[39] But Temple's point of view has received less attention probably—and ironically—because his has come to be thought of as the least controversial of the contributions.

The book was published on 21 March 1860. Liddon, who had just moved from being vice-principal of Cuddesdon to being Vice-Principal of St Edmund Hall in Oxford itself, had read it within ten days and begun to rally the opposition.[40] Nevertheless there was, naturally, some delay before it began to attract public attention. The *Guardian* referred to it in April and the *Literary Gazette* reviewed it in the same month. In neither case was the volume referred to in particularly excited tones. A variety of reviews, comments, and leaders in the religious and the national press continued to appear throughout the year but the most important of them were the reviews in the three most influential journals: the *Westminster and Foreign Quarterly Review*, the *Quarterly Review*, and the *Edinburgh Review*.[41]

The *Westminster* was the most radical and the one from which the essayists had expected the most sympathetic treatment. In fact, though, the article (which appeared on 1 October 1860) was written by Frederic Harrison, a very young man whom disillusionment with conventional Christianity had driven into agnosticism. He attacked *Essays and Reviews* as 'Neo-Christianity'—the absurdity into which all liberalism was

---

[38] Ellis, 109.
[39] Ibid. 102–56; and Altholz, 34–84.
[40] Ibid. 103.
[41] Ibid. 106 ff.

bound to deteriorate, not a rational form of religion but something which was neither religious nor rational. It was a brilliant and scathing article, apparently destroying any hope that the essayists might have had of being seen as defenders of Christianity against the rationalist attack. Harrison maintained that the volume could not possibly be 'a collection of pamphlets bound up into one volume or the farrago of a few kindred minds'. It was plainly, he insisted, a single and coherent party manifesto and it failed to convince. His article appeared, moreover, at almost precisely the moment at which it could do most harm. It was published just after the meeting of the British Association for the Advancement of Science at which Wilberforce and Huxley had debated Darwin's evolutionary hypothesis. It was followed by:

...a great gathering of the Oxford M.A.'s who had come up to vote in Convocation against the appointment of Mr. Max Müller to the Chair of Sanskrit. That distinguished Orientalist was suspected of 'Germanism', being in fact a German, and also an acquaintance of the Chevalier Bunsen, whose name (if only on account of Dr. Arnold's friendship for him) was a bugbear to many of the orthodox at the time. The clergy who came up on that occasion had their attention called to an article in the *Westminster and Foreign Quarterly Review*...The tenor of that article was calculated to excite their horror.

Then, in January 1861 came Wilberforce's review in the *Quarterly*. It was anonymous but its author's name seems to have become common knowledge fairly quickly. There were those, indeed, who thought it vile that a diocesan bishop should deliver an anonymous attack upon clergymen but most readers would have assumed that this was almost an official reprimand. Wilberforce pressed home all the reasons for thinking that *Essays and Reviews* expressed a unified and carefully thought out position. He attacked Temple's 'laboured similitude' which made the education of the human race analogous to the maturing of an individual. It amounted, he insisted, to a denial of the doctrines of the Fall and Redemption. And he condemned what he identified as the unifying theme of the volume, the elevation of private judgement and the abandonment of belief in the inspiration and authority of the Bible. He, too, was savagely sarcastic accusing the essayists of hypocrisy and dishonesty. 'They believe too much not to believe more, and they disbelieve too much not to disbelieve everything.' The third major review, Stanley's in the *Edinburgh* did not appear until April and by then much else had happened.

In the meanwhile, Temple was still quite sanguine. He wrote to Stanley on 14 January 1861 saying that the outcry against the book was not yet serious. His own school house was full until 1863 and he had a long list of applicants hoping for vacancies. He told his friend that some of the contributors were anxious to produce another volume but that he was not willing to write for it: 'People cannot swallow more than a certain amount at a time and another volume five years hence would be quite soon enough.' He talked of being upheld by the very large number of letters he had received from people who had found *Essays and Reviews* a help rather than a hindrance to belief. But, ominously, he said, 'I suppose Tait will not attack us. I do not fear damage from any other attack.'[42] He and Jowett went to visit Tait at Fulham Palace on 20 January: they gained the impression that Tait would be on their side.[43]

An enormous number of the clergy seem to have read Wilberforce's review and to have been influenced by it, particularly once it became known who the author was. Indignant clergymen wrote to the bishops. Some began to organize 'addresses' to the Archbishop of Canterbury, the Evangelical John Bird Sumner. These documents were rather like petitions for which as many signatures as possible were collected. And Wilberforce determined to press his opposition to *Essays and Reviews* even further. He had by this time been Bishop of Oxford for over fifteen years. He was, in any case, one of the most senior and significant bishops on the bench, known to have some influence at court through the Prince Consort, in spite of his High Church views. Early in February 1861 the bishops met at Lambeth and Wilberforce led the attack upon the liberals. Tait, of course, was present and, as Bishop of London, would have been the most senior of all after the archbishops, but Temple's trust that Tait would not attack them was doomed to be disappointed.

The bishops' meeting was neither a synodical nor a judicial gathering. The writings of the essayists were not being examined for heresy nor were they being tried for an ecclesiastical offence. The bishops, or some of them, might have to take part in a more official tribunal later. What they had to do, therefore, was to devise a way of expressing an episcopal opinion which would calm the fears of conservative churchmen without appearing to sit in formal judgement or to have prejudged the issue.

---

[42] Family papers in the possession of the Right Revd F. S. Temple: Letters to do with *Essays and Reviews*: Temple to Stanley, 14 Jan. 1861.
[43] See below, 77.

The best course seemed to be for the archbishop to answer one of the addresses he had received and for them all to sign his reply which would then be made public.

The address to which the archbishop was replying (emanating from a rural deanery in Dorset) had contained a paragraph complaining, without mentioning *Essays and Reviews*, of the spread of 'rationalistic and semi-infidel doctrines among the beneficed clergy of the realm'.

We allude especially to the denial of the atoning efficacy of the Death and Passion of our Blessed Saviour, Jesus Christ, both God and man, for us men and for our salvation, and to the denial also of a Divine Inspiration, peculiar to themselves alone, of the Canonical Scriptures of the Old and New Testament.[44]

Since there was no attempt to identify anyone who actually held these views, this seemed to the bishops to provide an ideal opportunity to condemn heresy and to imply they were opposed to the tendencies of *Essays and Reviews* without actually committing themselves to a judgement upon any specific statement in the book. It is true that they mentioned a 'book which contains' the views complained of and alluded to the possibility that judicial or synodical proceedings might follow. But no mention was made, anywhere in the address or the response to it, of the title of the book or of the names of the authors. In fact, the bishops were equivocating and inevitably their equivocation failed to achieve their real purpose which was to condemn *Essays and Reviews* without actually doing so. Moreover, those responsible for publicizing the bishops' statements handled it very badly. Worse still, at one point in the statement the bishops' original wording—'We cannot understand how these opinions can be held consistently with an honest subscription to the formularies of our Church'—had been changed to read 'We cannot understand how *their* opinions...', thus giving the impression that the views condemned were those actually expressed by the essayists, rather than the 'rationalistic and semi-infidel' opinions vaguely complained of in the address. In other words what had been intended as an unspecific episcopal reassurance to anxious parsons, had come to seem like a blanket condemnation of *Essays and Reviews*, its contents, and its authors. Tait's name appeared on the list of signatories immediately after those of the two archbishops.

---

[44] Quoted in full in Rowland Prothero, *The Life and Correspondence of Arthur Penrhyn Stanley*, 2 vols. (London, 1892), i. 35 ff.; and in Davidson and Benham, i. 281 f.

Almost as soon as the bishops' actions were known, Tait began receiving letters from good-natured people urging him to do something to rescue Temple from the position into which he had so foolishly got himself. One of the earliest came from Dr Richard Jelf, Principal of King's College, London, and formerly a Canon of Christ Church, Oxford, who seems to have been something of a friend of the Temple family.[45] In the 1840s, during the heated debate over *Tract XC*, he had been regarded as a fair and moderate man, but in the early 1850s he had been one of F. D. Maurice's principal critics in the controversy at King's about his teaching on eternal punishment. He had the reputation, therefore, of being both fair *and* orthodox. 'Can nothing be done', he wrote, 'to rescue poor Temple from his false position?'[46] Convinced that Temple did not share 'Powell's Atheism, or Dr Williams' perverse Deism' or what he called Wilson's 'Jesuitism' he nevertheless rejected the argument for 'limited liability' among the authors on the ground that the first essay contained a quite unmistakable 'key-note' to the whole volume. If it were not so, surely Temple would have said so.

I have no doubt that his silence originates in a chivalrous resolve not to desert his associates—and doubtless he could not do it without a most painful self-sacrifice. And yet, from my point of view, it appears to be a sacrifice which he owes to Christ and His Church, in recognition of the imprudence which has imperilled his high character. He might at least put forth some positive statement in evidence of his Faith, without so much as naming the *Essays*.

Jelf was, in fact, to become more vigorous in his opposition to the volume, being one of those responsible for urging Convocation to consider and censure it.[47]

Condemnation of the book and the extrication of Temple (and possibly Jowett) became a theme of many of Tait's correspondents. None of them seemed to realize how patronizing such a line would seem to Temple himself. It was to treat him as a bright and able youngster who must be rescued from the consequences of his own folly. It was all well-meant but it missed the real point: and, after all, Temple was forty years old and a headmaster.

The crisis appears to have placed Temple under intense emotional pressure. Friends like Jowett relied on him to stand firm with the

[45] Sandford (ed.), ii. 468.
[46] Lambeth Palace Library: Tait Papers, vol. 80, fos. 15–17. Letter dated 14 Feb. 1861.
[47] E. Abbott and L. Campbell, *The Life and Letters of Benjamin Jowett* (London, 1897), i. 344.

essayists. Friends like Stanley reminded him that it would have been wiser not to have joined them in the first place. Scott evidently felt betrayed by Temple's contributing to *Essays and Reviews*: it showed that he valued Jowett's friendship more highly than his own.[48] Temple himself had grown less buoyant. By 19 February he was telling Stanley that he did not mean to leave Rugby unless he was sacked and he did not think that the trustees had the actual power to sack him. He must have learnt on the same day of the bishops' statement, for he wrote a second letter to Stanley saying that he had seen it but could not make much sense of it until he had seen the address to which it was a reply. He even wondered whether it might not be sensible to sue for libel. Better still, he thought, the liberals might get up a counter-address to Tait, as the bishop whom they most respected, regretting that he could have signed the archbishop's letter. He told Stanley that he felt so totally betrayed by Tait that he could not even write to him 'indignantly'[49] but he did write, a day or two later, in extremely formal terms, demanding that Tait should tell him precisely which passages of his own essay were regarded by the bishops as exceptionable. It turned out that he had been confusing two different addresses to the archbishop. Temple had seen one which specifically asked for the condemnation of certain of his own statements whereas the document to which the bishops were actually responding had not. Unfortunately Tait's letter which made this clear and might have been used to avoid further controversy, went on to say that it was inevitable that the general public would regard the volume as a single whole and that, taken as a whole it was:

. . . in my judgement, not consistent with the true doctrine maintained by our Church as to the office of Holy Scripture. . . . I feel convinced that there is much in this volume, of which you as well as others of the contributors disapprove and I therefore the more regret that your high character and deserved influence

---

[48] Sandford (ed.), ii. 615.

[49] Family papers in the possession of the Right Revd F. S. Temple: Letters to do with *Essays and Reviews*: Temple to Stanley, letter dated 19 Feb. 1861. This account of the events of the first quarter of 1861 is pieced together from these family papers, from Tait's correspondence in Lambeth Palace Library and from Davidson and Benham, i. 280–312. Some letters quoted in the last-mentioned source do not appear in the relevant volume of the Tait papers and some of the letters in that volume are not mentioned or not given in full in Davidson and Benham. There are also small discrepancies between the version of certain letters given in the *Life* and the version in Tait's drafts. (It is possible that his chaplains may have polished the style in the final letters; alternatively, the polishing may have been done editorially by the writers of the *Life*, though Davidson was meticulous in his handling and use of documents and very anxious to be fair.) On the whole in such cases I have used the version in Lambeth Palace Library.

should, as matters stand at present, seem to give weight to the volume as a whole.... I shall be ready to state publicly if you desire it what is my opinion of your Essay taken by itself.[50]

Tait added that he would like to be able to publish their correspondence, explaining later that he believed that this would be a way of stressing the independence of the contributors from one another, without—though he does not state this explicitly—Temple's having formally to dissociate himself from the rest.

Tait's behaviour did little to mollify Temple. Once the latter discovered precisely what it was that Tait and the other bishops had been responding to, he told Stanley, 'I don't think A. C. London quite exculpated but his signature becomes quite a different thing. He is a coward but not a treacherous coward.'[51]

This was the point at which the crisis came for Temple. As in the last days at Kneller Hall he now suffered 'an attack of illness brought on by anxiety'.[52] Then he had undergone something of a breakdown. Crushed by frustrated ambition for the institution and a fear that he might be labelled as a failure, he had not found any easy comfort or escape. This time, things were even worse. Not only was he being made to feel immature and irresponsible but it seemed that he had committed himself to an act which, though he was sure it was morally right, had turned out to be imprudent and likely to destroy his position in the school. Once again there was a kind of breakdown.

One of the senior masters at Rugby wrote to Tait saying that the school was in some turmoil:

As the Address itself has not yet been published, no one can say who or what had been censured. Most of us think that Dr. Temple's essay is not included in the general censure. I am one of the few who hope that your lordships have only agreed in condemning certain specified opinions not maintained by Dr. Temple.... You will be sorry to hear that Dr. Temple was very far from well when the school met. As he is still in a very weak and nervous state we are very anxious about him. He had determined, for the sake of the boys, to disconnect himself in some way or other from the other essayists. Indeed, the parents are in such an uneasy state that something must be done to reassure them.[53]

---

[50] Lambeth Palace Library: Tait Papers, vol. 80, the correspondence between Temple and Tait on 21, 22, and 23 Feb. is to be found in fos. 25–31.

[51] Family papers in the possession of the Right Revd F. S. Temple: Letters to do with *Essays and Reviews*: Temple to Stanley, letter dated 22 Feb. 1861.

[52] Sandford (ed.), ii. 614.

[53] Quoted in full in Davidson and Benham, i. 293.

The penultimate sentence of the letter was in a sense misleading and may have given Tait the false hope that Temple could be persuaded to make some definite statement, separating himself from the other contributors to the volume. He replied immediately to the master, Robert Mayor, drawing his attention to the fact that the address had been published in the most recent number of the *Guardian*. 'You will observe that in that address there was no allusion to Dr. Temple nor to any opinion which his essay, as I understand it, maintains.'[54] Mayor then wrote again saying that Tait's answer had 'removed very general misunderstanding at Rugby and has been a great relief to Dr. Temple's own mind'. He reported that Temple was still confined to his bed but had managed to call the masters together and had spoken to them for about half an hour about his part in *Essays and Reviews*.

He told us that as soon as he read the other Essays he felt that he had made a great blunder. But he could not publicly say that he disagreed with the other writers, for his very object in promising to write in the vol.[sic] had been to get some who felt difficulties to speak out and that he had been prepared to tolerate much that he disliked. He implied that the writers had gone far beyond the limits he had proposed...He proposed to tell the boys that there was much in the book that he did not agree with and that they should not read it. He proposed to publish his sermons so that everyone may know what his teaching in the pulpit has been.[55]

It seems that Temple had spent the days of his illness coming to some sort of decision about what he ought to do to restore his position. He spoke to the boys, telling them:

It was perhaps a blunder in me not to reconsider my decision of letting the Essay be published when I came to Rugby, but inasmuch as it was a past act, it never occurred to me to reconsider it. I thought then, and I still think, even after what has happened that that book ought to have been published. The book contains opinions which had long been lurking in corners; it was time they were dragged to light and faced. We, the Essayists, knew who were going to write, but we did not know what each was going to write about. We agreed each to write what he thought, and that we were only responsible for our own essay; this was clear to us all because we knew before writing that we differed widely. In conclusion I would warn you against two things, against entering on the speculations

---

[54] Ibid. 294.

[55] Lambeth Palace Library: Tait Papers, vol. 80, fo. 33, letter from Robert B. Mayor dated 24 Feb. 1861. This letter is referred to but not quoted in Davidson and Benham. Sandford (ed.), i. 220 ff. contains the recollections of two other masters as to what Temple actually said.

contained in that book in a light and cursory way, and against supposing that I agree with all that is in that book. I am sure that you know me too well to suppose this for an instant.[56]

The breakdown, whatever it was, lasted some weeks. The correspondence between Mayor and Tait is dated between 21 and 24 February but Temple had written to Scott as early as 19 February saying that he had been very ill *in the previous week*. 'The fever brought back symptoms which eight years ago made three London physicians tell me that I could not expect to live out the year; *inter alia* long fainting fits.'[57] Once he had begun to recover, he was ready to do battle again. His correspondence with Tait was renewed. He wrote, on 25 February, what must have been a devastating letter to receive. Having told Tait that he remained completely unwilling that their correspondence should be published, he went on:

Surely the whole Bench of Bishops is enough to save the many from such influence without calling on the six contributors to give their aid.

The danger seems to me to be quite on the other side.

Many years ago you urged us from the University Pulpit to undertake the critical study of the Bible. You said it was a dangerous study but an indispensable[one]. You described its difficulties and those who listened must have felt a confidence (as I assuredly did, for I was there) that if they took your advice and entered on the task, you at any rate would never join in treating them unjustly if their study had brought with it the difficulties that you described.

Such a study so full of difficulties imperatively demands freedom for its condition. To tell a man to study and yet bid him under heavy penalties to come to the same conclusions with those who have not studied is to mock him. If the conclusions are prescribed, the study is precluded.

Freedom plainly implies the widest possible toleration.

I admit that toleration must have limits; or the Church would fall to pieces.

But the situation now is that the limits are not defined. One does not know when one transgresses. Suddenly without warning that one is on trial and with no opportunity to explain or defend.... the whole Bench of Bishops joins in inflicting a severe censure and in insinuating that they are dishonest men. And so utterly reckless are their Lordships how much or how little penalty they inflict that the censure is drawn in terms that are not intelligible without the production of another document.... How on earth is any study to be pursued under such treatment as this?

You complain that young men of ability will not take orders. How can you expect it when this is what befalls whoever does not think just as you do?

---

[56] Sandford (ed.), i. 220 n.   [57] Ibid. ii. 616.

I know what can be said against a wide toleration. It may be said that it will issue in wild and extravagant speculations. So it would in a few instances. But you know perfectly well that there is not the most distant chance of the great mass of sober Englishmen falling into anything of the sort. If therefore you tolerate extreme opinions their very existence in the Church is a guarantee that the moderate opinions are those held from conviction not from fear of consequences. But if you drive extreme views out of the ministry the inevitable result is to poison the minds of the laity with the suspicion that the clergymen who remain teach what they do, not because they believe it but because they fear the fate of the brethren. I for one joined in writing this book in the hope of breaking through that mischievous reticence which go where I would I perpetually found destroying the truthfulness of religion. I wished to encourage men to speak out. I believed that many doubts and difficulties only lived because they were hunted into the dark, and would die in the light. I believed that all opinions of the sort contained in the book would be better if tolerated and discussed than if covered and maintained in secret. And though there was much poor mixed up in these opinions yet certainly not more than in what is allowed and even encouraged. What can be grosser superstition than the theory of literal inspiration? But because that has a regular footing it is to be treated as a good man's mistake: while the courage to speak the truth about the first chapter of Genesis is a wanton piece of wickedness. A wide toleration would in time get all these matters in their true relation; for if neology had strong defenders, certainly the commonly received opinions have no lack of able men to maintain them.

But censures even on the right side will only do what you said more than fourteen years ago, gain you the aid of some treacherous waiters upon fortune.

In conclusion I must say a few words personal to you and myself.

If you do not wish to alienate your friends do not treat them as you have treated me. Do not if one of them seem [*sic*] to you to have done a wrong thing, ask him to your house, speak of the subject kindly, condemn in such a tone as to imply no severe reprobation, and then in deference to popular clamour join in an act of unexampled severity.

You might have spoken severely if you had thought severely. Having spoken leniently you were pledged to deal leniently. Nothing would have been easier than to imply to me what you were going to do, if you then had thoughts of doing it. And surely if your quiet perusal of the book had given you no such thoughts, the mere cry of the mob ought not to have influenced your judgment.

What you did had not the intention, but it had the effect of treachery.

You will not keep friends, if you compel them to feel that in every crisis of life they must be on their guard against trusting you.[58]

---

[58] Lambeth Palace Library: Tait Papers, vol. 80, fos. 37 ff.: the letter is also quoted in Davidson and Benham, i. 290 ff.

Temple told Stanley that he had had some correspondence with Tait which had ended in his writing 'rather angrily'. He did not know, he said, whether Tait would answer with 'equal wrath'. He also said that he was on the best possible terms with Lord Denbigh, the chairman of the Rugby trustees and that he did not think that he need have any fear about what the trustees might do.[59] The one thing he really regretted was that he had dragged the school into religious controversy for he feared that the boys might begin to dabble in critical questions before they were mature enough to cope with its implications. (This concern was something he repeated to various friends and correspondents.) 'In all other respects, Stanley, I do not and cannot regret that we wrote and published.'[60]

Both Tait and Temple were obviously deeply affected by this crisis in their friendship. Letters passed backwards and forwards between Rugby and Fulham Palace almost every day through the latter part of February 1861. Throughout the correspondence Tait tried doggedly to achieve two things simultaneously—to soften Temple's anger and restore their friendship; and to justify the bishops' belief that some things in *Essays and Reviews* were contrary to the formularies of the Church of England. Since these two objectives were incompatible he tried to reconcile them by demonstrating that Temple had very little in common with the other contributors. Tait's aim, therefore, was to obtain from Temple some sort of statement separating himself from them. This Temple was resolute in refusing to do.

Tait wrote again on 27 February with what was really an appeal to Temple to accept his former tutor's point of view:

I was in hopes that you would have felt with me that the Archbps [*sic*] and Bishops letter had so changed the state of the case that you and not you only but the other Essayists also might have publicly reiterated their demand to be judged each by his own Essay alone.[61]

But he insisted that the bishops, having been appealed to for an opinion, could hardly have said anything different from what they actually had said. 'What was issued was a condemnation of the book as one whole, leaving individuals each to speak for himself in exculpation.'

---

[59] The table of contents in *Essays and Reviews* listed Temple as 'chaplain to the Earl of Denbigh'.

[60] Family papers in the possession of the Right Revd F. S. Temple: Letters to do with *Essays and Reviews*: Temple to Stanley 27 Feb. 1861.

[61] Lambeth Palace Library: Tait Papers, vol. 80, fo. 41. Tait's draft of 27 Feb. 1861.

He thought Temple's attack on him—as one who now stifled biblical scholarship—was nonsense.

... there must be limits to the freedom of the conclusions to which clergymen come and which they teach. Suppose a man were unfortunately to arrive at the opinion as a result of his Biblical Studies that there is no God—and the Bible is from the beginning to the end a lie—am I to allow him to teach this as a clergyman of the Ch. of Egnd [*sic*]—or if I condemn the result of his studies am I to be said to discourage the study?[62]

A little desperately he pointed out that there is always a difficulty in harmonizing private friendships and public duties. Most people in public life try and solve it by socializing only with those with whom they are likely to agree. 'They escape thereby much danger of being misunderstood; but they rob life of what makes it of value.' And he reminded Temple that in the old days at Balliol, 'when there was many a painful difficulty of the same kind with Oakley and Ward' they had had an understanding that private friendships should neither prevent nor be broken by public acts.[63]

Tait tried to follow that same code in the events that followed. While these letters were passing between himself and Temple, the Convocation of Canterbury was in session. On 26 February in the lower house Archdeacon Denison, who had been such a critic of Kneller Hall, delivered himself of a comprehensive condemnation of *Essays and Reviews*. It was, he thundered, 'of all books in any language which I ever laid my hands on ... incomparably the worst. It contains all the poison which is to be found in Tom Paine's *Age of Reason*, while it has the additional disadvantage of having been written by clergymen.'[64] Tait's speech in the upper house two days later tried very hard to put his two incompatible points. He budged not at all from the conviction that the bishops had been entirely justified in their criticism of the book, while attempting also to suggest that his colleagues like Wilberforce, Hamilton of Salisbury, and Thirlwall of St David's were exaggerating its evils. He condemned in no uncertain terms the vituperative tone taken by some of the volume's critics. He expressed a faint hope that the more moderate essayists would dissociate themselves from the views of the more extreme. And of Temple himself he said:

---

[62] Ibid., fo. 48.
[63] The letter is printed in full in Davidson and Benham, i. 294 ff.
[64] *Chronicle of Convocation*, 26 Feb. 1861, 394 (and quoted in Davidson and Benham, i. 302).

I have known Dr Temple ... for many years in the intimacy of private friendship. The particular essay which he has written certainly does not express my views. I believe it was first preached as a University Sermon in St Mary's Church, Oxford. I dislike it, but, in my estimation, it is totally different in character from other passages which occur in this volume; and I cannot conceive by what motive the author could be restrained—if it should prove that he is restrained—from publicly declaring that he does not approve of various things which are to be found in this unfortunate book.[65]

Temple was utterly unwilling to take the hint. After the debate in convocation had taken place, he responded to the bishop's letter of 27 February, saying 'I do not care for your severity. I do care for being cheated. The greatest kindness you can now do me is to forget till all this is over that any friendship ever existed between us. That will at any rate save me from such mischief as yr [sic] speech in Convocation yesterday is certain to do me.'[66]

But Tait, no less than Temple himself, was suffering from a sense of friendship betrayed. He wrote in his journal, 'This week has been one of great trial. Temple's letter respecting the declaration of the Bishops have greatly pained me.'[67] And on 2 March he sent Temple a bitter complaint about what he had said to the masters at Rugby. He had somehow gained the impression that it had given a distorted account of the meeting between himself, Temple, and Jowett at Fulham on 20 January.[68] Temple replied to Tait's letter the very next day, saying that no one appeared to have told Tait that his last words to the masters were, 'You will see that if any public statement of my disapproving of the other writers in the volume is made, I shall probably find it my duty to contradict it.' There was no possibility of his having misunderstood Tait at Fulham: immediately after the meeting Jowett had said, 'Tait was very kind and on the whole gave me the impression that he agreed with me.'

Temple did, however, end his letter with what amounted to an apology for whatever might have seemed arrogant in his behaviour.

I owe you very much; more than I can ever repay. My heart swells sometimes when I think of lessons learned from your lips 20 years ago and of kindnesses

---

[65] *Chronicle of Convocation*, 28 Feb. 1861, 461 ff.
[66] Lambeth Palace Library: Tait Papers, vol. 80, fo. 51, letter dated 1 Mar. 1861 and printed in Davidson and Benham, i. 297 f.
[67] Quoted in Davidson and Benham, i. 307.
[68] Ibid., fos. 59 ff. Draft letter dated 2 Mar.

which perhaps were hardly thought of by you who did them, but were more than I can tell to me who received them. And you can hardly imagine the wound that it gave me to see your name under the Archbishop's letter... because my visit to Fulham made me feel sure that you would join in no such act.[69]

It was the beginning of a thaw and a return to an older and happier relationship. Tait thanked him for the 'more kindly tone' of his letter 'so much more like yourself' and conceded:

...that I appear to have left on your mind and on Jowett's an impression different from what I intended: though perhaps this difference between us may arise from your judging differently of the Bishops' protest from what I do. Remember the protest was directed against the general teaching of the book viewed as a whole and against certain doctrines in it and [an illegible word] stated to be extracted from it.

He then quoted from his journal of 20 January:

I find this entry which expresses my feeling at the time of yr [*sic*] and of Jowett's visit. 'Jowett has been with me for two days. The unsatisfactory part of his system seems to be that there is an obscurity over what he believes of the centre of Xty [*sic*] ... the central figure of the Lord Jesus; the central doctrine of the efficacy of his sacrifice; in fact St Paul's Xty—is this distinctly recognized by writers of his school? I have urged both on him and Temple who had been with me that they are bound to state for their own sakes and for the sake of those whom they are looking to influence, what is the positive Xty which they hold. It is a poor thing to be pulling down—let them build up.

He then apologized for possibly not making himself clear and so edged towards more friendly terms, signing himself 'Ever yours A. C. London'.[70]

The most difficult part of the controversy, so far as Temple was concerned, was the way in which he was pulled one way and another by old friends. Others, perhaps, claimed—as they delivered attacks upon him—a close and affectionate friendship which had never existed in reality. When the controversy was at its height and some of the conservatives produced a volume called *Replies to 'Essays and Reviews'*, Goulburn contributed what was a direct reply to Temple's 'Education of the World'. Goulburn was also an immense admirer of one of the

---

[69] Lambeth Palace Library: Tait Papers, vol. 80, fos. 63 ff.

[70] Ibid., fos. 65 ff. The correspondence between Tait and Temple in the early days of March 1861 is printed in Davidson and Benham, i. 299 ff. The letter in which there is an illegible word in Tait's draft appears on p. 301 but in a somewhat different form as though Davidson also had difficulty in reading it.

fiercest of all the conservative critics of *Essays and Reviews*, J. W. Burgon (soon to be vicar of the University church in Oxford) who, though older than Temple and Goulburn, had been at Worcester College when they were at Balliol.[71] He published in 1861 a volume of sermons, *Inspiration and Interpretation*, which attacked *Essays and Reviews* and he remained a bitter critic of Temple's for the rest of his life. After Burgon's death in 1888 Goulburn published a biography which painted a picture, at least by implication, of Burgon's continuing to feel a warm personal affection towards Temple in spite of being obliged to criticize his theology.[72] But it is clear that by 1870 Burgon had become openly hostile insisting that Temple was dangerous and dishonourable[73] and it is difficult to know whether there had ever been really close friendly relations between Burgon and Temple. The Sandford *Memoir* lists Burgon as one among a great many people with whom Temple had been friendly when he was an undergraduate and from whom he later grew apart. Goulburn is not mentioned at all except as having been his predecessor at Rugby. Temple certainly seems to have felt no animosity towards Goulburn for, when he was coming to the end of his time at Rugby and both Goulburn and Burgon had attacked his essay, he invited Goulburn to preach at one of the major occasions in the school year and went to some lengths to persuade former masters and old boys to attend the service.[74]

In March 1861 Macmillan undertook to publish some of the sermons Temple had preached since arriving at Rugby so that everyone might satisfy themselves as to the innocuous nature of the headmaster's teaching.[75] There was little now to be done except wait for the Rugby trustees to come to their decision but pressure was mounting against the essayists. Even most of those who wrote sympathetically to Tait about both Jowett and Temple were perfectly clear that they thought *Essays and Reviews* was an undesirable work.[76] J. C. Shairp, who had been a master at Rugby before moving to a chair at St Andrews,

---

[71] I am indebted to Colin R. Lawlor, who is currently doing research on Burgon, for drawing my attention to this information relating to the relationship between Temple, Goulburn, and Burgon.

[72] E. M. Goulburn, *John William Burgon, Late Dean of Chichester: A Biography*, 2 vols. (London, 1892), i. 149 f. and ii. 42.

[73] Bodleian Library, Oxford: MS Wilberforce d.47, fos. 261 ff., letter dated 'Oriel Feb. 11' [1870]. I am indebted to Colin Lawlor for drawing my attention to this letter.

[74] *The Meteor*, edited by members of Rugby School, No. 21 (3 Nov. 1868), 2.

[75] Sandford (ed.), ii. 614. The volume was published as *Rugby Sermons*.

[76] e.g. Lambeth Palace Library: Tait Papers, vol. 80, fo. 53, letter from J. P. Norris (Temple was godfather to his son), 1 Mar. 1861, also fo. 57, letter from the Dean of Wells.

suggested that, though 'The Education of the World' had aroused no criticism when preached, it contained things which, if looked at closely, were probably heretical.[77]

The trustees of the school were to meet on 19 April to discuss the headmaster's part in the book which was now thought of as having been condemned by the bishops. Lord Denbigh, the sixty-five-year-old chairman, was very much the grandee, a Count of the Holy Roman Empire as well as a peer of the realm, and eventually a Privy Councillor. The owner of estates in the region himself, he was related to many of the landowning families in the West Midlands. He had succeeded to the title as a small child and had been a trustee since Arnold's day. The other trustees, and there were a round dozen of them, were all in varying degrees of importance, local notables. They included:

the Earl of Warwick;
Lord Leigh, the Lord-Lieutenant of Warwickshire;
William Stratford Dugdale of Merevale Hall in Warwickshire, a former MP for North Staffordshire, a JP, and a member of an important local family;
Lord Howe, who was a Curzon but more importantly, in this connection, a relative of the Dugdales;
C. B. Adderley, Conservative MP for North Staffordshire and President of the Board of Health in the Derby administration of 1858/9 who had also been responsible for legislation on reformatories and young offenders;
Charles Newdigate Newdegat, Conservative MP for North Warwickshire;
the Hon. Charles Bertie Percy, brother of the fifth Duke of Northumberland, who had married the heiress of the Berties of Guys Cliffe, Warwick, and assumed the additional surname;
Sir Thomas Skipwith of Newbold Hall, Warwickshire, formerly MP for North Warwickshire;
Sir Henry Halford, whose father had been made a baronet for services rendered as Physician-in-Ordinary to George III, had changed his name from Vaughan, and was distantly connected to Denbigh by a complex series of links by marriage;

---

[77] Ibid., fo. 71 letter from J. C. Shairp 13 Mar. It is followed by part of another letter in what appears to be the same handwriting and is dated from St Andrews, so is probably also by Shairp.

the Revd C. Holbech, vicar of Farnborough in Warwickshire who had been an undergraduate at Balliol just before Temple's time there.

As the date of the meeting drew nearer Temple began to think that he might have been too optimistic about Denbigh's support as he had previously been about Tait's. He wrote to Stanley saying that in March the trustees had been in a panic and determined to get rid of him. 'However I think they are more at ease now; especially as they begin to see that the laws of nature are not suspended by the "vague anathema" of the Bishops.'[78] Stanley's defence of the essayists in the *Edinburgh Review* appeared shortly before the trustees meeting. He told the editor that he hoped 'to steer a middle course between the bottomless Charybdis of the Westminster and the barking Scylla of the Quarterly', adding that the contributions from Temple, Pattison, and Jowett were of a very different kind from the rest. Temple's original sermon, he thought, had been 'received with general approbation'; Pattison's contribution was 'a mere scholastic review of the eighteenth-century divines'; Jowett's 'had it appeared separately, and without his name, ... would, I am convinced, have been hailed as a considerable accession to Biblical scholarship'.[79]

Whatever Stanley's intention, the article seems to have carried little conviction. It may have been that he was too obviously concerned to rescue his friends Temple and Jowett or he may have seemed merely to be fence-sitting. If his intention was to defend the right of clergymen of the Church of England to express unconventional theological opinions, he conceded too much. He made it seem that he, one of the most broadminded of the Arnoldite Broad Churchmen, was unwilling or unable to present a coherent case for the views expressed in the book. He seemed to be apologizing for some of the essays and joining in the condemnation of the rest. Tait wrote in his diary for 21 April 1861:

Read over again the article in the Edinburgh on *Essays and Reviews.* Its logic is very poor—the writing forcible. It would be a good defence of Temple and perhaps of Jowett, if they stood alone or only with Pattison. As a defence of the book generally, it is quite powerless.[80]

Temple, always naturally sanguine took the opposite view. He told Stanley on 15 April that his article had been published at exactly the

---

[78] Family papers in the possession of the Right Revd F. S. Temple: Letters relating to *Essays and Reviews*, Temple to Stanley 15 Apr. 1861.
[79] Quoted in Prothero, ii. 33 f.
[80] Davidson and Benham, i. 307.

right moment, and said exactly the right things, to persuade the trustees.[81] But it was still far from certain that they would be appeased though the volume of *Rugby Sermons* had appeared just before the meeting, too. Temple told Scott that they were 'deliberating whether to dismiss the Headmaster. The headmaster declined to discuss with them any question but the welfare of the school. It had ended in a great growl, and for the present nothing more.'[82] He was playing down the seriousness of the situation though there was a precedent for his refusal to discuss anything other than the welfare of the school. In 1836, when Arnold's Broad Church views were under attack, the trustees had dealt with the situation by declaring themselves satisfied with his running of the school instead of examining his theology.[83]

The trustees' communication to the headmaster of 19 April went further. It expressed 'their satisfaction at the success of his exertions in the management of the School . . .'. But they added that, though they 'did not think themselves called upon to offer any opinion on matters of religious controversy connected with the objections made to some parts of the Volume, as tending to impair the reverence due to the Holy Scriptures. But they cannot be blind to the fact that such objections are entertained by the highest ecclesiastical authorities.' The communications ended with a reference to the statements Temple had made to the boys and the masters. The trustees claimed the right to be told what he had said as this might 'affect the best interests of the school'.[84] He told Stanley of their demand on 30 April, saying:

I have replied. They meet again on the 3rd but meanwhile those who write to me write in ominous language and Lord Denbigh, hitherto my fast friend, now quotes Bishop Thirlwall and Hampden and talks of my complicity in having distributed poison. If they go to consult the Bishop there is an end to the matter. [Henry Philpott, an Evangelical, had become Bishop of Worcester, in which diocese the school was, in March 1861] I hardly think they will turn me out. But so far from its being impossible, I fancy it will be a near thing. . . . I am clear that nothing will induce me to say one word in condemnation directly or indirectly

---

[81] Family Papers in the possession of the Right Revd F. S. Temple: Letters relating to *Essays and Reviews*, typed copy of a letter from Temple to Stanley, 15 Apr. 1861.

[82] Sandford (ed.), ii. 611.

[83] Family Papers in the possession of the Right Revd F. S. Temple: Letters relating to *Essays and Reviews*, copy of a statement signed by the trustees on 23 Mar. 1836.

[84] Ibid., copy of the letter addressed to Dr Temple at a private meeting of the Trustees held at Curzon House on 19th Apr. 1861.

of the other writers in the volume. It would be base and dishonest. But I much doubt whether they will be satisfied with less.[85]

When the trustees met on 3 May things went a little more smoothly than Temple had hoped. He had written to tell the trustees what he had said in his meetings with both boys and masters in the previous January. The trustees' reply expressed satisfaction with his explanation, though they did so in terms as demeaning as could be:

They are glad to find that he had warned the elder boys against reading the *Essays and Reviews* as being a Book unfit for their study.

They believe his name will never again be allowed to appear in connection with speculations of a questionable religious character, ascribing it to inadvertence that it has so appeared in the present instance.

They have pleasure in receiving his assurance that he retains the confidence (with very few exceptions) of those who have placed their sons under his care, and especially such as are Clergymen of the Church of England.[86]

Temple seems to have insisted that this correspondence should not be published: Denbigh hoped that it would be. On the very day of the meeting he wrote to Tait, regretting that it had been decided not to send it to *The Times* and went so far as to suggest that Tait need not treat the matter as confidential.

It is possible that Denbigh took it upon himself to spread the news to other grandees. He seems, at any rate, to have written to Lord Stanley of Alderley sending him copies of the trustees' correspondence with Temple.[87] Lord Stanley, Postmaster General in Palmerston's administration at the time, was Arthur Stanley's first cousin. His wife, whom Palmerston called 'Mrs Stanley' and described as 'joint whip' (with her husband) for his party in the Lords, was a leading campaigner for women's education and a great friend of Jowett who is known to have visited Alderley in 1861.[88] Why Denbigh should have chosen to keep him informed of what had happened at Rugby is not clear. That he was

---

[85] Family Papers in the possession of the Right Revd F. S. Temple: typed copy of a letter from Temple to Stanley, 30 Apr. 1861. There appears to be some confusion over dates. Temple refers to a meeting of the trustees on 28 Apr. but this is probably a mistake for 19 Apr. since the 'civil letter' asking for information is clearly dated on that day.

[86] Ibid., copy of a letter to Temple from the trustees, 3 May 1861.

[87] Ibid., Stanley to Denbigh, 5 June 1861. A note attached to the letter describes it as being from A. P. Stanley but the signature is plainly 'Stanley'—without initials or first name. The only other person who might have signed thus was the eldest son of the Earl of Derby, who had no obvious connection with any of the protagonists.

[88] Abbott and Campbell, ii. 339.

Arthur Stanley's cousin may have had something to do with it for he was plainly sympathetic to Temple, taking particular pleasure in the fact that only five boys had been removed from the school.

... and I should agree with Dr Temple that no publication of the correspondence was necessary. Considering the noise that has been made, and the prejudices of the public, it seems to me not less surprising than gratifying that the injury to the school should be so small.

Temple also seems to have felt a returning confidence that the damage had been contained. The trustees had declared themselves satisfied and could not now go back on that. Above all, he had not been compelled publicly to dissociate himself from the other essayists. The Bishop of Worcester was willing to come and take a confirmation in the school chapel and all places in the school were fully booked until 1866.[89] Relations with Tait had not yet been fully restored for Temple resented what seemed to him to be a verdict of guilt by association. Unless 'The Education of the World' could be shown to be heterodox, there was nothing for which to apologize, yet he was being asked to secure his own acquittal by publicly disavowing the other contributors.

Tait was equally caught in a trap. He had felt obliged to join the other bishops in the implicit condemnation of *Essays and Reviews*: there was now no way (except the one which Temple resolutely refused to consider) in which he could extricate himself from the appearance of having condemned his friend. This may account for what appears to be an increasingly irritable tone in letters written by Tait to Arthur Stanley in June and July of 1861; an irritation directed as much at Temple and Jowett as at Stanley himself.[90] Neither of the protagonists seems to have been able to leave well alone. Stanley had been from the first outraged by the bishops' statement, which seemed to him an affront to every principle of justice. Tait had then urged him to trust the bishops and to wait for six months for it to become clear, he said, that they had acted wisely.[91] He had been annoyed by Stanley's article in

[89] Sandford (ed.), ii. 614.
[90] The correspondence is printed in Davidson and Benham, i. 308 ff. and the originals are in Lambeth Palace Library: Tait Papers, vol. 80. Prothero's life of Stanley does not print them in full but merely refers to Davidson and Benham. Fos. 5–8 of volume 80 of the Tait Papers is a letter from Stanley to Tait which has been bound ahead of other letters from 1861 because it is dated 'Jan. 8', though without a year. But the letter contains a reference to Stanley's article in the Edinburgh Review so I have assumed (below) that it belongs to the beginning of 1862.
[91] Davidson and Benham, i. 284 ff.

the Edinburgh, which seemed to him to attack the bishops unfairly. But Stanley had not changed his mind. The moment he could claim that the six months were up, he wrote again saying that his opinion of the bishop's action had in no way altered.

It is quite clear that Tait was angered by this gadfly persistence. His tone was much more terse and impatient than in his earlier exchanges with Temple and the irritation resulted in a series of increasingly sharp remarks made to Stanley about Temple. He insisted that he had never changed his mind about *Essays and Reviews* nor expressed a judgement on it publicly which was different from his private opinion. It was Temple who had behaved inconsistently, distancing himself from the other essayists in what he had said to the masters, boys, and trustees at the school yet refusing to do so in public. The book itself he now denounced as a 'flippant and reckless assault on things universally respected which has aroused public indignation...'.[92]

The disagreement between Tait and Stanley dragged on for some months and, in a sense, was never resolved. Since Stanley was the bishop's examining chaplain[93] he might be thought to have every right to discuss the orthodoxy of various theological opinions with his principal. But neither man was really in any mood for discussion. Neither would give in and neither would even take the simpler course of being silent. At the very end of 1861 Stanley did indeed take steps towards healing the breach. Tait replied in much more cordial terms than before ('My dearest Stanley'), but still seemed to be irritated beyond bearing by any attempt to exculpate Temple.

My belief is that a great deal of bitterness was infused into the controversy in this way (quite unintentionally on your part) by the article in the *Edinburgh*, and if I may venture to say so, I think the same sort of irritation is kept by your quietly quoting, in the preface of your sermons, Jowett and Temple (without any sort of expression of the possibility of other people disagreeing from your estimate) as two of our best divines.[94]

Since Tait would not budge, nor would Stanley. He wrote to Tait again, with reference to the *Edinburgh* article, 'not to defend my

---

[92] Lambeth Palace Library: Tait Papers, vol. 80, fos. 87 ff., draft letter from Tait to Stanley. Tait's writing here is very difficult indeed to read, with many crossings out and corrections and fo. 91 has been placed in the wrong order. A version of the letter is printed in Davidson and Benham, i. 309 ff.

[93] Tait had offered Temple a similar appointment, which Temple had declined. (Lambeth Palace Library: Tait Papers, vol. 78, fos. 85 ff., letter dated 20 Oct. 1856).

[94] Davidson and Benham, i. 312.

position, but to explain it'.[95] He also asserted that the bishops had reacted to a storm in a teacup as if it were a typhoon.

It is my conviction that the Essayists—but especially Temple and Jowett—have been placed by the religious world under a ban, which it is the duty of all who think as I do to remove—and that the best mode of removing it is steadily to ignore it. Under such a ban Arnold was placed when Archbp [sic] Howley forbad him to preach at Lambeth and another Milman was placed under in 1829. Both of those have been now removed not from any change in the writers [opinions]—& (which is the case of Milman) not from any difference between them & Temple and Jowett, but simply because the religious public has been forced to acknowledge their seriousness, and because (to take Milman's case) he is in a high ecclesiastical position.[96]

It was clear that the *Essays and Reviews* affair had not really gone away. It was not even certain whether Temple could continue to rely on the support and protection of his former tutor who had thus far done everything to further his career. And if Tait could be so critical, others must regard Temple with very deep suspicion. Convocation had set up a committee to examine the book, and the committee would not report until 1864. The delay was caused by the prosecution of two of the essayists (Wilson and Williams) for teaching contrary to the formularies of the Church of England. They were found guilty by the Court of Arches but that judgement was reversed by the Judicial Committee of the Privy Council, as the court of appeal in ecclesiastical cases, and High Churchmen regarded that as blatant erastianism. That the whole process took three years had the unfortunate consequence from Temple's point of view that the censure by Convocation, when it came, was fresh in people's minds well into the decade.

[95] Lambeth Palace Library: Tait Papers, vol. 80, fo. 5.
[96] Ibid., fos. 5 ff., Stanley to Tait.

4

The School and the Schools Commissions

The stigma of having been a contributor to *Essays and Reviews* would always, in a sense, hang over Temple but the immediate threat had been removed and outside the world of unyielding ecclesiastical disputes he possessed a different reputation. By the time of the *Essays and Reviews* furore he had become both a Doctor of Divinity and a chaplain to the Queen. The Sandford *Memoir* attached no apparent importance to either distinction but being Chaplain-in-Ordinary to the Sovereign conferred on a headmaster an extra-diocesan position while it emphasized the fact that his was not a secular vocation. At that time a DD did not imply any major contribution to scholarship. It is clear from an anecdote, included in the *Memoir* in quite another connection, that the exercises Temple was required to complete in order to receive the degree were of a purely formal kind.[1] Both distinctions, in fact, simply reflected his general standing as a headmaster. In the educational world he could still rely on being treated as a responsible authority.

During the actual controversy over *Essays and Reviews*—just because it placed so much strain upon his closest friendships—his letters to the other actors in the drama provide a good deal of information about Temple's thoughts and emotions. Few of his relationships, however, survived the controversy unscathed and, partly for that reason, there are few sources from which to reconstruct the rest of his personal life at Rugby. Because his mother and elder sister were living in the school with him, there are none of the family letters which illuminate the earlier part of his life. The Sandford *Memoir* refers to the charming and protective way he treated his mother and there is a chapter on his 'Home Life at Rugby' but it is described in rather conventional terms. Even his letters to his friends about Dorcas's death in 1866 contain little

---

[1] E. G. Sandford (ed.), *Memoirs of Archbishop Temple by Seven Friends*, 2 vols. (London 1906).

description of deep feeling. Perhaps the most revealing phrases were in his letter to E. W. Benson.

I have never been long parted from her ever since I was born, and for the last twenty years she has lived in my house, and life does not seem the same without her. Very few mothers can be to their sons what she has been to me.[2]

The Temples are said to have lived a rather frugal and abstemious life with the headmaster always represented as a generator of friendship, laughter, and jollity. He is described as having a great affinity for young children and an ability to make easy contact with them.

Whenever Dr Temple was with nephews and nieces, whether in girls' cricket in the farthest garden, or in merry games in the Schoolhouse, he was the life and soul of the party, 'making them tenfold more delightful'. It was in these years that Lewis Carroll's *Alice in Wonderland* came out, and this he would read to the young people with such zest and spirit that the whole party laughed till they cried.

Nor was his joyousness and fun at this time kept for his own kith and kin. The boys would come in to some meal, or perhaps to that delightful institution—Sunday high tea. Despite the evening dress that was even in the holidays obligatory at this family meal, the boys were made happy, and talked freely to him, and looked as if they loved to listen to what he said. With his younger masters, too, he has left memories of sunny laughter mixed with serious talk.[3]

The language of 'merry games' and 'sunny laughter' may seem somewhat artificial but there is no reason to doubt that Temple possessed a gift for friendship and was genuinely loved and admired by most masters and boys. His relationship with his own sons[4] suggests that he really was fond of children and able to get on with them. His mother seems to have kept to her own rooms for most of the day and his sister, who must have been a remarkable woman, looked after them both with a self-effacing good grace which sought no position of dominance.

What is missing is any means of assessing what being the headmaster did to and for Temple himself. There is a great deal about how he was the life and soul of the party and the wise and skilful ruler but there is nothing—except in relation to *Essays and Reviews*—of what it cost him, whether he enjoyed it or found it a great bore, or about how his own personality developed as he met the challenges which Rugby provided.

[2] Ibid. ii. 603 f.   [3] Ibid. i. 231.   [4] See below, 162–5.

It is possible to reconstruct something of his work in the school but it is not easy to understand how Temple himself developed in that crucial decade. He was thirty-seven when he was appointed to Rugby, a sometimes hesitant, somewhat vulnerable, young man but possessing a growing confidence in his own abilities. He was forty-eight when he left it. He became, during those years, a formidable and assured person but there is no means of telling quite how and how quickly that self-confidence developed.

The most important source for discovering what Rugby was like when Temple was headmaster is the evidence which he and his colleagues gave before the Clarendon Commission on Public Schools which is always cited as belonging to the year 1862 but was appointed in 1861 and reported in 1864.[5] It was sitting, in other words, while the fury over *Essays and Reviews* was still raging but there is very little in its proceedings to indicate that Temple was regarded as anything other than an entirely respectable headmaster. One would not, of course, have expected the Commissioners to enter into theological subtleties with him but the Earl of Devon (Peelite secretary to the Poor Law Board until 1859), who was one of them and evidently devoutly anxious about the religious and moral welfare of the boys, does not appear to have been more suspicious of Temple than he was of other headmasters.

It is true that there were sometimes interesting exchanges between the Commissioners and the headmaster on the subject of the legal position of the trustees and the authority they exercised in the school. Lord Lyttelton (principal of Queen's College, Birmingham) questioned Temple about answers he had submitted in advance in reply to a questionnaire circulated to all schools by the Commission:

I find at the head of the second paragraph at page 10, 'The Head Master, with the sanction of the Trustees, exercises power over the whole school'; and at the head of the third paragraph, page 12, 'The government of the school is vested in 12 Trustees who shall have full power to appoint and dismiss of their own

---

[5] *Report of Her Majesty's Commissioners appointed to Inquire into the Revenues and Management of Certain Colleges and Schools and the Studies Pursued and Instructed Therein* (1864). Vol. iv contains the evidence relating to Rugby. The report is cited below as *Commission on Public Schools*. Other sources of information about Rugby are J. B. Hope Simpson, *Rugby since Arnold* (London, 1967) and 'Our Public Schools: vol. iv, Rugby', *New Quarterly Magazine*, N S, 2:255 ff. (The article is unsigned but was apparently by Arthur Sidgwick, see Sandford (ed.), i. 205 f. and cf. below, 97. It is therefore cited below as Sidgwick.)

pleasure the Head Master and all the under masters, and to make from time to time such rules and regulations for the government of the school as they shall think proper' (there I see no limitation whatever) in practice, however, no specified regulations are made, but the whole internal management and government of the school is delegated by the Trustees to the Head Master, who from time to time reports to the Trustees at their annual meeting any changes which he may deem to be necessary.[6]

Temple agreed that this was the case, and added that the head had no powers of his own: all his authority was delegated to him by the trustees. The trustees themselves had made no regulations but, he assured Lyttelton under quite persistent questioning, he would never do anything of any significance without consulting them.[7] Lord Devon got him to say that the trustees had never interfered in any matter in the school during his time as headmaster. And when pressed by H. H. Vaughan (professor of Modern History at Oxford) about whether he would consult the trustees *before* acting on any matter of importance, Temple insisted that he would.[8]

Even in the cold print of the published report of the Commission there seems to be something of an edge to this passage in Temple's evidence. It may be no more significant than any of the other points at which the Commissioners persisted with questions when they should have realized that they had got what they were going to get. But if they were hoping to discover what the trustees had done about *Essays and Reviews* Temple was giving nothing away. It may have been true that the trustees had never interfered in *matters related to the running of the school* during his time as headmaster. He had insisted, after all, on drawing a line between matters relating to the school (which he was prepared to discuss but the trustees were not) and his theology (which they wished to discuss and he did not). His answers to the Commission, if looked at in that light, suggest a grim determination not to admit that the trustees had hauled him over the coals. For all their persistence, however, the Commissioners failed to raise the matter explicitly and one cannot even be certain that it was in their minds.

It is not easy, either, to discover from the evidence given to the Commission exactly what changes Temple made in the running of the school. We know from other sources that he put the school's finances,

---

[6] *Commission on Public Schools*, iv. 245.
[7] Ibid. 246.
[8] Ibid. 247, para. 188.

including the fee structure and the salary scales for masters, on a sounder footing. He set himself to raise the academic standards because he recognized that otherwise Rugby would not be able to compete with other schools.[9] But in other respects one cannot always tell whether what was being described in the evidence was what was there when Temple arrived or whether it was a practice he had introduced since his arrival. The Commissioners were very anxious to discover, for instance, how well the masters were paid and whether the level of salaries made a significant difference to the ease with which they could be recruited. They had had some difficulty in understanding how salaries were calculated and, like all their kind, had tended to get themselves side-tracked on all sorts of minor issues. Professor Vaughan had devoted a good deal of time to trying to arrive at a round figure for the income of a senior classics master at the school. He had eventually come to the conclusion that it was approximately £1,600. This may have been of particular interest to Vaughan since it seems to have been roughly what his colleagues the canons of Christ Church (in some cases holding the canonry with a theological professorship) were paid at about this time.[10] Lord Clarendon (Chairman of the Commission and a once and future Foreign Secretary) questioned Temple about salaries and recruitment:

The answer at the bottom of page 16 is of considerable importance: 'The present number of masters is enough to teach the school reasonably well. But there can be no doubt that a few more would be a great improvement. It is, however, felt that it would be questionable policy to lower the salaries any further; even as it is, though first rate men can be got, they cannot be got so easily as three years ago. And it would be a great mistake to lower the standard of the men appointed to assistant masterships in order to make the size of a form 29 instead of 33.' I think as a principle that is perfectly right, but do you find that you have greater difficulty in getting masters now than formerly, the masters having, as Mr Vaughan has just been saying, salaries of something like 1,600£?

Temple's reply was as follows:

In the first place that only applies to the seven senior masters; and in the second place it is not nearly so much as they used to get. It is a pure question of the

[9] Sidgwick, 263 f.

[10] Herbert Danby, *Notes on the Chapter Fund, 1869–1944* (printed for private circulation in 1945), 5 indicates that in 1859 the dean and canons of Christ Church resolved that the yearly income of a canonry be fixed at £1,500.

market, and I can only say as a matter of fact that I find them harder to get than three years ago. I noticed that three years ago I had only to ask a man to come and he came. This last year I asked four men and they declined on the ground that the money was not enough. And this was in consequence of the reductions made in 1858, because before 1858 the number of pupils was unlimited and the school salary might rise above 336£.[11]

What is not immediately obvious in this exchange is that '1858' and 'three years ago' both refer, though not with complete accuracy, to a period soon after Temple's arrival at the school.[12] Temple had persuaded the most senior masters to agree, against their own selfish interests, to a fairer distribution of some of the income available for salaries.[13] It was this that had constituted the 'reductions made in 1858' (though he had actually carried out the equalizations in 1859) and Temple really meant that it had been easier to recruit masters before he equalized some components of the salaries.[14] Words whose meaning would have been perfectly clear in 1862 may be somewhat misleading now.

It is not surprising that the Commissioners had some difficulty in understanding the masters' salaries. One of the consequences of the school's gradual evolution into a well-known and flourishing public school of the nineteenth century, was its extremely complex financial arrangements. Part of the school's income came from the original endowment, which had been intended to provide free education for local boys: part came from the fees paid by the boys who were not local. The trustees administered the endowments, originally intended only for the benefit of boys who lived in Rugby or in certain neighbouring parishes but subsequently made available for anyone who lived within a radius of five miles. The headmaster seems to have fixed the fees, though they bore some relation to the notional *per capita* sum provided by the trustees.[15] In addition to the 'foundationers', there were exhibitioners supported by funds which were unrestricted as regards the recipients and a smaller number of scholarships (two in Temple's time) which were awarded as a result of competition and were financed by the masters.

---

[11] *Commission on Public Schools*, iv. 251, para. 322.
[12] Temple's evidence was given at a meeting of the Commission at Rugby on 12 May 1862: 1858 was the year of his arrival.
[13] Sandford (ed.), i. 187 f.
[14] Cf. Simpson, 45.
[15] *Commission on Public Schools*, iv. 244, answers to financial questions put to G. V. Hefford, clerk to the Clerk to the Trustees.

The masters themselves had been paid by a system which can only be described as very inequitable and was also a consequence of the history of the school.[16] It was this system which Temple had attempted to alter. It was inequitable because it had discriminated so markedly in favour of the more senior masters. Worse still, because there was a vested interest in preserving the *status quo*, it made it difficult to divert any money towards improving the pay of juniors or recruiting additional teachers. Only a comparatively small part of anyone's salary was paid directly from the trustees. The school fees were divided by a very complex scheme in varying proportions between the headmaster and his assistants and there were, in addition, various other sources of income. Masters in charge of boarding-houses made a profit out of the boarding fees and the custom had grown up of boys receiving private tuition from tutors, who were in fact the assistant masters wearing another hat. And there were also 'fellowships' awarded to some but not all masters and which were usually continued as a kind of pension after retirement. This was one of the topics which seemed to exercise a particular fascination for the Commissioners. Having once got their teeth into the question of the fellowships (which they obviously regarded as sinecures) it was as though they could not extricate themselves from it[17] even though it soon became plain that the headmaster himself thought they were of little benefit to the school and best got rid of.

The typical assistant master at Rugby in this era was a 'classical master' and the teaching of the classical languages was the school's chief business. Teachers of other subjects had been introduced from time to time, though in some cases only as a temporary experiment. There seems always to have been a feeling that they were not quite so essential for the school's existence as the *real* masters, who taught the classics. It is possible, in fact, to judge which of the teaching staff came closest to the classical masters in general esteem by comparing salaries. In 1863, about the time when Rugby was being scrutinized by the Commission, the headmaster received £2,967. 0s. 8d. from various sources. The senior classical masters (if they were also boarding-house masters) received— according to Vaughan's calculations—£1,617. 6s. 6d. If a classical master did not have a boarding-house his largest possible income was about half that. Significantly the mathematics and languages masters could receive much the same sort of salary as a senior, but house-less,

---

[16] Simpson, 14.
[17] *Commission on Public Schools*, iv. 244.

classical master, and the most junior of classical masters were only paid £340.[18]

Perhaps the most significant fact about the school was that by the mid-nineteenth century it existed as two quite distinct divisions: the day boys or foundationers and the boarders who, by this time, were much more important. It is true that the school appears to have tried not to emphasize the distinction. The foundationers did not have to wear a special uniform.[19] And it seems to have been almost an article of faith that they were not treated differently. Among those who gave evidence to the Commission were two former boys from the school. There is no means of telling why they were selected; whether they were thought to be typical of the boys as a whole, whether they were chosen at random, or whether they were suggested by Temple himself or his staff. (But one of them, Henry Lee Warner, went back to Rugby as a master in the year in which the Commission's report was published and his reminiscences form an important part of the chapter of the Sand-ford *Memoir* which deals with the relations between the headmaster and the boys. The other, Arthur Sidgwick, who also went back to Rugby to teach in 1864, wrote an important article praising the organization of the school under Temple in the *New Quarterly Magazine* fifteen years later.[20]) They were questioned closely on the matter of discrimination against town boys and both assured the Commission that there was none. Sidgwick (who had been at Rugby from 1853 to 1859 and had gone straight on to Trinity College, Cambridge where he still was when he gave his evidence) had himself been a 'town boy'[21] and he had gone home for all meals as well as for the night. There had been some local boys who were boarders but, in that case, full and proper boarders and not really town boys at all. There was no system of weekly boarders but the fact that a boy lived at home did not entirely free him from school discipline. There had been a kind of proctorial figure, Sidgwick told the Commissioners, whose duty it was to patrol the town at night and make sure that day boys were not out of their homes at a time when boarders would have been confined to school buildings.

The other young man's evidence was even more revealing. Henry Lee Warner had been a boy in the school from 1854 to 1860 and had gone on

---

[18] Simpson, 36 ff.
[19] *Commission on Public Schools*, iv. 252, para. 347.
[20] Sandford (ed.), i. 157 ff. and 205 ff.
[21] *Commission on Public Schools*, iv. 297, para. 2031 f.

to St John's College, Cambridge.[22] Having insisted that no distinction was made, in a social sense, against the sons of town residents, he was asked—by Lord Clarendon himself—whether these boys were the sons of tradesmen. Having gathered that they were Clarendon next asked, perhaps incredulously, 'And no difference is made whatever towards them?' And Warner answered. 'No, certainly not...', giving the game away by adding, 'only of course very few of the tradesmen's sons ever do rise [into the middle or upper school]; they come knowing no Latin or Greek, and they are taken away very soon, or else remain in the lowest forms.'[23]

The truth is that the school itself, and the town in which it was set, had changed so much that it was almost impossible to serve the original intention for which it had been founded. The town appears more or less to have doubled in population twice over in the previous quarter of a century. It had been about 2,000 in 1831; 4,000 by the mid-1830s; and was 7,818 according to the census taken in 1861. Someone who had lived in the town throughout that period believed that the increase in population had been partly due to the arrival of the railway but mostly because the school had attracted people wanting their children to be educated. Town parents had acquired the automatic right to enter their children as foundationers, which had got so out of hand that newcomers had had to be prevented from claiming that right immediately on arrival. There had also been a good deal of new building in the town and the value of existing property had risen steeply.[24] If this is an accurate impression, it presents a picture of a bustling, thriving town, with a rapidly growing middle-class population, many of whom wanted their sons to be educated at the school. But those whom the school would most want, would be those equipped by their earlier education to cope with a public-school curriculum based on the classics. The sons of tradesmen in the town, the very people whom the endowment had originally been intended to benefit, would not for the most part be so equipped.

When the Commission eventually made its recommendations it suggested that the school should cease even to attempt to make provision for local boys and that the funds intended to provide for free local education should be used instead to set up open scholarships. The

---

[22] *Commission on Public Schools*, iv. 286.
[23] Ibid. 286, para. 1151.
[24] Ibid. 252, paras. 355–65, evidence of Mr Hefford.

townsfolk objected to this proposal very strenuously. Thomas Arnold's reorganization of the school had already resulted in the disappearance of free education for boys under the age of twelve. What the Commission proposed would make things even more difficult. In order to know enough Latin and Greek to stand a chance of winning an open scholarship, a boy would have had to be very expensively educated. To win a scholarship would therefore cost a great deal of money. But Temple believed that scholarships restricted to certain localities or families were only too often wasted on those without ability.[25] And he was also convinced that providing free education indiscriminately for everyone, whether capable of it or not, was equally wasteful. To secure open scholarships and, at the same time, to be fair to the townspeople, he suggested a compromise. Some of the funds from the endowment might be used to create a lower school where a semi-classical and commercial education could be had and from which abler boys might pass by exhibition to Rugby itself. Neither the Commissioners nor the town much liked this suggestion but something of the kind was made possible by an act of parliament of 1868.[26] Meanwhile, five years after his appointment and three years after the publication of *Essays and Reviews*, Temple was turning away twice as many boys as he admitted to the school. The school's 'necessary charges' plus board and lodging came to about £90 a year.[27]

The general picture of Temple's place in the school that emerges from the Commission's report—and it appears to be a genuine one—is of a man easy in his manner, friendly in his dealings with the boys and masters alike, fair and just, and, above all, immensely hard working. This is also the picture that is conveyed by the Sandford *Memoir*, though the anecdotes contributed by those who had known and worked with him at Rugby, add the unexpected information that he was a man easily and deeply moved by emotion. The *Memoir* was plainly *intended* to present an attractive picture of the man for no one who sent the editors unflattering anecdotes about the archbishop would have expected them to be published. Nor is the consistency of the character sketch surprising, for those who provided the memoirs were often the very same people who had given evidence to the Commission.[28] It is difficult,

---

[25] See above, 40.
[26] Simpson, 57.
[27] *Commission on Public Schools*, iv. 253, paras. 393–401.
[28] See above, 97.

therefore, to say precisely why the picture presented in the report of the Commission is more convincing than that conveyed by the *Memoir*. The evidence has an immediacy (whereas the anecdotes of the *Memoir* were written down fifty years later) and was given under what was often very persistent questioning so that one gets the impression that the witnesses were not given time to think up diplomatic answers. And they did sometimes express opinions which were contradictory to or even critical of the headmaster's policies.

One thing suggested by the evidence is that it was the headmasters in the Arnoldite tradition who had had good relations with both masters and boys. Dr Wooll, Arnold's predecessor and headmaster from 1807 to 1828, was remembered as a total disaster during whose time there had been riots and a great deal of 'stealing of fowls'.[29] He had not consulted with the teaching staff at all except when there was 'disturbance'.[30] Arnold and Tait had consulted regularly: Goulburn had not. Temple consulted his masters even on the most important things, though the final decision was always his. It was regarded as significant that he had, for instance, held a meeting of the staff in order to draft the school's replies to the Commissioners' question-naire.[31]

The former schoolboys agreed enthusiastically that the headmaster was very approachable and showed a real concern for the boys' welfare. He was always around in the school close; he was often present at games. He encouraged the masters to be on good terms with the boys, to show an interest in games and even to play them. One of the younger masters was said to be the best footballer in the school.[32] But Temple was clearly no simple games fanatic. He evidently took special care that the school runs were not too long for boys' health and required them to have doctor's notes before they were allowed to take part in them. [During his headmastership, Temple did a great deal to make the game of rugby football a less violent and dangerous game, though he recognized that boys' games could not be made entirely safe.][33] He was to write to his eldest son, many years later, urging him to give up rugby. It was, his father said, 'a game for Boys and not for men. The violence of it suits the one and does not suit the other.... and it is too

[29] *Commission on Public Schools*, iv. 274, paras. 1129–31.
[30] Ibid. 274, paras. 1105–10, evidence of Revd C. A. Anstey and Revd H. J. Buckoll.
[31] Ibid., para. 1122.
[32] Ibid. 293, paras. 1848 f.
[33] See the chapter on 'School Games' in Sandford (ed.), i. 207 ff.

personal. Cricket stands altogether on a different footing. So does hockey.'[34]

Perhaps the most significant piece of evidence as to Temple's standing among the boys came, almost by accident, from Arthur Sidgwick. He was cross-questioned by Lord Lyttelton thus:

Did the upper boys communicate constantly and freely with the Head Master out of school?
Sidgwick. Whenever they wished.
Lyttelton. Did he go among them out of school in the games, or at other times?
Sidgwick. Yes.
Lyttelton. Did he ask them to his house in the evening?
Sidgwick. Yes.
Lyttelton. You think that the personal influence of the Head Master was perceptible?
Sidgwick. Yes; when I speak of the Head Master I mean Dr. Temple.[35]

Sidgwick had been a boy under Goulburn's headmastership for four or five years and for little more than a year of Temple's.

It also seems clear that Temple stood in the Arnoldite tradition in the way he regarded the chapel as central to the life of the school. That is not to say, of course, that the school (in the sense of the boys) regarded it as equally central. On the occasion when he invited Goulburn to preach in the chapel, the report in the school magazine decidedly suggested that the football match was the more important feature of the day's events.

The Fox Sermon was preached in the School Chapel this year, not on All Saints' day as is customary, but on the festival of Simon and Jude, Wednesday, Oct. 28. There was a large attendance, every available seat being occupied. A most eloquent and impressive sermon was preached by the Very Rev. E. M. Goulburn, D.D., Dean of Norwich, who took for his text, James 5:17, 'Elias was a man subject to like passions as we are'. The collection in aid of the fund was then made, which on this occasion amounted to £30 17s 6d. Among the congregation, beside many whose names will appear in the football column, were the Rev. B. Compton, formerly Assistant Master, Rev. T. W. Jex Blake, Principal of Cheltenham College; Rev. E. Benson, Headmaster of Wellington College, Rev. E. G. Sandford, &c

---

[34] Family Papers in the possession of the Right Revd F. S. Temple: letter dated 24 Oct. 1899.
[35] *Commission on Public Schools*, iv. 304, paras 2396–99.

This account is given in the *Meteor*,[36] described as 'edited by members of Rugby School' and 'a short chronicle of what was daily passing round us', 'price 6d'. The reference to 'the football column' was to an account of the Old Rugbeian match which appeared on page 8 of the same issue. The list of the Old Rugbeian team contained no less than twenty-five names, including certain players described as 'the great heroes of past days'. At least one of these 'heroes' was a clergyman and, plainly, his prowess at football made him far more important in the eyes of the editors than the master of Wellington, himself a former assistant master at Rugby. (The 'fund' referred to was almost certainly the fund for the purchase of a new organ for the chapel, which was the school's principal project at the time and was mentioned on both pages 5 and 10.)

Temple himself would never have been anything other than utterly serious about what happened in chapel. Like Arnold before him, he was officially the school chaplain and, again like Arnold, he seems always to have preached when he was present in chapel. His sermons, apparently, were appreciated by the older boys.[37] There seems to have been little which could be described as novel or entertaining in either his preaching or his services but he tried to make what he said intelligible and sensible. It was conventional, serious High Church devotion and it was simply what the Prayer Book prescribed. On Sunday morning the Litany was said at 8 a.m. Then came breakfast and, at 10.15, what was described as 'a lecture'. For the upper forms it seems indeed to have been an actual lecture given by the headmaster and form masters, each to his own form. (Temple seems to have chosen to lecture on the Old Testament.) For the juniors it consisted of 'saying something by heart' or hearing some chapters from the Bible. The important thing was, apparently, that no ordinary school work should be attempted during the hour allocated to lectures. After a brief break there followed, at 11.30, 'the rest of morning service', presumably morning prayer and Holy Communion. After dinner the boys were sent off on a long walk until 4 o'clock or 4.30, when there was chapel again and then more walking or simply being in the school close for the rest of the day.[38]

As chaplain Temple had to prepare the boys for confirmation. He did this as thoroughly as one would expect from someone whose own preparation for confirmation had been so demanding. The course lasted

[36] No. 1 (7 Feb. 1867), 1.
[37] *Commission on Public Schools*, iv. 290, paras. 1674 f.
[38] Ibid. 289, paras. 1654 ff.

for a considerable period: he saw the boys in small groups and also took them all together, once a week, for a talk or lecture. It represented, therefore, a significant slice out of the life of a busy headmaster.[39] And it would seem that the boys, both the candidates and others, took it equally seriously or, at least, believed that they should do so.[40] Attendance at Communion was not compulsory, yet there would be at least 100 boys present each Sunday and more than that at the beginning and the end of term and immediately after a confirmation.[41]

Rugby was proud of its system of school discipline which gave a good deal of authority to the members of the sixth form. It was also a subject which the Clarendon Commission was, not surprisingly, determined to examine very carefully. Temple devoted a good deal of his evidence, covering several closely printed large folio pages,[42] to the subject and both boys and masters were questioned about it. Before Arnold's time as headmaster the sixth formers had, in fact, exercised some authority but unofficially and in an unregulated way. Indeed the 'rebellions' of Dr Wooll's day seem to have been occasioned 'entirely on a point of discipline connected with the sixth form'.[43] The system had been legalized and regulated by Arnold and there was general agreement that it worked very well and resulted in a stricter discipline than existed in most schools at the time. Lord Devon, of whom Lyttelton said that one was more likely to get a joke from 'a bellwether or a Newfoundland dog',[44] pressed one of the masters very hard indeed on the matter. He was determined to establish whether the boys exercised their authority satisfactorily and whether the system contributed to maintaining the intellectual standards of the school. The master replied, 'It requires great watching no doubt, and great intercourse between the Head Master and the sixth form, and a certain friendship and acquaintance with them.' And though he admitted that he had known cases when sixth form power had been abused, he added, 'I do not know of a single instance in the present Head Master's time.'[45] The offender had a right of appeal, either to the sixth form as a whole or to the headmaster. The

---

[39] Ibid., paras. 1692–799.
[40] Ibid. 1693.
[41] Ibid. 290, paras. 1696 ff.
[42] Ibid. 254 ff.
[43] Ibid. 272, para. 1129.
[44] David Allsobrook, *Schools for the Shires: The Reform of Middle-Class Education in Victorian England* (Manchester, 1986), 183.
[45] *Commission on Public Schools*, iv. 275, paras. 1134, and 1127.

appeal could be made—and would be effective—up to the very moment that the sixth former's hand descended to deliver the stroke. Indeed 'stay the hand' seems to have become almost a technical term for making the appeal.

The most vivid picture of how the system worked is to be found in the evidence given to the Commission by Henry Lee Warner who since he was not, like Arthur Sidgwick, a town boy and since he had been a member of the sixth, must both have experienced and exercised the senior boys' authority. The questioning was begun by Clarendon himself:

Clarendon. They [the monitors] would consider themselves called upon to interfere if they saw anything going on that was very wrong, such as going into a public house?

Warner. They would at once interfere, and either send the boy up, or they have the power of licking him if they prefer it, only that of course is subject to appeal.[46]

He then explained that 'licking' meant with a cane and not with the fists. He was to add later that 'Of course you would not use a walking stick on a fellow.' 'Licking' was not often resorted to but it might be done in public if the boarding-house was interested in seeing justice done (as, for instance, in a case of bullying). And, in any case, one's study was too small for one to carry out the caning there. It is quite clear that the young man believed that the whole system was good both for the sixth formers and for those under them. He was also convinced that it actually worked and that it maintained a good moral discipline. There was very little bullying in the school, he thought, very little drunkenness, no 'gross immorality', no going into neighbouring towns overnight. Smoking was not really thought of as an offence but merely as something very silly. The only danger inherent in the system, Warner thought, was that the sixth formers 'might be rather priggish on first going up to the universities.'

One member of the Commission, Sir Stafford Northcote, had not been present at the sessions held in Rugby itself, but he attended the session in London at which the former schoolboys were questioned. Northcote, who had been a contemporary of Temple's at Balliol, had been Gladstone's private secretary in the early 1840s and had worked for him, as had Temple, in the Oxford election of 1847. But he had remained a Conservative and was at this time Member of Parliament

---

[46] *Commission on Public Schools*, iv. 286, paras. 1515 ff.

for Stamford and a recognized opposition spokesman in the House of Commons. When he was present he seemed to introduce a more relaxed, even jovial note into the proceedings. He was particularly anxious to know about the boys' beer, not—as other Commissioners might have done—in a disapproving way at all.

Northcote. After a game of football or cricket, did you get beer?
Warner. Yes, we generally went to the school house.
Clarendon. They are allowed beer there?
Warner. Yes, after football, those who played the biggest matches; of course all the small fellows are not allowed, unless they happen to want it very much, when a sixth fellow may take them.[47]

A little later Northcote asked, 'How is the beer?', to which Warner replied that it was very good indeed when he left.[48]

By this stage in the proceedings the Commission had turned its attention to the condition of the boarding-houses. When Temple had first arrived at the school, the boarding masters had become very independent of the headmaster's authority. Temple seems, without any fuss and without arousing much resentment or opposition, to have reasserted his control.[49] He seems, both as headmaster and as bishop, to have had an almost innocent belief that people would do as they were told—and it often worked. A housemaster naturally felt himself entitled to a certain independence. The house was not, after all, the property of the school but the personal, usually rented, accommodation of the master concerned. Part of his income was derived from any profit he was able to make. But it was equally important for Temple that there should not be enclaves of independent authority where an entirely different set of policies could be pursued from those which he was determined to implement in the school. It was also potentially dangerous for housemasters to be entirely free, for instance, to decide what food the boys were to be given. It was in their interest to feed the boys cheaply: it was in Temple's interest that they should feed the boys well.[50]

A housemaster might expect to make a profit of between £12 and £14 for each boy *per annum* and the average number of boys in a house was

---

[47] Ibid. 287 f., paras. 1580 ff.
[48] Ibid. 289, para. 1646.
[49] Simpson, 48.
[50] There is some evidence that Temple took pains to improve the quality of food in his own 'school' house: *Commission on Public Schools*, iv. 289, para. 1644 f.

about forty-five, so that this constituted a substantial part of a master's income. Most of the boarding-house masters (there were seven in all) were classical masters though there were exceptions. One of the modern language masters had a house but the other, who was a foreigner, did not. Asked whether this was *because* he was a foreigner, Temple replied, 'He has married an English lady.'[51] But he thought that it would be very undesirable if a majority of the houses were in the hands of other than classical masters. The head's own house, school house (which *was* the school's property), was much the largest of the boarding-houses, having seventy boys. And, since he had not to pay rent, his profit was also rather more—perhaps £17 a boy.[52]

There is some suggestion that the cost of running the boarding-houses had risen steeply since Arnold's day. This may have been partly because of the rise in prices of property in the town but it may reflect a genuine improvement. Temple estimated that there had been what he called 'a difference of habits which necessitate in the first place very much better accommodation, and therefore very much larger rents, and secondly a great many more servants of a different class'.[53] But this did not mean that life in these houses was sybaritic. They were heated by 'hot air flues' and were not actually cold. The boys received a 'standard-ized diet' (presumably meaning roughly the same in each house) con-sisting of bread and butter, tea, coffee or cocoa at breakfast; meat (almost a pound a head) and vegetables, cheese, or pudding, and sometimes soup at dinner; bread, butter, cheese, and beer at supper. They seldom got meat twice a day, 'unless sometimes when we had been out having a very long run, or anything of that kind, then they used to send some in'.[54] They were never fed from the 'pastry cook', which was obviously the equivalent of modern convenience or 'junk' food.[55]

There was, perhaps, more variation in the size of dormitories and bedrooms. Temple himself believed that there ought to be four or five boys together (because he thought that what he called 'publicity' was good for morals) but that each boy ought, ideally, to have his own separate study. These were tiny, box-like rooms—about the size of a large table—with walls going right up to ceiling and ventilated by an

[51] *Commission on Public Schools*, iv. 250, para. 310.

[52] Ibid. 315 ff.

[53] Ibid. 252, para. 321.

[54] Ibid. 289, para. 1650.

[55] Ibid. The evidence of Temple himself (pp. 250 ff.) and of the former schoolboy (p. 289) on the subject of food hardly differs at all.

opening, usually above the door. In practice they were usually occupied by one or at most two boys but there might occasionally be three.[56] When the Clarendon Commission was asking about dormitories, Lord Devon was, of course, anxious to know whether having several boys together in a bedroom made it difficult for them to say their prayers. Temple replied that he had only ever had one complaint and that was from a boy who had had to stop washing because someone else was praying.

Washing arrangements seem, indeed, to have been rather primitive. The boys had washstands in their bedrooms and sometimes had a sponge bath there. There were 'tubs' in what was described as the 'washing-room' and also something called the 'old bath'. It is not clear precisely what this was but it may have been rather like the Victorian public baths in parts of London. The boys also apparently used to bath in the Avon, which was very cold indeed. Only 'some very adventurous spirits' used it all the year round.[57]

Closely connected with the boarding arrangements was a matter which the Commission was very concerned to probe—the provision of private tutors. A boy's tutor was almost always his boarding master, except if he were in school house or in a house where the master was not a classical master for the tutor was really there to keep the boy's Greek and Latin up to standard. Boys in the lower forms sat in order of their academic performance and changed places if they were doing less well. Their promotion to higher forms depended on their having a satisfactory position in class. It was the tutor's job to ensure that they were promoted and eventually reached the sixth form. Though the sixth formers did not sit in order of merit, the private tutor system seems to have been so ingrained that even they continued to have one. Town boys, not having a boarding master, were not compelled to have a private tutor but it would seem that they invariably did so and that, if they could not afford the ten guinea fee, were able to apply for assistance in meeting it.

The problem with such a scheme as this was that it was extremely difficult to justify. Parents were, in effect, paying extra for services which were not 'extras' but central to the curriculum. If every pupil needed additional teaching in order to reach the standard required by the school itself, why should not the school provide it as a matter of course?

[56] Ibid. 253, para. 413.
[57] Ibid. Temple's evidence, on which this account of the boarding arrangements is based, is on p. 253, paras. 412–50.

Temple's answers under severe cross-examination seem to reveal his own uneasiness about the system.   Professor Vaughan asked him why it was necessary to have such a system at all:

Temple. It is the boys who seem to find it necessary, not the school authorities.

Vaughan. He finds it necessary because other boys have tutors, and they would take up their tutor's work?

Temple. Yes.

Vaughan. Supposing there were no boys who had private tutors, the whole system of promotion would go on through the whole school equally?

Temple. Yes.

Lord Lyttelton. But they do, in fact, have private tutors, because they get on better with them?

Temple. Yes.[58]

It seems likely that the vested interest which senior masters had in retaining the system was too strong for him. His other reforms had already created enough problems in the matter of recruitment. He was not yet ready to abandon the practice.

There were, in fact, only two good reasons advanced in support of its retention. One was that a private tutor could establish a personal relationship with the boys in his care which would encourage them to confide in him. Since he was not usually the boys' form master, he might seem less formidable. Temple thought this the chief advantage of the system. His ideas about the importance of a role model in education would, no doubt, have predisposed him to regard such a relationship favourably. But there was a catch in the argument. It was difficult to show why a boarding master could not establish such a relationship with the boys in his house without being paid extra for doing so. And the other attempt at justification was even more problematic. It was put forward by the young man Warner, who insisted that one of the advantages of retaining the system was that a good private tutor could compensate for having an 'inferior' teacher.[59] This was hardly an argument that the headmaster could advance. He might have been asked whether it would not be easier to get rid of the inferior form masters. In the event the Commission recommended the abolition of both private tutors and the practice of profiting from the boarding arrangements.[60]

---

[58] *Commission on Public Schools*, iv. 249.
[59] Ibid. 292, para. 1934.
[60] Simpson, 36.

Perhaps the most interesting part of Temple's evidence to the Commission was that which dealt with the relationship between classics and the other subjects taught in the school. It reveals how his ideas were developing and changing. The essential points are contained in one lengthy interchange with the two academics among the commissioners. Vaughan asked whether he thought that the physical sciences were of little value in disciplining and training the mind.

Temple. I think physical science is of very considerable value in that respect, but not to be compared with literature.

Vaughan. Supposing that a person of first-rate scientific attainment, but of inferior classical attainment, were to give an opinion of the value of classics as an elemental discipline, what value should you attach to such an opinion?

Temple. I cannot say that I should attach great value to it.

Vaughan. You consider that neither mathematics nor physical science touch the strictly human part of our nature. Do you not think that they tend to produce many wholesome moral emotions. I am speaking now of natural science, such, for instance, as wonder and admiration of the order of the world and so forth?

Temple. I think that in the present state of civilization, physical science to a very great extent tends to cultivate and refine all the emotions connected with the love of order and beauty; but I think that it never rises to touch the sense of personality or responsibility, the sense of being yourself a person and having to deal with other persons.

Vaughan. Do you not think that the contemplation of the physical laws of the universe tends to produce a high degree of awe and admiration, and, of course, so far as that is connected with the workmanship of an Omnipotent Being that it tends to produce feelings towards him of a very high order?

Temple. I think physical science does that very much, and that is what I meant by speaking of it as cultivating the love of order and beauty, which rapidly leads to a sense of religion; but I do not think it can be compared for one moment with the power of cultivating these emotions, with the study of literature, and, indeed, I think to a very great extent physical science itself owes already a great deal of that power in that respect to the literature which has been gathered round it. I think, moreover, that those emotions are but a small part of our moral nature.

Vaughan. Do you think that in any point of view literary studies produce that state of admiration and awe, and so far of worship, which physical science tends to produce. Do you think it brings before the mind works and evidences of a nature to produce the same moral emotions, or in the same degree?

Temple. The study of literature appears to me to cover almost all that physical science could cover, and very much more besides. There is hardly anything you will find in physical science, which you will not find in different departments of literature. There is no sense of awe or love of beauty which you will not find, I think, more powerfully brought to bear on the mind from the study of poetry even than from the study of any science, because in the study of physical science there is always that drawback, that in order to judge in those emotions, which the science is certainly able to excite, you are obliged for the time to quit the science, and to give yourself up to something with which the science itself has nothing to do. It is not the science which, as a general rule, cultivates the love of order and beauty so much as the objects to which that science is applied.

Vaughan. Does not the science bring out truths, which truths are almost necessarily the moving causes of those emotions, so that it would require a person to suspend the natural action of the mind, and to arrest it at that point to prevent those emotions. I mean the contemplation of the laws of gravity, or such laws as those. Do they not necessarily act on the mind to produce those emotions unless the mind puts a sort of force on itself to prevent them?

Temple. I should not be prepared to deny that. I do think that all that can be done by physical science in that way is covered entirely by literature.

Lyttelton. These two sentences in your answers seem to show what you mean. Man's chief business, it is said, is to subdue nature to his purposes, and these two [scientific]studies show him how; those who use this plea seem to forget that the world in which we live consists quite as much of the men and women on its surface as of the earth and its constituent materials. If any man were to analyse his own life he would find that he had far more to do with his fellowmen than with anything else. And if therefore we are to choose a study which shall pre-eminently fit man for life it will be that which shall best enable him to enter into the thoughts, the feelings, the motives of his fellows. It is in that special sense I take it that you use the word humanizing?

Temple. When I say that the study of literature humanizes, I mean that it cultivates that part of our nature by which we are brought into contact with men and with moral agents.

Vaughan. As in your judgment the opinion of a first-rate scientific man who is not a first-rate man in classical attainments depreciatory of the disciplinary value of classical attainments, is not of very high value, so would you think that the opinion of a first-rate classical scholar not having the same rank scientifically, and tending to depreciate the disciplinary value of scientific attainment was also not of very great value?

Temple. No, I do not think it would be in the same degree at all because it is essentially part of the one kind of study to know human nature and it is not a part of the other. The one is naturally led to the study of man, and to the study therefore of what is good for the discipline of the mind; the other has not studied man but things; and it is not his business to know what is good for the discipline of the mind. The study of the philosophy of the question comes properly within the sphere of one man's science, but not properly within the sphere of the other man's science.[61]

Vaughan tried hard to persuade him that this was unfair to science and, by implication, that Temple (as primarily a classicist and not a natural scientist) was not qualified to pass judgement upon science, but the headmaster would concede no ground. Finally Vaughan asked him whether he believed that classical learning necessarily involved a greater understanding of the way in which the intellect worked than scientific study. Temple answered this with a firm, 'I do'.

It is not surprising, then, to discover that, though he believed that the sciences and mathematics were given a proper place in the school, not everyone else agreed. A master called Wilson,[62] who had come to Rugby soon after Temple was appointed and whose job was to teach mathematics and science, found himself unable to do any laboratory work for the first two years. Even after he got his laboratory, he was unable to make proper use of it. He spent, on average, four hours a day with his maths pupils, in his classroom, and during part of that time the boys studying chemistry were in the laboratory next door. Some of them were very able indeed and most of them were above average but there was only one science set in the sixth form. This meant that he was having to teach a very varied group, some of whom had only just begun to study chemistry. He had tried to meet this problem by sending the more advanced boys off to the laboratory, unsupervised, while he gave introductory talks to the beginners. He was left, understandably, with the impression that the school was not really serious about science but was prepared to admit that his difficulties were not entirely the fault of the school. Because very few colleges at Oxford or Cambridge (only Magdalen and Christ Church at the former and possibly Caius at the latter) were willing to encourage the sciences, it was inevitable that schools would be reluctant to give time to them. There seemed to be no hope for his discipline at Rugby, so long as a thorough classical education was compulsory and science was permitted only as an optional alternative to modern languages. It seemed to him that there were many boys who gained nothing from classics and would benefit if the school were to allow them to do other subjects instead.

Wilson seems to have been justified in believing that the classical syllabus was very demanding. Boys going up from Rugby to the

[61] Ibid. 270 f., paras. 1037 ff.
[62] J. M. Wilson, afterwards headmaster of Clifton.

universities thought that they had read more Greek and Latin than boys from Eton or Harrow. They would have done some ten Greek plays, including four of Aristophanes; two books of Thucydides; sections of Herodotus; some of Xenophon's history; and three or four of Plato's dialogues. They would also have read roughly the same amount of Latin literature.[63] But they spent most of their time translating from Greek and Latin into English and not the other way round. There was, therefore, some doubt about their ability to write good Greek prose.[64]

Nor was Wilson alone in feeling that classics dominated everything else in the school. The boys themselves seem to have believed that, 'The classical fellows thought modern languages a bit "*infra dig*".'[65] And other masters, too, agreed that a number of the boys simply did not do well in classics and that no proper alternative was provided for them at all.[66] Some of the boys complained that they had little opportunity to study history and geography.[67] And all this is the more surprising when one remembers how Temple had said in his essay on 'National Education':

If refinement be the object of education, and if education cannot be continued beyond school to college, there can be no comparison between the youth who, at the age of seventeen, has to commence his apprenticeship to the world with a taste for the great English, and some knowledge of the great foreign classics and one who can just construe Horace and Euripides... The discipline of Greek and Latin is valuable; but... the discipline of learning physics and practical mathematics, English History and political economy, French and German, is, or may be made, equally valuable.[68]

It is only fair to add, at this point, that the Commissioners themselves thought that Rugby was the only school, amongst those they investigated, in which science was satisfactory and that Rugby and Harrow were the only two where history was taken seriously.[69] Nevertheless it seems clear that Temple had changed his mind significantly or, at least, had failed to implement at Rugby what he had believed to be important when he had been at Kneller Hall. It may be that there was always a certain conservatism hidden behind what appeared to be a radical cast

---

[63] *Commission on Public Schools*, iv. 291 f.
[64] Ibid. 292, paras. 1790–806; evidence of Henry Lee Warner.
[65] Ibid. 294.
[66] Ibid. 277, evidence of the Revd Charles Evans.
[67] Ibid. 292, paras 1891 ff.
[68] *Oxford Essays Contributed by Members of the University* (London, 1856), 265 f.
[69] *Commission on Public Schools*, i. 278.

of mind. It may be that he believed that there was a limit to the number of changes he ought to make in the school's traditions and methods. Or it may be that the difference is best accounted for by the fact that what he had written in his essay of 1856 referred quite specifically to *grammar* schools. The passage just quoted above began with the words:

Since the Grammar Schools were founded, there has grown up an English Literature, equal in many of its qualities to Greek and Latin, several foreign literatures of not less extent and value, and a whole army of physics and practical mathematics.

If he believed that a *public* school's function was primarily to prepare boys for the universities, so that they *would* continue beyond school to college and would not, like many grammar school boys, be put straight into 'an apprenticeship to the world', then he might have thought that a much more traditional syllabus was right for Rugby.

Two points made by the Clarendon Commissioners are particularly worth noting. In their report they described Temple as 'a Headmaster whose character for ability, zeal, and practical success promise to make him conspicuous on the list of Rugby Headmasters'.[70] And they recommended that the Rugby trustees should be replaced by a council. The implementation of that proposal provided Temple with a means of continuing to involve himself in the affairs of the school even when his headmastership had come to an end.[71]

Something of Temple's growing confidence in himself and his position is evident in his dealings with the Clarendon Commission. As Bishop of London and Archbishop of Canterbury, he was to develop a style in which the brusque and pointed rejoinder became a fine art. Though it must have been obvious that the Commission's opinion of his ability would vitally affect his reputation, damaged as it had been by *Essays and Reviews*, he was quite unwilling to be subservient. When the Commission sent out its questionnaire, even before it began taking evidence, Temple wrote to the secretary (Montague Bernard, professor of International Law at Oxford) in April 1862, 'Have you no consideration for busy men that you give us only seven days to send you back the proofs.' And he protested again in December of the same year:

... once upon a time there was a man called Juan Fernando who made the great discovery that no man can do more than he can do.

---

[70] Ibid. 298.   [71] See below, 134.

This complaint lacks the almost lapidary quality of some of his later ripostes but is typical of his blunt refusal to indulge in self-justification.

Temple was very soon to find himself a member of another commission with an even more extensive task to perform, the Schools Inquiry Commission under Henry Labouchere, Lord Taunton, who had been President of the Board of Trade in Russell's administration of 1847–52 and Colonial Secretary in Palmerston's from 1855 to 1858. The Commission was appointed in December 1864, apparently as a result of a deputation (including Tait) from the Social Science Association which had met Lord Palmerston in the previous June.[72] The Clarendon Commission's encomium may therefore have played a part in Temple's selection. He was in many ways an obvious choice because the new Commission was designed to do the very thing that he had suggested in his essay on national education, make the grammar schools the vehicle for the education of the middle classes[73] and it seems that he was actually consulted about who the other members and even the chairman might be.[74] The work to be undertaken by the Commission was enormous. It was to investigate virtually the whole field of secondary education in England and Wales save for the nine schools which had been examined by the Clarendon Commission. The Commission's secretary himself described the nature of the enquiry thus:

It took in…all school education above the National and British [i.e. the elementary] schools and below the Universities; and thus included many schools of the same general character as the nine (so-called) public schools. It dealt with girls' education as well as that of boys, and with private and proprietary schools as well as with endowed schools; but the so-called grammar schools, about 700 in number, were the principal subject of inquiry and report, and were all visited by assistant commissioners employed by the Commission.[75]

There was a faintly west-country character to the commission with Lord Taunton, Temple himself, T. D. Acland (Temple's old ally from the campaign to create the Oxford and Cambridge Examinations Board), and Stafford Northcote (MP for North Devon from 1866) among its members. The others were Lord Lyttelton who, like Northcote, had been on the Clarendon Commission; Lord Stanley, Derby's heir; W. F. Hook,

[72] Allsobrook, 180.

[73] See above, 40.

[74] Sandford (ed.), i. 133.

[75] Ibid. i. 133. The chapter of the *Memoirs* dealing with the work of the Commission was written by H. J. Roby, the secretary.

the Dean of Chichester who was best known as the former vicar of Leeds but had grown up in Whippingham on the Isle of Wight where his father had been rector; A. W. Thorold, vicar of a fashionable London parish and husband of Taunton's niece (who was eventually to become bishop of Winchester); the Chief Charity Commissioner, Peter Erle; W. E. Forster, Liberal MP for Bradford; and Edward Baines a somewhat militant Dissenter. Among the assistant commissioners sent to look into what actually existed and to report on its condition was a Rugbeian protégé of Jowett's at Balliol, Thomas Hill Green (later to be professor of Moral Philosophy at Oxford and the founder of the British Idealist school). Matthew Arnold, who held strong views about the importance of government intervention in education, was also an assistant commissioner but he was despatched to report on what was being done in Europe.

The business of discovering what was already there was vast enough: processing the reports that came in was a further burden; and compiling a single and coherent report with recommendations for the future was most daunting of all. The Commission met 115 times. Temple managed, in spite of the other demands that were continually being made upon his time, to attend about half of the sixty-eight sessions at which evidence was taken and all of the forty-seven sessions at which the broad outline of the report was agreed.

The magnitude of the Commission's task was not simply a question of the amount of ground which had to be covered. It also contained men of very different and strongly held views which had to be reconciled. It would seem that Lord Granville, Lord President of the Council and therefore responsible for the Committee on Education, had been anxious that none of the most vociferous theorists should set the direction for the Commission.[76] There were those who, like Matthew Arnold, believed that a government department of education was needed which would control the nation's schools. There were the vested interests of the Established Church and the National Society its educational agency. There were the contrary interests of dissent and the urban radicals. There were the trusts and trustees who were responsible for maintaining individual school foundations up and down the country and some of them were large and powerful. Then there were those, like Temple's former colleague at the Committee of Council,

---

[76] Allsobrook, 180 f.

Henry Moseley, who thought that the 'middle classes' chiefly needed technical education; and there were those who thought that such people—tradesmen and others—wanted their children to be upwardly mobile and therefore to be educated in the classics like their 'betters'.

What the Commission did was in some ways radical and in other ways fairly modest. It set itself, above everything else, to provide a uniformity of standard in schools throughout the country and to create some means of supervising and testing their competence. It made recommendations for government action, in itself a radical thing to do since it accepted that education was a matter which could only be dealt with properly by the State. The proposal that trust funds should be diverted from the objects for which they had originally been intended in order to benefit those who possessed proven academic ability, was equally radical: it touched the sacred rights of property. But many of the detailed recommendations—for the establishment of local boards of education, the involvement of the universities in supervising examinations, the use of conscience clauses to allow parents to withdraw their children from religious education—were not new.[77] And many of them had been suggested by Temple earlier.

The question therefore arises whether Temple was himself responsible for the line which the report took. It is quite clear that he was a dominant figure and that his personality contributed a great deal to the way in which discussion on the Commission developed. His rather boyish sense of fun seems to have led to a certain amount of teasing, perhaps particularly with Acland.[78] In the later stages Taunton and Temple with Lyttelton, Acland, Forster, and Baines had become a small and more closely knit rump.[79] The last four, who had all begun by holding strong though different opinions, became in the course of time more willing to compromise. It was these six who gave the Commission's findings their final shape. Temple drew up a skeleton report for the others to consider.[80] And the chairman is said to have told the secretary at the last meeting that, if there were matters of drafting detail about which he was uncertain, there would be no need to call the

---

[77] Ibid. 204.

[78] A. H. D. Acland (ed.), *Memoir and Letters of the Rt. Hon. Sir T. D. Acland* (London, 1902), 2. 265.

[79] Stanley and Northcote had taken office in Disraeli's cabinet. The others seem to have lost interest.

[80] Sandford (ed.), i. 134.

Commission together again.[81] It would be sufficient for him to secure Temple's opinion on the matter. The secretary himself (J. H. Roby) thought that Temple, Taunton, Lyttelton, Acland, and Forster, in that order, were the 'leading spirits'.

Roby also provided an account of how the report was put together, under very considerable pressure. His account is not always clear but it appears that he and Temple together drafted the second chapter, on the kind of education that was needed, and that Temple alone compiled the final chapter on the recommendations, though it is stressed that they had been 'very fully discussed'.[82] It has been suggested that the whole direction of the Commission's thinking was due to Temple and that what the Commission said can be treated as if it were simply expressing Temple's own ideas. The misapprehension probably arises from the mistaken idea that he had been the secretary of the Commission and composed rather than drafted crucial sections of the report.[83] Neither Roby's account nor the other available evidence suggests that the plan put forward by the Commission was solely Temple's work. Temple certainly believed, and the Commission seems to have accepted the idea, that grammar school endowments often provided free schooling for those who lacked the talent to benefit by it. He was always opposed to the idea of scholarships being awarded on any other ground than ability. In 1863 he told one of his masters, 'I shall always be glad if a poor boy gets one, but not if he gets it by a cleverer rich boy not standing.'[84] He also believed that undeserved financial support was as bad as indiscriminate almsgiving.[85] Nevertheless it was always Temple's way to give expression to the corporate view. In 1856, when he wrote his contribution to *Oxford Essays*, he had been the spokesman for many of his colleagues in the education office.[86] In 1862 he had consulted the

---

[81] Ibid. 136.

[82] Ibid. 135.

[83] Simon Green, 'Archbishop Frederick Temple on Meritocracy, Liberal Education and the Idea of a Clerisy', in Michael Bentley (ed.), *Public and Private Doctrine: Essays in British History Presented to Maurice Cowling* (Cambridge, 1993), 149 ff. and particularly 156, where Temple is described as 'secretary and virtual author of the concluding chapter'. In the rest of the article Green appears to assume that whatever the Commission said can be regarded as evidence for what Temple thought. Green may have been confused by the fact that Roby's account of the Commission's work appears in the chapter of the Sandford *Memoir* which deals with Temple's work with the Committee of Council and not in the chapter that deals with his time at Rugby.

[84] Sandford (ed.), ii. 535.

[85] *Report of Schools Inquiry Commission*, i. 592 ff.

[86] See above, 38.

masters at Rugby before replying to the Clarendon Commission's preliminary questionnaire. There is no reason to suppose that he ignored the opinions of the other members when drafting his share of the Taunton Commission's report.

5

Yet More Controversy

Given Temple's success as headmaster of Rugby it was inevitable that he would, sooner or later, be considered for a bishopric. In Temple's case, of course, his reputation as a heterodox theologian would weigh against an actual appointment. There were two important people who were anxious to ensure that consideration led to action—Tait and Gladstone—but they were on opposite sides of the most controversial issue of the late 1860s, the disestablishment of the Irish Church.

The association between Temple and Gladstone, though not anything that could be described as friendship, went back to the time when Temple had served on Gladstone's Oxford committee in the 1840s. Gladstone had disliked *Essays and Reviews*. Yet on the fly-leaf at the back of his copy of the book there is a list of names of clergymen who were all more or less Liberal in political terms. Some of them were also theologically liberal—Maurice, Jowett, Stanley, Pattison, Colenso,[1] and Temple himself. It is tempting to think that Gladstone may have been listing politically suitable episcopal candidates. The Prime Minister when the book appeared was Palmerston; and Gladstone was his Chancellor of the Exchequer. It is usually said that the great Evangelical layman, Lord Shaftesbury, was Palmerston's chief adviser on ecclesiastical patronage but the Tractarian Gladstone had clearly taken note of Temple in spite of *Essays and Reviews*.

Gladstone himself became Prime Minister in December 1868. He had forced a vote on Irish disestablishment in the House of Commons in March 1868 and won. In May Disraeli announced that there would be a general election in the autumn. It was perfectly clear that the future of the Irish Church would be a central issue. Feelings ran very high. Tait spoke at a public meeting in London against disestablishment and one of the very last things which Disraeli had done before going to the

---

[1] In 1860, when *Essays and Reviews* was published, Colenso's critical biblical commentaries had not yet appeared.

country had been to nominate Tait, then Bishop of London, to the see of Canterbury. Disraeli lost the election and resigned. Tait 'declined thenceforward to oppose the emphatic will of the nation'[2] and he had, in any case, to work with the new Prime Minister in ecclesiastical appointments. Yet in this instance the original suggestion that Temple be promoted does not seem to have come from Tait. Perhaps there was no need, for Temple had publicly supported Irish disestablishment. At all events, when Tait met Gladstone in early April 1869 he recorded in his journal:

From the little Gladstone s[d] about the Mastership of the Temple now vacant I gathered a more favourable opinion of his width of view in reference to Church appointments. He spoke in very high terms both of Temple and [?]Plumptre.[3]

Gladstone soon began to propose possible preferment for Temple. He offered him the deanery of Durham in July 1869, an appointment which would have made him warden of the university which had originally been founded out of the massive endowments of the cathedral.[4] When Temple declined this offer Gladstone wrote to Acland asking him to find out whether Temple would be willing to consider a bishopric. Acland apparently believed that there would be no very great public outcry at such an appointment but Gladstone was less sanguine. The choice of the particular see, he thought, 'requires care'.[5] In September 1869 there were four possibilities including the see of Exeter. Thirty years later Temple was to claim that he had been offered the choice, presumably in an unofficial way, and had chosen Exeter.[6] The west-country diocese must have seemed to Gladstone to provide the ideal opportunity to promote this somewhat risky West-Country clergyman. Temple was nominated. Gladstone's assessment of public opinion proved to be more accurate than that of Acland. In spite of the care taken, there was an outcry. Those normally mutually opposed leaders of ecclesiastical opinion, Pusey and Shaftesbury, combined

---

[2] R. T. Davidson and W. Benham, *Life of Archibald Campbell Tait, Archbishop of Canterbury*, 2 vols. (London, 1891), ii. 7.

[3] Lambeth Palace Library: Archbishop Tait's Journal, vol. 47, 14 f.: the entry is actually dated 10 Apr. 1869. Tait's handwriting is appallingly difficult to read and the second name is little more than 'Pl' and a squiggle. If the word is Plumptre it may refer to the Master of University College, Oxford or the professor of Exegesis at King's, London.

[4] E. G. Sandford (ed.), *Memoirs of Archbishop Temple by Seven Friends*, 2 vols. (London, 1906), i. 235.

[5] Ibid. i. 236.

[6] Ibid. i. 275 n.

forces to launch a campaign 'to prevent the scandal to the Church caused by the Premier's nomination of Dr Temple...'[7]

Not everyone, of course, was opposed to the appointment.[8] Tait wrote to express real pleasure. Arthur Stanley and Matthew Arnold exulted. But many of the letters Temple received, while offering congratulations and good wishes, also contained doubtful, even double-edged remarks. Samuel Wilberforce, whose former diocese of Oxford was one of the four on offer and whose place Matthew Arnold had hoped Temple would fill, wrote:

Often and often in my poor way I have defended you from what seem utter misconceptions of your character, and whilst I suppose there are matters on which we differ, I cannot forebear saying that I do firmly believe we shall not only sympathize with one another but work often together.[9]

Coming from the man who, more than anyone else, had been responsible for stirring up feeling against *Essays and Reviews*, this has an ironic sound. The Bishop of Ely, Harold Browne, whose sons had been at Rugby, wrote with a similar but less marked ambiguity, expressing his gratitude and respect but putting some emphasis on the way his ideas differed from Temple's. Even E. W. Benson wrote from Wellington School, in a letter bubbling with genuine and typical affection, 'I don't like to see (as at Rugby, I do) the sharp edges of the sword coming through the sheath, and at Exeter the scabbard may be mended...'[10]

Benson had been a master at Rugby under Temple. Temple had helped him get things going at Wellington in his first days at the newly founded school. There was always a surprisingly close friendship between these two very different men: Temple gruff, masculine, and brusque; Benson complex, introvert, and romantic. But Benson could only say, 'We are one—in hope—and in love.' 'One in faith' is the thought rather obviously missing from the sentence. Benson was later to write a very courageous public defence of Temple in *The Times*, insisting on his moral qualities. But even in that context he could not hide his doubts about *Essays and Reviews*. What Temple actually believed became more and more a matter of public concern.

---

[7] Ibid. i. 281.

[8] Sandford (ed.), i. 275 ff. contains many of the letters, both favourable and unfavourable, which Temple received when the appointment became public. Other letters, mostly from Temple's supporters, are among the family papers in the possession of the Right Revd. F. S. Temple.

[9] Sandford (ed.), i. 277.

[10] Ibid. i. 276.

Outwardly Temple displayed a stolid stoicism. Inwardly he was deeply distressed by the furore. Netta Temple, his sister and the one person perhaps who really knew how much he was hurt by the accusations of faithlessness, wrote to Benson after his letter was published:

All the storm has pained me so much—it is so unlike what I should desire for him. These two months, when his own prayers and the prayers of those who care for him or for the Church should have been invited, to be broken in upon by such discordant outcries has been very sad to me. God bless you for loving him, as I know you will do.[11]

As the time drew closer for his formal election by the cathedral chapter, more and more people urged him to make a statement. They wanted something that would satisfy those who admired his moral character but mistrusted his theology. *Essays and Reviews* had been censured by Convocation: it was odd, after all, to make him a bishop without Convocation's withdrawing the censure or Temple's withdrawing his contribution. Harold Browne exhorted him to make some statement which would make it easier for members of the chapter to vote for him. Samuel Wilberforce publicly expressed doubts about his suitability and then, when taken to task by Temple for going back on his earlier letter of congratulation, tried to pretend that he had temporarily forgotten that Temple's essay had been included in the official censure. Even Temple's friends began to put pressure on him. Stafford Northcote wrote on behalf of all those moderate people who were sure that Temple would make an excellent bishop. What they needed, he said, was a reason for *not* joining in the outcry.[12] He thought Temple's election might be carried only by a casting vote and that it might be followed by a secession from the Church of England. Only Gerald Wellesley, Dean of Windsor, who had backed him when he was at Kneller Hall, had the perceptiveness to say, 'It is difficult for a man to make explanations with a bishopric hanging over his head.'[13]

This was exactly how Temple felt. When Sir John Coleridge, Liberal MP for Exeter and, like Northcote, a contemporary of Temple's at Balliol, asked whether it would not be possible for his friend to make some pacifying statement, Temple replied in October 1869 in what was the clearest statement of his point of view:

If I speak at all, I must be just to the other writers, and I must be quite open to the Church.

---

[11] Sandford (ed.), i. 517.   [12] Ibid. i. 283.   [13] Ibid. i. 301.

Now I did not and do not consider myself responsible for the opinions of the other writers. I said so then. It was said in the Preface to the Book.

To say so again now would mean a great deal more. It would mean condemnation. I am not prepared to condemn them, though in not a few points I disagree with several of them.

Further it would mean that I thought that the Book had done harm. I think it has done much good as well as harm, and that the good preponderates.[14]

He feared, in other words, that if his own acceptability depended on his separating himself from others, he would in effect be declaring them unacceptable. And he reiterated the point he had made so often before that it had been necessary to bring questions and doubts into the open. Coleridge replied on 20 November 1869, 'I have watched the whole proceeding towards it with much interest—the opposition I believe was perfectly honest & I am sure will leave no unpleasant impression personally on your mind—but it seems to me singularly wanting in good judgement—and rather disgraced in the end in some quarters by pertinaciousness which might have embittered it.'[15]

If his closest friends in the West Country could be so understanding of the opposition, it is not surprising that there was a vigorous attempt in the diocese to prevent his becoming bishop. Many of the clergy were of Henry Phillpotts's conservative stamp: Tory High Churchmen of the 'old' school. The dean and chapter of Exeter had been instructed by the Crown to proceed with an election and had received the Crown's nomination of the candidate they were required to elect. Refusal to do so would have laid them open to a charge of *praemunire*. Some of them were, nevertheless, determined to make their opposition plain.[16] They were led by the Archdeacon of Exeter, Philip Freeman, and by W. J. Trower, subdean of the cathedral and formerly Bishop of Gibraltar. (Trower had virtually been performing all the bishop's duties in the diocese during Phillpotts's last years.) They received considerable support. There were local meetings of protest, particularly a large and vehement meeting of the clergy of the rural deanery of Plymouth. The *Exeter and Plymouth Gazette* took up the dissidents' cause. The *Exeter Flying Post* (probably motivated by the editor's quite evident dislike of Tractarianism and of the Pusey/Shaftesbury alliance) came out on

[14] Ibid. i. 285.

[15] Family Papers in the possession of the Right Revd F. S. Temple: 'On being appointed to Exeter'; Coleridge to Temple, letter dated Ottery St Mary, 20 Nov. 1869.

[16] See 'The Crown, the Chapter and Dr Temple by an Elector, with an Appendix by a North Devon Rector', repr. from the *Exeter and Plymouth Gazette*, 1869.

Temple's side, though with the same reserved air that some of his personal friends had displayed.[17] Neither Temple's politics nor his theology were to the newspaper's taste but he had done nothing, an editorial said, that was contrary to the law of England. The newspaper's support for Temple provoked Archdeacon Freeman into saying, 'I hate newspapers!'[18]

The dean, Archibald Boyd, took much the same line as the *Flying Post* and pointed out that, if the chapter refused to elect, the Crown had the power to override them and appoint by letters patent. Since Boyd was a firm but moderate Evangelical, and had considerable reservations about Temple, even this degree of support was significant. But the person on whom the chief burden of active support for the new bishop fell was a member of the chapter who had been a friend and colleague in the education office, Canon Cook.[19] Cook was among those who had wanted Temple to make some clear statement of orthodoxy but even for him Temple would not disown *Essays and Reviews*. 'A right-minded man cannot enter on such an office by beginning with what lowers him before his own conscience.'[20] So Cook had to become Temple's guarantor, as it were, persuading his colleagues 'of the strength of his belief in both the orthodoxy and the personal character of the Bishop-nominate'.[21]

In fact it seems that within a month of the nomination being made public the tide had begun to turn in Temple's favour. The editorial in the *Flying Post* on 3 November said:

The opposition to Dr Temple is practically at an end. Archdeacon Freeman is silent; the Gazette has given up. There is indeed a rumour in the wind that Dr Trower intends to carry out his opposition by proposing the election of Prebendary Mackarness; and this course is approved by Dr Pusey as an ingenious way of evading the statute of praemunire.

The manœuvre referred to was a clever one. John Fielder Mackarness, rector of Honiton and a prebendary of Exeter cathedral, had been nominated to the see of Oxford. He, too, was a Liberal in politics but he had not been censured by Convocation. The dissidents thought that,

---

[17] *Trewman's Exeter Flying Post*, 20 Oct. 1869. The paper also reprinted Temple's 'Education of the World' in the same issue and on another page there is a report of the protest meeting of the clergy of the rural deanery of Plymouth.

[18] Ibid.

[19] See above, 39.

[20] Sandford (ed.), i. 285.

[21] Ibid. i. 290.

by casting their votes for someone already destined for preferment by the Crown, they could make their point without appearing to challenge the royal supremacy.

The election took place, apparently without crowds or excitement, on 11 November 1869.[22] After the lessons had been read at morning prayer, the members of the greater chapter withdrew to the chapter house. They were: Boyd, the Dean; Canon Harington the chancellor; Archdeacons Freeman and Woollcombe; Canons Cook and Lee; Bishop Trower; Prebendaries Phillpotts, Downall,[23] Lyne, Ford, R. W. Barnes, Smith, Mackarness, Brereton, Tatham, Harris, Thynne, R. H. Barnes, Acland, Sanders, Cox, and Hedgeland. Four of these—Cox (who was ill), Smith (who was at his daughter's wedding), Thynne, and Ford—were not present. Trower made his protest but it seems that Mackarness was not, in the end, nominated. When the votes were cast there were thirteen for Temple. Trower, Freeman, Lee, Tatham, Harris, and Lyne voted against him. It all took about half an hour.

On 19 November Tait was taken desperately ill. He had been doing everything possible to make up for Temple's refusal to dissociate himself from *Essays and Reviews*, declaring that 'The Education of the World', taken on its own, would not have been condemned by Convocation.[24] His illness was serious—'a convulsive seizure of the most alarming kind' and it was followed by another a few hours later. His family plainly thought that it was merely a matter of waiting for him to die.[25] Nevertheless, as soon as he was strong enough, the archbishop continued to issue statements defending Temple's theological orthodoxy and trying to calm the fears of the dissidents in the diocese.[26] But it was quite clear that Tait was not going to be able to consecrate him. The consecration was set for 21 December, with the confirmation to take place at St Mary le Bow on 8 December, and Jackson, who had just moved from Lincoln to London, was appointed principal consecrator. Ironically, it was his successor at Lincoln, Christopher Wordsworth, who now took a leading role in the affair.

---

[22] The election is reported in the *Exeter Flying Post*, 17 Nov. 1869, and Trower's statement is printed in full in the same issue, immediately after the report of the Licensed Victuallers Association.

[23] Phillpotts and Downall were Archdeacons but not residentiaries.

[24] Davidson and Benham, ii. 61.

[25] Ibid. 50.

[26] The *Exeter Flying Post*, 24 Nov. contains a message sent from Tait to the clergy of a rural deanery in the diocese maintaining that Temple's published sermons were proof of his theological soundness.

On 13 November Wordsworth wrote to Temple begging him to restore peace to the Church by issuing a statement, which would not condemn *Essays and Reviews*, but would disavow his responsibility for everything in it except his own contribution. The bishop argued that the disclaimer in the preface had been cancelled by the publication of subsequent editions because Temple could no longer plead ignorance of what the others had written. Temple's reply recognized the moderation and generosity of Wordsworth's request but insisted that, as the law of the Church of England did not require him to make any statement at all, to do so gratuitously would be to accept responsibility for any ill consequences that might result. It was perhaps the least convincing of the reasons he had given.[27]

Wordsworth also wrote to Gladstone (and engaged in published correspondence in the press with Jackson), to which the Prime Minister replied on 16 December. Gladstone was ill in bed but had apparently been reading what had appeared in the newspapers since the start of the affair. He told Wordsworth:

Your first letter and that of the Metropolitan and that of the Bishop of London, all command my sympathy. I should have been very glad if Dr Temple had felt himself able to accede to the friendly and brotherly suggestion contained in all the three. I was unable to comprehend as matter of argument the ground taken by Dr Temple in his reply to you. Placing myself in his position I would have resisted any claim as of right... But I cannot conceive any such reason why Dr Temple should not have yielded to the appeal to charity, and I think such a yielding would have been a graceful and noble act.

These are my opinions, but I do not think I have a right to make a personal appeal to Dr Temple or to convey to him as a minister the wishes which as a man I entertain! It has however for some little time been my intention to make known my feelings to one of his intimate friends, a character to which I have no sort of title. I had meant to await, not to make, an opportunity of doing this. But receiving the appeal which your Lordship, a Bishop of the Province, has made to me, I cannot put that appeal aside as an ordinary suggestion. I will therefore by this evening's post send to the person I have in view a copy of your Lordship's letter and of my reply. Only adding that I think the call upon Dr Temple at this peculiar moment is to liberate himself not to administer censure to others.[28]

---

[27] The correspondence between Wordsworth and Temple is in Sandford (ed.), i. 292 ff. Temple signed himself F. Exon. (Elect).

[28] Lambeth Palace Library: Wordsworth Papers, MS 2148, fo. 85, Gladstone to Wordsworth, 16 Dec. 1869.

But whatever Gladstone may have asked the anonymous friend to say to Temple had no effect. He made no public statement about *Essays and Reviews*.

The ceremony of the confirmation on 8 December was crowded. Confirmation is merely concerned to establish that the bishop-elect is actually the person elected by the chapter and named in the royal mandate and that there is no obvious technicality which might invalidate his claim. The protesters, however, insisted on challenging Temple's worthiness in every possible way. Since bastardy was a technical objection possible under canon law, poor Netta Temple was obliged to appear before the court and testify to her brother's legitimacy. Robert Lingen had to give evidence as to Temple's moral character: his hatred of Tractarian ecclesiasticism must have made this a less than pleasurable experience. The court of confirmation refused to consider anything other than the most formal matters, declaring itself not a tribunal for establishing the orthodoxy of points of doctrine.[29]

The next act in the drama was the actual consecration, which took place in a crowded Westminster Abbey on a thick foggy day. There were two other candidates besides Temple, a Bishop for the Falkland Islands, and Lord Arthur Hervey the Bishop-elect of Bath and Wells. At the last moment, as the bishops assembled in the Jerusalem Chamber, the Bishop of London announced that he had received protests against the consecration from several bishops of the province and notably from the Bishop of Lincoln. Jackson declared that his own opinion, after taking advice from counsel, was that he had no option but to proceed with the consecration. He then asked the assisting bishops, Browne of Ely (who had at one time been in charge of a small theological college in Exeter), Philpott of Worcester (in whose diocese Rugby fell), and Thirlwall of St Davids, to give their opinion.

The Bishop of Ely, with his usual combination of modesty and learning, fortified his own judgment by the sanction of an appeal to a precedent of the primitive Church. With greater directness, the historian Bishop of St David's briefly pronounced: 'My judgment is that they cannot be received.'[30]

So the consecration proceeded. The sermon was preached by W. C. Lake, who had just been appointed to the deanery of Durham which Temple had earlier declined. He was in many ways a contentious figure;

---

[29] Sandford (ed.), i. 291.
[30] Ibid. i. 296 and see also *The Protests of the Bishops Against the Consecration of Dr Temple, Preceded by a Letter to the Bishop of London from J. W. Burgon* (Oxford, 1870).

radical not in theology so much as in matters relating to the reform of the university but credited with having played a part in preventing Jowett's election as Master of Balliol in 1854. A friend of Temple's and, like him, someone who regarded the natural sciences as important, he made no attempt to gloss over the controversy which had surrounded the appointment. He referred to Basil, Bishop of Caesarea (AD *c*.370) who had been, he said, denounced as at heart an unbeliever because he would not separate himself from his early friends. The charge was laid before St Athanasius (Patriarch of Alexandria and champion of orthodoxy).

How did Athanasius act? Did he exact from Basil some fresh assurance beyond the adoption of the Apostles' and Nicene creeds? No; he, the great father of orthodoxy, simply wrote to enjoin Basil's diocese to obey him...[31]

And Basil had been, Lake pointed out, a bishop full of wisdom and truth who had possessed throughout his episcopate the support of the laity.

The parallel may have been a little contrived but Lake could not have contrived the arrival at the Abbey, during their lunch break, of a party of working-class men who had come to show their support for Temple.[32] It was a very neat example of lay support.

A curious, but probably unreliable letter among Randall Davidson's correspondence provides a sort of footnote to the story of the consecration. Davidson's *Life of Archibald Campbell Tait* appeared in 1891 and he sent a copy of it to the Revd Robert Charles Jenkins. Jenkins had been rector of Lyminge in Kent from 1854 for over twenty years (being himself the patron of the living). He was also an honorary canon of Canterbury cathedral and may have had some place on Tait's staff at the time of Temple's consecration. He must, at any rate, have had some connection with the archbishop or there would have been no reason for Davidson to have sent him the book. Jenkins, in his letter of thanks, told Davidson (who had not become Tait's chaplain till 1877):

On one or two points, in which, being behind the scenes I knew more than those who were in front, I could have given you some enlightenment. One of these is the matter of the Consecration of Bp Temple—During the Abp's serious illness in 1869 (during which he appointed me an honorary Canon by a memorandum he had left with Bp Parry) the late Bp of Winchester then Bp. of Ely [Harold Browne] was appointed as the principal Consecrator of the new

---

[31] Sandford (ed.), i. 298.
[32] Ibid. i. 296.

Bishop. He was in great perplexity on account of the opposition of Wordsworth and others and their appeal to the canons of the first Councils, of which strangely enough the Latin Version was adopted. My old friend Mr J. B. Lee [legal adviser to the archbishop] (whom I knew from 1841 when he was my Parishioner at Willesden) was equally perplexed.[33]

Jenkins had, he claimed, pointed out to Lee and Browne that the Greek words used in the originals of the canons referred not to the consecration of a new bishop but to his election. 'I showed that the refusal to consecrate would be a resistance of the election and therefore bring its authors under a *praemunire*.' The Bishop of Ely, he said, had asked to be allowed to include this explanation in a statement he had drawn up for the bishops. Because Jenkins's memory was at fault in thinking that Browne had been the principal consecrator, there must be considerable doubt about the reliability of his account as a whole. But it is just possible that the paper he claimed to have written for the bishops was the source of Browne's 'appeal to the precedent of the primitive Church'.

One small event, with large consequences, happened soon after the consecration. Canon Cook told Archdeacon Freeman that no further edition of *Essays and Reviews* would ever appear again with Temple's contribution included in it.

After Christmas, which he seems to have spent at Rugby, Temple went to Exeter for his enthronization on 29 December. Once again his arrival at a new place was unconventional for, there being no carriage to meet his train, he travelled in a farm cart to the parsonage of his old headmaster at Blundells, Prebendary Sanders. Sanders had by this time become the incumbent of Sowton, a small village to the east of the city near where the motorway now runs. Temple spent the night of 28 December there preparing his sermon for the next day though, in the end he was to make no direct use of what he had written. Having to make himself heard in a packed cathedral he abandoned the prepared script but spoke on the same general theme.

There does seem to have been an unexpectedly large congregation. The *Flying Post* opined rather sneeringly that the opposition to Temple had only ensured that he had a bigger and better welcome than any other bishop could conceivably have received.[34] There seems to have

[33] Lambeth Palace Library: Davidson Papers (Official Correspondence), vol. 29, fo. 72, Jenkins to Bishop of Rochester (Davidson), 15 Jan. 1892.
[34] The report appeared on the actual day of the ceremony, 29 Dec. 1869 and gave the full text of Temple's sermon, presumably the original written version rather than what he actually said.

been no public protest or objection associated with the service itself, though none of the six members of the chapter who had voted against Temple appeared in the procession. Indeed, there are some features of the ceremony which suggest that Temple's supporters were determined to close ranks behind him. Mackarness walked alone in the procession, apart from the other prebendaries, as 'the Bishop-Elect of Oxford' as if to make it clear that he was in no sense Temple's rival. It is worth noting that the hymn 'Christ is made the sure foundation', not then as popular or well-known as it is now, was sung during the service. Having been translated by John Mason Neale and published by him in *Mediaeval Hymns and Sequences* in the 1850s, it was much approved of by the Tractarians.[35] And, of course, it proclaimed undoubtedly orthodox sentiments about the uniqueness of Christ. The same theme was taken up in Temple's sermon. His text was 'The word was made flesh' from the first chapter of St John's gospel. It was, therefore, a sermon on the incarnation and its theme was that, 'as the Bible was supreme above all other books, so, and in a yet higher sense, our Lord was supreme above all created beings,'[36] giving him the opportunity to insist upon his own personal devotion to Christ and upon the authority he attributed to the scriptures.

...I have desired with an exceeding desire for the day to come when I might meet you face to face, and to pour out before you all that is in my heart of devotion to you and to our common Master, our Lord God, the Son of God, Jesus Christ.[37]

It was the beginning of a long campaign to convince the diocese that he was no unbeliever. He had resolutely refused to make any concession so long as it might seem that he was purchasing his bishopric by reneging on what he had believed to be true and right. Having become the bishop, he was willing to go some of the way towards meeting the difficulties of those who had opposed his consecration. He intended, and had begun to tell his friends, that he would withdraw his essay. Archdeacon Freeman, perhaps disingenuously, perhaps through a genuine misunderstanding,[38] made this intention public in Convocation. Temple's enemies put the worst possible interpretation on the

---

[35] Leon Litvack, *J. M. Neale and the Quest for Sobornost* (Oxford, 1994), 27.
[36] Sandford (ed.), i. 300.
[37] Ibid.
[38] Ibid. i. 301.

announcement. Burgon wondered why Temple had not had the honesty to make it himself.[39] His liberal friends became very anxious in case a public condemnation of *Essays and Reviews* should follow. Stanley was alarmed. Jowett was already bitter. Two days after the enthronization he had written to Florence Nightingale:

I read Dr Temple's sermon without much satisfaction. Why should he make a declaration of the Doctrine of the Trinity in the first sentence? He knows that St Paul would not have used this language, nor would he himself ten years ago. His notion of the conscience is utterly confused. I don't like a man publicly devoted to Christ on 5000£ a year & leaving Rugby to Haman... this is not the young man whom I knew twenty years ago who used to talk to me about 'Untruthfulness being the great Sin of the world'.[40]

Temple was, as so often before, torn between two groups of friends. Freeman's announcement in Convocation in February forced his hand. He had to make a public statement explaining why he was withdrawing his essay. It said little that was new apart from an assertion that what it might be perfectly proper for Dr Temple to do might be an inappropriate action for the Bishop of Exeter.

The whole process had not actually taken very long. Gladstone had warned Tait on 2 October that he proposed to nominate Temple: the new bishop was in place by the end of December. To Temple himself it must have seemed a long and testing three months yet he had become simultaneously involved in a new controversy.[41] Jowett's remark about 'Haman' was a very donnish pun. Haman, 'the son of Hammedatha the Agagite, the enemy of the Jews', is the villain of the book of Esther in the Old Testament. Dr Henry Hayman was the person who had been appointed to succeed Temple at Rugby.

The trustees at Rugby were about to be replaced by the new governors and the appointment of Hayman was virtually their last act. Temple, who had not yet left the school, was incensed. It seemed to him a rash decision, taken by those who had nothing further to lose. Perhaps he felt that the appointment of Hayman would be tantamount to a

[39] Bodleian Library, Oxford: MS Wilberforce d.47, fos. 261 ff., letter dated 11 Feb. [1870].
[40] E. V. Quinn and J. M. Prest (eds.), *Dear Miss Nightingale: A Selection of Benjamin Jowett's Letters, 1860–1893* (Oxford, 1987), 182.
[41] The story of the controversy is told, in a version which is relatively sympathetic to Hayman, in J. B. Hope Simpson, *Rugby Since Arnold* (London, 1967), 64 ff. and see also S. R. T. Mayor (ed.), *Extracts from the Minute Book of the Governing Body of Rugby School Inspected, For the First Time, After the Bill Filed in Chancery, Shewing the True Character of Their Proceedings Towards the Late Head Master Dr Hayman* (London, 1875).

dismantling of everything he had achieved at Rugby rather like what he had already experienced in the complete destruction of his work at Kneller Hall. Hayman, he thought, lacked the intellectual calibre for the job. With the effortless self-confidence of an alpha mind, Temple declared his successor to be undoubtedly 'a good double second'.[42]

The man was not without experience. He had been headmaster of St Olave's, Southwark, of Cheltenham and of Bradfield, all very well-known schools, but he was from outside the Arnoldite circle. Either of the other candidates would have been acceptable to Temple. They were Theodore Walrond and John Percival. Walrond was Temple's own choice for the job. They had been friends and allies for a very long time. Walrond had been a fellow of Balliol and a colleague of Temple's in the offices of the Committee on Education and he had acted as Temple's campaign manager when he had been a candidate for the headmastership of Rugby, a decade earlier.[43] But Percival was scarcely less of a friend. He had been the first headmaster of Clifton since 1862 and was making it one of the leading public schools in England. And he had received useful help and advice from Temple who had warned him, for instance, that Clifton was too new for him to be able to get away with making public and radical political statements.[44] Two years before Temple's consecration, Percival had asked him to preach at Clifton and he had replied in a typically robust fashion, which makes it obvious that the two men were good friends and able to relax with each other.

I will preach your Sermon on Ascension Day if you cannot find a dignitary to do so. But I think you would do wisely to get a Dignitary if you can. All English folk prefer a man with a prefix. They feel sure of having the real thing.[45]

Walrond had impressive backing. His testimonials were from both Archbishops, the Bishop of Chester (Jacobson), the Deans of Westminster (Stanley) and Durham (Lake), from Scott (the Master of Balliol), from Jowett, and from Temple himself. There was, in other words, support which represented both the establishment and the liberal caucus. Hayman's testimonials were more hindrance than help. His own explanation was that, because he had only decided to apply for the post ten days before the election, there had been no time to secure a complete new set and have them printed. He had therefore used a set

---

[42] Simpson, 67.
[43] See above, 55.
[44] Lambeth Palace Library: MS 3219, Temple papers; fos. 69–73.
[45] Ibid. Temple to Percival, letter dated 13 Mar. 1867.

which had been written for him when he had applied for other positions.[46] The trustees seem nevertheless to have decided to appoint him. Hayman visited the school on 3 December, five days before the events at Bow church. This, no doubt, added to the tension of the occasion. Hayman met the masters, who seem to have made it clear that they would have preferred a more distinguished candidate. The meeting was cold and unfriendly. Hayman's encounter with Temple was worse, an explosive confrontation in which Temple announced that he proposed to tell the trustees that the appointment would be nothing short of disastrous. Twenty out of the twenty-one assistant masters also protested to the trustees.

Throughout December 1869, when Temple was in the thick of the controversy surrounding his consecration and was being pressed to make a statement dissociating himself from *Essays and Reviews*, he was also engaged in this row about Rugby. So far from, in Jowett's words, 'leaving Rugby to Haman', he was in fact doing everything he possibly could to prevent Hayman taking over the school. The press got wind of what was happening and the whole thing became public. G. G. Bradley (who had been a master at Rugby, was at that time headmaster of Marlborough, and was to be Stanley's successor at Westminster Abbey) wrote to *The Times* on 20 December saying that his testimonial for Hayman was a general purpose one, written three years before and never intended to be used in an application to Rugby. He had already written to the trustees to the same effect and fourteen headmasters of public schools including Eton, Winchester, and Harrow—according to Benson at Wellington—had protested at what they regarded as a subversion of the testimonials system.[47] The trustees met on the very day the letter appeared. With his consecration due to take place the following morning, Temple demanded the right to address the trustees and was refused. The trustees announced that they were perfectly satisfied with both Hayman and his testimonials.

Opposition to the new headmaster within the school continued for a long time and, sadly, Temple seems to have actively encouraged it. There were unseemly scenes when parties of boys called loudly for 'Three cheers for the Bishop of Exeter'.[48] Two School House tutors, Roberston

[46] Simpson, 69.
[47] Trinity College, Cambridge: E. W. Benson papers, Benson to J. B. Lightfoot, letter dated December 1869.
[48] Simpson, 74.

and Scott, led the opposition to the headmaster. On 5 December 1870 the trustees supported Hayman's desire to sack them but by 16 January they had received a large number of letters from present or former masters at the school backing the two tutors. They summoned the headmaster *and* the dissidents and in the end refused to allow Hayman to dismiss the tutors. It was hardly possible for him to run the school effectively after that. By 1873 the number of boys had fallen to about half what it had been when he had been elected and the trustees had been replaced by the new governors. Temple himself had been appointed a governor by the University of London and among the other governors were Bradley, Robert Lingen (Temple's former superior in the education office), and others who were opposed to Hayman.[49] Chairman of the governors, Henry Philpott, Bishop of Worcester, had at first supported him until he discovered that the headmaster was being less than honest in his campaign against the dissident staff.[50] Not surprisingly the governors then dismissed the headmaster who, in turn, sued the governors. In the hearing in Chancery, though the Vice-Chancellor found against Hayman, he commented very adversely on the behaviour of the governors and of Bradley and Temple in particular and there were many who felt that Hayman had been somewhat unfairly treated. Even Gladstone wrote to commiserate with him.[51] And one of Temple's admirers was afterwards to write that '... the form of their protest, by whatever motives prompted, was neither wise nor right'.[52]

The governors were not much affected by the adverse publicity. They appointed as the next headmaster T. W. Jex Blake, who had been headmaster of Cheltenham since 1868 and had been one of Hayman's most vociferous critics. Temple, as on so many other occasions, refused to account publicly for his actions. To someone who wrote to expostulate with him about the Hayman affair, he replied in the third person that his correspondent would 'hardly expect the Bishop of Exeter to answer questions until he has shown his right to put them'.[53] And yet he was not entirely insensitive to public opinion. He warned Percival that it was unlikely that the governors could appoint someone whom the former

[49] Simpson, 77, and Sandford (ed.), i. 241.

[50] J. R. de S. Honey, *Tom Brown's Universe: the Development of the Victorian Public School* (London, 1977), 329 f.

[51] Simpson, 88.

[52] Arthur Sidgwick, 'Our Public Schools: Vol. iv, Rugby', *New Quarterly Magazine*, N S, 2:266.

[53] Simpson, 66.

trustees had already passed over. It would look too much like a direct snub.

The school produced a ballad for the occasion. Modelled on 'Who killed Cock Robin' it began:

> Who killed poor Hayman?
> I, said Freddy,
> With my Governing Body,
> I killed poor Hayman

and ended:

> Who'll be his successor?
> I, said Jex Blake,
> And I'll be wide awake
> When I'm his successor.[54]

---

[54] Ibid. 100.

6

Bishop, Husband, Father

The first task of Temple's episcopate was to win over the clergy of the diocese. They were anxious, no doubt, about their new bishop's orthodoxy and yet it would not have been the points of pure theology which worried them most. Their chief concerns would have been such things as: the kind of sermons he would preach when he came to perform confirmations; his policies affecting the schools in their parishes; his attitude to everyday matters of morality; and, above all, his personal relations and dealings with themselves. For almost two generations they had been used to the forceful (sometimes cantankerous) leadership provided by Phillpotts who had believed that the orthodoxy of the High Churchmen was the orthodoxy of the Church of England and had had little sympathy with other schools of theology. Many of them had publicly committed themselves to the campaign to prevent the appointment and consecration of their new bishop. Some of them found it very difficult to relax their opposition lest they might seem to condone what they had formerly described as heresy. Others, recognizing that the appointment was *fait accompli,* and that Exeter was remote from the centres of theological and ecclesiastical power, would seize on any opportunity to make their peace with Temple.

For Temple himself the move to Exeter was a home-coming. He was the west-country lad who could plough as straight a furrow as any farmer in the parish. He was also, in spite of *Essays and Reviews,* the boy who had been brought up in the strict tradition of Church principles. In recent years he had claimed the right to think for himself and he continued to say that the Church of England was the most 'catholic' church there was, by which he meant that it was the most comprehensive. As a bishop, however, he also needed to insist, as he had never found it necessary to insist before, upon loyalty to the Church. His mother's early training had been calculated to instil just such an obedient loyalty. The world of Henry Phillpotts was not entirely new territory for him. It was as though, in his first few years in Exeter, he reverted in part to his High Church upbringing, seeking a compromise between freedom and ecclesiastical authority.

Moreover, at least in his own mind, *Essays and Reviews* had represented something very like such a compromise between freedom and loyalty. 'I was told', he had said, 'that it would be in the Liberal direction, but strictly within the limits allowed by the Church of England.'[1] He and Tait had disagreed furiously about whether the volume had actually remained within those limits[2] but they had agreed on two things. There must be a wide latitude for enquiry *and* that there must be limits beyond which latitude could not be permitted. So Temple could tell himself that he had never really changed his mind: he had simply come to articulate more clearly his belief that there were very clear limits to comprehension. In practice, moreover, there was only one way of determining what the permitted limits were and that was by discovering what the law said. Tait had become convinced that, in matters of ritualism at least, there was only one way to achieve peace within the Church and that was to seek a legally defined and legally enforceable standard.[3] Temple did not go so far, though he would vote for Tait's Public Worship Regulation Act of 1874:[4] he became a constitutionalist. One of his fundamental convictions was that only the law could preserve the rights of both the corporate body and the individual. To hold the balance between the two was one of a bishop's chief functions.

It was not long before Temple began to make serious efforts to get into the parishes and meet the clergy.[5] 'I am quite satisfied that when once I am among the clergy I can win many whom no honest declaration will win,' he had said when he was being urged to dissociate himself from *Essays and Reviews*. 'Much mischief may perhaps be done meanwhile. But I know what I can do and what I cannot. I cannot prevent it, but I can repair it.'[6] He made, however, absolutely no attempt to exercise charm in order to win over his opponents. The schoolboy at

---

[1] E. G. Sandford (ed.), *Memoirs of Archbishop Temple by Several Friends*, 2 vols. (London, 1906), ii. 605, and see above, 60.

[2] See above, 76–80.

[3] P. T. Marsh, *The Victorian Church in Decline* (London, 1969), 158 ff.

[4] R. T. Davidson and W. Benham, *Life of Archibald Campbell Tait, Archbishop of Canterbury*, 2 vols. (London, 1891), ii. 207.

[5] There is a description of Temple's first tour of the diocese in Sandford (ed.), i. 311 ff. A short extract from Sandford's first-hand account is reprinted in Jack Simmons (ed.), *A Devon Anthology* (London, 1983), 236 f.

[6] Sandford (ed.), i. 285, and cf. above, 122–3.

Rugby who described Temple as 'A beast; but a just beast.' had captured something of the gruff, uncompromising determination to be frank even when it made his life more difficult. Ernest Sandford, who went with him on his first journey round the diocese, provided a first-hand account of it which gives the impression that things had been allowed to go to seed during Phillpotts's last years and that those who were actually running diocesan affairs were barely conscientious. This is probably less than fair. There can be no real doubt that they had done their best. Sandford claimed that in the last ten or twelve years of Phillpotts's episcopate most of the clergy had not bothered to send in the required returns because no one ever looked at them.[7] But in the course of 1869 Trower had conducted a formal visitation of every parish in the diocese, rural deanery by rural deanery (and there were several hundred parishes in the two counties of Devon and Cornwall).[8] Even to collect the basic information assembled on such a visitation was hours of work and it meant that the essential facts about each parish were up-to-date and at Temple's disposal.

The new bishop set out very soon on a tour of the whole of the diocese, performing confirmations in almost every parish and encountering the clergy where their work was actually being done.

The remotest country parishes were visited—the inhabitants of which had never seen a bishop before—as well as the more populous towns. Sometimes it was but a handful of half-taught country boys and girls that was presented to him; but to these, equally with the larger congregations and fully prepared candidates, he poured out the full force of his earnest spirit in strong but simple words. Sometimes the leader and his young companion were brought into strange places, where there was but little culture even in the parsonage itself. 'Do you ever read any books?' 'Yes, we see the *Gardener's Chronicle* once a month.' Sometimes there was little evidence of pastoral care. 'How are you, my good woman?' said the not very diligent clergyman, wishing to make the best of himself before his Bishop, 'How are you and how is your rheumatism?' 'You haven't done much to make it better. You haven't been to see me these six weeks.'[9]

Sandford, the 'young companion', on whom that first tour of the diocese clearly left a vivid impression, talks of churches furnished

[7] Sandford (ed.), i. 350.

[8] Devon County Record Office, Exeter: Visitation Returns of a visitation of the Diocese conducted by Walter John Trower late Bishop of Gibraltar as commissary of the Right Reverend Henry Phillpotts, D.D., Lord Bishop of the Diocese.

[9] Sandford (ed.), i. 311 f.

with box pews with high wooden walls so that the building appeared to
be totally empty. Though there were actually a large number of candidates present 'no form was visible except that of the old leader of the
choir, perched up in the west gallery, with his bass viol.'[10] Sandford also
recorded a wonderfully evocative description of a confirmation in an
anonymous country parish, where

> … the candidates were said to be 'out in the lanes somewhere,' and had to be
> gathered into the church by the friendly schoolmistress of a neighbouring
> parish. The old rector himself hung his surplice over the end of a high pew in
> which he took refuge, whilst a kindly curate from outside superintended
> the order of the service. When all was over, the Bishop was invited by the
> aged incumbent, to 'come and take a glass of port', but was met, somewhat
> curtly, by the answer, 'Thankyou; I do not drink wine.' To the suggestion that it
> might be better for him to resign after so many years of service, he brought
> answer in person, when some time had been taken for consideration, that he
> was 'going to marry again', and that, 'the new wife would be as good as a
> curate'.[11]

The overall impression is that the diocese was not in bad heart
and that the clergy, on the whole, were diligent and conscientious:
Phillpotts had not permitted many really bad clergymen to survive.
Temple seems to have treated the clergy much as he would have
treated boys at Rugby, firmly and without much *politesse*; brusque and
abrupt with the lazy and the pushful; energetically encouraging with
the hesitant; pulling the legs of the pompous; making very great demands on the able. It was all rather boisterous and full of humour at its
best: somewhat rough at its worst.[12] After all, the only pastoral experience he had had was with the students of Kneller Hall and the boys
at Rugby. He seems to have been understanding with those clergymen
who were genuinely in need of care just as he had been with the
more fragile young men at Kneller Hall,[13] but he could be very impatient with those who were not prepared to put their backs into
things, shaming them by his industry just as he had shamed the
students by taking off his coat and cleaning the pigsty.[14] Even Sandford

[10] Ibid.
[11] Ibid.
[12] Ibid. i. 404 ff. There is a long chapter in two parts dealing with the bishop and his
clergy.
[13] See above, 33.
[14] See above, 31.

describes him as having a 'hard crust' and a 'rude exterior'.[15] And by the time he was translated to London he had earned a reputation of possessing 'very uncourtly manners'.[16]

Anyone who had supposed that his connection with *Essays and Reviews* meant that he would be a rather worldly bishop soon discovered their mistake. The standards which he set for the clergy were not chiefly about efficiency or the conscientious performance of duties. He was far more concerned that they should say their prayers; should have a genuine sense of vocation; should be rightly motivated; should preach well and read the scriptures intelligently. He hated the system of private patronage because it seemed to him to be a 'traffic' in what was not a commodity. He instituted a system of ruridecanal conferences in which he could discuss with the clergy the practicalities of their work. More importantly he also initiated a series of quiet days in which he could talk to them about spiritual values. He played an important part in the examining of candidates before ordination and would set out such impossibly high ideals for the clerical life that some of the best of the candidates tried to withdraw.[17] He was shocked by clergymen who had not understood that the ministry involved sacrifices. He loved to ask ordination candidates whether they would still wish to be ordained if they had an assured and substantial private income. He seemed to have retained, without its being diluted by cynicism or habit, the idealism he had felt before his own ordination. He had also retained the practical handiness which had been such a mark of his time at Kneller Hall. He was as willing to lecture the clergy about precisely how to stop a chimney smoking as about how to say their prayers.[18]

Temple was anxious to be thought of as a local boy who—in making good—had not ceased to be essentially local in outlook and sympathies. He made it very plain that his first concern was the diocese and its clergy. Apart from his own chaplains, he brought in no team of outsiders to take over the running of things.[19] Most of the preferment in his own gift was bestowed on local clergymen. In this he seems to have been following precedent set by his predecessor: most of the prebendaries at

---

[15] Sandford (ed.), i. 308.
[16] Lambeth Palace Library: Davidson Papers (Official Correspondence), vol. 29, fo. 72, the Revd R. C. Jenkins to Bishop of Rochester (Davidson), 15 Jan. 1892.
[17] Sandford (ed.), i. 418.
[18] Ibid. i. 448.
[19] Ibid. i. 311.

the time of Temple's election were parochial clergymen in the diocese. But Phillpotts had held one of the prebendal stalls himself and also the canonical stalls of the precentor and the treasurer, two of the four great offices within the chapter.[20] He had also conferred upon his eldest son, William John Phillpotts, an archdeaconry and another prebendal stall. Temple took no such offices for himself though he secured the precentorship for Cook and a prebend for his old friend and colleague John Percival, the only other person from outside the diocese to receive preferment. The now vacant treasurership went to the rector of Ideford, John Manley Hawker.

It is possible to detect in these appointments a tendency to promote those who had given him the strongest support at the time of his election and consecration. He also conferred the archdeaconry of Exeter on Sanders when Freeman died a few years later.[21] And Hawker became subdean on the departure of Trower (to become Bishop of Glasgow) and was in turn succeeded by Sandford in 1885 just before Temple himself was translated to London.[22] At the same time Henry Sanders was appointed to the chancellor's stall. These last two moves could be interpreted as a determined last minute attempt to leave the chapter packed with Temple's supporters were it not for the fact that Sackville Bolton Lee, one of those who had voted against his election in 1869, was made treasurer in place of Hawker.[23]

Temple's determination to be a good diocesan bishop is borne out by the fact that he seems to have sought no opportunity to play a part in national affairs or in the slowly developing central administration of the Church of England. He was assiduous in his attendance at the regular meetings of the bishops of both provinces which took place at Lambeth two or three times a year.[24] (He went to London only when there was good reason.) Yet, in spite of the regularity of his attendance, the record shows that he played little part in the proceedings. The first volume of

---

[20] Devon County Record Office, 37.14 N S Register of Institutions and Collations, 60, 64, and 71 showing the appointments of persons to hold offices vacated by Phillpotts's death.
[21] Devon County Record Office, 37.14 N S Register of Institutions and Collations, 104.
[22] Ibid. 209.
[23] Ibid.
[24] Lambeth Palace Library: Bishops' Meetings, vol. i. The minutes show that Temple was present at all except two or three meetings in the eight years covered by the volume. Vol. ii contains a table (fo. 121) showing attendance of bishops from May 1883 to June 1895, i.e. covering Temple's last two years at Exeter. It shows the same degree of assiduity in attendance and also suggests that his successor as Exeter attended only 22 times out of a possible 41 meetings.

the minutes of the bishops' meetings consists of very informal notes
kept by Tait and scrawled in his almost illegible handwriting. They were
informal only in the sense that they were kept by the archbishop himself
and not by a chaplain or secretary, as the later volumes were. In other
ways they are rather formal in style, for Tait was a formal person. His
notes always describe the members as 'Bishop of Winchester' or 'Bp of
Winchester', never simply as 'Winchester'. (There is a single exception to
this rule and it may be significant for he must have known Temple far
more intimately than he knew most of the bishops. In the record of a
meeting held on 19 January 1875 Tait noted '*Temple* withdrew his
amendment'.[25]) Tait's record also set the pattern for future volumes of
the minutes in recording who was present, who moved resolutions or
amendments, who was appointed to committees and who took part in
debates, but giving no indication of the content of speeches or who was
on which side of a debate.

During the fifteen years in which Temple was at Exeter his name was
only mentioned on eight or nine occasions in the minutes (apart from
the record of his presence). On 19 January 1875 he proposed, with the
Bishop of Winchester (Harold Browne), a resolution to the effect that
'the position of the celebrant at the Holy Communion' was not doctrinally significant. This anticipated the judgments in the ecclesiastical
courts that the rubrics in the Book of Common Prayer could not be so
clearly interpreted in favour of one position as to exclude the other, a
position later (1890) made official in the church by the pronouncement
of archbishop Benson.[26] This proposal they later withdrew. On 14
March 1876 he brought to the bishops' attention a draft bill 'for the
Union of Contiguous Benefices within certain Cities and Boroughs'.[27]
This was part of a plan for reorganization in the diocese of Exeter but
some bishops wished to have it extended to cover other parts of the
country. On 4 June 1878 he spoke in favour of a proposal to repeal the
laws which prohibited deacons, like other clergymen, from taking
secular employment for he was anxious that deacons should be allowed
to work as teachers. Temple, of course, thought of himself as the expert
on anything to do with education but, ironically, on this occasion the

---

[25] Lambeth Palace Library, vol. i. fo. 46—the emphasis is not in the original.
[26] There is some evidence that Temple himself was willing to approve the adoption of
the eastward position from the prayer for the Church onwards. See Sandford (ed.),
ii. 663 f.
[27] Lambeth Palace Library, vol. i. fo. 81.

matter was not pressed to a vote because Browne was not present 'who had paid great attention to the subject'.[28]

On 14 February 1879 Temple was appointed to a committee 'to consider what functions should be assigned to the office of lay reader' and what changes in the law would be necessary to permit them to exercise them. It seems likely that this matter was closely linked with the question of allowing a person in deacon's orders to be employed as a teacher in a 'secular' school. And the two together were of considerable importance for Temple's plans for the diocese. On the next occasion on which his intervention was noted, he spoke on the difficulties encountered in parishes where there were large areas but small congregations.[29] To license lay readers would, he thought, be tantamount to recognizing the ministry of Nonconformists and it seems that he may have thought it would be better to use deacons to take services. It is even possible that he was thinking of ordaining local schoolmasters for the purpose.[30]

(It is, perhaps, worth noting that in all the discussions of matters relating to the preparations for the Lambeth Conference of 1878 and the allocation of various responsibilities to individual bishops, Temple is not mentioned at all.)

On 4 February 1880, in a discussion of the reform of membership of Convocation, he pressed for the presence of more parochial clergy. Here again he may have had his reorganization of his own diocese in mind as on 6 February he intervened again on matters to do with cathedral chapters and prebendaries.

After ten years as a bishop, Temple seems to have begun to intervene on a wider range of issues, unimportant as well as important. In the same group of meetings he had something to say on the subject of girls' societies and central funding and he asked a question about a collection for the Irish famine. On 7 December 1880 he intervened in a discussion of a bill about burials and consecrated ground, which was a matter of particular significance in his own diocese, and took part in a debate about the 'Incarceration' of ritualist clergymen, a matter which was

[28] Ibid. fo. 124.
[29] The date of this is difficult to establish. It is recorded on the back of an agenda paper and is now early in vol. ii of the minutes of the bishops' meetings. Some of the papers in this volume do not have a folio number. The agenda paper appears to relate to the meeting of February 1878 but the assumption must be that anything in vol. ii relates to events later than those recorded in vol. i.
[30] This and subsequent items from the minutes are from Bishops Meetings, vol. ii. The binding of the volume obscures the precise point Temple was making about deacons.

convulsing the church as a whole. He spoke twice at the meetings in May 1881 but the record is written in a hand which is so cramped and small that it is impossible to tell what the subject was.[31] At the meetings in February 1882 he raised the question of the reordination of ministers of the Reformed Episcopal Church, which was also something that was particularly relevant to the diocese of Exeter. Temple had been having problems with clergymen of the Church of England who regarded their own ministry and that of the 'Free Church of England' as interchangeable.[32] He also spoke about the desirability of the bishops holding meetings with members of parliament when ecclesiastical legislation was pending and also on the subject of the imprisonment of clergy held to be in contempt of court in cases of 'ritualism'.

Fewer than ten recorded interventions in over thirty meetings spread across fifteen years is not a large number. (He may, of course, have said things that were not regarded as worth noting.) Moreover, almost everything he said concerned matters which particularly affected his own diocese. He seems to have been deliberately keeping a low profile in his first few years as a bishop and it is possible that he felt that the other bishops distrusted him and that he had to earn their respect. Some of those who were in office at his first meeting in 1870 would have been at the meeting which had condemned *Essays and Reviews* in 1861: others had formally protested against his consecration. But there may have been other reasons for his reticence. The distance between Exeter and London would not have made him an obvious person to be included in committees; and he was anxious to demonstrate that the diocese was his principal concern. When he became Bishop of London everything changed. He was appointed to a great many committees and was inclined to intervene on a very wide range of subjects. But by that time he had been a bishop for fifteen years, had served his apprenticeship, and was in any case more readily available. And the Bishop of London took precedence over all the others in the southern province.

The bishops' meetings were private. (They were also much more structured than the proceedings of Convocation. Temple himself complained bitterly that even the upper house of Convocation wasted a

---

[31] Tait's health was obviously failing at this time and there are some occasions when the notes taken are not in his hand. The illegible hand is probably that of Jackson, the Bishop of London.

[32] See e.g. *Free Church of England Magazine*, Oct. 1875, 189 f. I am indebted to the Revd Dr Grayson Carter for drawing my attention to this aspect of Temple's Exeter episcopate.

great deal of time because there was, for instance, no agenda paper and, therefore, no advance notice of what might be discussed.[33]) For that reason the minutes of the bishops' meetings, laconic though they are, may be a better guide to Temple's actual priorities and constraints than the record of his more public involvement in the national affairs of the Church of England. But something of the same pattern appears in his participation in the work of Convocation. He seems at first, like Tait, to have been somewhat indifferent or even hostile to Convocation and to have thought parliament a better and more effective forum for the settling of ecclesiastical affairs.[34] And Convocation seems equally to have treated his early intervention in debates with coolness and suspicion. A certain obstinacy was, however, always a feature of Temple's character. If he believed himself to be right—and that meant morally right—then he would make no concession to tact or diplomacy. Even if his judgement on the morality of an action turned out to be entirely idiosyncratic and no one else was able to understand why he had arrived at such a position, he remained absolutely unbending. He did what *he* thought to be right.

If in the diocese Temple's early actions seem to mark a shift towards authority and away from liberalism, his earliest speeches in Convocation tended in the opposite direction. Freeman's premature remark had virtually compelled him to try and explain both his initial contribution to *Essays and Reviews* and his subsequent withdrawal from it. But his attempt to convince Convocation that he had acted intelligibly, let alone properly, seems to have failed. The Bishop of Gloucester and Bristol (C. J. Ellicott who, though politically radical, had been one of the bishops who had raised objections at Temple's consecration) sent Tait a description of the debate which indicates that Temple, having done fairly well on the first day, somehow managed to alienate everybody on the second. He made, said Ellicott, 'a sad mess of it and delivered a hard oration which displeased everyone (even supporters like Dr Mackarness.')

The melancholy speech was received with profound silence. Our belief is that the unfortunate Bishop has been in the hands of very bad advisers, who have no heads or lose them in these public crises... Had he asked one of us he would have received... brotherly and politic counsel. As it is he withdraws his Essay, snubs his former friends, tries to explain away, fails,—and leaves the protesting

---

[33] Sandford (ed.), i. 572.   [34] Ibid. i. 556 f.

party (who managed the sequel very prudently and concessively) the moral victors.[35]

Even sympathetic hearers seem to have thought that he was simply arguing for total ('wanton' said someone who claimed to have 'stood by him in the fray') freedom of speech if not for 'free thinking' itself.[36]

The *Essays and Reviews* issue he could hardly have avoided. There was not the same necessity for him to become embroiled in the next controversy in Convocation. This concerned the Athanasian creed (or *Quicumque Vult* as it is more properly called), which the Book of Common Prayer prescribed for use at morning prayer in place of the apostles' creed on certain days of the year. Technically the Athanasian creed is not a creed; nor had Athanasius any hand in its composition.[37] It was composed perhaps in the fifth or perhaps in the eighth century, and is a rather tedious, repetitive, and over-anxious attempt to state the doctrine of the Trinity in a form which no Arian could accept. By the second half of the nineteenth century theological liberals were determined that its use should cease to be obligatory or, at the very least, that the so-called damnatory clauses should be removed from it, clauses which seem to state that salvation depends upon believing its precise verbal formulations. The problem was that to conservative Churchmen, and particularly to the followers of the Oxford Movement, any such proposal appeared to be a gratuitous abandonment of the 'catholic' faith. Athanasius's fourth-century struggle against Arianism was such an heroic and venerated episode in Church history that so long as the 'creed' was associated with his name its abandonment must seem like a tacit acceptance of heresy.

The *Quicumque Vult* was to be the subject of recurring controversy over many years and was a matter of acute, current debate when Temple first became a bishop. A royal commission to enquire into the rubrics and ritual of the Church of England had been appointed in 1867 and reported in 1870. The commission proposed that the use of the 'creed' be retained but that an explanation be made public to the effect that the damnatory clauses were to be understood as 'a solemn warning of the peril of those who wilfully reject the Catholic Faith'.[38] Tait, who always wished for a restored clerical discipline based upon a law whose observance could reasonably be expected to be obeyed, had reservations

---

[35] Lambeth Palace Library: Tait Papers, vol. 88, fos. 43 ff. letter dated 11 Feb. 1870.
[36] Sandford (ed.), i. 558.
[37] See J. N. D. Kelly, *The Athanasian Creed* (London, 1964), 7 ff.
[38] Davidson and Benham, ii. 128.

about this proposal. He thought that the doctrinal statements of the creed were valuable and important but believed that the creed 'should not retain its place in the Public Service of the Church'.[39] He was, nevertheless, irritated when Temple, together with the Bishop of Norwich (John Pelham), argued in the house of bishops that the explanation was not a satisfactory solution to the difficulty since it was not, and could not be, recited aloud together with the creed. Therefore those who found it difficult to assert the eternal damnation of anyone unable to *believe* the complex theological formulations of the creed, would find it no help to their consciences. Temple and Pelham forced the matter to the vote in spite of Tait's tetchiness and in spite of the fact that none of the other bishops supported them.[40] It seemed to be a gratuitous display of moral indignation and created the impression in Convocation (where the members were all clergymen and mostly senior clergymen) that the Bishop of Exeter remained distressingly liberal in theology. It was a long time before they ceased to regard him with suspicion.

Indeed, the freedom to think for oneself remained important to Temple. Ten years after becoming a bishop he was willing to ordain J. M. Wilson,[41] who had been an assistant master at Rugby during his headmastership, in spite of the fact that Wilson was agnostic about the miracles of the New Testament and even the physical resurrection of Christ himself. Wilson needed to be ordained in order to become headmaster of Clifton College and had already been refused ordination by the Bishop of Worcester. It seems that Temple was willing to accept him because he was assured that Wilson would not make a public parade of his doubts.[42] This distinction between what was held privately and what was publicly proclaimed accords with his assertion that what might be perfectly proper for Dr Temple might not be appropriate for the Bishop of Exeter.[43] Surprising and even hypocritical though it seemed to some of his former friends, such an assertion was wholly consistent with a constitutionalist position. If a part of a bishop's function was to maintain the balance between freedom and loyalty, that implied a need for public impartiality.

In his last five years in Exeter Temple began to play a significant part in the proceedings of Convocation, in connection with the reform of

---

[39] Ibid.
[40] Sandford (ed.), i. 558.
[41] See above, 111–12.
[42] Owen Chadwick, *The Victorian Church*, 2 vols., London 1968/70, ii. 144 f.
[43] See above, 131.

clergy discipline and the ecclesiastical courts.[44] Here, too, it seemed to him a matter of balancing conflicting religious liberties. 'Ritualist' clergy were being prosecuted for ceremonial practices.[45] Temple believed that a bishop's right to veto frivolous prosecutions in his diocesan court preserved a legitimate liberty to the clergy. But the laity should be free to *make* complaints even if they were subsequently disallowed. To most laymen his attitude would seem like a sensible compromise and to High Church clergymen it would seem to give them the much more important liberty. It did not, however, entirely overcome the suspicion with which he was regarded in Convocation.

Temple appears to have been even less successful in the House of Lords. His harsh voice, forceful manner, and awkward conscience would not have fitted very easily with the small-scale, intimate, and gentlemanly style of the upper chamber. The matters on which he spoke were of much the same kind as those on which he addressed the bishops' meetings: matters affecting Devon and Cornwall; the division of the diocese; private patronage (which the peers, as owners of extensive patronage, cannot have enjoyed); the amalgamation of small country parishes. In 1870 he spoke in favour of the relaxation of religious tests in the universities and, six years later, in favour of opening churchyards for the burial of Nonconformists.

Perhaps his most effective intervention in the Lords was a speech made, towards the very end of his time as Bishop of Exeter, on the merits and demerits of 'payment by results' in education. Since 1833 educational grants from public money had been made to the National Society for the Education of the Poor in the Principles of the Established Church (led by High Churchmen involved with the SPCK) and to the British and Foreign School Society (drawing upon the same interdenominational and evangelical constituency which supported the British and Foreign Bible Society). In both cases the grants were chiefly for the purpose of building new schools and training colleges. In 1846 minutes of the Committee of the Privy Council on Education, drawn up by James Kay-Shuttleworth,[46] made grants available for the training of pupil-teachers, who were in effect apprenticed to a schoolmaster and

---

[44] Sandford (ed.), i. 559 ff.

[45] Strictly speaking 'ritual' refers to the rite or words of a service: ceremonial to the accompanying actions. The offending clergy ought to be called 'ceremonialists'. But the term 'ritualist' was and is so widely used that it is now unavoidable.

[46] The minutes were subsequently reissued as a handbook for school managers and teachers.

learnt how to teach—as well as the content of what they ought to teach—by doing the job under his supervision. The head teacher also received payment for doing the training. In 1862 a so-called 'new code' was introduced in an attempt to raise the standard of education in elementary schools by an annual examination of individual school-children. Prescribed standards in basic subjects (the classic 'three Rs'—reading, writing, and arithmetic) were to be tested and the grants would in future be based largely on the results obtained. The fear, apparently widespread at the time, was that such a policy would impose an intolerable pressure on pupils and teachers alike.

Matthew Arnold, who very much disliked the system, had nevertheless pointed out that the worst pressures developed where pupils were taught in the wrong way. In his general report as an inspector of schools for the year 1882 (not one of his more poetic works) he wrote:

Attention has lately been called to the break down in India of a number of young men who had won their appointments after severe study and severe examination. No doubt the *quantity* of the mental exertion required for examinations is often excessive, but the strain is much the more severe, because the *quality* and character of mental exertion required are so often injudicious. The mind is less strained the more it reacts on what it deals with, and has a native play of its own, and is creative. It is more strained the more it has to receive a number of 'knowledges' passively, and to store them up to be reproduced in an examination. But to acquire a number of 'knowledges', store them, and reproduce them, was what in general those candidates for Indian employment had to do. By their success in doing this they were tested, and the examination turned upon it.[47]

The real pressures were being created by the continual demand for new subjects to be taught while the child 'remains as to age, capacity, and school time, what he was before'. The crucial thing, therefore, was that children should be taught by methods which encouraged them to think about and digest the 'knowledges' and not merely to regurgitate them. And that would depend on the judgement of the teacher far more than upon rules laid down by central government. Rules could define quantity: quality was to be obtained by 'More free play for the teacher'.[48]

Temple was bound to be against anything which encouraged the mere imparting of information or 'knowledges', so it is no surprise to

---

[47] Matthew Arnold, *Reports on Elementary Schools, 1852–82*, 2nd edn. with additional matter and appendices and with an introduction by F. S. Marvin (London, 1910), 227 f. The emphasis is not in the original.
[48] Ibid. p. xviii.

discover that his views, as expressed in the Lords two years after Arnold's report, echoed a good deal of what his friend had had to say. Temple concerned himself with the effect of the 'new code' upon those who had to teach rather than its effect upon those who had to learn. He denounced increasing pressures on masters and pupil-teachers, the rigid rules devised by government about how the teaching was to be done, and the tendency to impose restriction after restriction upon a teacher's own initiative and judgement.[49]

Education was, naturally enough, one of the bishop's chief concerns within the diocese. His arrival there came at a critical moment in the history of British education. On the one hand the recommendations of the Taunton Commission was being applied regionally: an assistant commissioner called Joshua Fitch visited Devon in 1870 to prepare a scheme for the reorganization of endowed schools there. On the other, at a national level W. E. Forster, as Vice-President of the Council in Gladstone's administration from 1868 to 1874, was tackling some of the constant problems implicit in designing a general educational system in the Endowed Schools Bill and the Elementary Education Bill. There was every reason for Temple to sympathize with Forster. It was not just that he was responsible for legislation to implement some of the recommendations of the Taunton Commission. He was also a personal friend and Matthew Arnold's brother-in-law. Forster may actually have consulted Temple about some of the provisions of the bills while the legislation was being drafted. Jowett, who believed that Temple 'had devised the scheme', commented that 'Forster's Bill is too complicated to pass in the face of a very strong opposition of private interests'.[50] These 'interests' included those who were threatened by the plan to divert endowments and those who wished to maintain denominational schools. Moreover, Forster's legislation would have important effects for Nonconformists as well as for the Church of England. It would not only affect religious instruction in day-schools funded by parliamentary grants, which was a matter of great concern to the Established Church, it would also have a far-reaching consequence for Sunday schools.

Sunday schools had originally been almost as much concerned with secular as with religious education. They were held on Sundays because so many young children worked in factories. In the eighteenth century

[49] Sandford (ed.), i. 576 f.
[50] E. V. Quinn and J. M. Prest (eds.), *Dear Miss Nightingale: A Selection of Benjamin Jowett's Letters, 1860–1893* (Oxford, 1987), 165.

Robert Raikes had faced down opposition from strict Sabbatarians and from conservative Churchmen to found a school in Gloucester where young employees could be got off the streets and taught to read and write. Subsequently he founded a school that was open every day of the week and the favourable publicity which it attracted meant that his approach to education was widely imitated. In Nonconformist circles it was common for churches to provide two sessions of school on Sundays: a morning session which concentrated on secular education and an afternoon session for religious instruction. Sunday schools amounted to free but very elementary teaching in letters and numbers which were, often enough, a sugar coating for the pill of religious instruction. Forster's act, providing free, secular, elementary education, meant that Sunday schools lost much of their appeal and a fair proportion of their clientele. Because the morning sessions were no longer so necessary as a means to basic education, children need no longer attend in the afternoons either.[51]

The perennial problem associated with every scheme for a national educational system also remained. If schools were to teach Christianity, then the Church of England claimed the right to determine the kind of Christian teaching to be given. Temple's predecessor, speaking in the House of Lords in July 1839 (when Temple himself was hardly more than a schoolboy), had taken this line. The Church of England, he said, would claim no right to *enforce* any system of education upon any part of the population:

But we have a right, my Lords, to demand that the State, acknowledging the Church to be the true Church, acknowledging it to profess and to teach the true Religion, and thereby implying the duty of the Church to inculcate—aye, and not only to inculcate but to spread, that blessed truth which it professes; we have a right to demand that the State shall supply the necessary means to enable the Church to discharge its high functions.... to educate all within its pale, who need public aid, and to offer to educate all without its pale, who will accept the offer, in that holy religion...which the State itself, acknowledge[s] to be true; and if true, of course, to be alone true.[52]

Naturally enough Nonconformists feared that a national system which permitted religious instruction would become an instrument of Anglican propaganda. On the other hand, if schools were forbidden to

[51] David Bebbington, *Victorian Nonconformity* (Bangor, 1992), 37.
[52] *Recent Measures for the Promotion of Education in England*, 10th edn., repr. in *Nineteenth Century Pamphlets Series* (no. 3) (Manchester, 1972), p. ix.

teach religion then there was an equally powerful fear that the nation would become irreligious. Moreover, because the act had the effect of enormously expanding the number of elementary schools, Nonconformist denominations would be unable to maintain the *proportion* of schools they had hitherto provided. In fact after 1870 the schools run by the British and Foreign Schools Society and most Nonconformist schools (except those of the Wesleyans) were handed over to the new school boards and became part of the system maintained by the State.

The new legislation was not, therefore, without its critics on all sides. It became law but not without amendment. Religious instruction in board schools was not to be given by clergymen or to consist of anything other than teaching the scriptures.

Temple was determined to encourage his diocese, and the city and county generally, to accept the new legislation and devise a local system for implementing it. But there were many in the diocese who preferred Phillpotts's high doctrine of the Church's responsibilities. Dean Boyd, though far from belonging to that school of thought, was also highly critical of the whole Liberal approach. At Cheltenham he had worked with Francis Close, a very prominent Evangelical, to provide free and religious schooling to the *deserving* poor children of the town. He believed that such resources as endowments or charity could provide should be used for the benefit of boys and girls chosen by right-minded clergymen and other suitable persons. He expressed these views, publicly and vigorously, maintaining that piously motivated patronage of this kind was still the way in which England should be educated. This, of course, flatly contradicted Temple's own views about endowments and scholarships and the views adopted by the Taunton Commission, which underlay Forster's legislation. Publicly, and in his usual gruff manner, Temple corrected his dean.[53] Much of his public speaking at that time, including many of his sermons, was devoted to the subject of national education. What he had to say received wide publicity even in the strongholds of early opposition to his episcopate.[54]

A year or two later he was lobbying the mayor, writing him a long letter to persuade him that the act, in spite of being a Liberal measure, was nevertheless educationally sound and likely to be beneficial to the

---

[53] Sandford (ed.), i. 331.
[54] e.g. F. Temple, *National Schools*, two sermons repr. from the *Western Daily Mercury* (Plymouth, 1870).

city.[55] Because Exeter (and indeed Devonshire as a whole) was relatively well provided with endowed schools it was possible, in fact, to devise a very good educational structure for it. The Forster Act provided elementary schools for the whole city; endowments were freed to provide exhibitions for clever children to proceed to secondary schools; existing foundations were reorganized so as to provide for the education of girls as well as boys; some elementary schools were upgraded so that they provided a better foundation for further education than most; the local grammar school was resited away from the centre of the city, where it could be given 'increasingly the character of an English Public School'.[56]

The act, as finally amended, had directed that religious education should be provided by the schoolteacher and should consist simply of teaching the Bible. It had not originally been part of the bill and was designed as a safeguard against denominational bias. Temple tended to interpret this provision very flexibly. His conviction that it was the State's duty to provide elementary schools where there were none, did not imply that the Church should withdraw in order to make way for board schools. During his episcopate education in the diocese was developed with enthusiasm. The standard of teaching in Church schools was raised and a team of inspectors, including his old friend Thomas Dyke Acland, saw that it was maintained. Even when circumstances made it essential for the Church to surrender control of a school the bishop did not think this need result in its complete secularization. 'It may be', he said, 'that in many cases the holders of school buildings will find it necessary to transfer them to School Boards to be supported but in all such cases the Act allows bargains to be made with the School Boards.' And he advised clergymen to offer their buildings on condition that they were allowed to continue to use them for Sunday school.[57] By the time he left Exeter there were more Church schools than when he had arrived and he encouraged schoolteachers in the State system to teach the Bible not simply by reading it aloud or recounting its contents as if the stories were true only at a literal level but by expounding its meaning out of their own understanding of the faith. Education in the diocese by 1895 was vigorous and far from secular.

Temple's experience as a bishop seems to have made him less radical, not least in matters of education. He went to Exeter, immediately after his work on the Taunton Commission, committed to Liberal policies. In

---

[55] Sandford (ed.), i. 333 ff.   [56] Ibid. i. 340.   [57] Ibid. i. 345.

his first few years as a diocesan bishop he began the long slow process by which he became, as archbishop, an apologist for the educational privileges of the Established Church.[58]

Temple's public disagreements with Dean Boyd about the Education Act had revealed his unwillingness to compromise, even when this alienated those whose support would have been invaluable. Nor was this the only matter in his early years at Exeter in which bishop and dean found themselves on different sides. In 1872 the dean and chapter commissioned George Gilbert Scott to design a reredos for the cathedral. It consisted of three panels sculpted in bas-relief. The left-hand panel, as one faced the altar, showed the transfiguration with Jesus raised above the disciples; the central panel was of the Ascension, depicting Jesus in an ogival frame, with the disciples gathered in a wider picture below; the right-hand panel showed the descent of the Spirit at Pentecost with, again, disciples gathered in the lower half. It is difficult to believe that the reredos can ever have fitted very happily into the existing double archway behind the altar. Above the pictorial panels there rose a towering canopy in Gothic style with a cross on the topmost pinnacle. It rose in line with the central pillar between the two arches, changing the whole appearance and perspective of the east end of the cathedral. William John Phillpotts, the chancellor of the cathedral[59] and the son of the former bishop, objected to the reredos and presented a petition against it. Temple chose to hear the case himself and on 2 January 1874 found the erection of the reredos illegal and ordered its removal. But the Judicial Committee of the Privy Council reversed his judgement and on 25 February 1875 declared the reredos to be permitted by law.[60]

Temple also began to exhibit, in the years at Exeter, an attitude towards sexual morality which was both stern and, in an odd way, legalistic. It may be that his experience as a schoolmaster had not really prepared him for the realities of the adult world. Unlike most later public-school headmasters he does not seem to have been obsessed by fears about masturbation and homosexuality.[61] Or it may be that his

---

[58] See below, 242.

[59] The entry for W. J. Phillpotts in the *Dictionary of National Biography* incorrectly describes him as the chancellor of the diocese.

[60] The case is reported in Cowell's Privy Council Appeals, vi (1875), 435–667. The reredos itself was nevertheless subsequently removed from the cathedral and is now in Heavitree parish church.

[61] J. R. de S. Honey, *Tom Brown's Universe: The Development of the Victorian Public School* (London, 1977), 167 f.

views were coloured by the naïve innocence he so often exhibited. Or it may simply be that here, too, he was a constitutionalist, believing that the Church of England had set clear limits which no one ought to transgress. He discouraged but would not prevent divorce and remarriage: the law, as it applied to the Church, permitted it. But requests for the least modification of traditional moral standards received very brusque replies.[62] And he delivered a speech to his diocesan conference in 1882 on the subject of marriage to a deceased wife's sister, which revealed both his innocence and the fierce sense of purity which governed everything he said on the subject. There was a proposal that the law should be changed to permit such a marriage. Temple maintained that it would destroy the ease of family life, encouraging a man to think of his wife's siblings as potential sexual partners. It would be impossible for him, then, to be on the same relaxed terms with them as he might be with his own sisters.[63]

He was also a vigorous advocate of total abstinence. He had first given up wine out of sheer poverty in his undergraduate days at Balliol but it had become a matter of principle. Like other Victorian Churchmen of modestly left-of-centre opinions (Manning, for instance, and Westcott) Temple had come to believe that giving up alcohol was a way of sharing the problems and temptations which confronted working-class men. Some of the younger clergymen who admired their bishop, like Ernest Sandford, also took up the cause so that it became almost a hallmark of Temple's episcopate. Unscrupulous clergymen were inclined to use their own teetotalism as a lever for obtaining favours from him.[64] And the local temperance association invited Temple's successor, E. H. Bickersteth, to address their annual meeting, assuming (wrongly) that he also would be a teetotaller.[65]

It seems that Temple enjoyed running the diocese. All the formidable energy which had been devoted to enlarging the syllabus at Rugby and getting its finances into order, were now employed in reforming

---

[62] e.g. Lambeth Palace Library: Davidson Papers, vol. 522, fos. 16 f., Temple to Bishop of Truro (Benson), letter dated 13 Sep. 1882, and cf. ibid., F. Temple Fulham Papers, vol. 55, fos. 89 f.

[63] F. Temple, *Marriage with Deceased Wife's Sister* (Exeter, 1882).

[64] e.g. the case of Archdeacon Colley's attempt to obtain a Lambeth doctorate from Temple after the latter had become archbishop. See Peter Hinchliff, 'Colonial Church Establishment in the Aftermath of the Colenso Controversy', in N. Aston (ed.) (forthcoming).

[65] See the report of Bickersteth's speech at the meeting of the Exeter Temperance Association in *Exeter Flying Post* for 12 Aug. 1885.

diocesan administration. Though he is not remembered in the standard textbooks as one of the great diocesan bishops of the nineteenth century, some of the things which he introduced at Exeter have become normal in the modern Church of England. He developed a system of consultation within the diocese by which every clergyman had an opportunity to make his views known to the bishop. In addition to his regular meetings in the rural deaneries, he further developed what Phillpotts had already done with diocesan conferences and issued pastoral letters which surveyed a whole range of current issues and urged the clergy to participate in discussing them.[66] The clergy were also given the responsibility of electing their own rural deans. In all these matters, it has to be said, he followed the pattern he had established with his masters at Rugby. Everyone was consulted but Temple took the final decision. He proposed to reorganize the cathedral chapter so that it became more directly related to the diocese and canons were given diocesan work to do. The cathedral itself was refurbished while, at the same time, the bishop held ordinations as well as confirmations elsewhere in the diocese so that every part of it might feel involved in what he was doing.[67]

In terms of organization, however, the division of the diocese was his greatest achievement. When he was first appointed there had already existed a strong movement for the creation of a new diocese for Cornwall. The western end of the diocese had been such a centre of opposition in his early years partly because it was feared that he would resist any move towards an independent Cornish see. 'We hoped', they said, 'for independence and were given Temple!' But, in fact, the new bishop was not against division. He bided his time; but once he had satisfied himself that the diocese was too unwieldy, he brought formidable drive and energy to the business of dividing it. Having perceived that previous attempts to create new dioceses had foundered on the problems of finance, he launched a fund-raising campaign. He also agreed to surrender part of the endowment of the undivided diocese so that an annual income of £800 would be available to a Cornish bishop. He enlisted support and benefactions from the local grandees like the Earl of Devon (who had asked so many questions about the boys' private prayers when he had been a member of the Clarendon Commission)

[66] e.g. F. Temple, *Pastoral Letter to the Clergy and Laity of the Diocese of Exeter* (Exeter 1879).
[67] Sandford (ed.), i. 350 ff.

and Lady Rolle, who was particularly generous. Very large sums of
money were given; initially from one or two very wealthy donors but
subsequently from considerable numbers of smaller ones too. He created committees to oversee the practical aspects of division. He spoke in
the House of Lords in the debates on the necessary legislation. And in
what was then regarded as a remarkably short time the whole process
was completed by 1876.[68] When E. W. Benson, his former assistant
master, was appointed as the first Bishop of the new diocese of Truro,
he was particularly pleased. He had helped Benson to set up the new
school at Wellington, he was now to help him set up the new diocese at
Truro. The unexpected friendship between the two men continued to
deepen and develop in their management of neighbouring dioceses.

Archbishop Tait died in 1883, having been far from well for some
time. To the general surprise, he was to be succeeded by Benson, who
had been a bishop for only half-a-dozen years. The account of these
events as given in the Sandford *Memoir* contains muffled hints about
two related matters—that relations between Tait and Temple had never
entirely recovered from the agonizing events following the bishops'
condemnation of *Essays and Reviews* and that there was some feeling
that Temple and not Benson ought to have been the next archbishop.[69]
There are no surviving letters of Temple's which suggest either that he
felt great sorrow at Tait's death (though his former tutor had, after all,
done a very great deal for him) or that he resented Benson's preferment.
His sole recorded comment was, 'Benson suits the clergy better than I
should have done.'[70] It may be the case, in fact, that one of the reasons
why Temple came to play a more prominent part in the life of the
Church of England in the 1880s was that Benson, accustomed to rely
upon his help and his gruff laconic advice, paid him more attention
than Tait had done.

Temple had begun his episcopate in Exeter knowing that his chief
task was to win over the clergy of the diocese. To achieve this he made
no concessions, used no tricks of tactful diplomacy, made no effort to
charm or beguile, but there seems little doubt that in the end he
succeeded. The Sandford *Memoir* is itself a somewhat biased work. Its
editor and contributors have no doubt that Temple was a great success.
They have countless anecdotes showing how one after another of the

[68] Ibid. i. 381 ff.
[69] Ibid. i. 592 ff.
[70] Ibid. i. 593.

bishop's former critics became his friends and supporters. Of these, perhaps, the most telling is the testimony of the man who had been a boy under Temple at Rugby, and had followed him to Exeter in order to be ordained.

How loyal to him and how proud of him we youngsters felt, as week by week the Bishop won his way and turned opponents into disciples, and hostile critics into admirers.[71]

More objective, perhaps, is the account of the farewell to Temple, reported in the *Exeter Flying Post* on 12 August 1885. The bishop had come back specially from London for a luncheon in the Rougemont Hotel at which the clergy of the diocese presented him with a silver service—' a large *jardinière*, two large candelabra, four small fruit bowls, in the style of George III and with arms of diocese worked on them'. The service cost £600, a very considerable sum for those days.

Temple had preached his final sermon in the cathedral on Easter Day at evensong, taking his text from Chapter 8 of the Epistle to the Romans: 'For I am persuaded that neither death, nor life, nor angels, nor principalities, nor powers, nor things present, nor things to come, nor height, nor depth, nor any other creature, shall be able to separate us from the love of God, which is in Christ Jesus our Lord.' In the context of a farewell its implication was clear—since Christians could not be separated from Christ, nor could they be separated from each other so long as each was united to Christ. It was a sermon on love and friendship and the life God gives in Christ; a life—Temple said—which he longed, but for his human weakness, to be able to live.[72]

In the midst of this busy and demanding episcopate Temple had, at the age of fifty-five and quite unexpectedly, fallen head over heels in love with a young woman half his age. There is nothing about his life up to this point to prepare one for this happening. He had lived at Rugby with his mother and his sister Netta: there is no record of his having been interested in any young woman during those years. His mother had died while he was still at the school. Netta continued to look after him when he moved to Exeter, even playing some part in diocesan education. Benjamin Jowett, who always rather liked intelligent, strong-minded women like Florence Nightingale and Lady Stanley of Alderley, wrote to Temple after her death:

---

[71] Sandford (ed.), i. 422.
[72] *Exeter Flying Post*, 5 Aug. 1885.

I think she was one of the best women whom I ever knew. She never thought of herself, and was so capable and self-sacrificing and did so much good in such a sensible manner. Your life was her joy and pride; and to a nature like this it was a real happiness to know that she had left you with one who could do more for you than she could in the late years of life. . . . Many things which she said to me have become impressed on my mind—one in particular that occurs to me while writing, 'That persons who wanted to do good must efface themselves.' I was very glad to have renewed acquaintance and friendship with her last summer. I was greatly struck by her clearness of mind and resignation to her great trial.[73]

It was often the case that strong-minded Victorian women did not enjoy good health. Netta Temple remained with her brother for the first three years of his Exeter episcopate and then found her health unable to cope. She went off in search of a kinder climate, lived in Clifton, then in France for a while and, finally, in Tunbridge Wells where she died in 1890 after seventeen years of poor health. It may have been the loneliness of his episcopal palace after Netta's departure which led Temple to consider the possibility of marriage but there can be no doubt that he was in love with Beatrice Blanche Lascelles.

She was the daughter of William Sebright Saunders Lascelles, brother of the third Earl of Harewood, and himself a Member of Parliament and a Privy Councillor. He had died in 1851 leaving his widow, Lady Caroline Lascelles, to bring up those of her nine children who were still at home. Beatrice was the fifth daughter and youngest child. Lady Caroline's youngest sister had become the second wife of the Earl of Taunton. Beatrice, then probably twenty-two,[74] had been staying with her aunt at Quantock Lodge in Somerset in 1867 when Temple came to visit Lord Taunton, presumably about the business of the Schools Inquiry Commission. After that they had not met again until the Easter of 1874 when Lady Taunton brought Beatrice to stay at the episcopal palace for a few days.[75] Temple seems to have been like an adolescent in love for the first

---

[73] Sandford (ed.), i. 518 f. The letter began 'My Dear Bishop', not yet an entirely relaxed and informal address but indicating a less frosty attitude to Temple than at the time of his consecration. When this letter was written Jowett was within a few years of his own death and Temple officiated at his funeral. The remark which Jowett attributed to Miss Temple became one of his own favourite aphorisms.

[74] There is some doubt about her date of birth; the standard works of reference do not usually provide dates of birth for daughters. F. A. Iremonger, *William Temple, Archbishop of Canterbury, His Life and Letters* (London, 1948), 2, gives the year of Beatrice's birth as 1845. Their marriage certificate simply describes them both as being of 'full age'.

[75] Family papers in the possession of the Right Revd F. S. Temple: letter addressed to 'My dear Robert' and dated 30 July 1876.

time. He was terrified of anticipating the joy of being in her company in case she should reject him. 'My Dear Miss Lascelles,' he wrote to her from Barnstaple on 27 July 1876, on one of his many journeyings round the diocese:

I find that I *can* come up to London on the 3rd whether there is business to be done or not which I do not yet know. And I wish to come very much if you will like to see me. But I cannot help having some fear that possibly when you find what I mean you will not desire it any longer.

I have become very fond of you. And I find that unless I can have you for my own altogether, duty to my own peace of mind and to the work I have to do requires me to keep away from your presence. For the charm of it haunts me day and night.

I know that you like my society. But you may nevertheless not like it enough to wish to be my wife. Possibly you may even resent my asking you, and think it somewhat hard that you cannot enjoy a pleasant friendship with one so much older without bringing on yourself such a solicitation as this.

I acknowledge if this be so I have no right to complain. I am a great [deal] older than you; I have no wealth to offer you for I have nothing but what I am. And what is worse my life and yours are so different that you would be unwise to change from yours to mine unless you could give me your very heart.

I can only plead your own sweetness and frankness and kindness which have made me dream of a happiness such as I never experienced in my life. And you can give me that happiness if you will.

Shall I come and see you on the 3rd? Ah, if you could understand how much depends on your answer.

She must have encouraged him for from that moment things moved very swiftly indeed. Two days later, on 29 July (there had just been time for a reply to reach him), he was writing to her again.

My dear Beatrice

How delightful it is to call you Beatrice. And the name suits you so exactly. For it means 'the blesser'. And you do bless me, my dear, with an exceeding blessing.[76]

And on the following day he wrote to a friend, 'I feel almost wild with happiness and can hardly think of anything else.'[77] Quasi-adolescent his behaviour might be but his acute awareness of the considerable difference in their ages sometimes displayed itself in an almost avuncular

---

[76] Both letters are among family papers in the possession of the Right Revd F. S. Temple.
[77] Ibid., letter to 'My dear Robert', 30 July 1876.

playfulness. He sent her a map of the diocese saying, 'I shall not require you to pass an examination in it, so do not look at it if you do not feel inclined.'[78] But, having been accepted by his beloved, there was no waiting. They were married by the rector of Morpeth in St Michael's, Chester Square, on 24 August 1876.

That blend of the adolescent and the avuncular remained characteristic of his attitude to her after they were married. He wrote to her in the spring of the following year a long letter full of rather solemnly humorous reflections like an improving tale in a child's book.

Never steal what you cannot enjoy. No doubt conscience is impartial and will sting you if you steal at all. But if you can enjoy what you have stolen there is some solace: the stings are a little blunted: or one does not feel them quite so much. But if there is no enjoyment, you are as it were, left alone with your wickedness, and it is dreadful. The woman who stole a brass kettle and was acquitted because the evidence was not quite complete was heard to say in a voice of much self comfort, 'Now it is honestly my own.' But I am sure it must have been a good kettle. There would have been no comfort in the acquittal if the kettle had been a leaky old thing.

... My black bag (Walrond's gift) is fitted with a blotter and when I wanted to write to you at Salisbury I took it out to write on. But it is limp and made a very poor sort of writing table. And I said to myself I ought to have a stiff pad ...

And yesterday while I was writing the carriage was announced. I suddenly remembered that I had no lozenges. I went as you told me, what an obedient husband I am! I deserve a kiss for that! and I got the key and found the lozenges. As I took them my eye fell on a stiff pad. 'The very thing' I cried, while the eighth commandment vanished from my memory. I took it up; I picked up my bag as I went, opening it and taking out the limp blotter. I ran down and got into the carriage, rejoicing, with the bag in one hand and the pad in the other. And there! I found that the pad was too long and would not fit comfortable [*sic.*] into the bag! My conscience suddenly awoke screaming and screaming at me. And the pad does not comfort me. My dearest, never steal what you cannot enjoy: or perhaps you may be made for ever to carry about an unusable pad as a dreadful punishment.

But the same letter broke off suddenly in the midst of his comments on what he has been doing.

My darling I cannot help stopping here apropos of nothing to say, I wish I could kiss you. It often comes across me quite suddenly when you know nothing about it. Oh I do so wish I could kiss you.[79]

---

[78] Ibid., letter dated 29 July 1876.
[79] Letter in Family Papers in the possession of the Right Revd F. S. Temple.

Age difference or no, it was the beginning of a long and happy marriage (Beatrice did not die till 1915) in which he came to rely upon her more and more. When he was made archbishop he was invited by the Queen to stay at Windsor Castle in order to do homage. He wrote to Randall Davidson (always Temple's chief adviser in anything to do with the royal family):

I wish if she invites me to stay the night, she would also ask my wife. It would help me much as my wife does much for me with her typewriter.[80]

It was probably in his relations with his children that his age made the greatest difference for he was fifty-eight when his eldest son (Frederick) was born in 1879 and his only other child (William) was born two years later. It was a difficult age-gap to bridge and it is touching to discover how hard he tried. When he was separated from the boys he wrote them letters in the form of nonsense verse.

To Frederick (aged ten):

Where are the Boys? Where are the Boys
What has become of their mischieday noise?
The mischievous Boys;
My torments, my joys;
My plagues when in sight;
My special delight;
My bother; my treasure;
My sources of pleasure;
Where in the world are the Boys?
The fact is that Fred is a jigmaree, and William is a pigwacket, and they are gone in a new foxiflash to see the other side of the brown bodibango where the fallallies live, and when they come back soap will be very cheap and we shall all dine on rowtowflows.
Where are the Boys? Where are the Boys'?
What has become of them and their toys?
Of what are they talking?
Where are they walking?
What have they to eat?
What is on their feet?
What have they to drink?
And what do they think?
The mischievous, mischievous Boys.

[80] Lambeth Palace Library: Davidson Papers, vol. 522, fo. 25, letter dated 14 Dec. 1896

I wonder what has come over this house. There is no sound in it, not even the sound of a mouse. I shall presently get on the tail end of a fiddle and ride to the middle of nowhere and look down the hole and see whether the Boys are at the bottom.
Silence! Hush! Don't!
It is
    Father[81]

Or this one which he sent to William:

> Once on a time a man came home
>   And growled for want of lunch:
> But his wife came in, and called him a goose,
>   And gave him a crust to crunch.
> What, what? said he, a crust for me;
>   I want a nice little boy.
> Your Boys, said she, are gone to the sea
>   To their own delight and joy.
>
> 'Oh dear! Oh dear! What a dismal cheer
>   To have no boys to eat'
> 'You shall have some toast; you shall have some cream;
>   And that will be a treat.'
> But the grumpy man was not content
>   And he growled like a Porly Jack.
> Till his wife cried out, I will go myself,
>   And bring those two boys back.[82]

No one, of course, could pretend that this is great literature but Temple was not a professional teller of tales to children. He was a very busy bishop of London making time to keep in touch with his sons whom he plainly adored. The verses addressed to Fred are, surprisingly, a little too young for a ten-year-old. Temple, the former schoolmaster, ought to have known better and he once wrote a letter in Latin to the ten-year-old William—not difficult Latin, nor saying anything significant, but Latin none the less.[83] Another indication that he found it difficult to judge what was appropriate to their age is a letter he wrote to William, then fourteen and a boarder at Rugby: 'Do you know a very

---

[81] Family Papers in the possession of the Right Revd F. S. Temple: dated from Fulham Palace, 7 June 1889.

[82] Ibid., letter from Fulham Palace, no date.

[83] Ibid., letter dated 26 Sept. 1891, which reads, 'Caro Gulielmo filio suo Episcopus Londinensis felicitatem vult. Hoc in loco omnia imbribus frequentissimus sunt humida. Me tussis saepissime qualit et vexat. Pueros meos desidero manoperere.'

bad Boy at Rugby who dares to write to me and send me impudent parodies of the Frogs of Aristophanes. They are not even good Greek.'[84] This seems just a little patronizing in style for a fourteen-year-old who had, after all, been *attempting* to parody the Greek of Aristophanes.

As the boys grew older, however, Temple seems to have found it much easier to relate to them. When they asked him serious questions in their letters home, he took them seriously. He wrote to Fred in 1896:

You asked me some little time ago what I thought might be our Lord's reason for teaching us in some of his Parables by the example of bad people. I have been so much overpowered by work ever since that I have not been able to answer you.

It seems to me however that it is a strong spur sometimes to ask good people who ought to be stirred by the best impulses to look to the conduct of those who are moved by mean or selfish impulses. The clearness of insight into means, the persistent unintermittent zeal of worldly men bent on their own comfort, or ambition, or gain puts to shame the languor, the feebleness, the hesitations, the frequent intermissions in our service of God.

We persistently, importunately, press our demands on other men for things that we want. We are cold in our prayers and hardly seem to care whether they are answered or not. The woman who petitioned the judge, the neighbour who wanted the loaves could not be shaken off: we are soon shaken off if our prayers seem to remain disregarded. The unrighteous steward had a keen eye to his worldly interests; where is our keenness for our eternal interests?

It does not seem to me that this mode of teaching presents serious difficulties: nor can I find it hard to understand why our Lord sometimes adopted it.[85]

He was perhaps at his very best in a letter to Fred when he was nearing the end of his time at Rugby and there was a possibility that he might enter for a scholarship to Balliol. The school was inclined to advise against it but Temple must have hoped to see the boy at his own old college for when William was at the same stage a little later, his father told him that a place at Balliol would be better than an exhibition at another college.[86] As archbishop and chairman of the school governors, he might have been expected to have wanted his own way. He might have rested on his reputation as an educationalist and insisted that he knew what was best for Fred. He might even have been jealous of the influence of others on the sons from whom he was separated by

[84] Family Papers in the possession of the Right Revd F. S. Temple: dated from Fulham Palace, 7 June 1889, letter dated 17 Feb. 1895.
[85] Ibid., letter dated Fulham Place, 10 Nov. 1896.
[86] Iremonger, 37.

sixty years. If he felt any of these things, he did not allow the feelings to show. After saying that he would not press Fred to attempt the entrance scholarship at Balliol, he added:

I cannot deny that I think [the masters] undervalue the teaching power of an examination. An examination does not merely test: it teaches. It gets knowledge already possessed into better order. The examined comes out with a clearer notion of what his own knowledge is and how it can be used than he had before he went in.[87]

But he admitted that the masters at the school would know his son's capabilities better than he could himself and that that was what really mattered. And it must have required considerable courage and an unpossessive paternal love to tell the boy that, in effect, it was better to expose himself to the risk of failure than to avoid the challenge.

The greatest tribute to Temple's success as a father is a remark of William's after he had arrived at Balliol. 'Father will never tell me his views because he knows how much I am tempted to accept them without thinking.'[88] Yet any reluctance which Temple may have had about imposing his opinions upon his sons was certainly not indicative of a lack of affection.

[87] Family Papers in the possession of the Right Revd F. S. Temple: letter dated from Lambeth Palace, 5 Nov. 1897.

[88] Iremonger, 3.

7

Religion and Science

At the moment of Benjamin Jowett's greatest bitterness at the sermon Temple had preached at his enthronization, he told Miss Nightingale that he had once hoped that Temple would have become a second Whewell. That hope he had by then abandoned.[1] In moments of disillusionment, of course, one exaggerates one's former hopes as well as one's present disappointment but the comparison was not entirely fanciful. Whewell had died in 1866, not many years before Temple's appointment to Exeter. He had been Master of Trinity College and formerly Vice-Chancellor of Cambridge. He had been a majestic polymath; outstanding mathematician, fellow of the Royal Society, once professor of Mineralogy and President of the Geological Society, a recognized if rather old-fashioned philosopher, author of several articles containing painstaking scientific observations about tides, thoroughly competent in the German language and at home with German contributions to mathematics and the natural sciences.

Jowett's remark about Temple, however, was not intended to indicate that he had once regarded him as a potential polymath: he meant that he had expected Temple to write something theologically significant about the natural sciences. Whewell's chief claim to fame was that he had written one of the treatises on 'the goodness of God as manifested in the Creation' founded by the will of Francis Egerton, Earl of Bridgewater. The Bridgewater treatises could be regarded either as works of natural theology or as attempts to show the essential compatibility of religion and natural science and in both those fields Whewell had been thought of as saying something of importance. His contribution to the Bridgewater series had been entitled *Astronomy and General Physics Considered with Reference to Natural Theology* and belonged to a world where there was no sharp distinction between theological reflection and

---

[1] E. V. Quinn and J. M. Prest (eds.), *Dear Miss Nightingale: A Selection of Benjamin Jowett's Letters, 1860–1893* (Oxford, 1987), 175, letter dated 1 Aug. 1869.

theoretical physics. Immanuel Kant's *Universal Natural History and Theory of the Heavens* was a product of the same world.

All the Bridgewater treatises belong, in fact, to the era of innocence before Darwin, or rather before the publication of Darwin's hypothesis. Darwin's long hesitation before publishing the results of his research may have been because he feared that it would seem destructive of religion (he, too, had been trained in the principles of natural theology) or it may have been because there were other and less serious theories abroad about how species evolved. He had done his work in South America in the 1830s. He had written up his results and begun to frame his theory of evolution by the mid-1840s. But he only published *Origin of Species* in 1859 after receiving a copy of Arthur Wallace's conclusions, independently arrived at, on natural selection. What was distinctive about the theories of Darwin and Wallace was that their concept of evolution was self-explanatory. They had moved into a new era in which each discipline was autonomous. Theology was distinct from theoretical physics. One sought biological (rather than religious) explanations for biological phenomena. Darwin's hypothesis posited an evolutionary process which was self-directing and served no goal or purpose. It needed no external divine mind, planning and shaping its course. New species came into existence by natural selection: changes in the surrounding conditions meant that certain forms of life, being better suited to the new conditions, survived; while others (less well fitted) did not. And the 'fitter' variant would appear to eliminate or supplant the less fit. Darwin's evolutionary process was open-ended, went where it happened to go, and could be entirely explained on its own terms. It needed no other force (no divine mind) to make it work.

There were others, equally convinced that life forms changed and developed, who nevertheless continued to maintain that a divine mind planned how it had all happened. In the interval between Darwin's explorations and his publication of *Origin of Species* there appeared Robert Chambers's (anonymous) *Vestiges of the Natural History of Creation* in 1844. Chambers book, which was bizarre enough to attract considerable attention, presented its readers with a picture of the natural world in which species changed both erratically *and* according to plan. God had created life so exuberantly explosive with possibilities of development and change that variations were continually occurring. A form of life might as easily evolve into a simpler as into a more complex variant. Chambers made no distinction between the sort of change which might occur in an individual life and disappear with it (things which might be called 'freaks', like a calf with two heads) and permanent mutations which resulted in the existence of a new species. So he argued that, if it was possible for a normal mother to give birth to a baby whose heart was defective (or, in Chambers's view, simpler and therefore more appropriate to a lower kind of species), it was equally possible for a normal mother to give birth to a baby whose heart was really appropriate to a higher form of life and thus create a new species.[2] But underlying all this exuberant pluriformity was a blueprint or programme which ensured that life arrived at the goal which the divine mind had intended from the beginning.

Chambers had picked up some notions of popular science but had provided far too many hostages to fortune. His work could be mocked and derided and it is possible that some of the attacks made upon Darwin's theory when it first appeared were a consequence of an assumption that his was little more than another absurd venture into science fiction. Nor did Darwin's work put an end to the more bizarre speculations in the field. Evolution became the modish term. Often misunderstood, it was seized upon as an explanation of all sorts of things to which Darwin himself would not have dreamed of applying it. Earnest amateurs in the Ethnological Society discussed such labyrinthine questions as whether Welsh was giving ground before the English language because the latter was 'fitter'; or whether black human beings were a different species from white ones and, if so, whether the cross-bred offspring, like mules, would be infertile. Misappropriated Darwinism seems to have been particularly attractive to those who were opposed to any attempts to ameliorate the harshness of contemporary society. There were those, for instance, who argued that the provision of universal free education would produce a nation of fools. If education had to be fought and struggled for (like scarce food in a drought-stricken plain) then the 'weaker' and the less 'fit' would be eliminated: if it was handed out to everyone the stupid would be enabled artificially to survive. The fact was that a great many people found the term 'fittest' beguiling.

The phrase 'the survival of the fittest' was not Darwin's own: it appears to have been coined by Herbert Spencer and was perhaps one of the most widely misunderstood phrases in the English language. There were those who assumed that 'fittest' meant 'strongest'. Others

---

[2] Robert Chambers, *Vestiges of the Natural History of Creation* (with an introduction by Sir Gavin de Beer) (Leicester, 1969), 219.

persuaded themselves that 'fit' possessed moral overtones. Indeed, there were a few, like W. H. Mallock,[3] who believed that evolution guaranteed the triumph of those who were both physically *and* morally 'fit' provided that no one meddled with its working. Nor were the ideologues the only ones who misunderstood. Far too many otherwise intelligent people made the mistake of thinking that Darwin's hypothesis implied the survival of the *strongest*. Benjamin Jowett once preached a sermon to the undergraduates at Balliol in which he sought to reassure them that Darwin's theory (which, he thought, was more or less right) need not destroy faith. Darwin taught the survival of the *strongest*, he said, but any intelligent observer would note that it was not always the strongest who survived. Sometimes what survived was the creature *best suited to the circumstances in which it found itself.*[4] Jowett thought he was improving on Darwin: he was really restating Darwin's own belief.

Straddling the controversy, with one foot among the social Darwinists and the other among the more serious thinkers of the period, was Herbert Spencer, an engineer by training, an individualist in politics, and a determined holist in his explanatory theories. Spencer was every bit as much of a polymath as Whewell had been, but a polymath representative of the new era rather than the old. If theology and geology, physics and metaphysics, had shaded imperceptibly into each other in the thought of former generations, Spencer perceived that each discipline dealt with and sought explanations for a different set of phenomena. But he believed that there was a uniform pattern or structure to them all which would allow biology, psychology, sociology, ethics, and metaphysics to be treated together in an overarching system or 'synthetic philosophy'. He was almost exactly Temple's contemporary, having been born in 1820. He would live until 1903, establishing before his death an immense reputation as the deviser of this synthetic philosophy. The basic groundwork for his system had been done in the 1850s, prior—that is to say—to the publication of *Origin of Species*. And he began to publish essays and articles in the course of that decade in which his grand scheme was touched on though not expounded in detail.

In 1861 Spencer also published a book called *Education, Intellectual, Moral, and Physical* which started with the purely physical level of

---

[3] Peter Hinchliff, *Benjamin Jowett and the Christian Religion* (Oxford, 1987), 118 ff.

[4] Benjamin Jowett, 'Darwinism and Faith in God', in W. H. Fremantle (ed.), *Sermons on Faith and Doctrine* (London, 1901), 1 ff.

things and worked up from there to the personal, the social, and the moral, applying at each stage what he had demonstrated as applicable to the previous level. It was, for its day, unusual. It delivered a savage attack on the conventional public-school curriculum, decrying the study of the classics and asserting that science was the only worthwhile knowledge for children to acquire. Spencer's primary intention was to try to demonstrate how children's natural inquisitiveness led them to learn things empirically, rather than by rote, and to show that rules are only subsequently derived from practical experience. He insisted that time was needed for acquiring knowledge; that children's minds needed to evolve gradually; that it was wrong to make them learn things by rote; and that the whole history of civilization was a process which led from enforced uniformity of beliefs to a state of affairs in which thinking for oneself was regarded as good. He characterized the process as being from 'the unanimity of the ignorant' through 'the disagreement of the inquiring' to 'the unanimity of the wise'[5] and suggested that Protestantism and the development of democracy were both signs of progress. The book appeared when the *Essays and Reviews* controversy was at its height and Spencer began to be talked of as someone with interesting ideas about education.

Spencer's complete scheme was initially set out in *First Principles*, which appeared in 1862 and was reissued in six subsequent editions before his death. It was intended as the first volume of a much larger project. Spencer had issued a prospectus in March 1860, describing the work in outline and soliciting subscriptions at ten shillings a year for which subscribers would receive four 'Numbers'.[6] The original idea—which never worked, partly because of Spencer's poor health—had been that the numbers should build up into a series of volumes, which would each be called 'Principles of' one or other of the disciplines to be surveyed. *Principles of Biology* appeared in two volumes but the second was not published till 1867. *Principles of Psychology* had already been issued in 1855 but was expanded into two volumes which appeared in the 1870s. *Principles of Sociology* was published in three volumes, of which the last was not issued until 1896. The volumes containing *Principles of Ethics* had been appearing concurrently with some of the other volumes during the 1880s and 1890s.

---

[5] Herbert Spencer, *Education, Intellectual, Moral, and Physical* (London, 1861), 59.
[6] Id., *First Principles*, 6th edn. (London, 1900), p. xvi.

Because *First Principles* appeared so soon after *Origin of Species* those who read it tended to confuse their authors' ideas. Here, they thought, was another book about 'evolution' and similar to Darwin's. Spencer himself did nothing to dispel that misapprehension for twenty years but in the fourth edition, published in 1880, he said:

To the first edition of this work there should have been prefixed a definite indication of its origin; and the misapprehensions that have arisen in the absence of such indication ought before now to have shown me the need for supplying it.

Though reference was made... to certain Essays [by Spencer himself]... yet the dates of these Essays were not given; nor was there any indication of their cardinal importance as containing, in a brief form, the general Theory of Evolution. No clear evidence to the contrary standing in the way, there has been very generally uttered and accepted the belief that this work, and the works following it, originated after, and resulted from, the special doctrine contained in Mr Darwin's *Origin of Species*.[7]

That, as Spencer pointed out, was not the case. His concept of 'evolution' and Darwin's were very different.

Since *First Principles* was intended as an introduction to Spencer's synthetic philosophy, it set out his fundamental premiss—that it was possible to make sense of everything by means of a single explanatory theory. But there already existed a variety of rival explanations, some of which related to aspects of the whole and some to the whole itself. To demonstrate the superiority of his own holistic theory, he had to eliminate this variety, either by reconciling divergent points of view or by getting rid of all but his own. And Spencer preferred the former approach. *First Principles* began, therefore, by attempting to reconcile the conflict between religion and science which he described as 'of all antagonisms of belief, the widest, the most profound, and the most important'.[8] The 'religious sentiment', he argued, 'is either directly created or is developed by the slow action of natural causes, and whichever conclusion we adopt requires us to treat the religious sentiment with respect'.[9] His preferred technique for overcoming divergence of opinion was to say that even false beliefs contained some grain of truth. Therefore he maintained that 'religions, even though none of them be actually true, are yet all adumbrations of a truth'.[10] And of science he said:

---

[7] Ibid. p. vii. [8] Ibid. 8. [9] Ibid. 11. [10] Ibid. 12.

To see the absurdity of the prejudice against it, we need only remark that Science is simply a higher development of common knowledge; and that if Science is repudiated, all knowledge must be repudiated along with it.[11]

Science had no limits: by definition it included anything which could be known and the cognizable regularity underlying natural phenomena provided the way of advancing one's understanding. Examining phenomena would provide an assumption: testing the assumption against all possible evidence and finding that it held good, would provide a 'fundamental proposition' (not deducible from something 'deeper' but based on observation). And that, in turn, would provide a basis for future action. Presumably he meant that if, for instance, one knew that the sun had always risen in the morning one was able to plan what to do after sunrise next day.

The primary truths, Spencer believed, were the persistence of force, the indestructibility of matter, and the continuity of motion. All reality was a kind of reciprocating exchange of forces—'forces which seem to be lost are transformed into their equivalents of other forces'; or 'conversely... forces which become manifest do so by disappearance of pre-existing equivalent forces'.[12] In other words, since matter is indestructible and motion continuous, nothing can really disappear: it can only become its opposite. There is no zero, only a balancing of the negative by the positive. From that proceeded two further steps in the argument. One was that evolution must be balanced by dissolution; to maintain the persistence of force there must be a negative as well as a positive, a regression as well as a development of life. The other—and more important for the structure of his project— was that the division of the whole into its parts is a mere matter of convenience.

While we think of Evolution as divided into astronomic, geologic, biologic, psychologic, sociologic, &c, it may seem to some extent a coincidence that the same law of metamorphosis holds throughout all its divisions. But when we recognize these divisions as mere conventional groupings, made to facilitate the arrangement and acquisition of knowledge—when we remember that the different existences with which they severally deal are component parts of one Cosmos; we see at once that there are not several kinds of Evolution having certain traits in common, but one Evolution going on everywhere after the same manner.[13]

---

[11] Spencer, *First Principles*, 13.   [12] Ibid. 433.   [13] Ibid. 438.

'After the same manner' are crucial words. Implicit in *First Principles* was the conviction, to be elaborated in the later volumes of the synthetic philosophy, that the pattern or structure observable in the most basic or purely physical level (the biological) reappeared at higher levels of life, the psychological or personal, the social and the ethical. Factors which operated in biological evolution must be expected to operate in social or moral development, too. The competitive drive—nature red in tooth and claw—which was observable at the biological level, was therefore appropriate at the moral level also. What was conducive to the survival of the fittest was rightly pursued in the social and moral sphere. Spencer drew the conclusion, not that everything was therefore reducible to the physical or material, but that the physical and the non-physical were united by some other overarching principle. Without much warning he introduced into the argument the notion of a 'First Cause'.[14] The capital letters which he gave to the words were significant though his First Cause was never quite the God of theism.

Eighteenth-century philosophers had pointed out that it was illogical to suppose that laws of causation inferred from phenomena observed in time and space necessarily applied beyond time and space. Spencer believed that he could ignore that difficulty and argue for the existence of an infinite something behind the whole persistent process of reciprocal forces which was what he meant by 'evolution'. It was implicit in the very nature of his synthetic philosophy though that observed phenomena should be evidence for what was beyond them. In his final summary of his entire argument he said:

Over and over again it has been shown in various ways, that the deepest truths we can reach are simply statements of the widest uniformities in our experiences of the relations of Matter, Motion, and Force; and that Matter, Motion, and Force are but symbols of the Unknown Reality. A Power of which the nature remains for ever inconceivable, and to which no limits in Time or Space can be imagined, works in us certain effects. These effects have certain likenesses of kind, the most general of which we class together under the names of Matter, Motion, and Force; and between these effects there are likenesses of connexion, the most constant of which we class as laws of the highest certainty. Analysis reduces these several kinds of effect to one kind of effect; and these several kinds of uniformity to one kind of uniformity. And the highest achievement of Science is the interpretation of all orders of phenomena, as differently

---

[14] Ibid. 27.

conditioned manifestations of this one kind of effect, under differently conditioned modes of this one kind of uniformity.[15]

The synthetic philosophy and its account of the evolving universe, physical, mental, and social, proved to have a lasting popularity. By the early 1880s the fourth edition of *First Principles* had been published (the edition which specifically explained that Spencer's notion of evolution was different from Darwin's) and the volumes on biology and psychology, and parts of the volumes on sociology and on ethics, had also appeared.

Spencer had, therefore, begun to acquire an international reputation when Temple was elected as the Bampton lecturer in the university of Oxford for 1884 and chose to give his lectures on 'The Relations between Religion and Science'. The Sandford *Memoir* says that Temple was 'urged to the task by Dr Jowett'.[16] This probably attributes too much to the Master of Balliol, though the Bampton lecturer was elected by the heads of the Oxford colleges, of whom Jowett was one. There is no record of Jowett's making any comment on the lectures—not even an unfavourable one—though as Vice-Chancellor he must have presided over at least some of them.[17] Nor is it even certain what sort of relationship existed between the two men by this time. The Sandford *Memoir*, again, is anxious to minimize any suggestion of a rift between them.[18] But it is clear that Jowett had developed doubts about Temple's reliability well before his appointment to Exeter. When he heard that Temple had declined the deanery of Durham he had said to Florence Nightingale:

I wish that he would speak out more plainly about theology. About ten years ago I had a conversation with him about the Atonement, but the sum of his argument was that it seemed to give great comfort to his mother (who was an excellent person). I did not care to talk to him any more about Theology.

And when he heard of the Exeter appointment he wrote:

I do not feel very glad at Dr Temple's bishopric (though I perceive that a general joy is diffused among liberals) because though a very able and clear-headed man

---

[15] Spencer, *First Principles*, 445.

[16] Sandford (ed.), i. 582.

[17] Hinchliff, 191.

[18] Sandford (ed.), i. 79. The explanation is unconvincing because Sandford suggests that the change was made because the original version of the dedication had been used to damage Rugby through its headmaster. But Rugby is not mentioned in the original version and Temple is specifically described as 'headmaster of Rugby' in the revised version.

he has done nothing for the cause of freedom of thought and has given up liberalism in Theology for liberalism in Politics, which is a far easier game, and he will get less and less liberal, more absolutely silent on any point which will ruffle the feathers of High Ch. & Evangelical. He may, perhaps, afford a haven for a few liberal Clergymen, but I doubt even this. He is one of those minds who run away from truth into practical usefulness, which if a man is capable of speculation, as he is, is a kind of treachery.[19]

The gradual restoration of the friendship between Temple and Jowett, evidenced by Jowett's letter to Temple on Netta Temple's death,[20] may well have begun by the 1880s. Jowett seems, however, always to have harboured some resentment. As late as 1889 he was writing to Florence Nightingale:

I had a very pleasant visit from Temple & his wife about a week ago. All his good qualities remain, but his defects have rather stiffened with the years. They are on the surface—but then the surface is what everyone sees.[21]

The lectures themselves must have been difficult to fit into the busy life of a diocesan bishop for all eight appear to have been given in the Hilary term of 1884.[22] This must have involved being in Oxford each weekend for the eight weeks of term and the preparation of the lectures must have taken up a good deal of time, too. Temple had, by this time, been Bishop of Exeter for fourteen years. He had, moreover, devoted himself very conscientiously to the diocese and its concerns. One cannot help but wonder how he had managed to maintain a serious interest in scientific developments while resolutely refusing to allow himself to be drawn away from Devon. He had never, of course, been a practising scientist himself, though a very able mathematician and, through applied mathematics, knowledgeable about some aspects of physics. He seems to have come, nevertheless, to think of himself as an expert on the *relationship* between science and religion.

There is some evidence that in his early days at Exeter he was in demand as a speaker on the subject; or it may be that that was the subject he chose to speak on when an opportunity offered. At all events he was invited to present the prizes at the Science School at Plymouth

---

[19] Quinn and Prest (eds.), 175 and 181.
[20] See above, 158–9.
[21] Quinn and Prest (eds.), 311.
[22] Sandford (ed.), i. 583, quoting Cosmo Gordon Lang who, as an undergraduate, was present at the lectures. Lang says 'Lent term' but 'Hilary' is the proper Oxford name.

within a year of his arrival in the diocese and the speech which he made on that occasion was thought worth publishing in pamphlet form.[23] [On Sunday, 1 July 1860, the day after the momentous encounter at Oxford between Thomas Huxley and Samuel Wilberforce, Temple preached before the delegates of the British Association, then meeting at Oxford. His sermon, which was subsequently published, advanced the same theme which had electrified the University only the day before: 'The Present Relations of Science to Religion'.[24] Curiously, Temple made no direct reference to Darwin's *Origin of Species*, nor to the confrontation of the previous day, at which he may have been present. Instead, he set forth in generous terms the most salient features of the debate between religion and science.[25] He gave full credit to scientists for setting out to discover every law in the universe which it was possible to establish, and promised to find 'the finger of God' in each one of them; for the Bible did not demand 'confirmation of minute details' but recognition of a deep identity of 'tone, character, and spirit' between scripture and nature.[26]] And alongside other sermons, lectures, and ephemeral publications which dealt broadly with science he began also to take up another and related theme. In its earliest form, which also belonged to his first year at Exeter, it was expressed in a sermon about revelation.[27] In its later and fuller form it was an assertion that the Bible and Creation were two parallel vehicles for God's revelation of himself.[28] These two closely related themes (the relationship between science and religion and the two parallel means of revelation) were subjects to which he returned repeatedly throughout the rest of his life.

There is still a puzzle, however, about how he managed to remain in touch with the world of the sciences. Even if he claimed no scientific expertise and even if his concern was with the theology of science rather than with the content of scientific developments, he can hardly have presumed to talk about 'the *present* relations of science to religion' without any knowledge of *present* developments within the sciences themselves. The explanation probably lies in two closely intertwined factors—the influence of Herbert Spencer's ideas and Temple's

[23] F. Temple, *Presentation of Prizes at Plymouth Science School by the Lord Bishop of Exeter*, repr. from the *Western Daily Mercury*, Plymouth 1870.

[24] Id., *The Present Relations of Science to Religion* (Oxford, 1870).

[25] James R. Moore, *The Post-Darwinian Controversies*, 89.

[26] Ibid.

[27] F. Temple, *On God's spiritual revelation to man (a sermon)* (Manchester, 1870).

[28] e.g. id., *The Revelations of Science and the Bible (an address)* (London, 1890).

membership of the Devonshire Association for the Advancement of Science, Literature and Arts.

He became a member of the Association after he had been at Exeter a little more than twelve months and was its president in the following year. It is significant that his presidential address, in which he disclaimed any right to be called 'a student of science', was really a plea that the Association should devote itself chiefly to promoting science. One could really only advance literature or art if one possessed the individual gifts of a writer or artist: science, being less 'individual', could be befriended and 'advanced' even by those who were not scientists.[29] The Association probably provided him with contact with other Devonian 'friends of science' and enabled him to talk about what the scientists were doing. When he died, the Association published an obituary in which he figured not as the archbishop but as its own past-president. In that capacity, the obituary said, he had attended every meeting both of the council and of the members generally and had had 'something apt to say on every occasion, and at the close of the reading of each paper'.[30]

His presidential address itself showed how his ideas about science were developing. He reverted, on the question of the relative importance of science and the classics, to something more like the view he had taken when at Kneller Hall. He noted, very perceptively, how the sciences had come to be regarded as setting the standards for all disciplines. The defenders of classical studies had once been disposed to maintain that classics were better instruments of education than science but now they argued that the study of classics was itself scientific.[31] He admitted that there were possible dangers in over valuing science. There was the danger of undervaluing everything else simply because science appeared to offer greater certainty. There was the more subtle danger of assuming that only those kinds of science which already existed were true science. They might, in fact, merely be the most elementary forms of science, the first steps in scientific knowledge. Knowledge of human nature (psychology, in other words), might be much more valuable than knowledge of material nature even though it had not yet become an exact science.[32] And so he came to his favourite

---

[29] *Transactions of Devonshire Association for the Advancement of Science, Literature and Arts*, vol. v. (Plymouth, 1872), 17.
[30] Ibid., vol. xxxv. 40.
[31] Ibid. 19 ff.
[32] Ibid. 26 ff.

topic: that science and religion were not incompatible. To the Christian, he said, it must be deeply significant that for centuries past 'science and Christianity have been given by God's providence to the same nations'.[33] Non-Christian peoples had no knowledge of the sciences. The bishop seemed to have forgotten for the moment about the contribution of Islam to mathematics.

In all this there were many hints that he had been reading Spencer and particularly *Education*. The book had appeared in 1861 and Temple, as a progressive headmaster, could hardly have failed to hear of it. He may not have read it when it first appeared, since the *Essays and Reviews* controversy was then at its height, but it seems almost certain that he had done so before he left Rugby for Exeter. By the time of the presidential address he had moved much closer to Spencer's idea that scientific education was all-important. Just as Spencer had argued that grammar was the 'science' of language so[34] Temple pointed out that the study of languages could be regarded as scientific in its methods.[35] If a pupil who could recite a proposition of Euclid but was unable to work out a simple problem from basic principles, could not be said to have learnt geometry, nor could he be said to have been taught classical syntax if he could recite the rules but not apply them. (There may have been an echo from his own childhood here.) Spencer's attack on learning by rote and his arguments in favour of 'natural' learning both struck chords with Temple and from this time on, one of his favourite themes was an obviously Spencerian one, that pupils need time to absorb what they learn.[36]

At Rugby, when he had given evidence before the Clarendon Commission, he had seemed to denigrate science somewhat but he had also been prodded into developing a *religious* argument for teaching it.[37] There was nothing particularly new or startling about that argument—that the sciences might make children aware of the wonders of creation and, therefore, of the majesty of God—but Temple seems to have paid it more and more attention over the years. Similar ideas were set out in some of the talks on the relationship between science and religion and

[33] *Transactions of Devonshire Association for the Advancement of Science, Literature and Arts*, vol. xxxv. 28.

[34] Spencer, *Education*, 52.

[35] *Transactions of Devonshire Association for the Advancement of Science, Literature and Arts*, vol. v. 19 ff.

[36] e.g. Sandford (ed.), ii. 82.

[37] See above, 109.

the two parallel means of revelation which he had given in his early years in the diocese. In the end the theme became the starting point for the Bampton lectures which were intended to show that religion and science illuminated each other. The text for the first of the lectures was from Psalm 104; 'O Lord, how manifold are Thy works; in wisdom hast thou made them all; the earth is full of Thy riches.' Here, too, was an echo of Spencer for Spencer had insisted that a true veneration of the creator logically required one to take creation seriously.[38] Nor would anyone who had ever heard Temple talk on the subject of religion and science have been in the least surprised by the opening statement of that lecture which was very like the argument which Spencer had used to claim that true religion and true science were never incompatible.

The believer in God...cannot find a more proper employment of time and labour and thought than the study of the ways in which God works and the things which God has made. Among religious men we ought to expect to find the most patient, the most truth-seeking, the most courageous of men of science.[39]

The lectures were not, in fact, intended to introduce his hearers to the latest scientific discoveries. Temple would not masquerade as 'a student of science'. Yet he possessed a sufficient grasp of basic principles to be able to give his audience a clear picture of a universe which originated as 'one or many enormous clouds of gaseous matter'.

And we have, nay all men have, been accustomed to assign to the original creation a great deal which Science is now disposed to assign to [its] history. But the distinction between the original creation and the subsequent history would still remain, and for ever remain, although the proportion assigned to the one may be less, and that assigned to the other larger, than was formerly supposed. However far back Science may be able to push the beginning, there still must lie behind that beginning the original act of creation—creation not of matter only, but of the various kinds of matter, and of the laws governing all and each of these kinds, and of the distribution of this matter in space.[40]

There are some problems in deciding whose ideas most influenced Temple. Ernest Sandford believed that the Bampton lectures showed an acquaintance with Hegel, and...Spencer, but the inspiration comes from Kant and Coleridge'.[41] As he was probably Temple's closest con-

[38] Spencer, *Education*, 50 ff.
[39] F. Temple, *The Relations between Religion and Science* (London, 1885), 4.
[40] Ibid. 106 f.
[41] Sandford (ed.), ii. 633.

fidant in the diocese at the time when the lectures were being written his opinion ought to be taken seriously. The influence of Spencer on the Bamptons is very obvious but there is, in fact, no direct mention of Hegel in them and no very obvious trace of his thought. That Temple was familiar with Hegel is, however, undeniable since forty years earlier he had set out to make a translation of some of his work in collaboration with Benjamin Jowett.[42] Kant and Hume were discussed at several points in the course of the lectures though Hume was usually mentioned only to be criticized. Kant, however, the bishop plainly admired. He was 'faithful to him to the end of his life and often based sermons on him'[43] but it is possible that he did not entirely understand Kant and for this, too, the influence of Jowett in the 1840s may be responsible.

Jowett had tried to convince his friends that Kantian ideas, which he had taken up with enthusiasm, were the key to understanding everything including theology. But he had not perceived that the effect of Kant's argument was to restrict 'knowledge' to that for which one could have empirical evidence. He used the passage towards the end of the *Critique of Practical Reason* which talks of the two things which excite awe—the starry firmament above and the moral law within—as the basis for a concept of God as 'personality clothed with law', the laws of nature and the moral law. It was an attempt to make Kant say almost the reverse of what he meant; to bring together the phenomenal world and the world beyond time and space. But, of course, it provided a wonderful means for someone who thought that science was one of the ways in which God revealed himself, to envisage morality and the natural world as harnessed together. Similarly Temple thought that he had obtained from Kant the idea that man's moral sense was evidence for the existence of God. But Temple's simple argument—that the fact that human beings possessed a moral sense meant that God must have planted it—was very different from Kant's progression of ideas—that the very existence of moral obligation implied freedom, therefore just rewards, therefore immortality, and therefore God. Temple frequently referred to the moral law within but though the phrase was, in a sense, Kantian the use he made of it was not.

It is just possible, however, that Temple derived his ideas about nature and morality from another source. A very similar idea had been incorporated in a book by the Scottish theological writer and

---

[42] Hinchliff, 80.
[43] Peter Addinall, *Philosophy and Biblical Interpretation: A study in Nineteenth-Century Conflict* (Cambridge, 1991), 21.

revivalist Henry Drummond, *Natural Law in the Spiritual World.* Drummond taught natural science in the Free Church college in Glasgow. His book, which used apparent examples of the way in which the world was ruled by law in both its spiritual and natural aspects, attempted to demonstrate the compatibility of religion and science.[44] It was first published in 1883, the year before Temple gave his lectures.

The most difficult statement in Sandford's account of the influences upon Temple's thought is his insistence that Coleridge was a paramount influence. The problem is that Coleridge was never directly referred to at any point in the Bampton lectures, though it is possible to guess that his ideas were in Temple's mind at times. Much the same is true of Coleridge's place in Temple's thought in general. Both Temple himself, and the Sandford *Memoir*, insist that it was both important and permanent. When Temple was an undergraduate he had found Coleridge's ideas so exciting that, after reading him, he could do nothing else but must go for a walk.[45] When he was nearly eighty and writing to his undergraduate son, he cited Coleridge as a great thinker with whose exciting speculations he had disagreed on one point only—the Trinity.[46] Yet there is no concrete evidence in Temple's lectures, his letters, or in the *Memoir*—except possibly once and that when he was a very young man[47]—as to precisely how Coleridge had influenced him: which of Coleridge's ideas shaped which of his; where a particular writing of Coleridge's made itself felt in which part of Temple's theology. The saying of Coleridge's which he was said to have found most inspiring was the very well-known 'Christianity is not a Theory, or a Speculation; but a *Life*. Not a *Philosophy* of Life, but a Life and a living Process.'[48] And that, of course, might mean little more than that he believed that Christianity had to be lived and not philosophized.

It was plainly the idealism of Hegel, Kant, and Coleridge, very different though each was, which attracted Temple. The opening sentence of his contribution to *Essays and Reviews* had acknowledged that a universe understood as consisting of 'mere phenomena, where all events are bound to one another by a rigid law of cause and effect'[49] was not a world in which it was easy to see God at work. Spencer nevertheless

[44] Ibid. 204
[45] Sandford (ed.), ii. 424.
[46] Ibid. ii. 690.
[47] Ibid. ii. 472.
[48] Ibid. ii. 670—quoting from Coleridge's 'Aids to Reflection'.
[49] *Essays and Reviews* (London, 1860), 1.

believed that it was possible to argue from phenomena to his First Cause. That First Cause, however, was hardly the dynamic divine being to whom Coleridge believed one should commit oneself as a way of life. In other words, two of the principal influences on Temple's thought— Spencer and Coleridge—were incompatible with each other. Coleridge's metaphysics and Spencer's empiricism sat very uneasily together and the resultant fundamental awkwardness was present throughout the lectures. It was not openly faced and that may explain why Coleridge was never directly mentioned.

Temple never seemed quite to understand the importance of the fact that scientific truths are universally demonstrable while religious truth is not. He recognized that the difference existed. He understood the implications, or some of them, for he argued, that since religious belief was not based upon sense perception, human beings must possess some other (spiritual) faculty on which the ability to receive God's revelation must depend. This was a shrewd point. His contribution to *Essays and Reviews* had made no real distinction between the general development of human knowledge and the more specific development of religious understanding nor between general advances in knowledge and individual genius.[50] His remark to the Devonshire Association that the advancement of art and literature depended upon individual talent suggests that he had come to understand the need to except genius from any general account of the progress of human understanding. In the Bamptons he went further, arguing that though religious knowledge evolved naturally, revelation was also necessary in order to develop and complete the natural process. The Old Testament itself, he argued, contained evidence of naturally developing ideas about God alongside others which clearly came from direct revelation.

He did not deal thoroughly with the crucial question whether the spiritual faculty was possessed by everyone, though he suggested that it was.

God has made man in His own image: that is He has given man power to understand His works and to acknowledge Himself. And it is in acknowledging God that man finds himself divine. He is a partaker of the divine nature in proportion as he recognizes the Supreme Law and makes it the law of his own will.[51]

---

[50] See above, 61–2.
[51] Temple, *Religion and Science*, 65.

It is interesting that when he came to discuss the actual content of what was revealed by God to man the examples given were mostly matters of morality—how one knows what is right rather than what one knows about God. And, in his final lecture, it began to seem that this special spiritual faculty was itself the moral law within. One wonders whether he may have read Newman and absorbed from him the idea that for its proper functioning, and for its understanding of truth, reason must possess a moral character.[52] But Coleridge, after all, had begun his *confessio fidei* of 1816:

I believe that I am a free agent, inasmuch as, and so far as, I have a will... Likewise that I possess reason, or a law of right and wrong, which uniting with my sense of moral responsibility, constitutes the voice of conscience. Hence it becomes my absolute duty to believe, and I do believe, that there is a God.[53]

Fundamental to Spencer's synthetic philosophy was a belief in the invariability of nature. Temple mentioned the fact often enough but did not really seem to have grasped that invariability is an absolute term. He sought to remove the great threat which science posed for traditional religious belief in Providence and miracle by asserting that the regularity of the world of nature was not absolute. In the first of his lectures he claimed that order (regularity and uniformity) is:

the stamp which, for reasons higher than itself, [God] appears to have put on His works. What is the limit to its application we do not know. There may be instances where this Order is apparently broken, but really maintained, because one physical law is absorbed in a higher; there may be instances where the physical law is superseded by a moral law. But we shall neither refuse to recognize that God has stamped his character on His works, nor let it on the other hand come between us and Him. For we know still that He is greater than all that He hath made, and He speaks to us by another voice besides the voice of Science.[54]

He thought that one could assert the possibility of miracle simply by going 'back to the beginning of things and saying: Here is an event which we cannot assign to that derivative action to which we have been led to assign the great body of events; we cannot explain it except by referring it to direct and spontaneous action, to a will like our own

[52] See Ian Ker, *John Henry Newman: A Biography* (Oxford and New York, 1989), 622; and Peter Hinchliff, *God and History, Aspects of British Theology* (Oxford, 1992), 36 ff.
[53] Samuel Taylor Coleridge, 'Aids to Reflection', in John Beer (ed.), *Collected Works*, Bollingen Series 75 (Princeton, 1973), 196 f.]
[54] Temple, *Religion and Science*, 33.

will.'[55] And in his third lecture, which was supposedly devoted to the question of the freedom of the will, he hinted that there was some analogy between God's action in the world and the fact that for the most part we act according to our nature and our will only 'interferes' very rarely.

This was undoubtedly the weakest point in the course of lectures. The real conflict between religion and science over freedom and determinism is not, at least from the perspective of a later age, whether an individual is capable of overriding his or her natural inclinations but whether the whole process of evolution is driven by forces which are both accidental and irresistible. But Temple was, in a sense, performing a species of conjuring trick. He was planting the idea that an occasional 'interference by the will', in the case of the human individual, need not be incompatible with the general uniformity of the nature of that individual, so that he could later assert that an occasional miraculous act, an interference by the divine will, need not be regarded as incompatible with the general uniformity of the nature of creation.

There was an uncomfortable dislocation, too, between Temple's attempt to rescue Paley's argument from design and his general devotion to Coleridge's thought. As is well-known Coleridge described Paley's *Natural Theology* as 'the utter rejection of all present and living communion with the universal Spirit'.[56] The supernatural rationalism of Paley's arguments seemed to Coleridge more conducive to unbelief than anything said by the opponents of faith. But when Temple came, in his fourth lecture, to a discussion of evolution, it appeared that one of his main objects was to defend Paley. He was concerned, in fact, not so much to expound evolution as to convince the anxious that they had nothing to fear from it. His generation, and others before them, had been brought up on Paley's *Natural Theology* with its famous argument from design about the watch and the watchmaker.[57] Darwin's work was thought to threaten Paley's argument and, for that reason, to be in conflict with Christian teaching. Temple described the problem clearly and succinctly:

[55] Temple, *Religion and Science*, 30.
[56] Addinall, 35.
[57] Whereas in the early nineteenth century the argument was *from* design to the existence of God, in the wake of Darwin it became an argument *for* design as compatible with the existence of God.]

If animals were not made as we see them, but evolved by natural law, still more if it appear that their wonderful adaptation to their surroundings is due to the influence of those surroundings, it might seem as if we could no longer speak of design as exhibited in their various organs; the organs we might say grew of themselves, some suitable, and some unsuitable to the life of the creatures to which they belonged, and the unsuitable have perished and the suitable have survived.[58]

Paley, Temple suggested, had added to his argument from design the assertion that the relation of universe to creator was more wonderful than that of watch to watchmaker—God's universe is like a watch which 'was so constructed that, in course of time, it produced another watch like itself'. In fact, said Temple triumphantly, evolution is even clearer evidence of design than that for it is as though the watch 'produced in the course of time not merely another watch but a better'. And he went on to produce his famous statement that God 'did not make things, we may say; no, but he made them make themselves'.[59]

There were moments in this lecture, it is true, when it seemed that Temple might fall into the same sort of mistake which Jowett had made in his sermon in Balliol chapel, that is, in attempting to improve on Darwin he was really restating Darwin's own belief. 'The very phrase', he said, 'which we commonly use to sum up Darwin's teaching, the survival of the fittest, implies a perpetual diminution of pain and increase of enjoyment...' But the point he proceeded to make avoided committing him to the belief that survival of the fittest implied the survival of the strongest or most fully developed. What he sought to suggest was that creatures 'fitter for their surroundings, most certainly will find life easier to live'.[60] His purpose throughout was not so much to remove the difficulties presented by evolutionary theories as to convince traditionalists that they would not have to give up the apologetic to which they were accustomed. Nevertheless it is clear by the end of the lecture that the evolution he was considering was Spencer's not Darwin's. The essence of Darwin's theory was that evolution went where it happened to go: the essence of Temple's argument, like Spencer's, was that there was a single developing pattern of life, a single plan, and single cause. 'The doctrine of evolution binds all existing things on earth into one.'[61] In his determination to rescue Paley, Temple relied on

---

[58] Temple, *Religion and Science*, 111.
[59] Ibid. 115.
[60] Ibid. 117 f.
[61] Ibid. 122.

Spencer's affirmation that evolution was somehow directed and controlled by the 'First Cause'. That meant that he did not have to abandon the notion of design and enabled him to offer comfort to the anxious disciples of Paley. But it sat very uneasily with his own devotion to Coleridge.

It is, perhaps, just possible to see how someone who was already devoted to Coleridge might, on coming to Spencer, interpret the two as compatible. Both Coleridge and Spencer had set themselves to overcome the distinction between the mental and the material. Coleridge, like a good idealist, strove to bring mental and material together in polarity. Spencer's attempt to advance from the analysis of material phenomena to an understanding of the whole of life was very different. Yet Coleridge, like Spencer, had written about how to arrive at a better science of nature. His *Hints Towards the Formulation of a More Comprehensive Theory of Life* rejected the arbitrary division of things into compartments. Parts presuppose a whole and individuation serves the 'one great end of Nature'. The work could be understood as stating a purpose not wholly different from that of Spencer's synthetic philosophy.

Temple was not entirely uncritical. He was capable of seeing the flaws in the arguments of even those whom he admired. He perceived, for instance, that if—as Kant claimed—the human mind imposed pattern and relationship upon sense impressions, ('as a kaleidoscope creates symmetrical designs out of scattered and fragmentary bits and pieces' said Temple[62]) there was the possibility that the resultant design might be a delusion. Yet he was really only critical of the parts of an argument which he did not want to use; the parts which he wished to use were taken over less critically. So he tended to gather together ideas from a wide variety of sources, Kant and Coleridge, Paley and Spencer, and to weave them together regardless of the fact that they were actually contradictory.

His attempt, in the sixth lecture, to deal with Darwin and evolution was the centre-piece of the course. As always, his statement of the question was clear and concise. One had only, he said:

to look at nature to see that things are constantly changing. If one is to maintain both the regularity of nature and the constantly changing character of nature then the changes must happen according to rules which can be inferred from observation. A change in the weather must happen in accordance with known

---

[62] Temple, *Religion and Science*, 16.

patterns of meteorological behaviour. The life cycle of animals and the growth of crops, the movements of the planets, do not happen irregularly but in accordance with known laws. Therefore all the various forms of matter, whether living or inanimate, must...be the necessary outcome of preceding forms of matter. This is the foundation of the doctrine of Evolution.

The bishop began his discussion by dividing the process by which the world arrived at its present state into two: the evolution of a physical world, capable of sustaining life, and the evolution of forms of life upon that world. In relation to the second of these points he argued for accepting Darwin's explanation. In view of his dependence upon Spencer this seems surprising but he proceeded to point out what he thought were significant weaknesses in Darwin's hypothesis. First, he maintained, there was no explanation offered as to the emergence of life from inorganic matter. 'The creation of life is unaccounted for.' It 'presents itself as a direct interference in the actual history of the world'.[63] Secondly, Darwin, having demonstrated that characteristics were, by and large, transmitted from progenitor to progeny, offered no explanation of why there should be minute variations in the progeny. Darwin had believed that variations in species were produced by variations in surrounding conditions: Temple maintained that it was difficult to conceive of a sufficient variation in conditions, at the very first, to produce the great variety of very different forms of life. He kept reminding his audience of the prodigality of the evolutionary process, forms of life proliferating exuberantly but being gradually eliminated by their inability to fit with changed and changing conditions. His purpose was to suggest that, if existing forms of life had been produced by a process which, in effect, had selected those which functioned best, there must be a plan or purpose behind it. In the end, therefore, he believed that he had accepted evolution and, at the same time, retained the notion of design.

Alongside that part of the argument Temple developed another theme relating to the existence of human beings. He did not completely reject the idea that humanity evolved from lower forms of life but he suggested that, if changes in species were the result of changed conditions, then 'the enormous gap which separates [man's] nature from that of all other creatures known, indicates an exceedingly early difference of origin'.[64] Moreover, similarity between human beings and members of other species did not necessarily prove that they were descended from a

[63] Ibid. 170. [64] Ibid. 176.

common ancestor: similarities might have been produced by similar conditions. Finally, Temple asserted that the existence of the moral law in human beings could not be the result of evolution 'any more than the necessity of mathematical truth can so come'.[65] In other words, moral truths exist objectively and not merely if and when human beings come to believe them. Though it is possible to understand how notions of pain and pleasure, liking and disliking, can have come to exist in human beings as a consequence of the evolutionary process, the sense of right and wrong cannot be so understood. Without finally and specifically committing himself to a belief in the special divine creation of human beings, the bishop was plainly hinting at it.

The lecture ended with a short section arguing that there was nothing about the theory of evolution, as modified by Temple, which was contradictory to Genesis. Advancing an idea that Charles Gore was to develop more fully in *Lux Mundi* five years later, the bishop suggested that it was the religious truths rather than the apparent facts contained in biblical narratives which scripture was concerned to convey—'... the purpose of the revelation is not to teach Science at all. It is to teach great spiritual and moral lessons, and it takes the facts of nature as they appear to ordinary people.'[66]

The last two lectures added very little that was not already in the earlier ones. The real point of the seventh lecture was to assert that religion, with its belief in things which were outside the scope of science, was no bar to the development of scientific knowledge. But it gave miracles a central importance which (notwithstanding Sandford's opinion to the contrary[67]) Temple would probably have rejected twenty years earlier. The final lecture, which summed up the course as a whole, also seemed to proclaim an attitude very different from 'The Education of the World'. It was very much a direct hortatory appeal to his hearers to love the Jesus as described in the Gospels; to subject their will to his; to devote themselves to his service.

Our Lord is the crown, nay, the very substance of all Revelation. If He cannot convince the soul, no other can. The believer stakes all faith on His truth; all hope on His power. If the man of science would learn what it is that makes believers so sure of what they hold, he must study with an open heart the Jesus of the Gospels; if the believer seeks to keep his faith steady in the presence of sc

[65] Temple, *Religion and Science*, 180.
[66] Ibid. 181.
[67] Sandford (ed.), i. 633 ff.

many and sometimes so violent storms of disputation, he will read of, ponder on, pray to, the Lord Jesus Christ.

It is difficult to avoid altogether the impression that Temple, after more than a decade as a bishop, was making the *apologia* for which so many people had asked before his consecration. The real theme of the lectures does not seem to be the relations of religion to science but whether it is possible to be a believing Christian without rejecting everything the scientists were discovering or, perhaps, whether it is possible to be a scientist without giving up religion. The lectures were about removing misapprehensions, in other words, and quieting fears. It may even be that they were designed to remove fears and misapprehensions about the Bishop of Exeter as well as about science.

The young Cosmo Gordon Lang, himself to become Archbishop of Canterbury in the twentieth century, was an undergraduate at Balliol, Temple's own old college, when the Bamptons were delivered. He was the son of a Church of Scotland manse who had come to Balliol on a Snell Exhibition. These exhibitions had been founded from the bequest of a seventeenth-century royalist and Episcopalian in the hope that they might expose Scots Presbyterians to the beguiling influences of Oxford and inculcate in them High Church and monarchist beliefs. Tait had been a successful product of its generosity and Lang was to become even more obviously so (though it is ironic that he was also to play a part in persuading a monarch to abdicate). He had become Bishop of Stepney at the time when the Sandford *Memoir* was being compiled. He contributed his recollections of Temple's lectures:

If I remember rightly, the audience at first was not unusually large; but it gradually increased until S. Mary's was crowded in every part. The force and massiveness of the man arrested and held the attention of the University. I was then a scholar of Balliol, entirely outside the ecclesiastical life of Oxford. But Temple was to Balliol men a College tradition. We had all heard of his undergraduate days and seen the staircase where he had read at night to save the oil in his own lamp. Stories were already in circulation of the bluntness of his manner and speech. The *Oxford Magazine* (recently started) reporting the first lecture said: 'The harsh tones in which the Bidding Prayer was spoken called up a recollection of the famous sonnet in the *Spectator* which apostrophized Dr Temple as "The Hammer of the Lord."' I well remember the effect which his voice had upon me. Certain characteristic phrases and intonations passed for the time into the currency of undergraduate talk; and increased the curiosity with which the Bampton Lecturer was regarded. But this curiosity soon gave place to the conviction that a personality of singular force and reality was standing Sunday after Sunday in the pulpit of S. Mary's. The magazine of May 14 asked: 'Who can say whether it is as a writer, as a bishop, or as himself that the Bampton Lecturer attracts such large audiences?' There is little doubt that most of us would have answered, 'As himself.' Indeed, my clearest recollection of the lectures is the impression made by the man who spoke them. To be quite honest, many of the arguments I have forgotten; some of them, I know, in those brave days of youthful confidence, we criticized with some severity and superiority. But the man himself made a deep and strong impression. We lived—and this is true not least of those of us who liked to be thought 'liberal'—in an atmosphere of philosophic phrases (mine were Hegelian). Here was a man whose words and phrases were his own, coined in his own rigorous mind, and stamped with his own personality. We were all supposed to be 'thinking for ourselves', and were apt also to suppose that this process was hardly consistent with any decided acceptance of the Christian Creed. Here was a man who was obviously thinking for himself, and thinking with vigour, freedom, and honesty; yet his thinking brought him to that Creed. Jowett, I remember, had said shortly before, in one of his quaint and characteristic Balliol Sermons, 'The search for truth is one thing; fluttering after it is another.' Here was a man whose earnestness rebuked all 'fluttering', who was plainly in honest and urgent search for truth, and who found it in the Word made Flesh. Few of us who heard the concluding words of his last lecture, summing up the long array of vigorous argument, are likely to forget the ring of absolute reality with which they were spoken—'read, ponder, pray to the Lord Jesus Christ'. In short, the strength, the sincerity, the simplicity of the man were the true *apologia* for the Christian Faith offered by the Bampton Lecturer of 1884; and there were many who felt its force.[68]

The fact that Lang did not quote Temple's final sentence in precisely the form in which it appeared in the published version of the lectures suggests that he really had remembered it over a period of twenty years.

In general, surprisingly little survives as evidence for the way in which the Bampton lectures were received or whether they made much impact on other people who were thinking about the relationship between science and religion. Sandford was probably right in thinking that the most significant fact was that they aroused so little criticism and did nothing to reawaken the sort of controversy which had accompanied the publication of *Essays and Reviews*. And he was also probably correct in suggesting that this was as much because of changes in public opinion as because of changes in Temple's own ideas.[69] The early 1880s were, after all, precisely the point at which the clergy and the

[68] Sandford (ed.), i. 583 f.   [69] Ibid. i. 582, and ii. 635.

educated laity in all British churches are said to have come to terms
with the new scientific ideas.[70] That most conservative of scholars, Dean
Burgon (who had claimed to be Temple's friend while savaging him for
contributing to *Essays and Reviews*[71]) remained unconvinced. He was
still dismissing Darwin's theories as absurd in 1888.[72]

More recent commentators have suggested that Temple's lectures
played a decisive part in the process by which evolution came to be
accepted. Owen Chadwick has claimed that they made evolution respectable in the Church of England.[73] But his argument is a complex
one. He points out that when Temple was appointed archbishop there
was none of the fury which had accompanied his nomination to Exeter.
The only protest came from a clergyman who had felt obliged to resign
his own orders because he had come to *accept* the truth of evolution and
believed it incompatible with Christian faith. It was, in other words, not
a protest against the liberalism of Temple's theology but a protest
against the supposed hypocrisy of his continued profession of faith.
John Habgood, in the Idreos Lectures for 1994 (delivered at Harris
Manchester College in Oxford) made Temple's Bampton lectures the
starting point of what he had to say and implied that Temple had come
to terms with an open-ended evolutionary hypothesis. But, in fact, at
every important point Temple actually preferred Spencer's version of
evolution to Darwin's, precisely because he could not reconcile Darwin's
theory with a divine plan and purpose. An open-ended evolutionary
process which went where it happened to go without any prearranged
goal was quite unacceptable to him as it was to most of those who
accepted some version of evolution.[74] Spencer's vision of a unifying
architectonic, relating every branch of knowledge in a single theory of
development moving towards a goal of perfection, was much easier for
them to make sense of. But it contained its own problem. To accept the
idea that biology, psychology, sociology, and ethics all evolved according to the same overarching pattern meant that one had to accept that
the competitive motor which drove biological evolution—the best-
adapted species surviving because they were more successful in competing for limited supplies of food—would, *mutatis mutandis*, be operative

[70] Daniel L. Pals, *The Victorian 'Lives' of Jesus* (San Antonio, 1982), 52.

[71] See above, 82.

[72] Owen Chadwick, *The Victorian Church*, 2 vols. (London, 1966/70), ii. 24.

[73] Ibid. 23 f.

[74] John Durant, 'Darwinism and Divinity', in John Durant (ed.), *Darwinism and
Divinity* (Oxford and New York, 1985), 21.

at the social and the ethical levels, too. Temple's Bampton lectures did not actually do this though the way in which he dealt with the profligacy of evolution suggests that he may sometimes have wavered in that direction. The implication of his argument was that creation-by-evolution ensured that, in the end, the species which survived were stronger and better and happier than would otherwise have been possible. There were times when political ideologues and Spencerian enthusiasts came very close to saying the same thing about the application of free-market principles to society.

The true Darwinians were very anxious that there should be no such thing as social Darwinism. Less than a decade after Temple's Bamptons T. H. Huxley (who became Darwin's most faithful and most intelligent publicist) gave the Romanes lecture in Oxford on the theme of 'Evolution and Ethics'.[75] It was a head-on confrontation with Spencer's concept, in which Huxley argued that every single advance in civilization made by the human race had been the result of going *against* the competitive thrust of biological evolution. The building of a good, just, decent human society, he maintained, was not achieved by competition but by the sharing of available resources. Since Huxley was the person who, more than anyone else, grasped the real truths for which Darwin's hypothesis stood it is significant that his lecture sought to demonstrate that the patterns and principles of biological evolution could not and should not be applied to sociological evolution.

[That Temple's lectures made little lasting impression on the religious public may, at first, appear surprising given their highly topical nature, and (if Lang's memory is to be trusted) the impact of Temple's singular personality upon his audiences. Moreover, at the time, the lectures must have provided some measure of comfort to those pondering whether one could remain a believing Christian without rejecting recent scientific discoveries, or practise science without giving up religion. Upon closer investigation, however, it seems clear that the lectures succeeded in advancing the debate very little beyond Darwin and Spencer. In other words, Temple's arguments remained unconvincing, his theories unoriginal (except perhaps to the extent to which he attempted to reconcile the irreconcilable).

Nor were the lectures altogether successful in restoring Temple's reputation as an orthodox High Churchman; the taint of liberal

---

[75] T. H. Huxley, 'Evolution and Ethics', in *Evolution and Ethics and Other Essay* (London, 1894), 80 ff.

heterodoxy which had dogged him since *Essays and Reviews* still clung to him, in the view of many suspicious Churchmen. While Aubrey Lackington Moore, then tutor of Keble College, Oxford, and one of the most respected exponents of the relations between science and religion, could find much to praise in the lectures, he regretted 'the sharp severance between the physical and the moral, which shows itself all through the Bishop's arguments, and at times becomes almost deistic'.[76] Moore admired Temple's efforts to rehabilitate Paley's argument from design, and he accepted that the only way to do this was on the basis of evolution. At the same time he remained critical of Temple's reasoning: to argue that God makes things 'make themselves' through 'one original impress' of his will on nature 'seems to imply, however little it was intended, that God withdraws Himself from his creation, and leaves it to evolve itself, though according to a foreseen and foreordained plan'. The consequences of such a position for Christian theology were, to say the least, damaging[77]

In short, the religious public appears to have concurred that the lectures fell short of achieving Temple's implied—and rather ambitious—objectives: a robust and intellectually credible defence of the compatibility of science and religion; the reconciliation of philosophical claims hitherto considered at variance, if not contradictory; the conflation of the argument from design and the theory of evolution; and the resolution of perplexing theological paradox. The debate over the relationship of religion and science went on. The establishment of a durable form of Christian Darwinism was not to be so easily achieved.]

---

[76] Aubrey Lackington Moore, *Science and Faith: Essays on Apologetic Subjects* (London, 1889), 99.
[77] For a review of Moore's response to Temple's lectures see James R. Moore, *The Post-Darwinian Controversies* (Cambridge, 1979), 220, 261 f.

8

The Ecclesiastical Edifice

After Tait's death Randall Davidson, who had been the archbishop's chaplain, was appointed Dean of Windsor. He was only thirty-six but was well on his way to becoming the Queen's favourite clergyman. He was soon on good terms with Sir Henry Ponsonby, her private secretary, and the two men would exchange bits and pieces of near gossip. Ponsonby would tell Davidson, for instance, what the Queen thought about the preachers in the chapels royal. On 7 January 1885 he sent a very curious letter to the deanery. It began with a page torn from Tennyson's verse play, *Becket*, containing the opening lines from the prologue:

> HENRY
> So then our good Archbishop Theobald
> Lies dying.
>> BECKET
>> I am grieved to know as much.
> HENRY
> But we must have a mightier man than he
> For his successor.
>> BECKET
>> Have you thought of one?

Ponsonby had drawn a pen stroke through the 'Arch' of 'Archbishop' for the letter was really about the death of Bishop Jackson of London. Unlike Theobald, however, Jackson was already dead, having died on the previous day. The letter itself read:

My Dear Dean,
   Would you answer the above question?
H.M. wants to learn your thoughts.
   I told her I thought the Bishop of Bedford?? [William Walsham How, Jackson's suffragan, probably never really a serious candidate].

I must show your letter in reply to the Queen—so if you quote Tennyson as I have done it must go before the Royal eye.[1]

Gladstone was again the Prime Minister and, as in 1869, had more than one vacancy to think about. The Queen was a far from passive recipient of prime ministerial suggestions. She often had firm ideas of her own and was inclined to object strongly to obviously political nominations. She made sure that she was well informed and the deans of Windsor were usually her principal source of insider information. Wellesley had played such a role and the Queen was coming to rely upon Davidson more and more.[2] The usual order of events was for the Prime Minister to make his proposals and then for the Queen to consult Davidson in order that he might tell her what he knew about the persons suggested.

Davidson replied to Ponsonby, though that letter has not survived, and on 24 January Sir Henry sent another, but barely legible, note.

Post off
Temple—London
Bickersteth—Exeter
New Dean
Dr King
Pastoral Theoly } Lincoln
Oxford
Please tell the Qn about these[3]

Davidson's reply was:

1. Bishop Temple for London. I have already as you will recollect written about him. I believe him to be (with the single exception of the present Bishop of Durham, if he is an exception) the fittest man in England to become Bp of London—Notwithstanding his rough exterior and harsh voice he has proved himself to be generally qualified to lead and influence men—He has gained the confidence of all those whose confidence is best worth having to whatever party they belong. Possibly the extreme Evangelicals don't like him much, but that is all. He is distinctly a Broad Churchman in theology, but the outcry which formerly arose about his connection with 'Essays and Reviews' has entirely

[1] Lambeth Palace Library: Davidson Papers, vol. 4, fo. 38, letter dated 7 Jan. 1885. The letter is quoted in G. K. A. Bell, *Randall Davidson, Archbishop of Canterbury*, 2 vols., 2nd edn. (London, 1938), i. 166 f. as is other relevant correspondence not given in full here.

[2] Owen Chadwick, *The Victorian Church*, 2 vols. (London, 1966/70), ii. 328 ff.

[3] Lambeth Palace Library: Davidson Papers, vol. 4; this scrap of paper has no separate folio number but is almost certainly the 'hastily scribbled' note referred to in Ponsonby's letter to Davidson of 25 Jan., fo. 40.

died away. His personal friendship (from early days onwards) with Archbp Benson will tend, if Her Majesty appoints him, to make everything work with the utmost smoothness, and Mrs Temple's links with as many more prominent in the political world will be a clear advantage socially. He is a man remarkable for earnestness of purpose and terse rigour and [*sic*] exposition, and though now 63 years old is physically very strong and active, a most necessary qualification for London.

He added that Bickersteth, who had just been nominated to the deanery of Gloucester was 'a most *liberal minded* Evangelical' and 'a man acceptable to all who know him as a refined Christian gentleman.' King, he said, had 'a strangely winning power'.

[He] has at Oxford succeeded beyond any other theological teacher in gaining the confidence of young men of all sorts of opinions—His own being decidedly High Church but he has never thrown himself into the *public* controversies on these subjects and he is so bright and cheery that he has done much to counteract the rather severe and gloomy views held about present and future which have characterized some of the other teachers who share his Church opinions.

Davidson went on to point out if those three were appointed at the same time there would be a balance between Temple, the Broad Churchman, Bickersteth, the Evangelical, and King, the High Churchman. Then he confided:

I confess to being myself a little surprised that Mr G is recommending a High Chman and did not submit the name of Canon Liddon with whom he is on such terms of friendship. Canon King however wd, I think, be a decidedly better Bp than Canon Liddon, and perhaps Mr Gladstone also thinks so … [but] An excluded leader is sometimes a source of danger and difficulty.[4]

There was such a flurry of notes exchanged between the castle and the deanery that Ponsonby's next letter was probably written before he had received Davidson's.

In great haste last night I scribbled Gladstone's proposals. He says he agrees with the Queen that Temple and Lightfoot are the 2 to be considered. He does not think Lightfoot would accept—If he did there would have to be a second translation as Durham is too high to go straight into—and the Church would lose the valuable books which Lightfoot now writes but could write no more in the busy hum of London.[5]

[4] Lambeth Palace Library: Davidson Papers, vol. 4, fo. 39, copy of letter from Davidson to Ponsonby, dated 25 Jan. 1885.
[5] Ibid., fo. 40, letter dated 25 Jan. 1885.

So Gladstone ended up by proposing the three whom Davidson had favoured and what Gladstone told the Queen that he would like to do, was what he did. Temple was translated to London with the minimum of outcry or opposition and to the obvious regret of the clergy of the diocese of Exeter.

Benson appears to have declared himself neutral in the choice between Lightfoot and Temple but it is clear that he thought the latter would be more help to him. Lightfoot, he said, was 'terrifically selfish in pursuit of utterly unselfish ends' and inclined to be ruled by younger people. 'Temple would often wound and bruise one without knowing it—and think if he knew you were hurt that it was your own fault—more brusque than people would like, or I should find pleasant.'[6] But he added that one would always be able to count on 'hearty sympathy, outspoken counsel, and any amount of time and trouble'.

By this time Temple had become disenchanted with some aspects of Gladstonian Liberalism. He thought that Gladstone's Home Rule Bill for Ireland 'degraded Ireland' and would make it both inevitable and right that the Irish would demand complete independence. He told Henry Lee Warner, 'He does not feel with us when we talk of our Empire as a gift from God, to be used for the good of mankind.' And added:

And I fear that the Liberal Party will long suffer damage from his action. He has not always been true to Liberal principles; I have never considered him true to Liberalism on the religious side. But up to this point his divergence from true Liberalism has always been within comparatively narrow limits; and, as no man is perfect, it has been possible to condone his divergences for the sake of his splendid services. We have come to the point at which such condonation is possible no more. By far the best thing for the country and for the Liberal Party would be his final retirement from public life.[7]

During his years in London Temple began to shift his allegiance, claiming to be a 'true' Liberal rather than a supporter of the Liberal party. It was a time, of course, when a good many people were alienated by the growing possibility of Home Rule and became Liberal Unionists but Temple's disenchantment was the product of much beside the Irish question.

The new Bishop of London was almost sixty-five, still upright, large-framed and beginning to be much heavier. Group photographs of the

---

[6] Bell, i. 169 f.

[7] E. G. Sandford (ed.), *Memoirs of Archbishop Temple by Seven Friends*, 2 vols. (London, 1906), ii. 639 ff.

period show him seeming, at first sight, to tower above others though, on closer examination, he was probably not much taller than they. His very erect stance, head thrown back in a characteristic pose, made him seem so. His hair was still very dark and the distinctive sideburns were black and sharp, delineating the shape of his cheeks and making his expression seem fierce and his gaze piercing. He was undoubtedly strong and vigorous. He *said* that it was possible to delegate much of the work but appears to have been reluctant to do so.

Jackson had improved administration and had arranged for the creation of an independent diocese of St Albans in 1877. He had obtained Walsham How's appointment as suffragan in 1879 and given him what was virtually an independent episcopal area in the East End of London. He seems also to have allowed a great deal of independence to Archdeacon Hessey of Middlesex. Walsham How had been given the title of 'Bishop of Bedford' (one of the titular suffragan 'sees' specified in the Act of Henry VIII) though Bedford was actually in the new diocese of St Albans. Temple obtained a second suffragan (Alfred Earle) who was given the equally unlikely title of 'Bishop of Marlborough'. When How became the first Bishop of Wakefield in 1888, Temple had hoped for the appointment of Sandford as Bishop of Bedford. Instead he was given Claudius Billing, rector of Spitalfields, who had been his second choice but whom he had not even warned that his name was under consideration.[8] Earle had been a clergyman in the diocese of Exeter, where he had originally been a vigorous critic of Temple's appointment, and it seems that the Crown was not willing for two suffragans to be imported into London from the West Country. The Bishop of Marlborough was chiefly responsible for the western half of the diocese, the Bishop of Bedford continued to look after the East End, and eventually a retired colonial bishop, Dr Barry, was made rector of St James, Piccadilly to keep an eye on the central area. But none of them was ever allowed anything like an independent jurisdiction. Temple said, 'I am the Bishop of the diocese and cannot divest myself of what belongs to my office', and 'I may delegate work, but responsibility I cannot delegate.'[9]

Hessey's letters to Temple were at first stiff and formal but he soon became a faithful lieutenant. Walsham How, who was to become more and more unhappy as he discovered that he no longer possessed any real

---

[8] Sandford (ed.), ii. 27, and Chadwick, ii. 345.
[9] Sandford (ed.), ii. 25.

independence, wrote initially to welcome the new bishop unreservedly saying, 'I have had the strongest wish, since my late dear master was taken away, that I might have the privilege of serving under you.' But he began to try and shape Temple's approach to the diocese. 'It would also be a very popular thing were you to appear first at some gathering among the poor folk in the East.' He invited him to come and stay in east London if he should be planning to visit before he took formal possession of his new see.[10] And when How wrote again in the following month, full of enthusiasm about a recent service for the commissioning of missionaries, Temple instructed his chaplain to arrange for the two bishops to meet—but at the Athenaeum.[11]

Others found it even more difficult to fit smoothly into the transitional arrangements than How did. Bishop Bromby, formerly of Tasmania, also wrote within a week or two of Temple's appointment to say that he had been asked to do confirmations by Jackson and supposed that he had better continue with the arrangements.[12] A further letter followed a few days later, written in a somewhat tetchy style and saying that Canon Gregory of St Paul's (who had been appointed 'official' to administer business during the vacancy of the see[13]) had now gone and made other arrangements, laying 'fresh burdens' on the Bishop of Bedford. 'All I can now say is that all my arrangements fall to the ground with Bishop Jackson's death, unless you would like my help after your arrival.'[14] Bromby claimed to be in sympathy with Temple's 'social and ecclesiastical views' and his son had been an incumbent in the diocese of Exeter and was now in London. A note of grumbling importunity began to creep into the letters. He had, he said, been given to understand that Jackson would move an incumbent of a city church 'with a sparse population' to another living and give the city church to Bromby. When Temple took no notice of the hint, Bromby began to complain that he had lost a canonry at Chichester while waiting for Jackson's plan to mature. He was also anxious to get his family to a more salubrious climate than that of Shropshire. Temple replied that it

[10] Lambeth Palace Library: Fulham Papers, F. Temple, vol. 55, fos. 204 f., letter dated 30 Jan. 1885. Most of the correspondence in this volume dates from Temple's first year as Bishop of London, much of it before he had actually moved from Exeter.

[11] Ibid., fos. 206 f., letter dated 3 Feb. 1885.

[12] Ibid., fos. 66 f., letter dated 31 Jan. 1885.

[13] A notice of the appointment appeared in *The Times* of 6 Jan. 1885.

[14] Lambeth Palace Library: Fulham Papers, F. Temple, vol. 55, fos. 68 f., letter dated 4 Feb. 1885.

was 'ill luck' that Jackson's scheme had come to nothing but was not going to commit himself to having Bromby as a perpetual assistant. Bromby clearly resented the 'ill luck' but was gradually reduced to saying that he would take anything in London that would provide him with housing.[15]

It is easy to understand why Temple's terse, blunt replies upset so many: more difficult to know whether they were intended to do so. He was asked by a young man whether the fact that his aunt had cancelled a trip on a liner which subsequently sank could be regarded as 'Providential interference'. Temple replied, 'Can't tell; didn't know your aunt.'[16] But there were times when these laconic utterances seem not to have been intended as anything other than perfectly serious responses. Masterly inaction had become his favourite tactic when confronted by clergymen seeking his patronage. He could be generous with those whom he judged to be deserving but was easily irritated by those who ought to have been able to look after themselves. The self-important and those who told him that their labours and sacrifices deserved a reward, received very short shrift. To one clergyman, whom he described as 'always wanting to do things and always spoiling everything he does',[17] he wrote, 'You spoil all sacrifices by perpetually asking to be paid for them!'[18] In these matters he was inclined to be a harsh judge, not giving those who importuned him the benefit of much doubt.

He also showed in these early days in London that his harshness was sometimes unpredictable. He had hardly been enthroned in April 1885 than a young curate in the diocese was accused of indecency with boys in the parish. Temple saw him and then wrote to his incumbent:

I learn that on first hearing of the charge made against him he instantly proposed to prosecute the accuser, and he instructed his Solicitor that very afternoon. This is exactly what an innocent man would do and I do not see what he could do more.

After carefully putting together all the statements that I have heard I have formed a very decided opinion that he is perfectly innocent.

[15] Lambeth Palace Library: Fulham Papers, F. Temple, vol. 55, fos. 70–5.

[16] Sandford (ed.), ii. 705.

[17] Family Papers in the possession of the Right Revd F. S. Temple; Frederick Temple's letters to his children; letter to William dated from the Old Palace, Canterbury, 5 Dec. 1898.

[18] Lambeth Palace Library: F. Temple Papers (Official Letters), vol. 21, fos. 351 f., Archdeacon Colley to Temple, date illegible. The archbishop's comment is written on Colley's letter to guide his chaplains when writing the reply.

There can be no question that his manner with Boys is silly in itself, and mischievous to him, and very mischievous to many of the Boys whom he is so fond of caressing.

But this is an altogether different thing from indecency.[19]

This letter displays an understanding which was not apparent in his earlier dealings with sexual misbehaviour, but it did not mean that, because he was older, he had lost his earlier fierce sense of purity. He could draw a distinction between foolishness and immorality but he could still be very fierce. He told the young man himself that he believed him to be innocent of the most serious charges but went on to say:

...I am bound to add my very grave censure on your conduct.
A familiarity with Boys who are not your own children which goes to the length of kissing them is likely to do them serious moral harm and certain to bring discredit on your ministry.
I hope you will at once and for ever give up all such unmanly practices.[20]

Moreover he had not mellowed at all towards those whom he thought to have behaved with something worse than mere foolishness. Because the boys would not bring charges publicly Temple was contemptuous of their complaints. No argument that they might have been at risk; no plea that priority had to be given to their safety, no claim that the boy who complained was really trying to protect his little brother, would move him at all. He thought their evidence was suspect and probably malicious. But his real anger was reserved for the clergyman (not the incumbent of the parish) who had brought the complaint to the notice of the ecclesiastical authorities in the first place. He was so severely critical of how he had gone about it that the clergyman sent back a furious reply, accusing the bishop of behaving in a manner 'autocratic and infallible'. Inevitably the letter was treated with masterly inaction. Temple's direction to his chaplain was 'Nil. Put away.'[21]

One cannot help feeling, either, that behind the gruff manner, there was sometimes a twinkle in the eye for those who had the courage to look for it. In Temple's second year in London, a curate—new enough to have been ordained by the new bishop himself—wrote to him with the touchy aggressiveness that only comes with complete lack of self-confidence. His writing paper was embossed with a burning heart

---

[19] Ibid., Fulham Papers, F. Temple, vol. 55, fos. 220 f. letter dated from Fulham Palace on 22 Apr. 1885 and marked 'copy'.
[20] Ibid., fos. 224 f., copy of a letter dated 4 May 1885.
[21] Ibid., fo. 234.

bearing the words 'passio' and 'pax' and surmounted by a cross surrounded by the motto 'non videre sed habere'—not, one would have thought, Temple's kind of thing. The young man's problem was that his vicar had forbidden him to hear the confession of a woman in the parish. Temple saw him and told him that he thought the vicar was right. The curate then asserted that he could not accept the bishop's licence because that would amount to a denial 'of the laity's right in the Church of England to demand that their confessions be heard'. To this Temple returned a rather odd reply. He told the young man 'I do not mean to blame you for saying what you have said', which seems not to have encouraged him very much for he went off to look for work with an insurance company, 'convinced that, in pushing the cause of Life Assurance, I shall still be labouring in the very real interests of Humanity'. He asked permission to publish the correspondence 'in the interests of those who may otherwise misunderstand my retirement' and he sent Temple a copy of a very dramatic farewell sermon appealing 'to God, to Jesus, to the Church Universal, to the plain meaning of the formularies of the Church of England, to the sense of Justice and Reason in the hearts and minds of her people'.

Any suggestion that a dispute or controversy might be conducted in public was always to Temple like a red rag to a bull. 'You are quite at liberty to appeal to the *Guardian* and *The Times*', he wrote, 'But as I do not consider myself justified in doing the same I am unable to answer correspondents who avow such an intention.'[22] But when the young man, after a delay of some weeks, wrote again to say that he had been told that he had misunderstood Temple's views on the matter of confession, Temple took the trouble to explain them all over again. He said, in effect, that he had heard confessions himself, though his way of describing it was quite different from the terminology which the average Anglo-Catholic would have used. And he explained that his real objection was to the notion that anyone had a *right to demand* confession for it might not be appropriate or wise to encourage that particular course in certain circumstances. It was a patient and courteous explanation, particularly as the correspondence had been going on for some three months by this time. But the young man had not yet done with the matter. He wrote again, greatly relieved to find himself mistaken and offering to publish an apology for his 'previous misconception of [the

[22] A quite different reply is published in Sandford (ed.), ii. 106 but the draft contained in the archives at Lambeth is as it is given here.

bishop's] teaching'. He had not really begun to understand Temple's attitude to the publication of *anything* but the bishop's draft reply was, for him, a model of gentleness and good humour.

I see no necessity for your making any apology, but in talking about your position among your friends it would be well that you should not let them suppose, as many people seem to suppose, that I either refused you a licence or implied that I would refuse you if you asked for one. It would be well also that you should modify your former statement that every layman has a right to require that his Confession shall be heard whether the Priest to whom he applies thinks it best for him or not.

I am quite ready to license you as a Curate.[23]

There was much that needed to be done in the diocese, which was, after all, the most demanding in England. The bishop took determined steps to discover exactly what its state was. For this, the rural deaneries were his primary instrument and the Archdeacon of Middlesex his chief agent. Temple gave a great deal of time to the rural deaneries and he took them seriously, as he had done in Exeter. After he had left the diocese he would admit that the work was extremely heavy especially as much of it had to be done at night. 'I had a Meeting of Clergy separately and of Clergy and Laity jointly in every Deanery every year.'[24] He also, as he had done in Exeter, undertook—against some opposition from the clergy themselves—to appoint as rural dean 'the beneficed priest who shall be recommended by the Clergy of that Deanery, and to make a fresh appointment every five years'.[25]

In the City and the East End, Walsham How already had things well organized and had given some thought to what still needed to be done to make administration effective. From time to time, however, attention had to be given to the City churches, amalgamating benefices where there were few parishioners, sometimes dismantling the buildings, selling the land and using the proceeds to build churches where they were really needed. A Diocesan Commission of clergy and laity was appointed to co-operate with the Ecclesiastical Commissioners in dealing

---

[23] The correspondence is in Lambeth Palace Library: Fulham Papers, F. Temple, vol. 55, fos. 14–41.

[24] Lambeth Palace Library: Davidson Papers, vol. 4, fos. 187 f. Temple to Davidson, letter dated 3 Nov. 1901.

[25] Lambeth Palace Library: Fulham Papers, F. Temple, vol. 45, fo. 1, letter from Temple to all clerical representatives to the diocesan conference instructing them to organize the elections. The letter is also printed in Sandford (ed.), ii. 8. See also Lambeth Palace Library: Fulham Papers, F. Temple, vol. 45, fos. 19 f., letter from Archdeacon Hessey, Mar. 1886.

with this.[26] The demolition of ten churches released three-quarters of an acre of valuable land in the City for sale. In each case a new church elsewhere in the metropolis had been built with the proceeds.[27] When St Benet, Gracechurch Street was amalgamated with another benefice (the population of both benefices put together amounted to only 481) its sale had realized £23,894. The Ecclesiastical Commissioners used £7,247 of that to build the new church of St Benet, Stepney; provided £9,000 as an endowment fund; and used the rest for grants towards other buildings.[28] In 1889 a Commission, under the chairmanship of the Archdeacon of London, was appointed to collect information about lectureships at the City churches which usually dated from the sixteenth or seventeenth centuries. Some of them were in the gift of City livery companies or of the local ratepayers; others were in the hands of the vestry, or of the churchwardens or trustees. In a number of cases the lectureship was held by the rector but sometimes only by an annual vote of the vestry. Lectures were still actually given in some City churches, often on a weekday, but attendance was not usually very large. The purpose of the Commission was to discover whether the endowments from which the lecturerships were funded could be diverted to some other purpose more useful in the late nineteenth century, such as the training of those preparing for holy orders, helping poorer parishes, or paying for curates where they were needed but the incumbent could not afford the stipend. It transpired, however, that only three of the lectureships were really valuable and most of them were restricted by the terms of the foundation to the giving of lectures in divinity.[29]

In the much larger archdeaconry of Middlesex Hessey knew the state of affairs pretty well and rural deans were also encouraged to be the eyes and ears of the bishop. Gradually precise information began to be gathered. At one of the bishop's early meetings with the clergy of the rural deanery of Ealing it was decided that the needs of the area must be properly surveyed. A subcommittee of the ruridecanal chapter was appointed which reported in 1886.[30] The report is a quietly impressive

[26] Lambeth Palace Library: Fulham Papers, F. Temple, vol. 25, fos. 135 ff., Report of the Commission.

[27] Ibid., fo. 144.

[28] Ibid., fo. 150.

[29] Ibid., fos 151–6, Report of the Commission: fos 156–96, questionnaire to which City incumbents were required to reply with information about lectureships in their parishes: 196–9, table of the parishes showing results of questionnaire.

[30] Ibid., fos. 123–8, Report of a subcommittee of the rural deanery of Ealing to consider 'the chief difficulties against which the Church in the Deanery has to contend and how to

document. The area was plainly in a state of flux. 'The old established families which till recently occupied the suburbs and were attached to the soil, have deserted them; their estates have been purchased not by wealthy men of business, but by Building Societies, under whose management gardens and parks have been divided into small lots for workmen's tenements and small villas.' And 'The vast majority of new buildings are intended for and occupied by working and labouring people or persons of small incomes not far removed from them.'

The changes were particularly obvious on the eastern side of the deanery. The population of the parish of Acton, for instance, had grown from 3,151 to 17,110 in the course of the previous twenty-five years and even Isleworth, on the other side of the deanery, had grown from 7,000 to 16,000. New churches and schools were desperately needed but the problems complex and the financial implications appalling. The committee reviewed the new church building of the previous thirty years but concluded that it had never managed to keep pace with the population. The clergy were having to find and pay extra curates (a curate's stipend was £120–£150 a year).[31] Church schools had become too small and school managers were unable to cope with the additional numbers. School boards had been formed and a rate levied. Former voluntary subscribers were unable to pay the new rate *and* continue their subscriptions. 'By degrees the Schools built at the expense of Church people are altogether lost to the Church.'

The social consequences of the demographic changes in the area were noted, sadly but without much hope that they could be avoided. The young were no longer disciplined. 'The large and unnecessary number of Public Houses is a great evil.' But as regards the Church the report was able to make quite specific recommendations. The previous bishop, it said, had worked hard but had not managed to visit some of the parishes in this part of the diocese at all. Because the archdeaconry was so big and because there was no suffragan for the area, there was no one to care for the incumbent, 'no one at hand of sufficient authority to rebuke his bitterness and encourage his zeal'.[32]

---

meet them'. The subcommittee consisted of the Revds A. Almack, L. W. J. Dale, A. H. Dunn, J. Jackson, and the Rural Dean, the Revd Henry Richards.

[31] Ibid., vol. 55, fos. 11 f., letter from the Revd Arthur J. Spencer and fo. 79 letter from the Revd W. E. Beaumont.

[32] Ibid., vol. 45, fo. 127.

'... to avoid waste of energy, to concentrate thought and enable the Church to advance with united purpose against her opponents, to stirr [*sic*] up the lukewarm, and encourage those who are earnestly trying, it needs that the Head of the Diocese should somehow come into closer communication with its outskirts as a first step to the removal of difficulties which would be of far less importance could this be accomplished.

There seems to be, in that last remark a hint that Temple could do more and the subcommittee was not afraid of criticizing the bishop. Its views on the subject of schools were flatly opposed to those which the bishop had been known to favour in the past.[33] The report suggested that either there should be legislation to protect the subscriber by exempting him from the rate or 'a fund [should] be formed at once to assist poor schools'. In particular the Endowed Schools Commission should be persuaded to abandon the unjust policy of taking endowments from the very poor in order to create scholarships for the children of tradesmen.[34] Temple seems to have taken note. His own attitude on schools began to change and Earle was appointed as suffragan for the area.

Temple must have enjoyed meetings with the clergy even when there was plenty of vigorous debate for he multiplied their number. He held a regular monthly session with his suffragans and archdeacons (like a modern bishop's 'staff meeting')[35] and, in addition to the meetings held in each of the rural deaneries, he also convened a conference of rural deans.[36] The rural deanery conferences were surprisingly formal with hard and fast rules about who might attend and what should be discussed. At Exeter he had used the diocesan conference to air his own concerns and obtain the reactions of both clergy and laity. In London this process was formalized. Each deanery conference was to 'discuss all questions referred to it by the Bishop' and 'any other question brought before it by a Member, subject to the consent of the Rural Dean'.[37] Again and again the agenda papers reflect the bishop's own interests—voluntary schools in relation to board schools; the religious instruction of children; temperance; the reform of private patronage; rescue and penitentiary work; and even such matters as

[33] See below, 241–6.

[34] Lambeth Palace Library: Fulham Papers, F. Temple, vol. 45, fo. 128.

[35] Ibid., fo. 31.

[36] Ibid., fo. 6, a memorandum dated 8 July 1885, 'Diocese of London. Conference of Rural Deans'.

[37] Ibid., fo. 60.

'clear and thoughtful reading of lessons in church services'. Sometimes the topics which the clergy wanted to debate—should hymns be omitted to make confirmation services less tedious?—were precisely those which one would have expected Temple to have found supremely irritating. But he seems almost to have enjoyed them and to have seized every opportunity to have the last blunt word—'Cutting off hymns would make the Service *more* wearisome!'[38]

He was capable of pointedly ignoring what he thought were silly or inopportune expressions of opinion, but he seldom allowed himself to repress honest debate. And he frequently used the diocesan conference as a vehicle for expressing his own theology. In the very first session after his move from Exeter he addressed the conference on three important issues. The first of these—religious equality—showed how his own ideas were changing. In 1869 he had spoken publicly in favour of Irish disestablishment. Demands for disestablishment in Wales had begun soon afterwards and by the time he became Bishop of London had developed into furious disputes about education and the payment of tithes. For Temple to speak on religious equality in 1886 could hardly fail to be interpreted as a statement about establishment which he now defended in a somewhat unusual way. There were other nationalized (he did not, of course, use the term) corporations like the post office or the naval dockyards against which private companies were prevented by law from competing because the national interest required that there should be a state enterprise with the sole right to do the job. The national interest similarly required that the religious life of the country should be in the hands of the Church of England. It was a strange argument from a man who thought Gladstone un-Liberal on religion and interestingly Temple went on to deny that the Liberal Party was in any way committed to the principle of religious equality: 'They will hardly', he said, 'sacrifice the religious welfare of the nation because there are sectional interests that dislike the Church.'[39]

In the following year the Central Council of Diocesan Conferences appointed a subcommittee on 'Church Extension and Defence in England and Wales' in which Temple took an interest and which published a booklet entitled *A Popular Story of the Church in Wales: Its Past History; Its Present Work; The Agitation for Its Disestablishment* (price

---

[38] Ibid., fo. 10 f., 'Conference of Rural Deans'.
[39] Sandford (ed.), ii. 10.

sixpence).[40] And in 1893, when there was even greater pressure for Welsh disestablishment, he addressed a public meeting on the subject and spoke firmly against it.[41] This was, perhaps, another straw in the wind of his changing political attitudes.

The other two matters on which he addressed that first diocesan conference were apostolic succession and private patronage. On the latter subject his views showed no sign of change whatever. He delivered some forthright, trenchant remarks on the sale of advowsons 'A patron buys an advowson with a view of putting in some friend of his own, and he therefore considers the interest of his friend instead of the interest of the parish . . . we constantly see a round man put into a square hole.'[42] Yet, in spite of his intense dislike of the system he was extremely conscientious and patient in working with patrons and in helping them find suitable clergymen for key livings. Most of the fifty volumes of correspondence that survive from his years as bishop of London are about matters to do with clergy and the parishes—exchange of livings, the needs of the clergy, requests for confirmations or for episcopal permissions, complaints from parishioners and every conceivable aspect of the pastoral duties of the clergy. Some of them deal with appointments of incumbents and their curates, and among these are letters which show how good the bishop's relations were with conscientious patrons.[43]

On the apostolic succession his characteristically pre-Tractarian High Churchmanship was very evident. Having said that the doctrine really signified the 'continuous life which exists between the Church that now is and the Church of the Apostles' and that the continuity was principally a matter of 'those traditions, those feelings, that way of regarding things in relation to spiritual matters, which we look upon as so precious an inheritance', he insisted that these things were as much inherited through the laity as through the clergy.

The doctrine of the apostolic succession of the ministry, if it is understood to imply this continuity of the spiritual life, is in its right place; but if it is taught as a means of separating the clergy from the laity and giving them a position of

---

[40] Lambeth Palace Library: Fulham Papers, F. Temple, vol. 45, fos. 1 ff., Report of the Subcommittee on Church Extension and Defence in England and Wales, 1887, and fo. 7 letter from G. H. F. Nye, 31 Mar. 1890.

[41] Sandford (ed.), ii. 168 f.

[42] Ibid. ii. 11.

[43] e.g. Lambeth Palace Library: Fulham Papers, F. Temple, vol. 1, fos. 31–6.

their own, it will become a hard, unspiritual thing which will repel many noble minds...[44]

It seems that even some of the younger clergy in the diocese appreciated (in both senses of the word) occasional expressions of 'old-fashioned' High Churchmanship. One of them, who was some thirty years younger than his bishop, wrote to him in 1895:

I was brought up as a boy under the influence of what is now sometimes called the 'Old-Fashioned' High Church School; the School that venerated the Sacraments as God-ordained means of Grace, without the extreme ideas and advanced ritual of modern times. As your Lordship says most truly, I am 'not a party man' at all; and prefer to call myself a Churchman, without any qualifying adjective.

I...most fully believe in the reality of Sacramental Grace as well as in the Sacrificial View of the Eucharist set forth in such writings as those of Hooker and Waterland.

With regard to the Sacrament of Baptism I will only refer to the able and helpful exposition of its nature which your Lordship gave to the Clergy of the Deanery of Hackney some few years back, as interpreting and expressing what I believe to be the Truth.[45]

That letter suggests three things. First, that Temple's position was well understood. Secondly, by its reference to Hooker and Waterland, that it was a classical High Churchmanship of a very traditional kind. And, thirdly, that this variety of High Churchmanship survived long after it used to be thought that it had ceased to exist.

It was as well that Temple did not dislike meetings for this was a period in which the sheer volume of committee work was growing exponentially as the Church of England developed, for the first time, a central, national organization. Previously there had been very few ways for disseminating ideas, let alone instructions, to the Church as a whole. Only those matters which were so important that they could be embodied in legislation could be imposed on everyone. The monarch sometimes issued a royal letter proclaiming a day of national prayer and fasting or directing the clergy to make a collection for some charitable object. No one else was in a position to send a communication to every parish priest in the country. But in the nineteenth century dioceses developed a stronger corporate sense. The office of rural dean was

---

[44] Sandford (ed.), ii. 10 f.
[45] Lambeth Palace Library: Fulham Papers, F. Temple, vol. 1, fos. 33 f. letter from the Revd H. E. J. Bevan.

revived. Diocesan prayer leaflets began to be issued.[46] Embryonic machinery for consultation and even decision making were created. The Convocation of Canterbury had begun to do business again in 1852. Diocesan conferences came into existence and by the time that Temple was translated to London there was even something called a Central Council of Diocesan Conferences to co-ordinate their work. And in 1885, the very year in which he moved from Exeter, a 'house of laymen' with representatives chosen by the diocesan conferences was associated with each of the Convocations. The whole character of the Church of England had changed. It had become a single corporation in a way in which it had never been before. A conscientious bishop like Temple spent a very great deal of time attending meetings of rural deaneries, of the diocesan staff, of the diocesan conference, of Convocation, and of the bishops of both provinces at Lambeth. The diocese was also beginning to acquire a structure of boards and councils—a diocesan council of evangelization, a readers' board, a board of education. And then there were such other committees, organizations, charities, and societies as arose out of his particular experience or interests.

Archbishop Benson often worried about the failure of the bishops to attend meetings outside their own dioceses. In his opinion they were not fulfilling any role as what he called 'bishops of England' as opposed to being bishops of the dioceses. They were not conscientious about attending meetings of such corporations as the S. P. G. or the Sons of the Clergy. They were seldom present even in the House of Lords and on one occasion, in particular, Benson thought their absence scandalous. There had been a debate in the Lords on the employment in theatres of children under the age of ten, a practice which Benson had attacked vigorously.

> ... we were beaten only by 7, and it is lamentable to think and indefensible, that only 7 Bishops were wanted and that *none* were there but myself. They had been all specially summoned.[47]

It has to be said that Temple was not one of the very few bishops whom Benson singled out for praise. Only the Bishop of Carlisle, who had furthest to come, seemed to meet with his approbation.[48]

---

[46] R. A. Burns, 'A Hanoverian Legacy? Diocesan reform in the Church of England c. 1800–1833', in John Walsh, Colin Haydon, and Stephen Taylor (eds.) (Cambridge, 1993), 265 ff.

[47] Trinity College, Cambridge: E. W. Benson Papers, Official Diary 1889, 5 Aug.

[48] Ibid. 22 June.

Benson lamented the fact that Temple did not go down well in the Lords and partly blamed this on the fact that Temple spoke so seldom.

It is painful, very painful to see the Lords always so unappreciative of the Bishop of London—the strongest man nearly in the House, the clearest, the highest toned, the most deeply sympathetic, the clearest in principle—yet because his voice is a little harsh, and his accent a little provincial (though of what province it is hard to say), and his figure square and his hair a little rough, and because all this sets off the idea of his independence, he is not listened to at all by these cold, kindly, worldly wise, gallant powers.... There is something sickening in seeing the House of Lords with its regulated tones and silken manners, which are well able to express as much contempt and animosity and selfishness, as they are able to express if they choose kindness and sympathy and chivalry, utterly unaware that they have greatness and strength in the Bishop of London. They talk, they look, they laugh at any allowance against himself which he makes. But I cannot but believe that if he would only speak a little oftener he must impress even their complacencies.[49]

Benson, however, recognized that the Lords were a 'cold audience, which weighs *every* man, and weighs them by their words and their knowledge of the world and their temper... the most formidable audience man can have'.[50] It is, perhaps, unsurprising that Temple did not attend more often.

At the bishops' meetings and in Convocation he took, as Bishop of London, a very prominent part in proceedings as was required of him, as the senior bishop of the province. When the Archbishop of Canterbury was not able to attend a bishops' meeting it was often the Bishop of London rather than the Archbishop of York who took the chair.[51] Moreover, developing forms of administration and government for the Church, required staff and buildings for their functioning. Temple took a prominent part in planning and raising funds for Church House in Westminster and in deciding how it was to be owned and run.[52]

---

[49] Sandford (ed.), ii. 176.

[50] A. C. Benson, *Life of Edward White Benson* (London, 1900), ii. 308.

[51] One can only judge this by the handwriting in which the minutes of the meetings were recorded. What looks like Jackson's totally illegible hand appears in the minutes of the early meetings in Lambeth Palace Library: Bishops Meetings, BM2, up to the meeting of 4 Feb. 1880, when Tait's hand resumes. Temple certainly presided at the meeting of 18 and 19 June 1891 in the absence of Benson.

[52] Lambeth Palace Library: Fulham Papers, F. Temple, vol. 55, fos. 115–39 (mostly printed papers) relate to the Corporation of Church House. MS material is chiefly about problems in raising the necessary money.

Busy ecclesiastics were not yet used to dealing with the new machinery of government and the ways in which the layers of the pyramid
were interdependent: nor had the Church of England as a whole entirely
grown out of the older, more informal ways of doing business. Soon
after his arrival in London Temple informed the diocese that he did not
feel able to preside at a meeting of the diocesan conference until he was
'better acquainted with the Diocese, its needs and character'.[53] His first
session was therefore set for February 1886 and he simply directed that
the clerical and lay representatives elected in 1882 for the sessions of
1883, 1884, and 1885 would retain their seats till 1886. This had a knock-
on effect. Since representatives were elected for three years and 1885 had
been the third year, elections would have to be held after the session in
1886 for representatives to hold office for the years 1887, 1888, and 1889.
In July 1885 the Convocation of Canterbury had decided to create the
'Provincial House of Laymen' and a year later a printed notice was sent
to the bishops requiring them to arrange for the election of diocesan
representatives to it.[54] Benson also sent a hand-written letter to Temple
saying that the process must be completed by 1 August when parliament
and the Convocations would be ready to meet and that 'it would never
do for the H. of laymen to be non-existent till October or have such a
contingent lacking as that from the London Diocese'.[55] This meant that
the elections for the representatives to the diocesan conference would
have to be held in a great rush so that they could then elect from their
own number those who would be members of the house of laymen. On
24 July, with only a week to go to meet the archbishop's deadline, the
clerical secretary of the diocesan conference, who was responsible for
organizing the election, wrote to Temple to say that the lay members of
the diocesan conference had met that day and had unanimously asked
that the election be deferred until October. The rural deaneries had not
all yet made their returns and so the electing body was incomplete: there
was simply no way in which the London representatives to the house of
laymen could be chosen in time.[56]

There were other drawbacks, too, in creating opportunities for consultation, however modest. They provided greater opportunities for the
eccentric, the bombastic, the insane, the devious, and the power-hungry

---

[53] Lambeth Palace Library: Fulham Papers, F. Temple, vol. 46, fo. 16, letter to Archdeacon Hessey dated 27 Mar. 1885.
[54] Ibid., fos. 55 f., printed notice dated 1 July 1886.
[55] Ibid., vol. 46., fo. 59, letter dated 6 July 1886.
[56] Ibid., fo. 71, letter from the Revd Dr Thornton, dated 24 July 1886.

to indulge themselves. And at best the participation of the clergy in diocesan business meant that things were often more complicated than if the bishop had simply taken all decisions himself. The files are full of technical questions about who was entitled to vote, what the procedures ought to be, whether the rural deaneries ought to be reorganized so as to provide constituencies of more even size, whether the chaplaincies in Europe were entitled to be represented, whether the officers would need to be elected by a rural deanery or would be members of the diocesan conference *ex officio*.

It was inevitable that party should sooner or later become part of the new machinery. In 1890 the Catholic party, led by Canon Gregory of St Paul's and a layman called Murray, attempted to gain control of the general purposes committee of the diocesan conference. The Archdeacon of London was furious because Murray issued the invitation to his meeting on paper printed in exactly the same type as the official papers of the conference and held it in the chapter house. 'The unwary were thus completely taken in; nobody was there to represent the existing General Purposes Committee and all present were pledged to vote for the High Church list.' 'There never was such a complete Committee outside the rooms of the English Church Union.'[57] The clerical secretary was again the returning officer and tried to deal with the matter by suggesting that it should be referred to the new general purposes committee, forgetting that the successful party would be reviewing its own behaviour.[58] The scrutineers protested vigorously to Temple proposing that he should treat the election as 'vitiated'.[59] But the force of this protest was somewhat weakened by the fact that both scrutineers were also defeated candidates and Temple's note to his chaplain wisely said that he did not think it would be right to interfere.

---

[57] Ibid., fos. 140 ff., letter dated 2 May 1890 from William Sinclair, Archdeacon of London.

[58] Ibid.

[59] Ibid., fo. 138, letter from Cust to Temple, dated 1 May 1890.

9

Ceremonial, Schools, and Sweated Labour

During Temple's time as Bishop of London the number of Anglo-Catholic clergy was growing fairly rapidly. They were gaining a foothold in more parishes and establishing daughter churches. Perhaps the most famous of these was St Cuthbert's, Philbeach Gardens where the curate in charge was Henry Westall. A curious relationship was to develop between Temple and Westall. The bishop had little sympathy with the ceremonial which Anglo-Catholics were introducing but as a constitutionalist he was unwilling to forbid anything to which they might conceivably be entitled by law. With much of their theology of Church, Sacraments, and Ministry, Temple, at least in part still influenced by his early High Churchmanship, had a good deal of sympathy but they tended to bring out in him a half-amused ferocity. The priests concerned, and Westall probably more than most, seem to have enjoyed goading the bishop to see what they could get away with. The resultant atmosphere, almost of a game, reduced complaining Protestant laymen to helpless fury.

When Temple arrived in London, Westall had already been at Philbeach Gardens for three years. A new church was in process of being built and part of it had been adapted for use in the mean time. The district had been carved out of the parish of St Philip, Earls Court and the trustees of the new benefice included Liddon, Lord Coleridge (the Lord Chief Justice—Temple's old friend), and a leading Anglo-Catholic layman the Hon C. L. Wood (later Lord Halifax). The building itself cost rather more than £9,000, a considerable sum for those times, and had had a great deal of conspicuous artwork lavished on its interior. There were at least two masses every day and three on Sundays, with a Bible class 'for servants' on Thursday afternoons and the Stations of the Cross on Fridays.

Westall opened relations with the new bishop by sending him in November 1885 a small engraving of the church, a programme of Advent services and a note saying, 'I hope you will admire our Church, which [is] one of the handsomest I think in London.'[1] By 1887 the building was almost complete. Westall asked that it should be consecrated and an application was filed with the Ecclesiastical Commissioners for the creation of a new parochial district. Temple indicated that he would come on 26 November 1887.[2] Because he could not do a confirmation at the same time he suggested that Westall might like to invite some other bishop instead. Westall ignored the suggestion but, because the chosen date would fall in Advent, asked whether the bishop could possibly come a week earlier, celebrate at 8 a.m. and then preach in the evening. He knew, he said, that Temple believed that to celebrate the Holy Communion in a new church was 'the great consecration'. Temple agreed to consecrate the church and celebrate, without a sermon, at 8 a.m. on 14 November. So far all seemed reasonably amicable and Westall even invited Temple to stay to breakfast after the service.

Four days before the ceremony it was discovered that some of the legalities had not been completed and the church had not been in-spected by the archdeacon.[3] Westall, who had only himself to blame, was frantic. The service had been widely advertised. The programme had been printed. Preachers had been arranged including the Deans of Durham (Lake) and Manchester (J. Oakley), the Bishop of Colchester (Alfred Blomfield), Archdeacon Hessey, the famous Anglo-Catholic missioner Canon Body, and the Chaplain-General of the forces (John Cox Edghill, who had a possibly undeserved reputation as an 'advanced' High Churchman). Westall begged Temple to persuade the Ecclesiastical Commissioners to meet on the Saturday so that the new district could be legally constituted in time. Temple refused to be panicked. He told Westall to keep to the programme of special services and said that he would come on Friday 18 November to consecrate the building.[4]

Even Hessey was willing to respond to the urgency of the situation. He inspected the church and told Temple that it was quite ready for consecration.

It is a singularly beautiful and majestic building, and I think you cannot fail to be pleased with it. The font has not yet arrived but there is a temporary one.

[1] Lambeth Palace Library: Fulham Papers, F. Temple, vol. 20, fos. 48 ff.
[2] Ibid., fo. 67, letter dated 9 July 1887.
[3] Ibid., fo. 73, a rough note detailing the difficulties, dated 10 Nov.
[4] Ibid., fos. 75 f., letter from Westall dated 10 Nov. with Temple's draft reply on it.

There is a side chapel, which appeared, I am told, in the plan signed and approved by your predecessor. Indeed it is absolutely [necessary] whenever, as on most weekdays, there is a small and early congregation. The Church itself would be very difficult to light and warm for that purpose, and very expensive, besides which the people want keeping together.[5]

Westall was duly grateful but he asked, as if he simply could not resist seeing how far he could go, whether Temple would agree to omit morning prayer and the litany from the consecration service. The bishop allowed a testy note in his reply. 'I do not think it well to alter the service except as previously arranged by omitting the sermon.'[6]

All seems to have gone well on the day but almost at once complaints began to reach Fulham Palace. One Martin Brown wrote:

I think it only right your Lordship should know what kind of service took place at 11.30 this morning at St Cuthbert's Philbeach Gardens almost immediately after your Lordship's consecration of this Church . . . Before the High Mass—for such it closely resembled in every minute detail—began, there was a procession in which the Crucifer, and numerous Acolytes took part, boys wearing blood red cassocks & slippers to match—boys carrying lighted candles, a number of Priests bringing up the rear—the officiating Priest wearing biretta, *full Eucharistic vestments*—his investment being held on either side by a small boy. The Mass was rendered with full orchestral accompaniment—there were 64! lighted candles on the 'altar'—the lesser lights being ceremonially lighted whilst the service was proceeding—the elements were lifted up far above the priest's head—endless genuflections took place during the service—the introduction of the Agnus Dei was a special feature in the service, to which much attention was paid—the bell was tolled at the Consecration prayer—and a small bell rung at another part of the service—the sign of the cross was made at various parts of the service—and the ceremonial mixing of the water with the wine, was done with much ostentation, and the ablutions at the close, occupied a considerable time. There was *much incensing* at different parts of the Mass, and acolytes bearing tall lighted candles came in at one part of the service—and there was much posturing and genuflecting throughout.[7]

Temple drafted a reply rather more fully than was his usual practice:

I regret as much as you do that there should be clergy who depart from the usages customary in the Ch of Eng. But there is a considerable number of laity

---

[5] Lambeth Palace Library: Fulham Papers, F. Temple, vol. 20, fos. 81 f., Hessey's report dated 15 Nov.

[6] Ibid., fo. 83.

[7] Ibid., fos. 85 ff., letter from W. Martin Brown dated 18 Nov. 1887. The writer's familiarity with all the technical terms is significant.

who support them. And majority of the laity as represented in parliament always steadily refuse to give the Bishops effectual power to interfere. A Bishop can do nothing which anyone may not equally do, namely, prosecute in the Ecclesiastical Courts. He may remonstrate but remonstrances not backed by power soon come to nothing.

There was worse to come. On 1 December Alexander Cobham, chairman of the Church Association (an organization founded to eradicate ritualism), sent a similar protest to Temple, more or less confirming the accuracy of the account given by Brown but extending the complaints so as to include the bishop himself.

On Friday morning November 18th your Lordship consecrated St Cuthbert's Church, Philbeach Gardens, and took part therein as 'principal Minister' at the celebration of the Holy Communion. During that service at which your Lordship so officiated Lights were burnt upon the Lord's Table, the sign of the Cross was made in the air with the chalice before offering it to each Communicant, a bell was tolled thrice at the words 'This is my Body', and again at the words 'This is my Blood', whereupon the Vicar-Designate, who was previously kneeling, prostrated himself so that his head apparently touched the step. In distributing the remains of the Consecrated Elements, the same gentleman knelt before each person while the bread and wine were being consumed. All this took place in your Lordship's presence, and you doubtless will have taken cognisance of the large crucifix suspended on the south wall of the chancel.[8]

Part of Cobham's complaint was that Temple had disciplined an Evangelical clergyman called Greenland who had behaved unlawfully, but would not act against the 'flagrant' illegalities of the Anglo-Catholics.

Temple's reply to Brown was published in an Evangelical newspaper alongside his letter threatening to inhibit Greenland.[9] The whole thing began to look like a prearranged trap and the protesters had, of course, done the one thing likely to make Temple furious. He ignored their letters. Cobham wrote on 20 December and again on the following day. Then, at last, came Temple's reply containing the characteristic passage:

Now I certainly do not consider myself called on to discuss the discharge of my duties in the newspapers. And if anyone publishes a letter to me or a letter from me on such a subject without my permission, my correspondence with him is always closed at once.[10]

---

[8] Ibid., fos. 90 f. letter dated 1 Dec. 1887, written in clerk's copperplate on official paper of the Church Association and signed by Alex W. Cobham.

[9] Ibid., fo. 92.

[10] The draft reply appears on the reverse of fo. 104, Cobham's letter of 21 Dec.

Everyone was behaving a little disingenuously. The Church Association was carefully orchestrating a growing volume of protest by means of which it hoped to compel the bishop to take action. The parish of Tottenham, for instance, presented him with a petition couched in overheated language which compared Temple with the 'Israelitish people of old' who would not choose between God and the Baals.[11] Temple reiterated to other correspondents his complaint that the bishops were unable to take action because parliament would not give them effective powers.[12] The truth was, however, that imprisoning ritualist clergymen for refusing to obey secular courts had proved a huge embarrassment. Tait and Jackson had agreed in 1882 that they would effectively veto every attempt at further prosecutions and the other bishops had followed suit.[13] Westall was sent for by Temple and asked to explain the crucifix about which Cobham had complained and which the bishop had been held to have condoned. He said that he had 'forgotten' that, at the time of the archdeacon's inspection, it had been hanging at the west end of the church.[14]

Complaints about St Cuthbert's continued to come in to Fulham Palace for several years. Temple refused to take action. Westall went on trying to manœuvre him into approving or allowing what was being done by pretending that he really wanted something else but did not like to ask for it.[15] The bishop's tactic was to try and prevent Westall from getting what he really wanted by giving him exactly what he had asked for.[16] The games-playing went on and the controversy, in a sense, was never settled. Westall and Temple were to confront each other again.[17]

The bishop was involved in another matter of 'ritualism' which must have seemed to him like *déjà vu*. A new reredos containing a crucifix had been erected in St Paul's Cathedral and in April 1888 the Church Association presented the bishop with a memorial containing some 9,000 signatures asking that he should proceed against the dean and

---

[11] The draft reply appears on the reverse of fos. 107 ff.

[12] e.g. ibid., fo. 121, Temple to Emma Falkner, letter dated Jan. 1888.

[13] Owen Chadwick, *The Victorian Church*, 2 vols. (London, 1966/70), ii. 349.

[14] Lambeth Palace Library: Fulham Papers, F. Temple, vol. 20, fo. 113, Westall to Temple 27 Dec. 1887.

[15] Ibid., fo. 123 f., letter from Westall dated 23 Apr. 1888 and fo. 130, letter from Westall dated 13 June 1889.

[16] See Temple's reply on fo. 130.

[17] See below, 277–8.

chapter in the archbishop's court. There were widespread protests, some of them very highly coloured. One of his correspondents wrote:

...I love the Church of my fathers, and recognize in it a section of that spiritual temple, even the Body of our Lord Jesus Christ, which can boast of a noble army of martyrs, whose very blood calls to us from Smithfield and Oxford to maintain in its entirety our Protestant Reformed faith of which the Bible is its standard and the Prayer Book [and] its admirable XXXIX Articles its formula...May God help your Lordship to hold aloft the Bible as the religion of Protestants and so help by your prayerful determination to resist the tide of Romish error & practice which is coming in like a flood upon us.[18]

Excited remonstrance of that kind did not move Temple. He replied that he did not agree with such a 'view of true Protestantism. I see nothing inconsistent with Protestantism in such a Reredos as it is proposed to erect in St Paul's Cathedral. And the Courts of Law have so decided.' He was, in fact, harking back to the Exeter case, in which his own initial judgement had been overturned. He regarded himself as bound to obey that earlier decision: it would be unconstitutional for him to forbid the chapter to do what the courts had allowed.

Archbishop Benson thought, in fact, that Temple had explained too much. On 26 May he wrote in his diary:

Bishop of London's reply to the memorialists who remonstrate foolishly against the reredos of St Paul's as idolatrous, and belabour him to have a case heard in my court. He declines, but I think argues rather too much in declining. Unreasonable people must have their unreason negatived—but neither they nor the reasonable ones are grateful or forwarded by argument.[19]

The protesters then applied to the Queen's Bench, where a majority of the judges including Lord Coleridge, were willing to grant a *mandamus* which would have required Temple to proceed with the case. On appeal, however, which eventually went to the House of Lords, it was held that the bishop's discretion was absolute and that he could not be compelled. This decision was not reached until 1891. In the meantime Temple agreed to go to St Paul's to dedicate the offending reredos.

The chapter at St Paul's was in some ways a great centre of moderate Anglo-Catholic opinion. R. W. Church had been the Dean since 1871

[18] Lambeth Palace Library: Fulham Papers, F. Temple, vol. 41, fos. 53 f., letter from V. Taylor dated 17 Aug. 1888: fos. 35–219 of vol. 41 are all devoted to the matter of the reredos.
[19] A. C. Benson, *The Life of Edward White Benson, Sometime Archbishop of Canterbury*, 2 vols. (London, 1900), ii. 282.

and was by this time seventy-three. He had been a colleague and close friend of Newman's in the 1840s and, as junior proctor at Oxford for the academic year 1844/5, had vetoed the attempt to strip Newman of his degrees. He was regarded as, and in a real sense was, a figure from an earlier era in the Church's history. Gregory, leader of the 'Catholic' party in the diocesan conference who would succeed Church as Dean, was the treasurer and had put the fabric of the cathedral in good order. H. P. Liddon, the person who had first launched the attack on *Essays and Reviews*, was the chancellor. Scott Holland, one of the younger Anglo-Catholics and a member of the group which would produce *Lux Mundi* in the following year, was the precentor.[20] They were, perhaps, anxious to bind Temple to their cause. Dean Church wrote to him to say that they would be willing to help with his legal expenses in the case before the courts.[21] Temple, however, was not easy to manipulate. When Scott Holland let the bishop know what the plans were for what he called the 'opening' of the reredos he made it all sound as un-ritualistic as possible. The chapter would meet the bishop at the west door and escort him into the cathedral during the introit. There would be no actual form of blessing of the reredos itself and only the most modest additions to the Communion office. The Te Deum would be sung with the bishop standing before the altar and the chapter below him, facing east.[22] But Canon Gregory was indiscreet enough to refer to 'the ablutions' which provoked Temple into demanding to be told, 'What are the ablutions?' Gregory tried to divert him by saying that they would not really be going beyond 'our little humble washing of the cup and paten'.[23] Temple was not to be diverted: the washing would be better done, if done, after the clergy had left the church.

An unexpected by-product of the controversy was that it made Temple, for a brief while, the hero of the English Church Union. Letters came in from all over the country thanking him for the firm stand he had taken in exercising the episcopal veto against the attempted prosecution. He was also praised for defying those who wished to banish art from churches. The Norfolk branch of the English Church Union sent him a copy of resolution which it had adopted, thanking him for 'his forcible and out-spoken utterance as to the breadth and simplicity

[20] Lambeth Palace Library: Fulham Papers, F. Temple, vol. 41, fo. 12, letter from Church to Temple, 11 Oct. 1886.

[21] Ibid., fo. 129, letter from Church to Temple, 11 June 1888.

[22] Ibid., fos. 61 ff. letters from Scott Holland, 16 Jan. 1889.

[23] Ibid., fos. 63 f., letter from Gregory undated.

of the principles of the Reformation, and his confident appeal to the commonsense of ordinary religious Englishmen in the matter of the figure of our Lord upon the Cross'.[24] It may have been because of this support from the English Church Union that Temple gained a reputation as someone who protected ritualists by persistent use of the episcopal veto. The Sandford *Memoir* went to some lengths to defend him against the charge, pointing out that the reredos case was the only one which he had ever vetoed.[25] The truth was that he thought that litigation almost always made the situation worse. Captain Cobham was tireless in drawing his attention to Anglo-Catholic illegalities and he was the one person against whom Temple's favourite policy of masterly inaction never worked. If Cobham received no reply to a letter, he wrote again immediately, and continued to write until he provoked some kind of response. One of his letters complained that Temple's refusal to take action against ritualists amounted to 'a deliberate abandonment of the duties belonging to his high office'. It received the reply, 'The Bishop of London is much obliged by being informed of the view which Captain Cobham takes of the duty of a Bishop.'[26]

At much the same time as the St Paul's reredos was attracting public attention, Bishop King of Lincoln was prosecuted for certain ceremonial practices which were alleged to be contrary to the law. When King had been appointed, at about the time when Temple had been translated to London, Davidson had described him as likely to make a good bishop because of 'his unassuming manners and his power of ready sympathy'.[27] It had proved to be an extremely accurate prophecy. At Lincoln he quickly earned for himself a reputation as a saintly, pastoral bishop, who was known to take a direct and personal interest in prisoners, the poor, and the sick. He was accessible as few Victorian bishops were. Davidson's report to the Queen had been correct, too, in describing him as far from extreme. His style was more like that of the early Tractarians and he was not over-concerned about ceremonial.[28]

The complaints against King were brought by the Church Association. It was, in a sense, a last determined effort on the part of that body. Its funds had been considerably depleted by its earlier efforts which had, themselves, turned out to be somewhat self-defeating.

---

[24] Lambeth Palace Library: Fulham Papers, F. Temple, vol. 41, fo. 126.
[25] Sandford (ed.), ii. 112.
[26] Ibid. ii. 110.
[27] See above, 196.
[28] J. A. Newton, *Search for a Saint: Edward King* (London, 1977), 58 ff.

Ritualist clergymen had been willing to go to prison rather than accept the rulings of courts which they regarded as purely secular tribunals and the resulting embarrassment had led to the bishops' refusal to allow further prosecutions. Courageously the Association decided to carry the fight into the enemy's camp and to prosecute King in a court which was outside the normal judicial structures, the archbishop's own court of special jurisdiction over his suffragans. That court could not be rejected by the High Churchmen as Erastian and incompetent.

Benson was in a difficult position. He did not belong to any particular Church party but he was certainly no rabid Protestant. Tradition, beauty, and order mattered to him enormously. Moreover it would require considerable fortitude to find against one of his fellow bishops and risk serious division in the Church. He had particular links with Lincoln, where he had been a canon of the cathedral during the episcopate of King's predecessor Christopher Wordsworth (the chief objector at Temple's consecration). Moreover, this was not the Church Association's first attempt on King. In an earlier case, the Bishop of Lincoln had vetoed an attempt to prosecute a clergyman in his diocese and the Association had appealed unsuccessfully to Benson then. A further refusal on the part of the archbishop to take any action might look like partisan behaviour. Yet King and his supporters were deeply upset by any suggestion that the archbishop should proceed to hear the case. King felt that he could not do his normal work properly with the case hanging over him. His friends were convinced that Benson ought to use his veto to stop the prosecution. But Benson was convinced that he must proceed. He engaged in a great deal of negotiation behind the scenes to convince everyone that it was better to constitute the court than to exercise any supposed archiepiscopal discretion.[29] The court itself, however, was of a somewhat dubious kind. It had only been invoked once since the Reformation and then in a very different kind of case. The prosecution was widely regarded as mischievous: there was some popular sympathy for King but little for his opponents.

There were other problems, too. King believed that he had a duty to maintain obedience to the 'Catholic' tradition rather than to the law as it applied to the National Church. The archbishop wrote in his diary 'The Bishop of Lincoln's point apparently is that he extends liberty by breaking the law—very sad!' His own opinion was:

---

[29] See e.g. Trinity College Cambridge: E. W. Benson Papers, Official Diary 1888, entries for 3–5 Aug.

That our Church of England was free to make her own orders as to rites and ceremonies, and that she had made them; that they commanded our obedience and were not to be altered into conformity with the usages of another Church; that her dignity and our loyalty were engaged; that we are free to use other means, argument, preaching, and writing, to get the law altered; that this freedom was especially English, but the liberty to break the law was not real liberty, nor an English habit.[30]

But King told the clergy of his diocese:

...it is not, and it has never been, my desire to enforce any unaccustomed observance on an unwilling congregation; but my hope now is that this prosecution may, in God's providence, be so overruled as ultimately to promote the peace of the Church by leading to some authoritative declaration of tolerance for certain details of ritual observance, in regard to which I believe that they are either in direct accordance with the letter of the Prayer Book, or at least in loyal and perfect harmony with the mind of the Church of England.[31]

King also issued a formal protest against the form of the court. He claimed that *all* the bishops of the province should sit together to try one of their number whereas Benson was convinced that he should be the only judge. In spite of the dubious precedent he must ensure that the lawyers were satisfied that it was the *archbishop's* court. He had also to persuade the High Churchmen that he, as Metropolitan, was exercising a purely spiritual jurisdiction over a bishop of the province. To do that he must sit *in person* for allowing one of his legal officials to appear on his behalf would run the risk of making the court appear to be part of the secular legal system. Moreover the Judicial Committee of the Privy Council, when asked by Benson to determine whether he really possessed 'the doubtful looking jurisdiction', had agreed that he had but must exercise it in person on account of the bishop's dignity.[32] The best compromise seemed to be for Benson to sit as the only *judge* but to appoint five of the bishops of the province as assessors—Temple, Stubbs of Oxford, Thorold of Rochester, John Wordsworth of Salisbury, and Browne of Winchester. The last of these was not well enough to act and his place was taken by Atlay of Hereford.

The trial began at Lambeth on 23 July 1889. Benson seems almost to have enjoyed the whole thing, in spite of the obvious stress which it placed upon him. He enjoyed deciding how much formality and

[30] A. C. Benson, ii. 325.
[31] W. E. Russell, *Edward King, Sixtieth Bishop of Lincoln* (London, 1912), 166 f.
[32] Trinity College, Cambridge: E. W. Benson Papers, Official Diary 1888, 3 Aug.

ceremonial there should be;[33] what he should wear; and the sheer intricacy of the scholarship which he needed in order to decide the issues. King was accused of performing certain actions during the celebration of the Holy Communion which were unlawful in terms of the directions of the Prayer Book. They were: mixing water with the wine in the chalice *during the service* and then consecrating the mixed cup; facing east during the first part of the service, with his back to the congregation; standing on the west side of the altar during the consecration prayer so that the congregation could not see the manual acts being performed; causing the hymn *Agnus Dei* to be sung after the consecration prayer; performing the ablutions of the chalice and paten at the end of the service and in the presence of the congregation; using lighted candles—which were not needed for the purpose of giving light—on the altar, or on the retable behind it, during the service; making the sign of the cross with an upraised hand, facing the congregation, during the absolution and the blessing.

It is difficult to discover just how much part Temple played in the decisions arrived at by the archbishop's court, though the Sandford *Memoir* said that it was 'an open secret' that he was Benson's principal adviser throughout the hearing.[34] Interventions made and questions asked by the assessors during the formal proceedings do not necessarily imply any significant effect on the findings. The question is whether the assessors really influenced the archbishop's thinking and it is not easy to discover what went on behind the scenes—whenever, for instance, they were free to express an opinion whenever they wished to do so or whether they were able to offer advice to the archbishop only when he asked for it.

Stubbs, the Bishop of Oxford and a serious professional historian, is the person whom one would have expected to be most at home in these issues. Davidson, who thought that Temple's behaviour at the opening session was 'admirable'—'strong and clear and helpful'—described Stubbs as 'quietly sneering and carping at the whole thing from the strength of his very conscious omniscience'.[35] And it is probable, in any case, that the archbishop thought of *himself* as the real expert on many of the matters raised. Benson's diary is unhelpful. For one thing it tends

[33] A. C. Benson, ii. 348.
[34] Sandford (ed.), ii. 54.
[35] G. K. A. Bell, *Randall Davidson, Archbishop of Canterbury*, 2 vols., 2nd edn. (London 1938), i. 135.

to be, like most diaries, self-concerned. It is Benson's own thoughts rather than what other people said which occupies most of the space. The archbishop said that he found the case so distasteful that he did not want to keep his own account of what happened: it was enough that there was an official record.[36] This did not prevent his writing at length from time to time about what he regarded as the illogicalities of King's arguments or attitudes but he rarely mentioned the discussions that took place with the assessors behind the scenes. One of the very few instances relates to an early point which the court had to determine, whether a bishop was a 'minister' in terms of the Prayer Book rubrics. On this point the archbishop had some doubts about the Bishop of Salisbury's opinion but thought that the other assessors were sound.[37] And a day later he described Stubbs as amending the precise wording of the court's decision in the matter. Wordsworth had 'held that a Bishop is bound in honour to observe the rubrics but not in law. But there is not in him, as the Bp of London says "one atom of law".' That hints at a discussion between Benson, Stubbs, Wordsworth, and Temple but is not enough to allow one to form an impression of how significant Temple's role in the whole matter was. There is little else to go on.

It is interesting to note that that particular entry in Benson's diary ends with the words, 'The country would have been indignant if we had not found a Bishop to be a Minister—to be outside the law.' It shows that the archbishop clearly had an eye upon what was politically acceptable as well as what was strictly legal. It would have been extremely helpful to know whether Temple concurred in such an attitude. He was later to arrive at findings of his own which paid little regard to anything other than what he thought the law required.[38] On the crucial matter of whether breaking the law was conducive to the increase of liberty, however, he was of exactly the same opinion as Benson.

Weighing the actual charges involved two kinds of scholarly enquiry. There were, first of all, general issues of canon law—whether the rubrics were legally enforceable requirements or no more than general directions as to the kind of action which was appropriate; or whether a bishop possessed the authority to perform, or to permit others to perform, liturgical actions not provided for in the rubrics. For issues

---

[36] A. C. Benson, ii. 353.
[37] Trinity College, Cambridge: E. W. Benson Papers, Official Diary 1889, 23 July.
[38] See below, 257–8.

of that kind the archbishop had to examine medieval and, where possible, primitive precedent. But on matters of liturgical detail, because the Judicial Committee of the Privy Council in earlier ritualist cases had taken the view that rubrics were, in effect, clauses in an act of parliament, there had also to be an examination of the post-Reformation history of the Church of England. Because High Churchmen looked behind the Reformation to the early and medieval church and because Evangelicals regarded the Reformation as the real beginning of the Church of England, the historical enquiry had to be carefully balanced. It would be virtually useless unless it were recognized by all the parties as relevant to the issue. The High Church party had to be persuaded to recognize that the post-Reformation history of the Church of England had a bearing on the way nineteenth century 'Catholic' priests and bishops ought to behave. The Low Church party had to be persuaded that the liturgical and canon-law traditions of the pre-Reformation Church were relevant to what happened in the Church of England in their own day.

The archbishop did not deliver his judgement until towards the end of 1890, nearly eighteen months after the actual hearing. The laconic entry in his diary—'Delivered Judgment in Lincoln Case'[39]—hid the fact that he was immensely proud of the scholarship displayed. The judgement went against the Bishop of Lincoln on the matter of the mixing of the chalice and the use of the sign of the cross at the blessing and absolution. He was told that it was not enough that he did not intend to hide the manual acts at the consecration: he must intend that they should be visible. And there were various *obiter dicta* unpalatable to the High Churchmen, such as Benson's opinion that anything that gave the ablutions the appearance of being part of the service—which, as he pointed out, was not in question in the case—would be illegal. On most other points, including the eastward position and the use of lights, his findings were in King's favour.

There was general agreement among the learned that the judgement displayed considerable and accurate scholarship. Benson himself seems to have been chiefly concerned to achieve two things. First, to demonstrate that an understanding of the historical context was essential for the proper interpretation of the rubrics. And, secondly, to establish that judgements of the Privy Council could be reversed.[40] Ironically, the

---

[39] Trinity College, Cambridge: E. W. Benson Papers, Official Diary 1890, 21 Nov.
[40] Bell, i. 149.

Church Association appealed to the Privy Council which did not deliver its judgement until 2 August 1892. The archbishop received a telegram saying, 'Their Lordships upheld the decision of your Grace's court in all its findings and dismisses appeal on all points. Judgement unanimous'.[41] He was jubilant and characteristically delighted by the congratulatory letters he received.

Temple himself seems to have been ambivalent towards Benson's findings in matters of detail. He appears to have argued fiercely with the archbishop about the position of the celebrant in the Communion service and, in the end, decided loyally that he must simply hold his tongue and not dissent from the archbishop's judgement.[42] He would not change his own practice of celebrating at the north end, even in churches where it was usual for the celebrant to face east. When he was present, he expected his clergy to conform to his practice. (He was equally adamant in saying the full words of administration to each communicant and in delivering the cup into the communicants *hands*.) He would not, as he made clear to Canon Gregory, permit the ablutions to be done during the service. Yet he loyally expounded the judgement to his clergy, giving a little historical excursus on each of the seven points of ceremonial covered by the judgement, in a way that suggests that he had absorbed much of Benson's technique as well as the conclusions to which he had come. But he made it quite clear that he did not intend the clergy to regard the archbishop's findings as a positive direction to indulge in more elaborate ceremonial. He said very firmly that no priest ought to change the customs of his parish without securing the bishop's approval. Where Benson had declared some practice to be permissible, and a priest had come to believe that it was what the rubrics directed, Temple would probably approve its adoption. The essential thing was for the clergy to get his consent. 'In thus acting they were entrenching themselves in a perfectly secure position, seeing that without the Bishop's sanction no one could prosecute them.'[43] He was anxious to avoid anything like a witch-hunt. He told his rural deans that there was to be no inquisition about matters of ceremonial and that they should only report matters to the bishop if they received complaints from parishioners.[44] But what he really felt about ritualism may

---

[41] Trinity College, Cambridge: E. W. Benson Papers, Official Diary 1892, 2 Aug.
[42] Sandford (ed.), ii. 663 ff.
[43] Ibid. ii. 54 f.
[44] Lambeth Palace Library: Fulham Papers, F. Temple, vol. 45, fo. 8.

be revealed by the fact that he told the rural deans that they were to behave in exactly the same way about lazy or neglectful clergymen.

He was equally ambivalent about the application of the law. He thought that there was nothing to be gained by prosecutions: they only made things worse. It worried him that so many of the ritualists were people of deep spirituality and moral integrity. Yet he always believed, with unexpected naïvety, that if the bishops were firm and clear about what the law *said*, illegality would soon disappear. He could not understand why others did not share his enthusiasm for legality nor why ritualists agreed with King's opinion that to break the law was to extend their freedom.

Temple's ambivalence, however, did not mean he was inconsistent. With religious communities he was often unexpectedly sympathetic but always insisted that they were to do what the bishop required of them. At the very first of the bishops' meetings which he attended after being nominated to London the whole matter of the relationship between the episcopate and the growing number of religious communities in the Church of England had been thoroughly discussed. The bishops had been insistent that there should be an episcopal visitor for every community (most communities had one already) and that he should normally be the bishop of the diocese in which the mother house was situated. They had also been anxious that no 'external work' (work done, presumably, outside the community's houses) should be undertaken without the bishop's permission. And they were very dubious about vows taken for life.[45]

As Bishop of London, Temple was to have a difficult time with the Sisters of the Church at Kilburn, whose patron he had been invited to become in 1892. Having heard nothing but good of their work, he accepted the position. Up to this point he had been helpful and sympathetic. The warden of the community wrote to him in 1890 to ask whether the sisters might be professed publicly and wear a ring to symbolize their profession. The warden had himself been accustomed to hear the vows until he had discovered that Bishop Jackson felt strongly that life-long religious profession was improper in the Church of England. He had then discontinued the practice but the sisters, he

---

[45] Lambeth Palace Library: Fulham Papers, F. Temple, vol. 45, fo. 8., Minutes of Bishops' Meetings, BM3, loose pages numbered 1 to 5, Report of committee on relations of sisterhoods and brotherhoods to the episcopate, inserted at minutes of meeting on 2 Feb. 1885.

said, longed for it to be reinstituted. Temple used his favourite tactic. He wrote nothing to the warden and put 'Nil' on every letter. But he seems, by word of mouth or by not actually forbidding things, to have allowed the custom to begin again. When he was thanked for permitting the professions he did not protest or demur. Nor did he raise any objection when, in May 1891, he was thanked by the warden for approving a revised form of service for the profession of a novice.[46]

But two years later Temple began to hear rumours, which were rife at the time, that the sisters were paying £40 for each illegitimate child handed over to them. The mother superior proved evasive when Temple tried to discover what was the truth of the matter. By November of 1894 the bishop had not only obtained a copy of an offensive circular in which the sisters advertised for such children but also had heard about the conditions in which the children were kept, virtually imprisoned in wire cages. He wished to send the Bishop of Marlborough to inspect the house. The sisters objected not only to the bishop but to every other inspector whom Temple suggested and finally on 25 January 1895 they wrote to say that 'they had determined to dispense with all Patrons (including Abp: of York and me) on the grounds that they did not wish their friends to bear any of the unpopularity which in these days attended their philanthropic efforts. All the time I kept receiving letters from former orphans and others representing partly the great kindness, partly the severity of the sisters.'[47] In fact he took no notice of the decision to discontinue the office of patron, the mother superior herself recognized the importance of having a full enquiry, and in the end the sisters' statutes were amended and Temple, as bishop of the diocese for the time being, was made visitor of the house.

It is clear, in fact, that had it not been for the unfortunate business of the sisters apparently buying illegitimate children, Temple's relations with them would have been perfectly happy and straightforward. There were other religious communities in the diocese and he seems not to have had any problems with them. The community of the Sisters of the Faith at Stoke Newington seem to have had a particularly happy and trusting relationship with the bishop even when there were problems

---

[46] Ibid., Fulham Papers, F. Temple, vol. 48, fos. 330–8, letters from the Revd W. H. Cleaver.

[47] Ibid., fo. 296. This is evidently Temple's own summary (but dictated, for it is not his handwriting) of his difficulties with the sisters. Fos. 296–349 all relate to the Sisters of the Church. See also Minutes of Bishops' Meetings, BM3, 19 June 1895, for memorandum describing Benson's dealings as archbishop, with the same community.

relating to children left in their care.[48] And his dealings with the Convent of St Mary at Twickenham were equally comfortable and untroubled. Perhaps because women's religious communities tended to ask permission and to do what the bishop asked that they should do, he was normally genial and relaxed with them. But when he felt that they were being difficult or insisting on going their own way, he reacted to them much as he reacted to ritualist clergymen.

Temple seems to have been particularly upset about the activities of the Kilburn sisters because he had initially been so pleased with their work among the poorest in his diocese. He always had a reputation for being sympathetic to 'working' people. He was known to favour state pensions for the elderly.[49] After he became archbishop he gave public support to co-operatives in which workers were also partners in the business. And there are anecdotes about his generosity and his willingness to go out of his way to help the disadvantaged.[50] But hard evidence which would enable one to make a proper assessment of just what that reputation rested on is simply not available. There are letters amongst his correspondence from East End parishes, and from districts like Fulham and Paddington where there were some very poor areas; and from charitable institutions and workhouses; but it is difficult to discover whether he had clear ideas about the nature and causes of poverty in London or ideas about what might be done. The Sandford *Memoir* has a chapter about 'social problems' in Temple's London years. Most of the matters with which it deals are what Temple himself regarded primarily as moral issues—temperance, prostitution, and the kind of stage performances which 'suggest what had better not be suggested'[51]—though many of them were closely related to poverty and unemployment. (He particularly disliked 'the ballet', saying 'When you have persuaded the ballet-dancers to practise their art in proper clothing the case will be altered.'[52])

When he dealt directly with social and political issues, he showed absolutely no sentimentality. He recognized the complexity of problems of poverty and unemployment:

The choice is constantly this: Shall a man get wages on which he cannot live, or no wages at all? I think he ought, in that alternative, to get no wages at all; for

[48] Lambeth Palace Library: Fulham Papers, F. Temple, vol. 45, fos. 350–9.
[49] Chadwick, ii. 285.
[50] e.g. Sandford (ed.), ii. 179.
[51] Ibid. ii. 130.
[52] Ibid.

then he will be driven to transfer his labour to some place where he can get wages on which he can live. The principle for which I would contend is this, that if a man employs another man he must give him wages on which he can live; but there are businesses I fear which would cease to exist if this principle were universally adopted, and the workers in them would get nothing. I think it imperative always to bear this in mind.[53]

That statement probably reveals the weakness in his attitude. He could deal with issues clearly and directly when he looked at them as questions of personal morality: he found it much more difficult—as did most churchmen of his day—to recognize that there were questions of morality implicit in social conditions and political programmes. In a public address delivered in Birmingham towards the end of his time in London he compared the behaviour of tramps—who spent the summer in the country 'looking for work' and the winter in London calling themselves 'the unemployed'—with the behaviour of the upper classes who also got out of the city in the summer months.[54] To the twentieth century eye this seems insensitive but neither the editor of the *Memoir*, nor the contributor of the section concerned, seem at all uneasy about Temple's attitude. It is always difficult for those who believe in the importance of market forces to recognize that freedom is more accessible to the rich than to the poor.

At about the same time as his Birmingham speech Temple also delivered a lecture, in his own diocese, on the clergy and party politics. He might have been expected to take the simple and obvious line that the former should avoid the latter. In fact, his premiss was that clergymen were primarily 'ambassadors of Christ' and that there would be times when that role would decidedly require them to engage in political matters. But they had also to remember that they must not gratuitously offend those whom they were meant to help.

In a word, the clergyman will join in politics in his capacity as an ambassador for Christ, and, consequently there will be a place and a time when in that character he will leave politics aside to speak of something that must be always for him, and for all men, higher than any politics whatsoever.[55]

On the whole, however, he was not enthusiastic about organizations. Because he believed very strongly that helping the poor must be done secretly, he disliked any sort of public campaign, like that of the

---

[53] Ibid. ii. 126.
[54] Ibid. ii. 126 f.
[55] Ibid. ii. 133.

Salvation Army, the Anti-Sweating League, or other bodies who had a policy or programme for solving the problems of poverty in the capital. Most programmes he found too simplistic and likely to make things worse. Help must be directed towards those individuals who could be counted on to do their own best to improve themselves. Large-scale schemes, he thought, would discourage self-improvement and would be mischievous. Yet there were some organizations which, having once convinced him of their value, he supported enthusiastically and vigorously. The Church of England Temperance Society and other such bodies, for obvious reasons, received his whole-hearted support. But it is not always easy to know why he chose to back some organizations and not others. Both he and Beatrice, for instance, became involved with the Colonial Emigration Society which recruited lower middle-class young women, who had no 'prospects' of job or marriage in England, and arranged for them to go to Canada and elsewhere.[56] Well-intentioned, no doubt, this organization was curiously innocent about the immense social problems involved in such an undertaking. It is odd that the bishop, whose critical eye detected so many flaws in the manifestos of so many other charities, expressed no doubts about this scheme.

The most important of the social issues in which Temple became involved was the London Dock Strike of 1889. It is one of the great puzzles about the bishop's life, like his immediate reaction to the storm over *Essays and Reviews* or his behaviour in the period between his nomination to Exeter and his consecration. It seems curious that so decided and blunt a person, about whose courage there can be little doubt, should have behaved in what seems so ineffectual a way.

The strike began on 14 August and lasted for a month. It was a very tense time in the country generally and Christian leaders were anxious about the possibility of serious social and political disorder. On 21 August Benson wrote in his diary:

Spurgeon [the eminent preacher and theologically conservative Baptist leader] told me the other day that Lord Shaftesbury had said to him 'You will see the streets of London swim with blood'. Spurgeon had said in answer 'I think not', and he remarked on the [illegible word] of people who in some form or other are trying to do good. There is abundant evil among rich people of rank—enough to bring a revolution if it stood alone: and they are not much worse than some other classes. But the difference is that in Paris it did stand alone. The

[56] Lambeth Palace Library: Fulham Papers, F. Temple, vol. 48, fos. 193 ff.

piety of the pious did not touch it. The dévots were looked on as nearly idiotic. And the poor suffered horrors unapproachable.[57]

The matter at issue in the strike was the wage paid to casual unskilled dock labourers whose conditions were so appalling that when they *were* able to obtain work they were sometimes in such a state of malnutrition as to be unable to work a full day.[58] What made the strike significant was that skilled labourers, who made no demands of their own, came out in sympathy. The Lord Mayor (Sir James Whitehead) established a conciliation committee which met for the first time on 6 September. It consisted of Whitehead himself, Cardinal Manning, Temple, Sir John Lubbock (later Lord Avebury, a Liberal and an influential figure in the banking world, who represented the Chamber of Commerce), Sir Andrew Lusk (a 'self-made' businessman and himself a former Lord Mayor and Liberal MP for Finsbury who had become a Liberal Unionist), and Sydney Buxton (Liberal MP for Poplar and a member of a family which had played an important part in social-reforming movements earlier in the century).[59] Temple was on holiday in Wales and came back to London specially for this meeting.

The committee concluded that the demand for increased wages ought to be met but not until the following 1 March—almost six months away. This the strikers' representatives were unwilling to agree. A compromise date was put to both sides—1 January. What the committee was not apparently told at this stage was that even this date was likely to be unacceptable to the strikers.[60] It would mean that the rise would only come when the busiest time on the docks was over. Whitehead, Manning, and Temple (assuming that 1 January was acceptable to the labourers) communicated the proposals to the employers who took nearly twenty-four hours to accept them but then insisted that the strike committee must also signify its agreement that very evening. The leaders felt that they must consult the strikers as a whole since there were various reasons, including the unacceptability of 1 January, why they did not feel they could speak for them. Unfortunately this made it

---

[57] Trinity College, Cambridge: E. W. Benson Papers, Official Diary 1889, 21 Aug.

[58] H. Llewellyn Smith and V. Nash, *The Story of the Dockers' Strike* (with an introduction by Sydney Buxton, MP) (London, 1889), 47 f. The authors are described as 'two East Londoners' and the account given is plainly sympathetic to the strikers but Sir Herbert Llewellyn Smith and his co-author were obviously not in the normal sense of the term 'East Londoners'.

[59] Buxton's own account of events is printed in Sandford (ed.), ii. 142 ff.

[60] Smith and Nash, 145 f. implies this.

seem that the leadership had acted with less than complete honesty and the conciliation committee assumed that the employers would regard the 'offer' as rejected. Whitehead, Temple, and Manning signed a letter to the strike leaders to that effect, though Manning—who had been on the side of the strikers throughout—did so very reluctantly. It was assumed that the attempt at mediation had failed. The full conciliation committee 'repudiated' the actions of the strike leaders and broke up. Temple went back to his holiday in Wales. Manning, however, refused to accept failure, and with Buxton persuaded the conciliation committee to meet a widely representative group of strikers. A settlement was arrived at and the strike was ended. Temple did not attend that meeting and refused to have anything further to do with the matter. His reason appears to have been that the men's renewed demand to be given their rise from 1 October was a repudiation of their leaders' earlier acceptance of it.[61]

The story of the strike has been most often told from Manning's point of view and the outcome was quite plainly a great achievement on his part. His sympathy for the strikers and his willingness to persist when others had given up, were probably decisive.[62] But, unfortunately, in telling the story from the cardinal's point of view, his biographers have usually quoted Benson (actually on holiday in Switzerland at the time) who wrote in his diary, 'Why has my dear Bishop of London gone back and left it to [Manning]'.[63] To be understood properly that entry in Benson's diary needs to be read in full:

Cardinal Manning has done well for London. But why has my dear Bishop of London gone back and left it to him? Are the dockers on strike Roman Catholics all?[64]

It also needs to be read against another entry from earlier in September 1889 which reveals the archbishop's lack of sympathy with the strikers and his intense dislike of Manning.

The Strike of the Dock Labourers continues. The Sweating Committee brought out that the casual labourers at the Dock Gates are no real labourers, but men who have rendered or found every better position or work in life impossible for themselves. It is not here that the seriousness of the thing lies; but in the

[61] Sandford (ed.), ii. 145 f.

[62] Ibid. ii. 146 f.

[63] Robert Gray, *Cardinal Manning* (London, 1985), 306 ff., and Shane Leslie, *Henry Edward Manning, His Life and Labours* (1921), 373.

[64] Trinity College, Cambridge: E. W. Benson Papers, Official Diary 1889, Sept. 17.

well-paid regular men never out of employment joining with them, and well-to-do artisans, unconcerned in the whole thing, with *them*. This, and the fact that they are ready to starve for the cause is what shows that the movement is social; not a matter of wages alone. Manning, as is his wont, appears on the scene, drives through the crowd, enters the Committee Room; all that passes is to be confidential; reappears, drops (as if he didn't intend it) the word that 'he hopes he has done some good,' is loudly applauded by the crowd, drives off. Those who know the man, and his resourceless brain, his character and knowledge of dramatic effect, will not be deceived. Others will.

The Church which is really working heart and soul, mind and body, without flaunting and without screeching, but for the good of the poor victims at once of social pressure and of base orators, is at present nothing in common talk but 'the Parsons'. Perhaps it is good for us that it should for a time so continue.[65]

A number of points emerge. First of all, the 'gone back' plainly refers to Temple's resumption of his Welsh holiday. Secondly, Benson's dislike of the cardinal explains why Manning's biographers have not quoted more extensively from the archbishop. It also suggests that the real reason why Benson was upset by Temple's departure was that he lost the kudos which Manning acquired. The archbishop also plainly hated the unpopularity which the Church of England was suffering. Thirdly, Benson regarded Manning's sympathy with the strikers as subversive of social stability. All in all, his reaction, from so far away, was probably as distorted as any could possibly be.

The explanation of Temple's behaviour is almost certainly that he believed that the strike leaders had not been entirely open with the conciliation committee. He was often impatient when faced with complex issues and if he came to the conclusion that one party had not acted honestly, he was quite capable of adopting an irreversibly hostile attitude.[66] Having made up his mind, he would not budge: nor would he do anything to justify his actions publicly. That was a characteristic he had displayed over and over again: he preferred to be misunderstood than to explain. In the end it is possible that he came to realize that he had simply made a mistake about the intentions of the strike leaders for there is some evidence to suggest that he remained on good terms with at least one of them.[67]

---

[65] Quoted in A. C. Benson, ii. 280 f.
[66] See the case of the boys who accused the young clergyman of abusing them, above, 200–1.
[67] Sandford (ed.), ii. 149 n.

Because Temple found it impossible to understand any deliberate breaking of either the law or one's own word, he often disconcerted those who thought that, as a former contributor to *Essays and Reviews*, he would be sympathetic to clergymen who had ceased to believe in some part of the traditional faith of the Church of England. Charles Voysey, who had been deprived of his living in 1871 for unorthodox teaching, and had begun to form what eventually became the Theistic Church in London, wrote to Temple soon after his translation, claiming to be 'one of the clergy ministering in your Lordship's diocese' and thanking him for his Bampton lectures.[68] He retained, he said, a deep attachment to the alliance between Church and State but used his own liturgy. Temple gave him short shrift, or no shrift at all, for he said he could not accept him as though he were a clergyman in the diocese.

I should look on the separation of Church and State in this Country as a very serious evil; but such a reform of the Church as would include your opinions (as far as I understand them) would be in my opinion an evil far more serious.[69]

But he added a very odd remark, 'I cannot receive the Revd Charles Voysey, the Clergyman of the Church of England; but the Revd Charles Voysey, Nonconformist Minister will be very welcome.' And '...I entirely concur in your view that Natural Religion is the only foundation on which belief in Revelation can be built up.' These remarks Voysey found sufficiently encouraging to return yet another letter in which he claimed that at law he was still a clergyman. He also sent Temple a copy of his 'little book' on the Lord's Prayer.[70] This was too much for the bishop. His rough draft for a reply said that he was far too busy to argue and very much disliked the little book which he believed to be incompatible with the doctrines of the Church of England.

Temple's distinction between 'the Revd Charles Voysey, the Clergyman of the Church of England' and 'the Revd Charles Voysey, Nonconformist Minister' has to be taken seriously. It shows very clearly that his devotion to what was constitutional and legal was more than mere legalism. What he could not stomach was the breaking of the promises which clergymen of the Church of England made at their ordination, and continued to make at intervals throughout their working lives. He

[68] Lambeth Palace Library: Fulham Papers, F. Temple, vol. 55, fos. 322 f., letter dated 9 May 1885.

[69] Ibid., fos. 324 f., copy of Temple's reply dated 10 May 1885.

[70] Ibid., fos. 326 f., letter dated 11 May.

reminded his clergy in his visitation charge of 1895 that they had undertaken to use no other forms of service than those provided by the Prayer Book 'unless ordered to do so by lawful authority'. 'It is distinctly dishonourable', he said, 'to break such a promise as this.'[71] 'Distinctly dishonourable' was no lightly used term. It expressed the emotional as well as the moral attitude with which he would regard those who claimed, as Voysey did, to be clergymen of the Church of England but refused to be bound by what the Church required. The law was not something to be obeyed for its own sake but because the law was the only way in which it was possible to determine what the Church did require. He was probably being quite literal when he said that he could *welcome* Voysey so long as he made no claim to be a clergyman of the Church of England. He took a very similar line in the case of another clergyman, Alfred Momerie, who was professor of Logic and Moral Philosophy at King's College, London but was thought to be unorthodox in his lectures which were compulsory for theological students in the college. Some members of the college council, including Gladstone, were anxious to censure Dr Momerie formally. Temple, who was involved as Bishop of London, saw Momerie twice and persuaded the council to transfer the chair which he occupied from theology to another department. Momerie appeared to be attacking the doctrines of the Church as 'crude definitions of doctrines' emanating 'from narrow schools of thought'. He was doing, in other words, much what Temple had conceived himself to be doing when he wrote his contribution to *Essays and Reviews*. He was not being untrue to his promises as a clergyman but he could be said to be failing in what was expected of him as a professor in the Theology department. Removing the compulsion on the students, therefore, seemed to resolve the whole matter.

The bishop's position in relation to King's College involved him in higher education, in which he had not hitherto claimed any expertise. He may have had, though, a good opinion of his own ability as a scholar. The Sandford *Memoir* tells the story of a lecture which the bishop once gave to a very large audience at Oxford House in Bethnal Green. In the discussion afterwards 'a secularist lecturer' asserted that 'Christ had borrowed all He taught from the philosopher Pythagoras'. Temple's reply was:

[71] Sandford (ed.), ii. 111.

I have read all we have that Pythagoras is supposed to have written, and I do not think it would cover a single page of the New Testament. Perhaps my friend there has discovered much more.[72]

The man's 'mates', we are told, called out 'What price, Pythagoras?' after the unfortunate secularist as he fled. It was no doubt a devastating riposte but it wasn't a difficult one for a Balliol man to achieve in an East End settlement.

Nevertheless, partly because he was recognized as a person with some expertise in matters of education, partly just because he was the bishop of the diocese, he was unavoidably involved in questions of university education in the metropolis which were raised early in his London episcopate. The theological department of King's College had originated as a means of training ordination candidates who were not yet graduates. The principal, Henry Wace, was the bishops' principal adviser on examining these and other candidates of one kind and another. And the relationship between college and diocese was so close that the diocesan conference normally met in the college buildings. When it was proposed to move to Sion College (to save some money) Wace protested to such effect that the conference continued to meet at King's.[73]

This is a great Church College [wrote Wace] and we rejoice in any thing which binds us more closely with the Church and its work; and we are pleased to accommodate our arrangements at any time as far as possible, for such a purpose, as we have done, for example, in another matter—the Bishop's Examinations for Holy Orders, which have of late been held here.[74]

In 1887 a proposal that the University of London should become a teaching university was put forward jointly by King's and by University College (originally a deliberately secular college sometimes referred to as the 'irreligious' institution in Gower Street). Up to this point each college had done its own teaching and the university had been very little more than an examining and degree-granting corporation. A commission was appointed under the chairmanship of Lord Selborne (who had been Lord Chancellor under Gladstone from 1872 to 1874, and again from 1882 to 1885; a High Churchman who, as a barrister, had appeared in a number of important ecclesiastical lawsuits) to decide, in effect, whether it would be better to reconstitute the University of London or

---

[72] Sandford ii. 91.
[73] Lambeth Palace Library: Fulham Papers, F. Temple, vol. 46, fos. 87 ff.
[74] Ibid., fos. 95 f.

to create an entirely new institution. Its advice was that the constitution of the existing university should be modified so as to permit it to become a teaching university. But the university dragged its heels. The government then initiated plans for creating a new institution to be called the Gresham University but, again, the proposal came to nothing, this time because of internal divisions within the Tory party. A third commission was therefore appointed in 1892, under the chairmanship of Earl Cowper. He had been Gladstone's Lord-Lieutenant of Ireland in the stormy years of 1880–2 but had opposed his Home Rule Bill of 1886 and was actually a very distant connection of the bishop's. The whole matter dragged on until after Temple had been translated to Canterbury but he had in the meanwhile given evidence before all the commissions.

His evidence before the Selborne Commission had been full of ideas which he had adumbrated in earlier phases of his career. He insisted that the most effective educational instrument was contact with 'great masters of the subjects to be taught' or 'of mind with mind', the personal influence of the teacher. He insisted, too, that education must proceed at a steady pace, allowing 'the study to sink in': cramming information into the mind was not education. And, because no examination could actually test what really mattered—understanding rather than information—the examination should follow the teaching, not *vice versa*. All this was entirely in line with the things he had been saying since his days at Kneller Hall. It was in some of the detail that he appeared to have changed his mind. Asked whether he thought that the reconstituted university should have a theology faculty, he said that he thought that that would not be necessary and, indeed, that it would be impossible to devise one which would be independent of denominational creed.[75]

This is a surprising line for Temple to have taken or, at least, it is surprising in the man who at Kneller Hall had insisted, in the face of High Church criticism, that he would take men from all Christian traditions and instruct them together in religious studies. It is also, perhaps, surprising in the man who had, by implication at any rate, written his contribution to *Essays and Reviews* because he believed that open and intelligent discussion of critical questions in religion was an important part of theology. His interest in apologetics and in the relationship between science and religion, moreover, would also have led one to expect a willingness to regard theology as something which

---

[75] Sandford (ed.), ii. 74 ff.

was open for rational discussion. The truth probably is that Temple had never finally resolved the tension implicit in the guidelines with which he was provided when he was asked to join *Essays and Reviews*—'in the Liberal direction, but strictly within the limits allowed by the Church of England'.[76] As bishop of Exeter he had already begun to develop the idea, almost indistinguishable from Tait's, that there were clear limits beyond which clergymen of the Church of England must not stray. And in London he became more and more convinced that the law could determine what those limits were. Almost imperceptibly—perhaps, even, imperceptibly to himself—he had become more concerned about the traditional teachings of the Church and less about maintaining freedom of enquiry. Being a bishop had done that to him, and particularly being a bishop of a diocese where ritualism was so strong. But it is possible that he was also beginning to distinguish between educational method (in which his ideas had hardly changed at all) and the *content* of what was to be taught (in which his ideas changed fairly frequently). He had changed his mind, after all, on several occasions about the relative importance of classics and science while not changing it at all on how subjects were to be taught—cultivation, the role model, not learning by rote and so on.

Temple again gave evidence before the Cowper Commission and again his views appear to have changed and, on this occasion, in matters of principle as well as detail. He still insisted on the importance of having teachers of the highest possible calibre and on the value of colleges as communities of scholars, on the nature of education as cultivation rather than as the imparting of information, on the need for time and space for real learning and on the importance of a moral dimension to education. But he had come to think that it would be possible for the university—and he recognized that it would have to be a secular university—to maintain a faculty of theology. The Commission proposed this as a faculty of theological *science* which would make no attempt to teach dogmatic theology or the creed of any particular Christian tradition. The faculty would teach the books of the Old and New Testaments and the languages in which they had been written, ecclesiastical history, the history of doctrine, the philosophy of religion, the comparative history of religions, ethical systems, psychology, and logic.[77] In other words the courses were to concern themselves with

---

[76] See above, 60.   [77] Sandford (ed.), ii. 80.

teaching what *had been* believed by Christians rather than *ought* to be believed by Christians. With this Temple was more than happy, particularly because King's would retain its own department of theology. He further developed his ideas on this point until he came to believe that the colleges within the secular university ought to be denominational and ought, indeed, to be allowed to impose their own religious tests. If the college were required to abandon its traditional religious character, its whole nature would be altered and the intention of its founders destroyed. When it seemed likely that King's would lose an annual state grant of £1,700 if it remained a denominational institution and some of the bishops were tempted to agree to a change, Temple persuaded them to stand firm and to send himself and the Archbishop of York as a deputation to Gladstone to argue the case.[78]

He must, in fact, have been conscious that this was a surprising position for someone who had argued in the 1850s for the abolition of religious tests in Oxford and (as he had argued again in the matter of endowed schools) for the right to alter the objects for which endowments had originally been given. He wrote, trying to justify his apparent change of opinion, to a man who had known him when he was a young fellow of Balliol:

... when I was an earnest advocate of the abolition of tests at Oxford I acted in the interests of justice. I thought it unjust that Nonconformists should be excluded from educational foundations which dated from times when our religious divisions were unknown. But I heartily concurred with Dean Stanley in the hope that denominational colleges would be founded afterwards as Keble College and Mansfield College have since been founded.

The inclusion of denominational colleges in an undenominational University appears to me to be the true development of Liberal principles in application to education. The true advancement of Liberal principles is not to exclude from National purview the most important of all possible subjects, but to reconcile the inclusion of such subjects with strict justice to all.[79]

It may be that this renewed conviction was the really important thing which emerged for Temple out of the whole complicated business of a university for London. It seems that his approach to the problem of a national system of elementary education came to be more and more expressed in very similar terms. He came to believe that in schools, as in the new universities, justice required that a single, secular system should embrace Church institutions alongside institutions of any and every denomination or of none.

Forster's Elementary Education Act of 1870, in which Temple had had such an important hand, had been an uneasy compromise between those who desired an entirely secular system of national schools and those who believed that the schools provided by the Established Church should be enabled to survive in competition with them. Temple's ideas had changed over the years on this very point. In his famous essay on national education of 1856 he had vigorously attacked the supporters of denominational schools. But as the new Bishop of Exeter in 1870 he had urged his clergy to squeeze favourable terms for their schools out of the new system. By the 1890s he had come to realize that Church schools were losing an unequal struggle against subsidized board schools. In addition, as a matter of principle, he had come to believe that it was essential for children to be taught religion by believing teachers, in the context of a Church school.[80] The arguments with which he defended this position were recognizably derived from his views about the importance of the teacher as role model and the necessity of a moral dimension in education. In the new context, however, they were used to support a point of view which differed very little from the 'Oxford ecclesiasticism' he had so despised forty years earlier. Temple was moving away from, or reinterpreting, his earlier political Liberalism. At the beginning of his London episcopate he had said that in the matter of religious equality he had come to believe that true Liberalism was rather different from the policies pursued by Liberals. By the early 1890s he was saying much the same thing, *mutatis mutandis*, about 'the true development of Liberal principles in application to education'.

The truth was that the Forster Education Act had not worked or had worked very much to the detriment of voluntary schools. The evidence was incontrovertible. Everyone agreed that Church schools were simply unable to compete with board schools. There simply was not the money to enable them to do so. The Established Church was being put, for the first time in history, in a position of real disadvantage in the world of education. What the subcommittee of the ruridecanal chapter of Ealing had said in its report was echoed all round the country. Nor was it simply a matter of the resources available. There was a positive determination to destroy Anglican dominance. Those who had favoured secular education or had resented the Church's former privileges had

---

[80] Sandford (ed.), ii. 86.

taken up the cause of the school boards with passionate fervour. In 1888 Benson believed that there was a real crisis looming, 'There is approaching a grave struggle against the Church for the School Boards, a determination not to allow any saving to be made by supporting Voluntary Schools.'[81]

Throughout the early 1890s the bishops devoted a large part of their informal meetings at Lambeth to the question. Most of them thought that it would be wrong for the Church to oppose any legislation to provide free education so long as the independence of voluntary schools was not interfered with.[82] They simply failed to grasp the reality that voluntary schools could not compete with board schools. In February 1890 Temple introduced a discussion on 'free or assisted education'. Eighteen months later (from the chair because the archbishop was absent through illness) he initiated a major debate about proposed legislation which would have made some more money available for voluntary schools but not, in Temple's opinion, sufficient to make a real difference. His principal argument was that earlier legislation had created board schools whose standards had continually improved. But higher standards also cost more so that the State was virtually compelling voluntary schools to spend more in order to compete.[83]

The minutes of the bishops' meetings were normally little more than a record of subjects discussed and conclusions reached. The greater detail recorded for this one debate suggests, therefore, that the bishops—or perhaps the chairman—thought it a particularly important issue. They were willing, as never before, to get to grips with the problems but, at the same time, different—sometimes vigorously different—opinions were emerging. When Temple asserted that it would be possible to build new voluntary schools provided more time was allowed for finding subscribers, Bishop Ridding of Southwell (a former headmaster of Winchester) asked whether the time had not come for the Church to give up her schools and 'throw her weight into the School Boards'. A division of opinion along these lines between North and South was to become a matter of great importance in the future, so it is interesting that Temple retorted that perhaps the time had come for the managers of voluntary schools in the North to 'throw themselves on the liberality of the laity for the increased subscriptions needed'. Westcott of Durham

---

[81] Trinity College, Cambridge: E. W. Benson Papers, Official Diary 1888, 30 July.
[82] Lambeth Palace Library: Minutes of Bishops' Meetings, BM3, 11 Feb. 1890.
[83] Ibid. 18 and 19 June 1891.

asserted that the Church's policy would have been far more effective 'if from the first she had thrown her whole energy into the School Boards'. What really mattered, he said, was that the Church should put its energies into the training colleges in the hope of securing the highest possible level of religious teaching in board schools.

What was so different about this phase of the dabate was that it took place in the context of a Conservative rather than a Liberal government. Most previous attempts to reform national policy on education had been regarded as exuding traditional Whig or Liberal hostility to the Established Church. Conservative attempts at reform were regarded as opportunities to obtain further privileges for voluntary schools. There was also a question, within the wider issue of whether the government ought to provide subsidies for voluntary schools, whether such sub sidies should come from central government or from local rates. Temple had asserted, in his essay of 1856, the superiority of rates over grants. Then, as a fervent Liberal, he had believed in the importance of market forces. It is a little difficult to discover precisely what his opinion was forty years later. The Sandford *Memoir* represents him as 'a pronounced advocate of State aid as opposed to Rate aid' who by 1896 was willing to compromise in the matter because the Convocations (and the houses of laymen) had publicly preferred the rate-aid method.[84] In practice he seems not to have minded whether the money came from central government or from local ratepayers provided there was as much of it as possible.

There had been an interlude between August 1892 and June 1895 in which the Liberals were once again in power. The bishops, nevertheless, had continued to make plans for what they should do whenever they should again have the opportunity to ask for financial help. In February 1893 the Bishop of Salisbury (John Wordsworth) sketched a rather complicated plan to co-ordinate voluntary schools with board schools. Voluntary schools might receive some rate aid in return for ratepayers being given a share in their management. At the same time non-Anglican parents would be entitled to ask for separate religious instruc-tion for their children. In spite of Temple's fears that 'the present time and circumstances were not favourable for the introduction of the question of applying for voluntary schools to obtain share [*sic*] of rates as opponents would be likely to take advantage of such proposal', the

---

[84] Sandford (ed.), ii. 90.

two bishops proceeded to try and obtain legislation on the subject. In June 1893 they were still trying to explain to their colleagues the advantages of the elementary education bill (religious) then at the committee stage in the House of Lords, which provoked a further attack from Westcott (who did not wish to see any separation of religious and secular education), Ellicott, and King. The bishops as a whole were very conscious of the pressures on voluntary schools but were unable to devise a concerted policy because of different conditions in different parts of the country.

The archbishops appointed a voluntary schools committee which reported early in 1895 and the Conservatives returned to power in June of that year (and were to remain in office for the next decade). There was therefore some hope of new legislation favourable to Anglican interests but Nonconformist support for board schools as against voluntary schools became even more vigorous. Educational policies moreover, became entangled with other matters in which it was widely believed that the Established Church was attempting to entrench its own privileged position or was encouraging anti-Protestant feeling. Ritualism and disestablishment became sub-themes to the debate.

There were also divisions within the cabinet and the Conservative and Unionist Party. By September 1895 Arthur Balfour, Leader of the commons and First Lord of the Treasury in Salisbury's ministry, was openly anxious to provide relief for voluntary schools and their subscribers. Anglicans pressed hard for more financial support but were quite unwilling to accept centralized control of their schools. Benson, who had his own doubts about the matter, convened a conference in October which narrowly rejected 'rate aid' in favour of 'State aid' and sent a deputation with a memorial to wait on the Duke of Devonshire, Lord President of the Council and therefore minister in charge of education. Salisbury showed some sympathy but Nonconformist opposition had not abated and Joseph Chamberlain (who had resigned from Gladstone's Liberal government in 1886 on account of the Irish Home Rule Bill and had then taken office in Salisbury's Unionist ministry in 1895) believed that any proposal to increase subsidies for voluntary schools would destroy the compromise of 1870, split the party, and allow the Liberals in.[85] The bill, therefore, which was finally introduced in March 1896, was an untidy compromise. Increased State

---

[85] G. I. T. Machin, *Politics and the Churches in Great Britain, 1869 to 1921* (Oxford, 1987), 26.

aid would be provided for voluntary schools and under-funded school boards, alike. What was described as 'reasonable arrangements' for religious instruction were to be provided in all schools. So vigorous was the attack from all sides that the bill had to be withdrawn again in June. A very much simpler law to provide additional funding for voluntary schools was enacted early in 1897 and was followed by a bill to assist 'necessitous board schools'.

Temple's most fixed conviction in this period seems to have been that, if religious instruction were to be given within a secular educational system by teachers appointed without any religious test, then it might become 'such as could hardly be called religious instruction at all'.[86] He also maintained, somewhat paradoxically, that board schools gave good religious instruction but only did so because Church schools were there. Their existence proved that some people cared about the importance of religious instruction.[87] He had supported Balfour's original proposals of 1896 on the ground that, unlike previous legislation, which had always left it entirely to the local school boards to determine what was or was not done about religious instruction, this bill would have given parents the right to demand proper arrangements for it. It was a secular system containing provision for the denominational teaching of religion. 'I have no hesitation in saying', he had declared in the previous year, 'that I would very much rather that a child were brought up as a religious Nonconformist than that he should go without any religious instruction at all.'[88]

Temple does not appear to have been particularly interested in other Christian denominations. He seems always to have spoken sympathetically about English Nonconformists but one gets the impression that he was so sure that the Church of England was the true and proper expression of Christianity and the natural guardian of the religious life of the nation that he simply was not interested in going into questions of relations with other churches. He was always willing to work with their representatives on committees concerning matters of national importance. (As archbishop he would pay an official visit to the General Assembly of the Church of Scotland but it was intended to serve the cause of temperance rather than ecumenism.[89] He always spoke in friendly terms of other bodies, particularly where they might seem to

---

[86] Sandford (ed.), ii. 89.
[87] Ibid.
[88] Ibid. ii. 163.
[89] Ibid. ii. 231 ff.

have something of the same history as the Church of England. But he hardly ever concerned himself with examining in any detail the theological differences between, or the non-theological factors dividing, the various Christian traditions.

Soon after his arrival in London he had received the Very Revd Namadalla Sabli, vicar-general of the Maronites (a Uniat community of Syrian origin) in Cyprus.[90] In view of his own upbringing in the Mediterranean this may have had a particular interest for him but it does not appear to have led anywhere. When he was asked to promote closer relations with the Old Catholics, he replied warmly but without committing himself to taking any action.

My impression is that the Old Catholics of Switzerland are reforming themselves on the lines of the English Church. They can hardly be said to be advancing slowly: but they have not jumped at once in [*sic*] Anglicanism.

I should be glad to see a kindly feeling between them and our continental chaplaincies.... Probably the chaplains of the Colonial and Continental Society look on the Old Catholics as still Papists. The real danger seems that they should advance too rapidly.[91]

He took considerable pains to establish good relations with the French Huguenot congregation. For this there were probably two reasons. The Huguenot congregation had been using one of the City churches and for that reason got caught up in Temple's plans to reorganize and rationalize the use of those churches. The bishop of London had also possessed, by royal patent and for a very long time, a special relationship with the congregation in which he acted officially as their superintendent.[92] Moreover, the Huguenots were a small religious community in permanent exile and theirs was very much a special case.

Temple also appears to have devoted little time or attention to other provinces of the Anglican Communion. This was probably as much a consequence of historical developments as of a lack of interest on Temple's part. Traditionally the bishops of London had had oversight of the Church in the colonies but after the first Lambeth Conference in 1867, which had itself laid down various models for the development of independent provinces in other parts of the world,[93] those provinces

---

[90] Lambeth Palace Library: Fulham Papers, F. Temple, vol. 55, fos. 283 ff.
[91] Ibid., fos 247 f.
[92] Ibid., vol. 25 fos. 200–12 all relate to the French Protestant congregation.
[93] Peter Hinchliff, 'Church–State Relations', in Stephen Sykes and John Booty (eds.), *The Study of Anglicanism* (London and Philadelphia, 1988), 360 f.

tended to deal with the archbishops of Canterbury, through their own metropolitans. Where there were isolated dioceses, not part of a province, they were treated as directly subordinate to Canterbury. Matters arising from 'the colonies', therefore, no longer came to the bishop of London as a matter of course but went straight to Lambeth. One request which did come to Temple's attention directly from colonial Anglicans related to the Church in Natal which had been split by the controversy surrounding Bishop Colenso. In that case, however, there were particular reasons why one of the parties was anxious to preserve a rather old-fashioned relationship with the Church of England itself and refused to recognize the South African province.[94] Almost the only other trace of any involvement with Anglicans outside England which survives among Temple's London papers is a letter from a clergyman in the diocese of London who had been offered an appointment by the trustees of a congregation in Aberdeen. It was part of a body known as 'English Episcopal', who refused to recognize the Scottish bishops and claimed to be subject to the Bishop of Carlisle. The clergyman asked for Temple's advice and was firmly told that he ought not to accept the appointment.[95] But this, too, was not an official communication from an overseas province. It was a personal request from one of his own clergy.

In some parts of the Anglican Communion the smell of *Essays and Reviews* still seems to have clung to Temple even more than at home. At the Lambeth Conference which met in June and July 1888, he was given the job of introducing a report on 'the definite teaching of the faith' which included such issues as the authority of scripture. It is not clear how he came to be given that job. In one sense he was the obvious choice since he had been speaking publicly on these matters for nearly thirty years. In another sense, for those who still regarded *Essays and Reviews* as heretical, it was a provocative choice. The minutes of the bishops' meetings, at which the plans for the Conference were approved, do not mention Temple's being given this particular assignment but he was a member of the committee which had met with the archbishop to decide the details and may even have asked to be given the job.[9]

---

[94] Peter Hinchliff, 'Colonial Church Establishment in the Aftermath of the Colenso Controversy' (forthcoming).

[95] Lambeth Palace Library: Fulham Papers, F. Temple, vol. 55, fos. 105 ff. letter from William S. Carter, 7 Nov. 1885.

[96] Ibid., Minutes of Bishops' Meetings, BM3, 80, 8 June 1886.

Alternatively, it may have been Randall Davidson, still Dean of Windsor, who handed Temple what turned out to be a poisoned chalice. He had, as Tait's chaplain, done a good deal of the organizing of the previous Conference and was appointed to assist Ellicott, the episcopal secretary, in 1888.[97] His journal, a splendid record of what happened behind the scenes, records his claim that he played the chief part in deciding what the subjects should be and who should be the speakers invited to open each subject.[98]

Davidson was somewhat ambivalent about Benson. Though he regarded him as a clever and diplomatic president of the conference he thought him less impressive than Tait. When the bishops went to Canterbury for a service Davidson wrote:

The Abp's address from S. Augustine's Chair was wise and generous if somewhat obscure. Seldom to my mind has the contrast been more remarkable than between the big simplicity of the words spoken in 1878 [by Tait] and the somewhat eager, apologetic & involved utterances *read* from the same chair in 1888. But it was thoroughly *good* all the same & no one is more effective looking in a function of this sort, or more genial & kindly as the centre of such a gathering.[99]

His account of Temple's attempt to secure the passage of his report was clearly sympathetic. In what was the usual practice at Lambeth Conferences the matter had first been discussed by a committee or section of the whole gathering. When the matter came before the whole Conference on the morning of 24 July, Davidson thought Temple's report 'quite admirable'.

His speech clear and strong, perhaps a little too strong to please some of his hearers. The Bp of Winchester [Browne] proposed an amendment, saying the same thing in a more timid, guarded and circumlocutory way. Bps of Gloster [*sic*] & Minnesota [Henry B. Whipple] & Abp of York [Thomson] strongly opposed *any* commending of the Report, the last named referring (with what seemed to me bad taste) to Essays and Reviews decision. A splendid ringing speech from the Bp of Manchester [Moorhouse] beseeching the Conference not to reject the Report, tho he had not been in the Ctee and has nothing to do with

---

[97] Ibid.

[98] Ibid., Davidson Papers, vol. 574, Journal commencing January 1888, 31. The pages of the journal have been numbered twice. The numbering used here is the series which has located numbers even to the blank folios. The passage is quoted in e.g. Bell, i. 120, and . M. G. Stephenson, *Anglicanism and the Lambeth Conferences* (London, 1978), 177.

[99] Ibid. 33.

drafting the Report. A whole sheaf of amendments were proposed in turn and I now (12.45) have not an idea what the ultimate resolve will be. It is to me intensely disappointing to see what are the remarks which meet with applause. The Bp of Minnesota's speech was the most applauded, I think, of all, and he took a quite uncompromising line of opposition to the part referring to Genesis 1. 1 o'clock—A great fight over the question whether the Reports of the Committees cd be *amended* by the Conference. This [presumably a resolution to amend the report] was (Deo Gratias) rejected by the Conference but only by 61 votes agst 54. 1.15 After much wrangling it has been resolved to refer back the Report to the Committee. Tho' no instruction was given, it was clearly meant that the last part of the Report as to Inspiration &c shd be cut out. God grant it may not be so. Some of those who voted in the majority meant it as a civil way of shelving the whole subject. But I hope the Bp of London may defeat this pious intent.[100]

After that, apparently, Davidson had no time to devote to his journal, so involved was he in the winding up of the Conference, until he was spending a weekend at Osborne on 12 August. Then he recorded that Temple's report had come back to the plenary session on the final Thursday afternoon (25 July) and 'after a stormy and most unfortunate debate rejected'.

I missed the discussion [but]...I came back to Lambeth just in time for the division—a rather close one—which finally 'put away' the Bp of London's Report. I am intensely sorry for that decision as the Report seemed to me to be on the whole the best bit of work the Conference had done. Many people thought it due to the fact that its author was the Bp of London—one of the authors of Essays & Reviewaws [*sic*] I dont myself think this made much difference to *most* people. tho' it is more than possible it may have given cause for the Bp of Gloster and Abp of York's opposition which was strenuous.

The Bp of London behaved splendidly, only asking the Bps not to circulate the Report anywhere, as it would be most unfortunate if it shd obtain publicity as a thing which had been proposed and rejected.[101]

Bishop Perry of Iowa thought the report 'in some respects the most able and masterly of all the reports offered...' and attributed the rough handling which it received to two things—the fact that it asserted only the *substantial* truth of the New Testament and its 'seeming to concede that the opening portions of the Word of God, like its close, were

---

[100] Lambeth Palace Library: Davidson Papers, vol. 574, Journal commencing Jan. 1888. fo. 35.
[101] Ibid. 45 ff.

vision or an allegory'.[102] When the committee submitted a revised version of its report it was still rejected by the Conference. The bishops seem to have made up their minds that the committee was unsound and were determined to make no concessions to unbelievers. Others besides colonial and American bishops still remembered the supposed heterodoxy of *Essays and Reviews*. Ellicott had been one of the bishops who had objected at Temple's consecration so it should not have surprised anyone to find him a 'strenuous' critic of the report. What *is* surprising is that a piece written very nearly thirty years earlier by the young headmaster of Rugby, should have come back to haunt the sixty-seven year old Bishop of London.

Once Temple was over seventy, even his powerful physique began to show signs of strain. He was forced to seek medical advice towards the end of 1894 and was told that he was suffering from an 'affection of the kidney and one which we know is liable to become acute without much warning'. The doctors told him that he should do no work at all for the time being and must expect never to be able to do anything but the lightest work in the future. Being Bishop of London was too demanding, both physically and mentally, and he must be particularly careful not to exert himself in the winter months of the year. He might, they said, live for some while to come but only if he took their advice.

I write this letter only after very careful consideration of all the facts of your illnesses past and present, and in the earnest desire as your doctor and sincere friend to give you the best advice in my power. I know that it will be a great grief to you to withdraw from the work which you have so entirely at heart and which has prospered so well under your guidance but I consider that the state of your health demands it.[103]

It is, of course, one thing to seek advice and quite another to take it. Temple does not appear to have reduced his work load very greatly, even during the winter months. There were small signs, perhaps, that he was beginning to feel the strain though he would not admit to it, himself, until after he had left London. Arthur Winnington-Ingram, who was a priest in the diocese and was eventually himself to become Bishop of London, said 'it was plain enough to all who knew him that the long strain of his twelve years in London was on the point of breaking him

---

[102] Quoted in Stephenson, 83. Stephenson dismisses the whole affair as 'part of the Geology and Genesis controversy'.

[103] Lambeth Palace Library: Fulham Papers, F. Temple, vol. 55, fos. 42 f., J. Vere Nicholls, 2 Nov. 1894.

down when respite came in the call to Canterbury'.[104] The mysterious illness which he had suffered as a young man and which caused a breakdown on at least two occasions, rendered him a bad risk in the eyes of doctors and insurance companies until he was middle-aged.[105] When that had cleared up after he had become a bishop, he seems to have developed a heart condition and some problem with his eyesight which got worse in the last few years of his life. All in all, it is not surprising that his doctors were worried about him.

The Archbishop of Canterbury, who was eight years Temple's junior, died first. He was staying at Hawarden with Gladstone and was thought to be particularly fit and well. He had been to an early celebration of the Holy Communion on Sunday, 11 October 1896. Later in the day at morning prayer he became comatose and died while he was being carried to the incumbent's house. The news took some hours to reach London and arrived at Fulham Palace with the post on the Monday morning. Beatrice wrote to tell William:

Poor Father is very sad today, he and the Archbishop were friends for 40 years—it is such a great loss to him, as a friend, as well as from their being together in their work—At first, on seeing the flag half mast high, and hearing the bell toll, I thought it must be for the Queen—then Nana told me the postman had brought the news—and I thought it better to tell Father at once—he looked as if he had received a blow—he was quite over come at prayers—& couldn' begin the Lesson at first—then he read part of the XV Chap I Cor (or I think from the 50th verse) and at the end his voice sounded quite steady, & as if he was reading a Hymn of Praise—It is all so bewildering because so much coming work depended on the Archbishop.[106]

The sense of community between the living and the dead was some thing which mattered to Temple. He had written a prayer, using phrase from the Prayer Book and the Authorized Version of the Bible, which he used each day with his family. It began with the words, 'We also praise Thy Holy Name for all Thy servants departed from amongst us in Thy faith and fear...'[107] He told Lord Salisbury that Benson had been his 'most intimate friend for forty years'.[108] He was very nearly seventy-five and not many of his generation were left. Jowett was dead. Stanley was

---

[104] Sandford (ed.), ii. 193.

[105] Ibid. ii. 247.

[106] Family Papers in the possession of the Right Revd F. S. Temple: letter dated 12 Oct 1896.

[107] Sandford (ed.), ii. 712.

[108] Ibid. ii. 246.

dead. John Coleridge was dead. Acland had not much longer to live. Labouchere had been dead for over twenty years. Most of the people with whom he had shared ambitions and achievements had gone. Now Benson, who had been in touch nearly every day and had consulted him on all kinds of issues, was dead, too. He was not really intimate with any of the other bishops except possibly Davidson. He was suddenly a man alone.

10

The Rest Cure

Lord Salisbury was Prime Minister when Benson died. There was the usual exchange of ideas between the Queen's household and Davidson, who by that time was Bishop of Winchester. What must have added an extra piquancy to the discussion was that on this occasion Davidson was himself a possible candidate and one whom the Queen favoured. His opinion was that, though there were several very good men among the recent appointments to the bench of bishops, none of them really possessed the qualities needed for the primacy. The good ones (Talbot of Rochester; Creighton of Peterborough; Jayne of Chester) were too young: the older ones, like Moorhouse of Manchester or the Archbishop of York, were not up to it. The only other possible was Westcott though his health too poor and Temple's was hardly better.

Foremost beyond question both in powers and in influence stands the Bp of London. His largeness of sympathy and truly liberal views outweigh for those who know him all faults of manner and if it be possible to secure him for the post for a time it would in my opinion be well for the Church but he is 75 years old and his eyesight is failing.[1]

In a later letter Davidson again advised that Temple's appointment 'even if he only held the office for a year or two would be hailed with universal acclaim'.[2] The Queen was reluctant. She was probably putting pressure on Davidson to allow himself to be nominated for he had to send her a telegram insisting that Temple must be the new archbishop. The Queen's telegraphed reply on 21 October said that she was thinking it all over.[3] But she cannot have thought for long. On 22 October Salisbury wrote to Temple saying that he had been authorized to offer

---

[1] Lambeth Palace Library: Davidson Papers, vol. 4, fo. 154 Copy of letter from Davidson to the Queen dated 18 Oct. 1896 and see G. K. A. Bell, *Randall Davidson Archbishop of Canterbury*, 2 vols., 2nd edn. (London, 1938), i. 282 ff.
[2] Lambeth Palace Library: Davidson Papers, vol. 4, fo. 155.
[3] Ibid., fo. 157.

him the appointment and the next day Temple sent his chaplain
round with his acceptance.[4] Salisbury sent a telegram to the Queen
and she to Davidson on 23 October. Hers was in code this time (one
imagines the postmaster at Balmoral thinking that some international
crisis must be brewing) and when decoded read—'Somewhat to my
surprise London has accepted Canterbury.'[5] On the following day she
sent Davidson her account of what had happened. She had wanted
Davidson but Salisbury had insisted that he was too new a bishop and
already very rapidly promoted. There was a hint that Salisbury had
persuaded her that to put Temple in for what could not be more than a
brief primacy would actually be the quickest way of getting Davidson
into the archbishopric. And she said bluntly, 'I do not like the choice at
all and think the Bishop of London's presence eminently *unsuited* to the
post.'[6]

The announcement was made public on Monday 26 October. The
whole thing had been settled within a fortnight of Temple's hearing that
Benson was dead. He had, nevertheless, as dean of the province, employed the interval to write a prayer for use in parishes during the
vacancy of the see of Canterbury and sent it to all the bishops. The
prayer was for those who had the responsibility of choosing the new
archbishop:

Guide them we pray thee to him whom Thou hast chosen; and so replenish
him with the truth of Thy doctrine and endue him with innocency of life,
that he may faithfully serve before Thee in his high and holy office and may
rule Thy Church and people with a perfect heart to the glory of Thy holy
name.[7]

The boys were naturally elated about their father's preferment. William, who was fifteen, wrote to his mother:

We are very much excited. When do people begin to call him 'Your Grace'? We
went and told some people this afternoon and Ginger said 'What a sell for Mrs
Peterborough!' We shall have an ideal archbishopess, she'll be at home in the
purple.[8]

---

[4] E.G. Sandford (ed.), *Memoirs of Archbishop Temple by Seven Friends*, 2 vols. (London,
1906), ii. 245 f.
[5] Lambeth Palace Library: Davidson Papers, vol. 4, fo. 158.
[6] Bell, i. 284.
[7] Lambeth Palace Library: Davidson Papers, vol. 522, fo. 20, typed copy of prayer with
MS additions, 19 Oct. 1896.
[8] F. A. Iremonger, *William Temple, Archbishop of Canterbury* (London, 1948), 23.

Mandell Creighton, whom both the Prince of Wales and the Archbishop of York had wanted to succeed Benson, was to receive a consolation prize. The Queen thought that he would not quite have done for Canterbury but might do for the vacancy in London which Temple's appointment had created.[9] Salisbury appears to have wanted Davidson but the Queen forbade him even to offer it lest it ruin his health. She took the extraordinary step, however, of sending Davidson a copy of Lord Salisbury's submission.[10] In the end Queen and Prime Minister agreed that London should be offered to Creighton.

Temple's confirmation as archbishop took place at St Mary-le-Bow on 22 December 1896. The Archbishop of York presided and declined to hear a protest made on the ground that Temple 'was a self-confessed believer in the full doctrine of evolution'.[11] There was no need, therefore, for any response to be made to the protest though Temple had briefed one of his suffragans to say that the archbishop designate had never believed the 'full' doctrine of evolution.[12] Although Temple may have intended publicly to commit himself to Spencer's theory of evolution, he was no doubt primarily being evasive.

By this time Temple was really very conservative in comparison with what had come to be perfectly acceptable to other Churchmen. *Lux Mundi*, whose contributors were much more willing to embrace evolutionary ideas, had already been published. And in matters relating to the Bible (the area in which *Essays and Reviews* had been most suspect) his ideas were much more modest than those of a new generation of New Testament scholars. By the 1890s the scholarship of Westcott and Hort was beginning to sound cosy and comfortable compared with what was being said by other English authors. The year of Temple's confirmation was the year in which the third edition of William Sanday's Bampton lectures, *Inspiration*, appeared. It contained a categorical denial that the Bible 'as a whole and in all its parts was the Word of God' or that 'in history as well as in doctrine it was exempt from error'. Nothing that had been said in *Essays and Reviews* was nearly so radical. When Temple talked about the relationship of the synoptic gospels to one another his views would not have been unacceptable to

---

[9] Bell, i. 284.
[10] Lambeth Palace Library: Davidson Papers, vol. 4, fo. 159, copy of a paper from the bishop of Salisbury, dated 26 Oct. 1896.
[11] See above, 184–8.
[12] Sandford (ed.), ii. 253.

Eusebius, the fourth-century historian of the church.[13] Though he knew what German scholars were saying, he thought their theories rather fanciful.

His contemporaries seem to have been aware that he, who had once been suspected of having such advanced and radical ideas, had become very conservative by the end of his life. And it did not seem to them that it was just that he had got left behind by a new generation of radicals. Ernest Sandford argued that responsibility and pastoral experience had made him less radical not only in relation to theology and the Bible, but about politics and education, and about a range of ecclesiastical issues. 'Never limited by partisanship in his political creed, he became absolutely unfettered as the responsibilities of his life multiplied.'[14] The headmaster of Berkhamstead put the matter more bluntly, saying of Temple, 'old age Toryizes'.[15] Neither had it quite right, for Temple's ideas do not seem to have become *uniformly* more conservative as he got older. His ideas changed, not because his responsibilities had *increased*, but because they had come to lie in a different direction. He complained, for instance, that Gladstone was not a true liberal in religion.[16] If he had said this thirty years earlier, when he was expounding the policies of the education office, he might have been referring to Gladstone's Tractarian 'ecclesiasticism': by the 1890s he was more likely to be thinking of his support for disestablishment. He had become *the* spokesman for the Church of England. In matters of education he came to support the Tories because Church schools needed help. He seems to have felt no obligation at all to assist Conservative administrations when they got themselves into difficulties.

By the time Temple became archbishop his own brand of High Churchmanship [(which would later—and more accurately—come to be known within the Church as 'Liberal Catholicism', to distinguish it from the more conservative and ceremonial 'Anglo-Catholicism' which arose out of ritualism)], with its belief that the wide tolerance of the Church of England had clear limits defined by law, had had to be modified. As a bishop he had become an interpreter of the law and then, as he became more influential, a maker of the law. In neither role could he simply treat the law as a given. But it was not that he became

---

[13] Ibid. ii. 98.

[14] Ibid. ii. 639. Sandford deals with Temple's changing views in ii. 632 ff.

[15] Lambeth Palace Library: Davidson Papers, vol. 54, fo. 90, Dr T. C. Fry to Davidson, 28 Feb. 1898.

[16] See above, 34.

steadily more conservative (or 'Tory-ized') about everything. There were ups and downs. He seems to have been most firmly a political Liberal, believing in the importance of the free market and its ability to solve social problems, in the latter part of his time at Rugby and during the years at Exeter. That was the period when he was most influenced by his experience on the Taunton Commission and by Spencer's thought. During the latter part of his time as Bishop of London, under Benson's influence, he seems to have been willing to work with Tory governments on education and to modify his preference for the strict application of the law in matters of ceremonial. But, in fact, he seems to have changed his mind—when he did—for quite specific reasons which applied to particular matters rather than as part of a general process of becoming older.

Davidson seems to have been the person who influenced him most during his years as archbishop. Temple and Davidson were no more alike than Temple and Benson had been and their relationship was full of paradox. Davidson's biographer says that Temple formed the impression in 1896 that Davidson had wanted the primacy for himself. The story is based on Davidson's own correspondence with Arthur Benson, the former archbishop's eldest son.[17] The rift is said to have lasted for a year or two and that even then, 'the resumption of friendship did not mean the resumption [by Davidson] of the former position of intimate counsellor'.

Several things need to be said about this account. It is, first of all, quite clear that if Davidson had wished to be archbishop he could have encouraged the Queen to press even harder. Salisbury might still have won the argument but it would have been a tougher fight. Moreover Davidson was certainly shrewd enough to have perceived that the appointment of Temple might well be the best way to further his own ambitions. As it was, his behaviour had been impeccable and there was certainly no reason for Temple to have harboured such suspicions.

Secondly, there is nothing to support the belief that Temple and Davidson were on bad terms in the months immediately following Benson's death. Temple certainly consulted Davidson about two matters which were of a very personal kind. One was the Queen's invitation to stay at Windsor for his homage, when Temple wanted to be allowed to bring Beatrice with him.[18] The other was in connection with the Lambeth Conference of the following year. The American bishops wished to

---

[17] Bell, i. 288 f.   [18] See above, 162.

present Temple with a mitre, a proposal which greatly embarrassed him. He asked Davidson to try tactfully to persuade the Americans not to pursue the matter.[19] It may be argued that Davidson was the obvious person to consult in just these matters but they were also the matters which such an intensely private person as Temple would have found it difficult to share with someone with whom he was not at ease. If there was ill feeling, it was hardly very deep.

It is quite clear that within three years relations between the two men were sufficiently close to be able to withstand disagreement. In 1900 Temple wished to hand over some of the land adjoining Lambeth Palace to the London County Council to be permanently opened as a public park (he had done something similar while he was Bishop of London). Davidson opposed the scheme but was very apologetic about doing so. Temple's response was of the blunt, honest kind which can only be written and received where there is real friendship:

Do not let us quarrel because we cannot agree on such a matter as this. If you can stop what I propose to do, by all means stop it. I shall be vexed, but I shall not feel any resentment, nor rely less on your friendship.[20]

The archbishop got his way over the land and he, at any rate, felt no ill-will.

There is, in any case, reason to question the truth of the whole story for its source is suspect. Davidson had been thrown together with Arthur Benson, who was a housemaster at Eton, by the events immediately following the former archbishop's death. They must have known each other before, of course, but seem to have become particularly friendly at this time. Davidson had been much involved in archiepiscopal business under Tait, whose chaplain he had been and whose daughter he had married, and under Benson, who had allowed him the permanent use of rooms in the Lollards Tower at Lambeth as a *pied-à-terre* and continued to use him as an unofficial chief-of-staff. He had therefore possessed a very privileged position from the time of his appointment as chaplain in 1877 until Benson's death in 1896. To be less involved would inevitably seem a kind of ostracism and while Temple—'genuinely, though brusquely'—invited the Davidsons to retain their rooms at Lambeth he made it very clear to everyone that he intended to run things in his own way.

[19] Lambeth Palace Library: Davidson Papers, vol. 522, fos. 36–40.
[20] Bell, i. 299.

The new archbishop retained the services of Benson's chaplain, Ernest Ridge, for the first four years of his primacy. Other members of Benson's staff were not so lucky. A layman called Phillips, who had been Benson's private secretary for twelve years, wrote several letters in both sorrow *and* anger to Davidson in the weeks after Temple was nominated. He complained that the archbishop designate had told him 'baldly' that he would not be needed after Christmas. These are sad letters. The complaints are repetitive as though the writer was becoming obsessed. Phillips begged Davidson to intervene on his behalf and then bewailed the fact that there was nothing that anyone could do.[21] He was precisely the kind of fussy, loquacious person whom Temple could not bear. Mrs Benson interceded, indirectly and without effect, for those who had been particularly useful to her husband.[22]

Benson had attracted great personal devotion from his employees. When the health of one of them broke down he wrote rather smugly in his diary, 'People have a habit of working too hard for me.'[23] Temple was probably correct in thinking that those who had been devoted to his predecessor would find it difficult to work for him. He and Benson had got on very well together almost because their personalities were so different but the people who were close to one of them did not necessarily appeal to the other. If Temple found some of Benson's entourage difficult to work with, the Benson family seem to have thought Temple uncouth.

The principal purveyors of the story that Temple suspected Davidson of jealousy were Davidson himself, Arthur Benson, and Ridge. Because of the tensions between the new archbishop and his predecessor's household, this is bound to raise doubts about its reliability. In November 1896, when Davidson was feeling very much that he had been pushed out of the charmed circle, he wrote to Ridge:

Mind you keep me in touch so far as you can with what goes on, for to me it is strangest of all the changes of my life to find myself out in the cold as regards the central affairs of the Church of England, after nearly twenty years of closest knowledge.[24]

[21] Lambeth Palace Library: Davidson Papers, vol. 522, Phillips to Davidson, 2 letter written on 28 Oct. 1896; one on 30 Oct. and one on 10 Nov.

[22] See Phillips's last letter to Davidson of 10 Nov.

[23] Trinity College, Cambridge: E. W. Benson Papers, Official Diary 1888, 31 July.

[24] Bell, i. 287.

Arthur Benson wrote to Davidson on 22 January of the following year saying that Ridge had told him that Temple was in high spirits about the move to Canterbury 'as a headmaster might accept a deanery...'[25] He felt obliged, he said, to add that Ridge had also told him that Temple thought that Davidson resented his appointment. The letter protested that he hated to impart such news but feared that he 'might do more harm by being silent than by speaking out'. Davidson replied that he simply did not believe the story; and that, if it were true, it would imply that Temple must think him 'the most doubledyed humbug and hypo-crite unhanged'.[26] Yet his relations with the Temples continued to be so warm and friendly that he believed Ridge must be deluded. He spoke to Ridge who convinced him that it was not a delusion.

Arthur Benson confided malicious snippets of gossip about all sorts of people to his diary and he was particularly fond of stories which made Temple look senile or incompetent. About the middle of 1897 he wrote:

I must not forget that Ridge at Eton told me several very amusing things about the Abp. He reads novels, puts letters into bundles, unanswered, plays patience as much as ever. He was really very ill in Dec, and nearly died and spent nights of horrible pain. The household turned upside down next day by Mrs Temple because of a book the Abp wanted—a book he had been reading—asked for a preciser description, all he could say from his bedroom, was that he couldn't remember title or author's name, but it was about nigger being shot down by a schooner. It was found at last, a little children's story book about pirates at SPCK?

When ill he went about the house in a black flannel shirt no collar, grey worsted stockings and carpet slippers—looking a horrible old ruffian—a sort of dissipated coal-heaver. Very tiresome about health, will take no precautions.

There was, complained Benson, very little entertaining at Lambeth. No one came to luncheon or dinner and guests staying in the house were given breakfast and left to sponge elsewhere for other meals. But:

Mrs Temple is delightful: most kind and motherly to the Abp, who won't let any of his three chaplains go, though he only gives them one hour's work a day, behaves to them, says Ridge, as a goodnatured *great-uncle* who has three rather troublesome schoolboys home for the holidays.[27]

[25] Ibid. 88.
[26] Ibid.
[27] Magdalene College, Cambridge, A. C. Benson diaries, vol. 2, 149 ff. I am indebted to Dr Stuart Mews for drawing my attention to these diaries.

Instead of the 14,000 letters written each year in Archbishop Benson's day (Ridge was presumably the source of this information, too) Temple's staff were only writing about 5,000. Ridge had plainly been indiscreet for he also told Benson that people were in despair about ever getting answers to their letters.

Benson continued to gather information about Temple and to record the least attractive bits of it. About two years later he was describing an occasion in Canterbury at which he had been present where the archbishop, 'very hairy and dirty and quite blind' took the service reading 'the prayers very dully'.[28] And he loved to get stories from others in which Temple figured as rapidly failing and becoming ever more brusque and ungracious. The provost of Eton told him a story of the archbishop giving an address at a farewell service for two missionaries in which he gave them no word of encouragement but shouted at them that if they did not keep up their reading they would become 'ROT-TEN'.[29]

Arthur plainly loved and admired his father. When *he* had been archbishop and people were in a crisis they thought at once, he said:

of the kind mannered, anxious, masterful man at Lambeth, and what he would wish or advise—all this is gone and nothing seems to be taking its place—but I have no doubt that a *change* is good, and that my father's rule did *not* foster independent action but tended to bureaucracy.

Temple was bound to seem a less heroic archbishop to anyone whose mental picture of Benson combined 'masterful' with 'anxious'.

When Arthur Benson wrote to Davidson to tell him that Temple harboured these peculiar suspicions, Davidson was smarting under the sense of being in exile and may have been too ready to believe what he was told. Ridge was also, in a sense, the nearest thing to a Trojan horse within Lambeth Palace which the Bensons possessed. The Benson picture of a shambling, senile, near-blind, unkempt and unwashed archbishop is certainly a caricature. Yet there are recognizable fragments of truth in it. Guests at Lambeth may have been encouraged to be out for other meals for the same reason that, as an undergraduate, Temple had entertained his friends at breakfast—wine was not on the breakfast menu. Davidson thought it absurd that the archbishop spent time each morning tidying his dressing room and folding up his

---

[28] Magdalene College, Cambridge, A. C. Benson diaries, vol. 3, 235 ff.
[29] Ibid., vol. 9, June 1902, 29 ff.

towels[30] but Temple had been thoroughly trained in duty and obedience as a boy in the farmhouse at Axon. And if one is taught that one may not relax until one's duty is done, relaxation—even with novels or patience—is a sign that one has done what has to be done. One may also become impatient with those who manufacture unnecessary work or come running with questions which they ought to be able to answer for themselves. Ridge's remark about headmaster and deanery was intended to imply that the new archbishop was relieved to be going to a less demanding job. Temple was certainly convinced, as Tait had been before him, that Canterbury would be less taxing than London. He told his friends that he believed that he had five years more of work in him.

After his illness of December 1896 his health appears to have improved except for his eyesight which got worse and worse and which probably accounted for some of the odd things he did. He would suddenly find that he lost control of the muscles of his eyes and could not focus on what he was doing. He would sometimes have to stop, even in the middle of signing a cheque, till he could recover. The condition is peculiarly exhausting. When one cannot glance at a page and take it all in, or look round a room and note quickly who is present, one's mind, too, seems to focus more slowly. It was easy to think him senile as one of Balfour's secretaries complained that he was.[31] And even the Sandford *Memoir* permitted a hint of pathos to creep into its description of Temple in old age—'the grim, gaunt, tender-hearted man of seventy-five, entering with the quietness of strength upon the great task before him'.[32]

There is no genuine evidence of senility. His instructions to his chaplains, when he gave them, were clear. His wit could still be biting and his jokes read like the captions to cartoons in *Punch*:

Waiter. May I give your Grace some of this cold chicken?
Archbishop. No, you may not; wherever I go they give me cold chicken and 'The Church's One Foundation', and I hate them both.

Bishop at the Lambeth Conference. I think, your Grace, it may save time if I rise to move...
Archbishop. You can save more time by sitting still.[33]

---

[30] Bell, i. 291.
[31] G. I. T. Machin, *Politics and the Churches in Great Britain 1869 to 1921* (Oxford, 1987), 51.
[32] Sandford (ed.), ii. 247.
[33] Ibid. ii. 705.

William, as a sixth-former and undergraduate, was sent letters discussing Darwin's evolutionary hypothesis and Kant's philosophy. They showed no signs of mental disorder but a very great deal of pleasure in being able to talk about serious things with his son. What he said was clear and sensible even if it had not developed very much since the days of the Bampton lectures.[34]

The archbishop's work was, no doubt, much more of an effort every year. What had once been masterly inaction, sometimes became inaction pure and simple. Yet Davidson, in spite of his complaints about Temple, insisted that he always did what his office required.

For a diocesan Bishop, who means to be diocesan almost exclusively, this gives ample opportunity of strenuous service. The daily round of Confirmations, preachings, and other branches of diocesan administration is his, whether he will or not, and the difference between a good diocesan Bishop and a bad one depends upon how far he really rises to the adequate discharge of duties which in some form or other, adequately or inadequately, have got to be discharged.... In all such work Frederick Temple excelled. He was strong, thoughtful, self-reliant, forcible in speech and action, a great educationalist, and above all an enthusiastically earnest Christian man.[35]

And that description conveys very neatly Davidson's role during Temple's primacy. He was both critic and admirer: perhaps he had every intention of being his successor, too. He wanted Temple to do the job well (for everyone's sake, including Temple's). Temple's blunt, forthrightness was sometimes just what was needed and was sometimes disastrous. Davidson, who was superb at getting others to do what he wanted them to do, was not always above manipulating Temple—though, of course, for his own good. Davidson's real complaint was that Temple's very self-reliance made him too independent of others—and even of Davidson.

His chaplains had no knowledge of his correspondence, though a certain number of letters, not many, were given to them to write. He told them little or nothing and they had to pick up facts as best they could.... I fear that in his later years the reply was merely that the matter would receive consideration, and nothing more was heard of it.[36]

Even as Primate, Temple took his duties as a diocesan bishop very seriously. He insisted on performing a regular share of confirmations each year, so that he visited the parishes. He entertained the cathedral

---

[34] Sandford (ed.), ii. 687 and 693.   [35] Bell, i. 290.   [36] Ibid. 291.

community, canons and choristers alike, at Christmas. He carried out regular visitations of the diocese. And, above all and against a good deal of opposition, he got rid of the archiepiscopal country residence at Addington and re-established a house in Canterbury where the archbishops had had no residence for some 200 years. On the day of his enthronization he told the mayor that he very much regretted that there was nowhere for him to live in the city.[37] Some of his predecessors had also lamented the fact: Temple acted. The residence at Addington was sold. The chapter allowed him the use of a house on the site of the former palace of the archbishops. At the age of seventy-five he oversaw its enlargement and rebuilding and undertook the business of moving house and the rearrangement of his domestic life. It required considerable mental and physical energy and he knew what he was doing. When he was asked whether he thought that his successors would *like* living in Canterbury, he replied, 'No, I don't. I want to make 'em.'[38]

Immediately after he became archbishop, Temple was compelled to tackle one issue left over from the Benson era which he would probably have preferred to ignore. Leo XIII's *Apostolicae Curae* of September 1896 had declared Anglican orders to have no validity. Anglo-Catholics passionately wanted an answer to be made which would prove the contrary. Temple had not been among the bishops who were anxious to take the matter up. He was always convinced that the Church of England was unquestionably preferable to any other manifestation of Christianity. What a Pope had to say was not of much interest. John Wordsworth, Bishop of Salisbury, who had been trying since 1889 to persuade Dutch Old Catholics to take a favourable view of Anglican orders, felt differently.[39] He had written two papers on Anglican orders, one in 1890, with the help of Bishop Stubbs, *De Successione Episcoporum in Ecclesia Anglicana,* and the other four years later, with Benson's encouragement, *De Validitate Ordinum Anglicanorum Responsio ad Batavos.*[40] Both had been addressed to the Dutch. Later in the same year he had been in touch with 'friendly clergy of the Church of France'

---

[37] Sandford (ed.), ii. 210.

[38] Ibid. ii. 264.

[39] Wordsworth's account of events is in Lambeth Palace Library: Davidson Papers, vol. 100, fos. 39–53, Typescript entitled 'Archbishop Temple and the Responsio Archiepiscoporum Angliae ad Litteras Apostolicas Leonis Papae XIII' and inscribed by hand 'The Archbishop of Canterbury [Davidson] with affectionate regards from John Sarum'. The typescript probably dates from 1905 since it is bound with papers from that year.

[40] The letter was published and a second edition appeared in 1895.

including the Abbé Portal, editor of *Revue Anglo-Romaine*. A friendship between Portal and Lord Halifax (president of the English Church Union) had led to very informal talk about the possibilities of reunion. It was widely believed that *Apostolicae Curae* was intended to put a stop to these activities. Wordsworth, then, had both some experience of drafting documents on the subject and some knowledge of what was happening within the Roman Catholic world.

When the bull appeared, Mandell Creighton (still at Peterborough)—knowing of Wordsworth's contacts with the Dutch and the French—suggested to Benson that he and Wordsworth should join with Stubbs in writing a response. Having obtained the archbishop's approval, Creighton wrote to Wordsworth, who was on a visit to Glasgow and who at once left by train for Peterborough, drafting as he went. But Creighton was soon to be translated to London and in the upheaval of the move and with all the additional work involved was no longer able to take a very active part in writing the *Responsio*. Wordsworth had, therefore, virtually to draft it on his own.

I finished my draft on Friday 9th October at Tyneham, Dorset, where my brother then was, and posted it to Archbishop Benson at Hawarden. It just reached him on the Saturday but was never opened by him. He died, it will be remembered, on the Sunday morning of October 11th in Hawarden Church. It will also be remembered that his last public act was to write a short memorandum commenting on the Papal Bull and informing the public that it would be answered.[41]

Wordsworth had written to Benson a few days earlier, saying that he had seen the archbishop's statement and that he had prepared a draft which he would send to him as soon as it had been copied. Meantime he urged Benson that whatever was sent should take the form of a letter from the archbishops *addressed directly to the Pope*. The draft was sent back to him after Benson's death and he had then sent it to Archbishop Maclagan of York.

Two days after Temple's appointment was made public Wordsworth had sent him the draft response to the bull but it was not until after the ceremony of confirmation on 22 December that the new archbishop was able to give it his attention. Wordsworth had met with Stubbs and Creighton at the Athenaeum on 4 November to consider the draft which had already been printed up 'on slips'. 'It was possible to send a

---

[41] The letter was published and a second edition appeared in 1895, fo. 46.

slip or portion of a slip to any scholar and obtain his judgment on any particular statement without putting the whole in danger of premature publication.' A good many scholars were evidently consulted on various details which caused some delay but resulted in an improved text. Then Wordsworth went to meet Temple at Church House on 4 January 1897. He had been anxious all along that the response should be unaggressive and doubted his own ability to achieve the right tone. He was somewhat apprehensive about the changes which the brusque and undiplomatic new archbishop might introduce. Their session together lasted for four hours and Wordsworth found it exhausting. Temple was, he said, a 'delightful fellow-worker' who concentrated on the tone of the letter, insisting that every trace of bitterness be eradicated—and Wordsworth was convinced that this was not merely a matter of policy but because of 'deep Christian feeling'.[42] On the sections of the *Responsio* which compared the communion office of the Book of Common Prayer with the Roman canon of the mass and the English ordinal with the Roman pontifical 'Archbishop Temple gave very sound and careful advice. Though he obviously had not time to make any fresh researches it was clear that the subject was familiar to him from old reading and his quick perception of what was a good and valid argument and what was an undue refinement was most helpful.' The fact was, of course, that though Temple's academic reputation was as a mathematician interested in the natural sciences, he was—like every able Balliol man of his generation—primarily a classicist. Getting the nuances of the Latin right would be an interesting exercise in mental gymnastics.

At the end of January the three bishops met again with both archbishops, who signed the document on 19 February. Wordsworth had to arrange for the document to be translated into English, French, and Greek—and Temple apparently checked them and approved[43]—and for its publication. The council of the Church Association complained that there was no need for an official reply and that the Pope had been right in thinking that the ordinal of the Church of England had no intention to create sacrificing priests.[44] The archbishop ignored the letter.

The *Responsio* was not the only piece of business left unfinished by Benson's death. The Lambeth Conference had been planned for 1897

---

[42] Ibid., fo. 50.

[43] Ibid., fo. 52 f.

[44] Ibid.: Davidson Papers, vol. 47, fos. 349 ff., *Some Criticisms by the Council of the Church Association on the 'Answer' to Pope Leo made by Archbishops Maclagan and Temple.*

rather than 1898 (which would have been a decade after the previous Conference) because it was the thirteenth centenary of Augustine's landing in Kent in 597. The date could not be changed. All the arrangements had been discussed by the English bishops, the jobs allocated, the financial decisions taken and Davidson appointed secretary to the Conference. It was not, therefore, really *Temple's* Lambeth Conference. Indeed when he tried to transfer some of the meetings to Church House he was attacked, with an absurd fury, by Westcott who said that with all these menacing innovations looming, it would not be surprising if the next Conference were to be held in New York (by implication the most terrible thing that could happen). Temple characteristically made no attempt to justify his actions but sat quite still with his hand over his face. But he took the Bishop of New York home to dinner at Lambeth Palace.[45]

He had to chair the Conference and play host to it. One of the bishops described his manner as 'wholly honest and humble and very strong'.

He did not pay much attention to smaller rules of procedure but guided it in a commonsense way. He could not stand 'gas' and would put anyone down, in the manner of a Schoolmaster. The American Bishops were nettled at first, but they soon saw the big nature of the man and his utter freedom from pretence or desire for power.[46]

The Conference took some very important decisions about the future structure of the Anglican Communion,[47] but it ran along its own tramlines. The archbishop's most important contribution to its actual business was that he drafted the encyclical letter addressed to the wider Anglican world. It was clearly marked with his strong, austere views on morality (after the preamble the first four paragraphs were headed 'Temperance', 'Purity', 'Sanctity of Marriage', and 'Industrial Problems') and it was adopted by the Conference with very little amendment.[48]

Davidson, who had thought Benson a less powerful personality than Tait but a more genial host, found Temple abrasive and ungracious. The archbishop plainly thought that this was a job to be done and he would

[45] A. M. G. Stephenson, *Anglicanism and the Lambeth Conferences* (London, 1978), 95 f.

[46] Bishop H. H. Montgomery quoted in Stephenson, 96.

[47] *Conference of Bishops of the Anglican Communion Holden at Lambeth Palace in July 1897: Encyclical Letter from the Bishops with the Resolutions and Reports* (London, 1898), Report of the Committee on the Organisation of the Anglican Communion, and the resolution setting up a 'Tribunal of Reference', 53 ff.

[48] Ibid. 13 ff.

get it done as expeditiously as possible. Davidson was shocked that it had not occurred to Temple to say a few nice things about Benson at the opening session.[49] When he prompted him the archbishop said, ' "Then I will do it" and spoke some admirable and telling sentences.' For Davidson it was all like that.

I had been appointed the Episcopal Secretary and was conversant with every-thing, yet he hardly consulted me about anything, leaving me a perfectly free hand about things that were in any sense within my province and saying absolutely nothing to me, unless under pressure, about the policy, or the plans, or the order of proceedings, for which he would have to be, when the time came, technically responsible, but in which I was necessarily closely concerned. The whole thing was done by him like other things in his life, vigorously, brusquely, and effectively but with no attempt to touch any vein of sentiment or to recognize the work of Archbishop Benson in the programme laid down or the matters selected for discussion.[50]

Yet even Davidson was bound in the end to come to the conclusion that what he achieved 'was due to his single-hearted outspoken devotion to the sacred principle of duty, inspired by a quite overmastering sense of the presence and help of God'.[51]

The bishops must, on the whole, have felt as Davidson did. If they resented Temple's brusqueness, they put up with it. The American bishops, who had treated him in such a cavalier fashion at the previous Lambeth Conference, wished on this occasion to present him with a mitre as a gesture of their admiration and a recognition of his quasi-patriarchal status. In spite of his obvious embarrassment, Temple was inquisitive about some of the aspects of the use and abuse of mitres.[52] In the end he asked for, and was given, a sick communion set—something, he said, which he had never possessed. The inscription on the case spoke of 'his wise leadership his justice his generosity his gracious hospitality'.[53] He had tried very hard to be hospitable and to entertain the bishops to more than breakfast. He had invited parties of about twenty-five bishops to stay at Lambeth Palace for three days at a time 'from Mondays to Wednesdays and from Wednesdays to Saturdays. The

---

[49] Bell, i. 303.
[50] Ibid.
[51] Ibid. 304.
[52] Lambeth Palace Library: Davidson Papers, vol. 48, fo. 253 and vol. 522, fos. 38 ff., and Sandford (ed.), ii. 272 f.
[53] Sandford (ed.), ii. 272—there are no commas in the original.

Archbishop kept Sundays as days of rest.'[54] Entertaining the bishops was by implication very hard work and one wonders whether they knew it.

Dealing with colonial bishops was a part of the archbishop's work which Temple seems to have been least enthusiastic about. It is difficult to avoid the impression that he regarded them as rather second-class bishops, perhaps a little less significant than English suffragans. Colonial bishops who wanted to resign their sees and 'come home' were a frightful nuisance because successors had to be found for them and because they wanted some quiet but dignified position such as a residentiary canonry. Davidson thought his treatment of the overseas bishops quite dreadful. Even on the most complex issues, Davidson complained, he would act quite on his own, if he acted at all, ignoring the missionary societies or those who understood the problems. The bishops complained that they could not get an answer, or an answer that was any help.[55] It was not that the archbishop thought that what was usually called the missionary work of the Church was unimportant. He preached often and enthusiastically on the subject. He was assiduous in attending the functions of the missionary societies. But he was impatient with people who complained of being overworked or in poor health. When a clergyman told him that his doctors had warned him that a particular job might damage his health, Temple replied, 'Oh, but we don't think of that, do we?'[56] Colonial bishops complaining of ill health were probably fortunate if they did *not* receive a reply. If it was insensitive to assume that everyone was like himself, Temple was probably insensitive. He set no value on conversation or correspondence which was aimed at making him *feel* better: if it achieved no practical end, it was a waste of time. He could not believe that others were different. A bishop somewhere in south-east Asia, at the end of his tether physically and facing a hundred problems he had no hope of solving, might have been encouraged by a letter containing what Temple would have regarded as meaningless polite platitudes. On the other hand, a practical problem, however tiresome and intractable, was likely to receive practical attention.[57]

Among the most complicated of matters requiring attention in his early years as Primate was the Queen's Diamond Jubilee of 1897. [David

---

[54] Sandford (ed.), ii. 271.

[55] Bell, i. 291.

[56] Sandford (ed.), ii. 193.

[57] See e.g. Peter Hinchliff, 'Colonial Church Establishment in the Aftermath of the Colenso Controversy' (forthcoming).

Cannadine has suggested that between the 1870s and 1914 a profound change affected the public image of the monarchy, 'as its ritual, hitherto inept, private and of limited appeal, became splendid, public and popular'.[58] To some extent, this change had been facilitated by the Queen's retirement from active politics. However difficult and intrusive she had been, she now wielded far less effective power. Consequently, the way was open for the monarchy to surround itself with magnificent and affecting ceremonial. In short, royal power had been exchanged for royal popularity.[59] The Diamond Jubilee, whatever its complications, assumed great symbolic significance in the national life.] The Jubilee was not Temple's first experience of royal occasions. He had taken part, for instance, in the marriage of Prince George to Princess May of Teck. But this was the first time he had played a central role and from it he was distracted by the small matters of detail.[60] Half amused half irritated, he told Fred that he was being overwhelmed by petty requests from the army. They had asked that troops involved in the Jubilee parade might make use of a piece of open land attached to Lambeth Palace.

Every demand seems to grow. I was asked to let the soldiers take their dinner in the field after the great procession on the 22nd. Then came a petition that they might also come before the procession. Then they wanted to have their breakfast there. Then they wanted to come at 5 in the morning. Then they asked to send some men in the night before to have everything read[y]; and now it is 'possibly two nights before'. Verily in this world should [a man] take care how he consents to say A; assuredly he will presently have to say B; and if time suffices he will have to go to the end of the Alphabet.[61]

So far as the service itself was concerned the biggest problem was that the Queen had become incontinent and could not leave her carriage, so a ramp was to be constructed to allow her to drive up to the west door of St Paul's for the singing of a *Te Deum* and some prayers. And Temple became seriously concerned that no one seemed to be dealing with the practical implications of such a service.

[58] David Cannadine, 'The Context, Performance and Meaning of Ritual: The British Monarchy and the "Invention of Tradition", *c*.1820–1977', in Eric Hobsbawm and Terence Ranger, *The Invention of Tradition* (Cambridge, 1995), 120.

[59] Ibid. 120 f.

[60] Lambeth Palace Library: Davidson Papers, vol. 49, fo. 346, Temple to Davidson, 5 Feb. 1897.

[61] Family Papers in the possession of the Right Revd F. S. Temple: Temple to Frederick, dated from Lambeth Palace 22 May 1897.

I have heard absolutely nothing from anybody about the proposed ceremonial on the 22nd June. That a short service with fine music just outside the West Front of St Paul's could be made exceedingly impressive, I have no doubt. But what on earth shall we do if it be a rainy day?[62]

Temple's anxiety that something should be *done* was partly met by the appointment on 15 February (by the Prince of Wales) of a committee consisting of the Archbishop, the Bishops of London (Creighton) and Winchester (Davidson), the Dean of St Paul's (now the former Canon Gregory), Reginald Brett (the future Lord Esher; at this time secretary at the Office of Works and a member of the Queen's intimate circle), and two senior military officers. Since Temple issued the notice convening the committee he presumably acted as chairman.[63] But the problems turned out to be far greater than had been supposed. A fortnight later the Queen's secretary was telling Davidson that there was little enthusiasm for the service. The Prince of Wales thought it might be better to have simultaneous services in every cathedral and parish church and there was popular resentment that so much of the space in front of St Paul's would be taken up by the ramp, the official procession of carriages and princes on horseback, troops, bands, dignitaries, and choirs, that there would be little room for the public.[64]

The Queen also had her reservations. Davidson told Gregory that she was insisting that the service should not last more than a quarter of an hour, 'or at all events under 20 minutes, she repeated several times. She dreads sitting there in her carriage long w. all the Princes on horseback round her.' The Queen had been timing various settings of the *Te Deum* and had come to the conclusion that ten minutes was quite enough and that it ought to be simple, 'with no additions or flourishes...'[65] The dean was to tell Dr Martin, the organist, to bear that in mind when composing a special setting. Martin was not pleased—'Though my *Te Deum* takes only ten minutes, yet I think the Queen would not like it, as it is not simple and I am afraid it begins with a dreadful flourish.'[66] Davidson smoothed that one out by insisting that Dr Martin's *Te Deum* was part of the plan originally approved which could not now be altered except by royal command. Temple's most prominent part in the actual

[62] Lambeth Palace Library: Davidson Papers, vol. 49, fo. 352, Temple to Davidson, 13 Feb. 1897.

[63] Ibid., fo. 354.

[64] Ibid., fo. 358 f., letter dated 29 Feb.

[65] Ibid., fo. 361 f.

[66] Ibid., fo. 365, letter from Martin to Gregory, 8 Mar. (emphasis added).

service, which itself went smoothly, was to cope with the one snag no one had anticipated. Seventeen other carriages had to be got out of the way before the Queen's could leave. There was, therefore, a horrible gap after the final hymn. The archbishop called for three cheers for her majesty 'and the threatened hiatus was filled in a way that brought the tears coursing down the cheeks of the dearly loved and venerable Queen'.[67]

More serious, perhaps, were Temple's dealings with the Queen and the royal household over matters to do with the South African War. Again Davidson was the intermediary with the Queen's staff whose reaction to the archbishop is never easy to assess. When they told Davidson that the Queen thought the archbishop 'so wise' were they being ironical? Behind the issues raised by Temple and others were hidden problems which needed delicate handling. The nature of war itself was changing. What was happening affected 'ordinary' homes and families as previous wars had not done. Or it may be that august personages had never realized how war affected ordinary people. There were also those who regretted the war as an unwarranted, aggressive interference in the rights of two small independent republics. The behaviour of British colonial politicians, like Cecil Rhodes, was not above reproach. There were two things, in particular, in which Temple was passionately interested and for which he wished to enlist the Queen's support. First and foremost was the need for money to care for the casualties of the war and their dependants. He wished the Queen to authorize an appeal to the churches for a collection to be made throughout the country. Sir Arthur Bigge, the Queen's secretary, was alarmed because there were so many other interests to be considered. Colonel Tully of the Imperial War Fund was saying that there was far more money already than would ever be needed. Hospitals and other charities were complaining that the response to their own appeals were drying up because everyone was giving to war victims. The government were most anxious in case the archbishop should say something which might have unfortunate political implications. (A Conservative government fighting a war of which some Liberals had been highly critical, might well wonder whether Temple's Liberalism might revive.) Bigge wrote to Davidson, 'I do hope the Archbishop is not going to make The Queen godmother to an unwelcome child. Of course we can still

---

[67] Sandford (ed.), ii. 268.

smother it.'[68] Davidson must have passed these comments to Temple for Temple wrote back very firmly that some of the money had been diverted to the Patriotic Fund and that, though £257,364 might be enough to care for widows and orphans of those *killed* in the war, £60,000 would hardly be sufficient to care for the dependants of reservists who might actually survive but be too crippled to support them. And £30,000 was 'but a poor provision for the permanently disabled'. 'I think Her Majesty need not fear that we shall have too much for these purposes.'[69] Temple understood the realities of modern war.

Having won the Queen's support Temple raised a related issue and it was Bigge who then needed Davidson as a go-between. He sent him a message on 23 December 1899 saying that the archbishop was now asking that 7 January 1900, the day when collections were to be devoted to caring for the dependants of war casualties, should be made a national day of intercession. The only precedent for such a thing was that the Crown had sometimes proclaimed a day of prayer, fasting, and humiliation when the nation seemed to face probable defeat or disaster. The Queen was opposed to anything which might suggest that Britain was losing and so was the government. The Queen wanted the bishops, instead, to arrange prayers in their own dioceses. Davidson made it clear that it was Temple's own idea—'It is his way to act independently.'[70] And to everyone's relief and satisfaction the bishops at their January meeting at Lambeth, agreed to choose a day (which satisfied Temple) on which each bishop would ask his own diocese to use prayers for the nation at war but would be careful to avoid the word 'humiliation' (which satisfied the Queen).[71] So in the end the matter was amicably settled.

Yet another question arose about the South African War. One of the official forms of prayer issued for use in churches had included one for the fallen—'that they with us may enter into that rest which Thou hast prepared for those who believe in Thee'. Temple was asked a question in the House of Lords about prayers for the dead and whether they had ever been permitted in the Church of England. Remembering among the dead those whom one loved was something with which Temple had

---

[68] Lambeth Palace Library: Davidson Papers, vol. 69, fo. 230.
[69] Ibid., fo. 235 f., Temple to Davidson, 9 Dec. 1899.
[70] Ibid., fos. 264 ff., draft of a letter from Davidson to Bigge.
[71] Ibid., fos. 302 f. draft of a letter from Davidson to Bigge, 16 Jan. 1900.

great sympathy. It was, perhaps, the point on which he came closest to the ritualists though he was never happy with anything like a requiem mass. With an air almost of triumph he produced for the Lords two eighteenth-century prayers authorized by the Crown and containing very similar words.

Ritualism remained the least amicable issue of the day and caused political tensions, too. Balfour found it an embarrassment when he tried to devise an education bill which did not disadvantage the Established Church. Sir William Harcourt, a leading Liberal politician and a severe critic of the government's policies in South Africa, was an equally vigorous opponent of anything remotely smelling of ritualism and resented the bishops' use of the veto against prosecutions. In the summer of 1898 he wrote a series of letters which were published in *The Times* in which he complained bitterly of the bishops' apparent reluctance to do anything to stop the growth of ritualism. At about the same time there were a number of other incidents in which various Anglo-Catholic practices—incense, lights, reservation of the Sacrament, confession, and prayers for the dead—attracted a great deal of publicity.

Temple's views on most of these questions were not in doubt. A charge delivered at the visitation of his diocese in the autumn of 1898 made it quite clear that he disliked most of these practices though he declared that some of them—notably the doctrine of The Real Presence in the Eucharist—were lawful in the Church of England.[72] He was also unwilling to budge from his rather naïve earlier conviction that prosecutions only made matters worse. In a sense, then, he played into Harcourt's hands by appearing to condone what he condemned. And he also continued to hold to his opinion that if the bishops were firm in declaring that practices were illegal, the clergy would give them up. The preface to the Book of Common Prayer suggested a procedure to be adopted when there was doubt about how to 'understand, do, and execute' its rubrics and directions. The archbishop let it be known that he hoped that it would be followed. The preface said that the parties should:

.. resort to the Bishop of the Diocese, who by his discretion shall take order for the quieting and appeasing of the same; so that the same order be not contrary to anything contained in this book. And if the Bishop of the Diocese be in doubt, then he may send for the resolution thereof to the Archbishop.

---

[72] Sandford (ed.), ii. 291, and Owen Chadwick, *The Victorian Church*, 2 vols. (London, 1968/70), ii. 356.

It appears that Temple got this idea from Benson, who had thought that it might provide a way of dealing with controversial issues without having to resort to litigation.[73] An application to the archbishop would not be a prosecution: no one could be sent to prison but, Temple hoped, a solemn decision from the archbishop, made in accordance with the instructions of the Book of Common Prayer, would have a very powerful influence on the behaviour of the clergy. He had reckoned without the determination of some of them.

When he was asked for an opinion, it was obviously not an entirely spontaneous affair. Certain bishops in both provinces applied, each to their own archbishop, for a decision. In each case it was said that the bishop had directed a clergyman in his diocese to cease to perform certain actions and the clergyman concerned had claimed to be doing only what was directed in the rubrics of the Book of Common Prayer. The bishop having failed to settle the matter was sending it 'for the resolution thereof to the Archbishop'. Because both archbishops had received similar requests (in what was legally no more than a coincidence) they sat together at Lambeth to hear the questions on Monday, 8 May 1899 and several subsequent days. The questions concerned the use of incense and the carrying of lights in procession.

The Archbishop of York was William Maclagan, who had been Bishop of Lichfield from 1878 until he became Archbishop in 1891. He was a High Churchman but discouraged the sort of ceremonial that the younger Anglo-Catholics believed important. He had become interested in reunion and particularly in creating good relations with Old Catholics, having attended a conference with them in Bonn in 1887.

Everyone seems to have found it difficult to remember that this was not a court and that there was no prosecution. When the archbishop was about to adjourn for luncheon on the second day of the hearing, John Kensit of the Protestant Truth Society (a notorious pursuer of ritualists) intervened.

Mr Kensit. Before your Grace adjourns may I enter a protest against the holding of this Court, a protest which I will hand up to your Grace. May I read this Protest, or hand it up to your Grace?

Archbishop of Canterbury. You may do what you like with it.

Mr Kensit. Then by your permission I will read my protest against the holding of this Court. 'I John Kensit'—[*great laughter*] I have the permission of his Grace. If you do not know how to behave it is a pity you do not.

---

[73] Sandford (ed.), ii. 294.

Abp of Canterbury. This is not a Court, Mr Kensit, at all. I think we had better go to luncheon.[74]

Officially the hearing was called 'In the matter of the Revd Henry Westall, St Cuthbert's, Philbeach Gardens London and in the matter of the Revd Henry Ram, St John's, Norwich before His Grace the Archbishop of Canterbury and His Grace the Archbishop of York.' Westall was, of course, Temple's old adversary.[75] Ram was a clergyman in the diocese of Norwich. Technically, Creighton the Bishop of London and John Sheepshanks the Bishop of Norwich were each applying to his own archbishop for a ruling. Learned counsel appeared to argue the case for the clergymen and for the bishops. The bishops' team included Lewis Dibdin, who was to be one of the most eminent ecclesiastical lawyers of his day. Appearing with him, in addition to his junior, was a Professor Collins who was an ecclesiastical historian but there as counsel not as an expert witness. The other team was led by H. C. Richards, QC, MP, with two juniors. By far the greatest part of the hearing was taken up with speeches from counsel though there was evidence from experts such as Walter Frere, a member of the Community of the Resurrection and a leading liturgist (eventually Bishop of Truro), and several prominent Anglo-Catholic figures interested in liturgical matters, like W. Birkbeck and Athelstan Riley.

The argument and the evidence traversed the whole question of the use of incense and of ceremonial lamps or candles, from biblical evidence, through the usages of the Early Church, to the rubrics of the Book of Common Prayer. But the central question was the precise meaning of the so-called Ornaments Rubric of the Book of Common Prayer of 1559 in Elizabeth's reign. That rubric said that until the Crown should direct otherwise the ornaments of the church buildings and of the ministers should be the same as those which were in use by authority of parliament in the second year of the reign of Edward VI. Edward's reign had begun on 28 January 1547 and if the years of his reign were calculated strictly from the actual date of his accession, the second year was from 28 January 1548 to the end of January 1549. But if

---

[74] Lambeth Palace Library: Verbatim Account of Archbishops' Hearings on Incense and Reservation, 1899; (VZ IB/3/1–3), vol. I, 219. The account was done professionally by shorthand writers of the firm Marten, Meredith and Henderson of 13 New Inn, Strand, W.C. It is in several hands and parts of it are typed. Shorthand writers sometimes inserted descriptive comments in brackets. In vol. 1 there are two sets of page numbers. The numbers at the top of each page are used here.

[75] See above, 214–18.

one were to calculate the second year of his reign from the first day of
the new calendar year, then it ran from 1 January to 31 December 1548.
The Prayer Book of 1549 had been passed by parliament on 21 January
1549 so that by the first calculation it fell within the second year and by
the second it did not. It could be said that there was real doubt as to
whether the 1559 book reimposed the vestments of the 1549 book. There
was also the question whether the Crown had ever imposed 'further
order'. And it was genuinely doubtful whether it had. Elizabeth's archbishops had issued directions: she herself had not indubitably done so.
It was Westall's contention that he had been directed by his bishop to
discontinue the use of lights and incense which he believed that he was
actually required by law to use. Ram's case was much the same, though
it applied only to the use of incense.

It is plain that Temple found the proceedings tiresomely long drawn
out. He intervened far less often than Maclagan did with questions to
counsel and witnesses. Moments of knockabout comedy, as with Mr
Kensit, were rare and there was little to break the monotony of the
technical arguments, both historical and legal. He made little attempt to
disguise his impatience at the length and number of speeches which
counsel found necessary nor at the number of days occupied by the
hearings.[76] But there is nothing to suggest that he missed any of the
finer points and he sometimes pulled counsel up when he thought they
had been inaccurate.[77] The hearing on incense continued into a fifth day
and was adjourned on 13 May.[78] It resumed on Tuesday 6 June 1899
when there was a very similar performance on the subject of proces-
sional lights. Both archbishops were again present in spite of the fact
that Westall's practice alone was being considered.[79]

Temple delivered his ruling on both incense and lights on 31 July and
drafted the document himself though he had sent it to Maclagan for
comment and signature. In both instances he found, in effect, against
the clergymen concerned, declaring all three practices illegal. In some
ways his style and reasoning were reminiscent of Benson's in the Lincoln
case, but he made none of Benson's allowances for what was politically
expedient nor had he Benson's veneration for history. He brushed aside
arguments about what had been custom and usage in the sixteenth

[76] See Temple's exchange with Dibdin: Lambeth Palace Library: Verbatim Account of
Archbishops' Hearings on Incense and Reservation, 1899; (VZ IB/3/1–3), vol. i. 396.

[77] Ibid., vol. ii. 461 f.

[78] Ibid. 187.

[79] Ibid. 189.

century, saying that it had been a time of great excitement and unsettlement and no doubt Elizabeth's act had been imperfectly obeyed. But, he thought, its precise and clear statements had gradually prevailed and the forbidden ceremonies had gradually disappeared. In places his findings read almost as if he were describing the correct policy for dealing with late nineteenth-century excitement and unsettlement: clear statements of the law would prevail and the forbidden ceremonies disappear. So he went by the strictest possible interpretation of the law and there seemed to him no loophole for ritualism. Nor would he budge an inch when in January 1900 he was presented with a memorial signed by 14,000 laymen protesting against his rulings.

Meanwhile there had been a further hearing on the subject of the reservation of the Sacrament, starting on 17 July 1899 and affecting clergy and bishops from both provinces.[80] The archbishops sat together but again the drafting was primarily Temple's. The ruling was delivered at Lambeth on 1 May 1900 and ended with the words:

In conclusion, after weighing carefully all that has been put before us, I am obliged to decide that the Church of England does not at present allow Reservation in any form, and that those who think that it ought to be allowed, though perfectly justified in endeavouring to get the proper authorities to alter the law, are not justified in practising Reservation until the law has been altered.[81]

Throughout the period in which the hearings had been taking place, the government had been under pressure to compel the clergy to obey the law. A Church Discipline Bill had been shelved for the time being though with the implicit threat that, if the bishops were not able to enforce discipline, new legislation would be enacted. Balfour, who had been Leader of the Commons throughout the crisis and under considerable pressure from some of his own backbenchers as well as from Harcourt and others in the Liberal party, found Temple's masterly inaction very difficult to deal with. He wanted an assurance that the bishops would act against lawlessness. Parry, Balfour's secretary, complained to Davidson that Balfour needed something which he could use to appease the law-and-order lobby and could get nothing from the archbishop. Davidson's reply was as near to open disloyalty as he could ever be.

---

[80] Lambeth Palace Library: Archbishops' Hearings on the Reservation of the Sacrament, VZ 1B/3/3.
[81] Ibid. 513.

...I can never be responsible for anything [the archbishop] does or leaves undone. He is inscrutable—and perhaps most incrutable of all to us who are supposed to have most to do with him. He cannot be regarded as like other men! grand as he is.[82]

Temple pursued his own policy regardless. He had come, he was quite sure, to legally correct conclusions. He was convinced that, in due course, the good sense of the clergy would make them see the foolishness of illegality. He could not believe that any good purpose would be served by giving Balfour ammunition for public attacks on the ritualists. So he ignored all pleas that he should do anything more than his duty required. Anglo-Catholics, however, ignored the hearings and the anger of their opponents was undiminished.

[82] Bell, i. 349.

11

A Crowning Achievement

Queen Victoria died at Osborne on 22 January 1901. Temple had preached at a service in St Paul's to mark her eightieth birthday in the previous May and he was present in the Lords on 25 January when the house was officially informed of the Queen's death by a message from the new King. On the following Sunday he preached again in St Paul's on the Queen's life and her service to the country. The body was taken to Windsor for burial and the service was conducted by Davidson. Temple does not seem to have been present at the funeral.[1]

Creighton, who had been thought too young for the primacy in 1896, had died in the previous week. Temple was extremely anxious that Davidson should agree to move to London and wrote to him, urging him to agree, and to Salisbury saying that there was no doubt at all but that it should be Davidson.[2] When Salisbury actually offered to appoint him, however, Davidson's doctors were adamant that he ought not to agree.[3] Davidson, therefore, remained at Winchester and Arthur Winnington-Ingram was appointed to London in the hope, perhaps, that—having Anglo-Catholic leanings himself—he might be able to control the ritualists.

[The coronations of Edward's three immediate predecessors had not been particularly memorable occasions. George IV's coronation, although conceived in the grandest possible manner in a desperate attempt to gain popularity, 'was so overblown that grandeur merged into farce', the pathetic attempt of Caroline to gain access to the Abbey being only one example.[4] William IV, no lover of ceremony and

---

[1] G. K. A. Bell, *Randall Davidson Archbishop of Canterbury*, 2 vols. (London, 1938), 356 ff.

[2] Lambeth Palace Library: Davidson Papers, vol. 4, fo. 187, Temple to Davidson 3 Nov. 1900 and fo. 188 Temple to Salisbury, same date. Also Bell, i. 360 ff.

[3] Lambeth Palace Library: Davidson Papers, vol. 4, fos. 191 ff.

[4] David Cannadine, 'The Context, Performance and Meaning of Ritual: The British Monarchy and the "Invention of Tradition", *c.* 1820–1977', in Eric Hobsbawm and Terence Ranger, *The Invention of Tradition* (Cambridge, 1995), 120.

ostentation, had tried to dispense with the ritual altogether. When his coronation did occur, it was so abbreviated that it began to be referred to, contemptuously, as the 'Half-Crownation'.[5] Nor was Victoria's coronation much more impressive. It was unrehearsed; the clergy lost their places in the order of service; the music was very inferior; Archbishop Howley placed the ruby ring, designed to fit her little finger, so hard upon the fourth finger that she could only get it off painfully after soaking it in ice water; and two of the trainbearers talked throughout the entire ceremony.[6] By the fourth quarter of the century such lukewarm attitudes to national occasions had begun to give way. Old ceremonials were staged with much greater expertise and a sharp eye to their public appeal; there was an interest in 'invented tradition', the deliberate concoction of new rituals to meet popular demand. Rapid and unsettling social change, Cannadine argues, produced a desire for the 'preservation of anachronism', in which 'the deliberate, ceremonial presentation of an important but venerated monarch as a unifying symbol of permanence and national community, became both possible and necessary'.[7]

The coronation of Edward VII, therefore, required careful consideration, planning, and consultation. As Jocelyn Perkins, the sacrist at Westminster Abbey from 1899 to 1958, later wrote:

Anything even remotely suggestive of...brilliant muddling was unthinkable...Things accepted without question in 1838 could not fail to meet with stern condemnation in 1902...The attainment of a lofty standard of worship and ceremonial at the solemn sacring of Edward VII was felt on all sides to be imperative.[8]]

The coronation was originally fixed to take place on 26 June 1902 but the King was taken seriously ill, was operated on for appendicitis and the ceremony had to be postponed to 9 August. Not only was the King still far from strong when the deferred date arrived but Temple was over eighty and known to be infirm and the Dean of Westminster, G. G. Bradley, was himself old and ill. With three of the principal players in doubtful health the proceedings were bound to be fraught with anxiety

---

[5] Cannadine, 'The Context, Performance and Meaning of Ritual', 118.

[6] Ibid., E. Longford, *Victoria R.I.* (London, 1964), 81.

[7] Cannadine, 'The Context, Performance and Meaning of Ritual', 108, 122.

[8] Ibid. 132.

[9] Described in some sources as 'perityphlitis' which is defined as 'inflammation of the secum or appendicitis'.

A great deal of the burden, both of planning the arrangements and of carrying them out on the day, would rest on Davidson. He, being Davidson, was determined to see that the coronation was as perfect as it could be made. The King was unpredictable in more than health: he could be impatient about matters of religion and he could also be suddenly devout—as when he asked for a celebration of Holy Communion in his mother's bedroom after her death. His chief and immediate concern seemed to be to shorten the service in every way possible. Temple, too, was thought to be an unceremonious sort of person, even when in the best of health. There were fears, therefore, that this might be, from a liturgical point of view, one of the worst coronations on record.

Lord Halifax wrote to Davidson:

What a pity Abp Benson and Arthur Stanley are not respectively at Canterbury and Westminster when the Coronation takes place. They would have been interested in all the historical and religious traditions and associations and would have seen that all was as it should be. Now, the present Archbishop is useless, and the dean of Westminster more useless still.[10]

He thought that the two crucial things were to get a small commission appointed to take charge of the liturgical side (St John Hope of the Antiquarian Society, W. Birkbeck an expert on the Orthodox Church, and Canon Armytage Robinson at the Abbey) and to get a new set of cloth of gold copes for the Abbey from Russia—'far finer and more splendid than anything to be got in the West'. *The Times* said of Temple that 'it could be anticipated that he would bring to the subject a devotional mind and strong English commonsense; but, when it was known that he had received a general instruction to shorten the service, rumours of a disquieting kind began to spread and irresponsible persons asserted that serious mutilations of the ceremony were contemplated'.[11]

In fact Temple seems to have been looking forward to crowning a new sovereign for some years. When he was writing to Davidson about the proposed gift of a mitre from the American bishops he had said that the only occasion on which he could conceive of wearing a mitre was at the coronation ('if I live to see one') and wanted to know what bishops did about putting mitres off and on at the crowning.[12]

---

[10] Lambeth Palace Library: Davidson Papers, vol. 278, fo. 1 ff., letter dated 27 Apr. 1901.
[11] *The Times*, 5 May 1902.
[12] Lambeth Palace Library: Davidson Papers, vol. 522, fos. 36 and 38.

In fact the three most serious problems connected with the coronation were the shortening of the service, whether bishops should wear
mitres, and how many parts of the King ought to be anointed.[13] The
bishops' mitres proved an almost intractable problem, haberdashery as
always bringing out the worst in everyone. Correspondents wrote from
all over England urging Temple to make the bishops wear them or not
wear them. Even Westall of St Cuthbert's, Philbeach Gardens drew
Temple's attention to a story which the Anglo-Catholics had got hold
of (eventually proved to be unreliable) that silver mitres had been worn
at the coronation of George II.[14] The King seemed to favour mitres. So
many people had strong opinions that Temple was forced to do an
immense amount of research on the matter—or have it done for him.
Amongst his papers is a kind of score sheet, showing what headgear, if
any, the bishops wore at each coronation from the Reformation onward.
Whoever wrote it also seemed to think that mitres were worn at the
coronation of Edward the Confessor but not at that of Harold, his
successor.[15] In the end the archbishop ruled firmly that all bishops
would carry square black caps, not purple, and not even velvet. That
was not the end of the bother, though, for in June the Society of St
Dunstan wrote to say that they possessed the copyright on a new square
cap designed by the Revd Percy Dearmer and modelled on the portrait
of Cranmer in the National Portrait Gallery. They informed Temple that
the canons of Westminster and four of the bishops had already ordered
these caps. He had only to send his head size and they would supply
him with one forthwith. Thereafter they wrote roughly every ten days
giving him an update on the number of bishops who had ordered caps
and hinting that the supply might soon be exhausted. There is no
evidence to show whether Temple ever ordered one.

There appeared to be no end to the questions people wanted Temple
to answer. The firm of Ravenscroft wished to know whether he wanted
to order wigs for his coachman and the bishop of London's chaplain
asked Temple's chaplain what the coachman was going to wear. (Temple
scrawled on the letter—'ordinary dress'). A Mr Miall wrote to say that

---

[13] The most useful sources for material relating to the coronation are Lambeth Palace
Library: F. Temple Papers, vols. 57 and 58, and the Davidson Papers, vols. 4 and 278; the
Family Papers in the possession of the Right Revd F. S. Temple includes a file of papers
relating to the coronation and the royal family, many of them printed copies of service
papers, etc.
[14] Lambeth Palace Library: F. Temple Papers, vol. 57, fos. 222 ff.
[15] Ibid., vol. 58, fo. 76.

he proposed to make a picture of the archbishop in coronation dress (he made his living from water-colours) and needed to know which cope he would be wearing and what colour his eyes were. (Temple's note was 'Do not know'.) The *Ladies Field* wanted a photograph of him for a coronation number which would be presented to the Queen. Even the editor of the *Somerset Herald* wanted full details about the embroidery on his cope though he did not disclose why he needed the informa-tion.[16] Opulent costume obviously fascinated contemporary society. The *Daily Chronicle* of 20 June provided full details of each bishop's cope. Only when it was all over did Temple reveal to anyone that he had worn a cope borrowed from another bishop.[17]

The question of which parts of the service might be omitted was more serious. Part of the problem was that Victoria's long reign meant that no one remembered the last coronation. The Privy Council ap-pointed on 26 June 1901 a very large 'Coronation Committee' but then authorized any five of them to act for the whole. The Coronation Committee met on 1 July. It asked Temple to prepare a form of service and it appointed an executive headed by the Duke of Norfolk who, as Earl Marshal, was in overall charge of the coronation and actually took legal possession of the Abbey for the period—which, because he was a Roman Catholic, outraged some extreme Protestant opinion.[18] The executive committee was still very large and consisted of courtiers like Lord Esher; civil servants like Sir Schomberg McDonnell from the Office of Works; senior military and naval officers; and Francis Knollys, the King's secretary. Davidson was the only cleric, which put him in a very powerful position.[19]

Temple acquired copies of the forms of service used for William IV and Victoria but evidently found the business of revising very difficult and he was moving much more slowly than he or anyone else had anticipated. Davidson started to take a hand in the planning. The king wanted the service to be as short as possible. Davidson, perhaps because of Halifax's suggestion, started to consult Armytage Robinson, who could be a very difficult person but was throughout all the preparations for the coronation a model of helpful, unassuming good sense. There were two kinds of curtailment possible. One was uncontroversial; a

[16] All these letters appear in Lambeth Palace Library: F. Temple Papers, vol. 57, fos. 230–6.

[17] Ibid., Davidson Papers, vol. 4, fo. 205, Temple to Davidson, 12 Aug. 1902.

[18] Ibid., F. Temple Papers, vol. 58, fo. 365.

[19] Ibid., vol. 57, fos. 72 ff.

matter of cutting out the parts of the ancient ceremonies which had no sacral significance and which had traditionally taken place in Westminster Hall, like the King's Champion challenging his rivals. The other was more difficult; what could be done to shorten the actual service to meet the King's demands, whether arising from his ill-health or his impatience. London was full of rumours that the King was demanding that there should be no Anointing and no Communion. St John Hope wrote in shocked tones from the Society of Antiquaries to say that only King John and King James II had not received Communion at their coronations—not good precedents![20] No one seems, however, to have seriously thought that there might be no Communion.

Armytage Robinson's advice about abbreviation was invaluable. He possessed a considerable knowledge of liturgical history and a strong antiquarian bent. He was able to suggest several seventeenth- and eighteenth-century accretions to the service, most of them liturgically unsound, which could be omitted with positive advantage. He was also in a position to tell Davidson which of the royal suggestions for shortening should be resisted at all costs.[21] By late November Davidson was in a position to advise Temple on what should be done.

One would have been glad to abbreviate yet further, for I still think it will be regarded in August Quarters as too long; but I do not see how we can properly *suggest* the omission of anything more. Of course if a definite command came to you to that effect you will consider what else is possible (e.g. in the Litany) but, if I may say so, I think you would do well to emphasize in writing to the Executive Committee and sending your draft, *what a great deal is omitted*, and this, with a greatly shortened sermon, and a direction against redundant anthem-music, will I hope be regarded as 'tolerable'.... What I would suggest for your consideration is that either Eyre and Spottiswoode or the University Press ... should be told by you to set up the Service in type. And not to expand it over quite so many pages! It would be well that it should not *seem* too long when inspected by the Great Personages.[22]

There was still very little to show the committee[23] and by Christmas the King was demanding to see something. In the end Temple used the form of service from William IV's reign and marked it in red ink to

---

[20] All these letters appear in Lambeth Palace Library: F. Temple Papers, vol. 57, fo. 64.
[21] Ibid., Davidson Papers, vol. 278, fos. 28–41. This is a lengthy document with a Robinson's proposals and is almost identical to the form of service actually used.
[22] Ibid., F. Temple Papers, vol. 58, fos. 29 ff., Davidson to Temple, 23 Nov. 1901.
[23] Ibid., Davidson Papers, vol. 278, 78 f., Temple to Davidson 1 Dec. 1901.

show the changes that were suggested. But then there was a possibly alarming development: the King suddenly began to take a serious—and apparently informed—interest in liturgical details and particularly the Anointing.

This was a difficult question because Temple and Davidson held different views. Temple was convinced that one Anointing was enough; and on the forehead. 'That and that alone is Biblical and the Biblical is best for Englishmen.'[24] Davidson would have preferred a triple anointing (head, breast and arms), which he thought dated from the reign of Richard I but which Temple was (wrongly) convinced was William III and Mary. Unable to persuade Temple at the preliminary stage, Davidson allowed him to make his proposal to the committee. But the committee's job, of course, was to make a recommendation to the King and the King, inevitably, asked for Davidson's advice—as a personal friend rather than as a member of the committee—before returning his own comments on the draft form of service. Temple wrote to Davidson in February 1902, greatly surprised, saying he had seen the King and his Majesty was very keen to have the triple anointing. Davidson was probably not much surprised.

There were many details to be settled before Temple went in state to present the final form of service to the King. It was arranged that the Bishop of London should preach the sermon, according to precedent, but that he should be allowed no more than five minutes. The Archbishop of York was to crown the Queen not of *right* but at Temple's invitation.

Temple's grasp of practical matters was as shrewd as ever. He said to Davidson:

...I do not think that the king or even you have quite appreciated the cause which makes the whole office so long. You all seem to fancy that you can really shorten by omitting parts of the prayers etc. that are to be said. But the length of the service is not caused by the words to be said but by the deeds to be done. A rubric directs certain people to do certain thing [*sic*], & every one of these people will use up at least five minutes. And there are a good many of them and many of these folk have rights to do these things.

There are only two ways of shortening ceremonies. One is to have two or three rehearsals and to drill all these performers; the other to amalgamate many of the separate ceremonies.

[24] Ibid, fo. 80, Temple to Davidson, 13 Dec.

In the event both expedients were tried. Several careful rehearsals were held, though the archbishop was not required to attend, and various ways of cutting down or amalgamating ceremonies were tried. In the grand procession into the Abbey most of the regalia would be carried by important ecclesiastical dignitaries or officers of state but to bring it all to the Abbey and to get the lesser pieces of equipment into position a much less eminent procession set out long before the service started. It happened that one of the canons of Westminster was James Welldon, formerly headmaster of Harrow and Bishop of Calcutta. The order of this lesser procession was rearranged so that Welldon brought in the ampulla containing the oil for the anointing and, depositing it on the high altar and being himself a bishop, consecrated the oil then and there thus relieving Temple of having to do it during the ceremony later. [Similarly, the musical arrangements for the coronation were planned and executed with great care under the watchful eyes of Sir Frederick Bridge, organist at the Abbey, and Sir Walter Parratt, Master of the King's Musick. The service was adorned with specially commissioned works by Stanford, Parry, and Elgar, providing the assembled congregation with a reminder of the recent renaissance in English sacred music.[25] Moreover, the Abbey itself had experienced something of a renaissance since the last coronation. The organ had been twice rebuilt, in 1884 and 1894; the choir had been remodelled and lit with electricity; the choristers had been provided with red cassocks in 1897. In 1899, Lord Rosebery had presented a new cross for the High Altar. As one enthusiastic witness described the scene of the coronation:

From end to end did the altar blaze with a display of alms dishes, flagons, chalices ... Upon the amateur ritualist of the nineteenth century, with his tailor-made vases, his feeble floral decorations, the scene bestowed a sorely needed lesson.[26]]

The service itself got under way smoothly. Temple entered in the procession, walking before the Queen and her attendants, wearing his cope and carrying his cap and accompanied by his sons in court dress. (Precedent directed that the archbishop should be attended by two gentlemen and it must have been a relief to his wife, in the gallery, to know that Frederick and William—now in their early twenties—would

---

[25] Cannadine, 'The Context, Performance and Meaning of Ritual', 130. For a full account of the music at the coronation of Edward VII see *Musical Times*, 43 (1902) 387 f, 577 ff.

[26] Ibid. 132.

be near their father.) Because of his poor eyesight Temple had to have the questions to be put to the King written in very large letters on specially prepared scrolls which Davidson held for him. Even so he stumbled over the words occasionally. Arthur Benson, who was in the congregation but too far away to see what really happened, noted every mistake that the archbishop made.[27] All went reasonably well through the long ceremonies until after the crowning itself. When the archbishop went to pay homage he could not manage to get up from his knees again. Exactly what happened is difficult to decide. The Sandford *Memoir* made it sound as though it simply took the archbishop a little while to stand up again until the King leaned forward and helped him. The *Daily Chronicle* of 11 August said that the primate 'was seen to stagger and reel as if in a faint, and would doubtless have fallen but for the assistance rendered him by his supporters. But his Grace rallied after a little, and was assisted down upon his knee in presence of the King, to whose left cheek he gradually and cautiously found his way and imprinted upon his Sovereign a faithful kiss. Then he was helped to rise and assisted to his bench—there to rally and resume his service after it had been taken for a while by another prelate.' The *Daily Mail* of the same date claimed that 'it cost him three efforts to fall upon his knee, and when he had given the kiss he could not rise unassisted. But the King had his hand, and firmly holding it appeared to raise him almost by his own strength. With a touching grace the King kissed his hand before he let it go.' The *Western Mail* (for whom Temple was a local boy made good) gave a rather different account, saying that the King failed to raise him and it was Davidson and (implausibly) Dean Bradley who lifted him up. Temple himself seems to have insisted that he did not faint but suddenly found that his legs had no strength. 'I had made up my mind to get up on my right leg and they pulled me over on to my left leg. It was kindly meant but it upset me.' When Davidson offered him a 'meat lozenge' he is supposed to have said that it was his legs not his stomach which were the problem.[28] What is very clear is that he found it an emotional moment. When he had been Bishop of London he had disapproved of the then Prince's life-style so much that he had tried to persuade the bishops to make some sort of quiet protest.[29] Now

---

[27] Magdalene College, Cambridge: A. C. Benson diaries, vol. 16, 105. Internal evidence suggests that Davidson was his informant.

[28] Ibid., Benson implies that he was told this by the archbishop himself 'afterwards, at tea'.

[29] Lambeth Palace Library: Minutes of Bishops Meetings, BM3, 235 and 237.

he said, 'God bless you, Sir; God bless you; God be with you!'[30] Afterwards the King conferred honours on both Temple and Davidson in recognition of their services.

On the next day after the ceremony Beatrice Temple wrote to Davidson:

Kindest and most helpful of friends. I am so grateful to you—so thankful that all went off as well as it did and I feel, from my heart, how much of it is owing to your thoughtfulness and watchful attention—

He is tired, of course, but I do hope and believe none the worse. He walked to, and from, morning Ch [*sic*] here—

I trust that you were not overstrained—I felt for you in those anxious moments! and hoped they were not adding to the burden and fatigue...[31]

The archbishop wrote more soberly and at greater length, dealing with practical matters left over from the service and adding:

...I am conscious that the debt of gratitude for all your labour is due to you from me more than from any other person. I cannot easily express how much I feel that I owe to you. You have been indefatigable in your endeavour to save me from overwork. To the end of my life I shall be sensible of your unselfish kindness.[32]

That 'end' would not be very long delayed but it was not yet. Temple does not seem to have diminished his schedule of commitments at all. The Sandford *Memoir* prints his list of engagements for October and November 1902 which included a visit to Wales; a formal visitation of the diocese; temperance work; sermons; presiding at a meeting of the governors of Rugby; a service of thanksgiving at St Paul's for the King's complete recovery; the regular bishops' meeting; confirmations in the diocese and meetings in London.[33] Beatrice was ill during much of the time and for that reason the archbishop returned to Canterbury over night whenever he could. His eighty-first birthday fell on Sunday 30 November and he preached in the cathedral that morning for what was, in fact, to be the last time.

On the following Thursday he went up to London for a meeting of the ecclesiastical commissioners at 11.30 a.m. At 1.30 he saw the new bishop for Auckland, Dr Neligan, and at 2.45 there was another

---

[30] E. G. Sandford (ed.), *Memoirs of Archbishop Temple by Seven Friends*, 2 vol. (London, 1906), ii. 374.

[31] Lambeth Palace Library: Davidson Papers, vol. 4, fo. 201, letter dated 10 Aug.

[32] Bell, i. 371.

[33] Sandford (ed.), ii. 375 ff.

interview. And then he went on to the House of Lords for a meeting of the governors of St Augustine's College, Canterbury at 3.30. He had, no doubt, deliberately arranged his schedule so that he could be at the House of Lords for the debate on the Education Bill that afternoon.

Since the previous Education Act the Conservative administration had made two attempts to devise a comprehensive scheme and, failing a permanent solution, had put temporary measures in place to give some public assistance to voluntary schools. The bill of 1902 was yet another attempt to devise a national educational system which would incorporate the Church schools and yet protect what the Established Church was most anxious to retain—independence from state control as regards religious education. Balfour, who became Prime Minister in July, planned to draw voluntary schools into the national system by means of a scheme devised by Robert Morant (shortly to become permanent secretary to the Board of Education). By the act school boards would be abolished and all schools placed under a local authority which would maintain buildings and pay salaries in return for the right to appoint a minority of the governors. The Church was to continue to provide religious instruction in what had been voluntary schools though there was a conscience clause which allowed parents to withdraw their children from it.

The bill aroused powerful Nonconformist opposition which claimed that it would place denominational teaching 'on the rates'—indeed John Clifford (the eminent Baptist preacher) went so far as to call it 'Rome on the rates' because there was a widespread fear that the proposed legislation would subsidize Roman Catholic and Anglo-Catholic teaching in schools.[34] Like so much else in this period the Education Bill was complicated by the political implications of ritualism. A deputation from the National Council of Evangelical Free Churches called on Balfour on 12 June. Andrew Fairbairn (principal of Mansfield College, Oxford) delivered an address which does not appear to have had any noticeable effect on government policy. Balfour, once he became Prime Minister, proceeded with the legislation despite Nonconformist (and Protestant Anglican) opposition and the Liberals' determination to exploit an opportunity for splitting the government.

[34] G. I. T. Machin, *Politics and the Churches in Great Britain, 1869 to 1921* (Oxford, 1987), 61.

Temple, therefore, had a difficult task to perform. He had to present the case for the Church of England schools and explain why they needed financial assistance in the circumstances that then existed. It was widely believed that he had advised the government about earlier bills they had devised: it was reported in the press that the advice which Benson had given Salisbury about draft legislation in the 1890s actually came from Temple.[35] This is entirely plausible. It would explain how Temple had contrived to establish himself as *persona grata* with a Unionist and Conservative administration so that, by the time he became archbishop, Salisbury and Balfour would feel able to trust him in spite of his Liberal past. It was certainly the case that many of the things for which he had been asking since becoming Bishop of London had been incorporated in the bill of 1902. He had become the champion of state aid for voluntary schools. His name was associated with what was being attempted.[36] He had, therefore, to defend the proposed legislation almost as if he were responsible for it. At the same time he had to try and meet the objections of Nonconformists and those who thought that the Established Church was being given the best of both worlds.

Temple's own ideas, by this time, had changed almost completely since his essay on national education in 1856. Those with whom, in the past, he had shared friendship, educational experience and political opinions—J. M. Wilson, by this time Archdeacon of Manchester, and John Percival, Bishop of Hereford—were far more willing to agree to complete public control of Church schools. But it had become clear to Temple that opinion within the Church of England was that the bill did not go far enough.[37] As always he felt obliged to represent the collective opinion. Yet he continued to behave as if he thought of himself as a reconstructed liberal whose chief concern was for justice.[38] He still expounded his 'Coleridgean' educational ideals in his preaching.[39] And pleading for justice was the one course which would enable him to reconcile the two contradictory points he needed to make. He could

[35] Sandford (ed.), ii. 90.

[36] D. W. Bebbington, *The Nonconformist Conscience: Chapel and Politics 1870–1914* (London, 1982), 142.

[37] For a thorough and careful analysis of the spectrum of Anglican reactions to the bill see D. R. Pugh, 'The Church and Education: Anglican Attitudes 1902', *Journal of Ecclesiastical History*, 23 (1972), 219 ff.

[38] See above, 241.

[39] e.g. F. Temple, *The True Ideals of an Educator (a Sermon)* (London, 1898).

argue that voluntary schools needed aid because they had been placed in an unfair position: he could try to appease Free Church opinion by pleading for justice for Nonconformists, too.

Nothing, of course, could have prevented his speaking on the subject. He rose early in the debate to praise the importance of the advance made by the bill towards a national system of education and of the help which it was giving to voluntary schools. He repeated the arguments for preserving thoroughgoing religious education within the national system. He underlined the injustice of making supporters of voluntary schools pay rates as well as subscriptions. Before he could complete what he had to say, however, he was compelled to slump back into his seat. He forced himself up on to his feet again and tried to draw his speech to a proper conclusion. But he was too weak to carry on and had to be taken home to Lambeth. He sent Davidson back to the Lords next day with a message that, if he had been able to continue, he would have argued that Nonconformists ought not in any way to be disadvantaged by the bill.

A good case can be made for saying that Temple's 'Coleridgean' ideal of education by cultivation remained with him all his life but his thinking was probably never doctrinaire. What he wrote for publication was usually addressed to the political realities of the time and it is possible that sometimes it was not so much his own personal opinion as the corporate mind of the department, a commission, an institution, or the Church of England, to which he was giving expression. What he said to his friends as a young man was full of ideals and enthusiasm. In his middle years, on the Taunton Commission and at Exeter, when he was most politically Liberal, he believed that market forces and competition might bring about the necessary reforms. But he became disillusioned with that approach and as an old man he was much more cautious, primarily concerned to protect the vested interests of the Church of England. If there was one thing for which he cared deeply throughout the whole of his life it was probably that talented young people—who might suffer from the relative poverty and lack of polish which had handicapped his own struggle for education—should be allowed the opportunities he had been given.

A week after Temple's collapse in the Lords the Archbishop of York came to celebrate the Holy Communion in his bedroom. Davidson, Winnington-Ingram, some of the staff at Lambeth, and the archbishop's wife and two sons were all present. On 15 December Beatrice Temple wrote to Davidson, 'he is quite himself but sleepy—and one cannot tell how he will be as to clearness in another hour...'[40] On 18 December the Education Act received the royal assent. Temple died a little after eight o'clock on the morning of 23 December ('So the old Warrior did not last till Christmas...', said Winnington-Ingram[41]) and was buried near the cathedral in Canterbury four days later. On the last day of the year Balfour wrote to Davidson saying that he intended to propose his name to the King as the next Archbishop of Canterbury.[42]

[It is not easy to assess Temple's archiepiscopate, which lasted six years to the day. In the first place, his nomination by Lord Salisbury was accompanied by limited expectations, at least on the part of the Church, and probably on the part of the government as well. As Temple's most creative years were now over, this was to be something of a caretaker archiepiscopate, a recognition of his eminent standing in the Church of England, rather than a protracted appointment from which great initiatives and complex reforms were to be anticipated. The new archbishop was, after all, seventy-five years old at the time of his confirmation, and not in robust health. To be sure, his term of office would not all be smooth sailing. The forthcoming Lambeth Conference would require careful planning and skilful diplomacy. Ritualists continued to press for liturgical innovation, threatening still further to unsettle the Church's delicate *via media*. Ecumenical considerations were becoming more prominent. A coronation was considered a distinct possibility. And Temple, unlike his most recent predecessors (and unlike Davidson his successor), had never enjoyed the confidence of the Queen, nor been granted access to the inner circles of the Palace. Yet these various difficulties, however serious they might have appeared to the public, were never reckoned by knowledgeable insiders to lie beyond the grasp of the new archbishop. Temple was undeniably elderly, but he was certainly capable.

To some extent, Temple was further disadvantaged by the fact that he succeeded Tait and Benson, both inspired leaders of the Church and both temperamentally better suited to the delicate duties, public and private, of an archbishop. But Temple was not without his own considerable attributes as archbishop, and while his occasional brusqueness, his notorious impatience with the finer details of ecclesiastical

---

[40] Lambeth Palace Library: Davidson Papers, vol. 4, fo. 202. The letter is dated 'Mon 15th' without month or year, but since 4 Dec. 1902 was a Thursday it is very likely that the letter was written on Monday 15 Dec. 1902.

[41] Bell, i. 383.

[42] Ibid. 384.

administration, his inability to delegate, and his comparative lack of social polish, might have offended some, his forthrightness and common touch endeared him to many more.

The last years of the nineteenth century, while not lacking in ecclesiastical tensions or opportunities, were not years in which an able—and ageing—archbishop was likely to advance his already considerable reputation in the Church or within society itself. There were, at the time, few great stages on which to perform, few complex dramas to be scripted, few important parts to be played. Church and State relations had improved considerably, if only temporarily. The threat of disestablishment and disendowment had begun to fade. Liturgical reform would not reach crisis point until the late 1920s. The Church had by now negotiated something approaching an informal treaty with liberalism. Nor were the extreme ritualists continuing to be subjected to protracted proceedings in the ecclesiastical courts, the Lambeth Opinions (1899–1900) providing a more eirenic and sensible approach to the problem of ceremonial 'innovation'. All in all, the context permitted an efficent and relatively peaceful archiepiscopate, if not a particularly memorable one.

Temple, of course, continued to sit in the House of Lords during his archiepiscopate, and this proved of some considerable use in advancing his pet causes, such as educational reform. He also presided over the Lambeth Conference of 1897, but this was never destined to be an extraordinary, or particularly historic, conference, and so it proved.

His crowning achievement lay perhaps in his ability to maintain a conservative, High Church defence of the historic episcopate. After his consecration as Bishop of Exeter, and more especially during his time as Bishop of London, Temple had become increasingly appreciative of the episcopal office, and the need for bishops to remain above reproach doctrinally and in their private lives. By the time of his elevation to Exeter he understood fully that what might be acceptable in a headmaster of a public school might well not be acceptable for a bishop of the Established Church. As archbishop it became impossible for Temple to fulfil the intellectual and theological expectations which some had held out for him, particularly his old Balliol friends like Jowett and Stanley, many of whom were now dead. His would not be an archiepiscopate dominated by Jowett-inspired liberalism. Instead, Temple, now a figure of great stature in Church and society, would strive to uphold the rather more traditional and conservative High Church principles which he had first imbibed from his mother, and which were later advanced by his most influential teacher and mentor, A. C. Tait. Nothing which occurred during his archiepiscopate diminished that stature.]

INDEX

Throughout the index, FT refers to Frederick Temple.

Acland, Sir Thomas Dyke 15
Acland, T. D. 41–2, 114, 116–17, 120, 125, 153, 253
Adderley, C. B. 83
Addington palace, disposal 265
Aitken, W. Francis 1
Almack, A. 204 n. 30
Amiens, Treaty (1802) 3
Anglo-Catholicism:
  and education 291
  and English Church Union 220–1
  growth 214–15
  and Liberal Catholicism 257
  and St Cuthbert's, Philbeach
    Gardens 214–18, 277, 284
  and St Paul's Cathedral 219–21
  and validity of orders 265
  see also ceremonial; ritualism
Arnold, Matthew:
  and Broad Churchmanship 84–5
  friendship with FT 19, 32, 56
  and FT's preferment 121
  and payment by results 149–50
  and Schools Inquiry Commission 115
Arnold, Thomas:
  banned from preaching 89
  and biblical interpretation 67
  on history 64
  influence on FT 19, 21, 64
  and Oriel Noetics 16
  and Rugby 17, 21, 23, 36, 44, 52–5, 57–8, 99–103, 106
Ashley, Lord (later 7th Earl of Shaftesbury) 27
Athanasian creed 146–7
Athanasius, St 128, 146
Atlay, James, Bishop of Hereford 223

Baines, Edward 115–16
Balfour, Arthur 245, 246, 275, 279–80, 291–2, 294

Balliol College, Oxford:
  and Civil Service 28
  FT as fellow 23–8
  and FT's Bampton lectures 189
  FT's scholarship to 14–18, 82
  influences on FT 21–3
  and Jowett 22, 35–6, 44
  and Tractarianism 18–20
Bampton lectures:
  (1866) 62
  (1884) 174–6, 179–93, 236, 264
  (1896) 256
Bardsley, John Wareing, Bishop of Carlisle 210
Barnes, R. H. 125
Barnes, R. W. 125
Barry, Dr Alfred 198
Basil of Caesarea 128
belief, development 61–3, 67, 69, 182
Bellairs, H. W. 42
Benson, Arthur 258, 259, 260–2, 289
Benson, E. W.:
  and Anglican orders 265–6
  as Archbishop of Canterbury 142, 157, 196, 262, 294
  as Bishop of Truro 157
  and Convocation 212
  and Davidson 249, 269
  death 252–3, 254, 255–6, 258, 259, 266
  friendship with FT 54, 91, 121–2, 196, 197, 252–3, 258, 260
  and Hayman 133
  and House of Lords 210–11
  and King of Lincoln 222–7, 278
  and London Dock Strike 232–3, 234–5
  and national education 245, 292
  and ritualism 219, 276
  staff 260
Benson, Mrs Mary (wife of E. W. Benson) 260
Bernard, Montague 113

Bevan, H. E. J. 209 n. 45
Bible:
    authority 69, 71, 130, 248–51, 256–7
    critical study 62, 67, 76–7, 79, 84
    and science 176
    and truth 188
Bickersteth, E. H., Bishop of Exeter 155, 196
Bigge, Sir Arthur 273–4
Billing, Robert Claudius, Bishop of
        Bedford 198
Birkbeck, W. 277, 283
Birmingham Education Association 42
Blomfield, Alfred, Bishop of
        Colchester 215
Blundell, Peter, and scholarships 14–15, 56
Blundell's School:
    FT as pupil 7, 9–14, 23–4
    and Old Boys' meetings 4–5
Body, Canon George 215
Book of Common Prayer:
    and Athanasian creed 146–7
    FT's regard for 19, 237, 267
    and ritualism 142, 223–5, 275–8
Boswell, James 14
Boyd, Archibald, Dean of Exeter 124–5,
        152, 154
Bradley, G. C. 133, 134
Bradley, G. G., Dean of
        Westminster 282–3, 289
Brereton, Prebendary J. L. 125
Brett, Reginald (later Lord Esher) 272, 285
Bridge, Sir Frederick 288
Bridgewater treatises 166–7
British Association for the Advancement of
        Science 61, 69, 176
British and Foreign Schools Society 148, 152
British West Africa 6–7
Broad Churchmanship 21, 52–3, 195–6
    and Arnold 84–5
    and *Essays and Reviews* 66, 84
Bromby, Bishop of Tasmania 199–200
Brown, W. Martin 216–17
Browne, Harold:
    as Bishop of Ely 121–2, 127, 128–9
    as Bishop of Winchester 142–3, 223, 249
Bull, George, *Defensio Fidei Nicaenae* 12–13
Bunsen, Christian Karl Josias, Baron 66, 69
Burgon, J. W. 82, 131, 191
Buxton, Sydney 233–4

Cambridge University:
    and grammar school examinations 41–2
    see also universities

candles, ceremonial 216–17, 224, 276–8
Cannadine, David 270–1, 282
Carveth, Richard (maternal grandfather of
        FT) 8
catechism, FT learns 12
Catholic party 213
ceremonial:
    ecclesiastical 148, 214, 258, 276–9, 295
        and King of Lincoln 221–7
        see also ritualism
    state 281–2, 284–5, 287–8
Chadwick, Owen 29 n. 12, 191
Chamberlain, Joseph 245
Chambers, Robert, *Vestiges of the Natural
        History of Creation* 167–8
Christology 81, 130
Church Association 217–19, 221–2, 227, 266
Church Discipline Bill 279
Church of England:
    as comprehensive 53, 136–7
    and establishment 207–8, 236, 245, 257,
        294
    history 226
    and loyalty 136–7, 147, 155, 223, 227, 240
    and national education 29, 150–1, 241–6,
        291–2
    and national organization 141, 209–10,
        211–13
    and overseas provinces 247–8, 270
    parties 213
    and prayer for the dead 274–5
    and religious communities 228–9
    and Reservation of the Sacrament 279
    validity of orders 265–7
    see also Broad Churchmanship;
        Evangelicalism; High
        Churchmanship; Oxford
        Movement
Church of England Temperance
        Society 232
Church House, Westminster 211
Church, R. W., Dean of St Paul's 219–20
church schools 29, 205–6, 241–6, 257, 291–2
Church and State 34, 207–8, 236, 294
    and education 37–8, 151–3
Cirencester, agricultural college 47
Civil Service:
    and FT 28–9, 50–1
    and Jowett 28
Clarendon Commission on Public Schools
        92–101, 103–5, 107–14, 118, 156, 178
Clarendon, George William Frederick, 4th
        Earl 94, 98, 104

class, socio-economic, and education 40

classics:
at Rugby School 96–9, 106–8, 111–12
FT's ability in 5, 8, 10, 163, 267
and middle-class education 10, 116, 170, 177, 240

clergy:
discipline 146, 216–18, 279–80
imprisonment 143, 144, 148, 218, 222
and party politics 231

Clifford, John 291

Clifton College 132, 147

Close, Francis 152

Clough, Arthur Hugh 19

co-operatives, FT's support for 230

Cobham, Alexander W. 217–18, 221

Colenso, John William, Bishop of Natal 119, 248

Coleridge, Sir John 122–3, 214, 219, 253

Coleridge, Samuel Taylor:
and education 44–5, 292, 293
influence on FT 19, 45, 181–2, 183, 184, 186

Colley, Archdeacon 155 n. 64, 200

Collins, Prof. J. C. 277

Colonial Emigration Society 232

colonies:
and Anglican overseas provinces 247–8, 270
attitudes to 2, 6
see also British West Africa; Sierra Leone

communities, religious 228–30

Compton, Beardmore 54

conferences:
diocesan 156, 206–8, 210, 212–13, 220, 238
ruridecanal 140, 156, 206–7
see also Lambeth Conference

confession, in Church of England 27, 202–3

Conservative party:
and national education 244–5, 257, 291
and South African War 273

constitutionalism, and FT 137, 236–7

Convent of St Mary, Twickenham 230

Convocation of Canterbury:
and Athanasian creed 146–7
and clergy discipline 147–8
and *Essays and Reviews* 79–80, 89, 122, 125
and FT's speeches 145–7, 211
and house of laity 210, 212
membership 143

proceedings 144–5
revival 210

Cook, Canon F. C. 39–40, 124–5, 129, 141

Cowper, Francis Thomas de Grey, 7th Earl 239, 240

Cox, Prebendary 125

creation, and scientific understanding 61–3, 66, 77, 167–8, 176, 179, 183–4, 191–3

Creighton, Mandell, Bishop of Peterborough (later London) 254, 256, 266, 272, 277, 281

crime, and education 47–9

Crimean War, effects on Rugby 53–4

Dale, L. W. J. 204 n. 30

Danby, Herbert 94 n. 10

Darwin, Charles:
and alternative theories 167–9, 171, 174
and argument from design 184–5, 193
and *Essays and Reviews* 61, 68–9
and evolution as open-ended 167, 191
and FT 176, 186–7, 264

Darwinism, social 168–9, 191–2

Davidson, Randall Thomas:
as Archbishop of Canterbury 294
as Bishop of Winchester 253, 254–6, 272, 281
as chaplain to Tait 55, 128, 196, 249, 259
and coronation of Edward VII 283, 285–7, 289–90
as Dean of Windsor 162, 194–7, 221, 249–50
and King of Lincoln 224
and Lambeth Conference (1897) 268–70
relationship with FT 258–62, 264, 279–80, 281, 290, 293
and South African War 273–4

Dawes, Richard 39–41

deacons, and secular employment 142, 143

Dearmer, Percy 284

Denbigh, Lord W. B. P. 78, 83–6

Denison, George Anthony 29, 50, 79

development, and religious belief 61–3, 67, 69, 182

Devon, Temple family resident in 5, 7–9, 14, 136, 140

Devon, William Reginald Courtenay, 11th Earl 92–3, 103, 107, 156

Devonshire Association for the Advancement of Science, Literature and Arts 177, 182

Devonshire, Spencer Compton Cavendish, 8th Duke 245
Diamond Jubilee celebrations 270–3
Dibdin, Lewis 277
dioceses:
  diocesan conferences 156, 206–8, 210, 212–13, 220, 238
  structure and organization 210
Disraeli, Benjamin 119–20
divorce, FT's views 155
Downall, Archdeacon 125
Drummond, Henry, *Natural Law in the Spiritual World* 180–1
Dugdale, William Stratford 83
Dunn, A. H. 204 n. 30

Earle, Alfred, Bishop of Marlborough 198, 206, 229
economics, free market 2, 41–2, 230–1, 244, 258, 293
ecumenism, and FT 246–7, 265–7, 276, 294
Edghill, John Cox 215
Edinburgh Review:
  and Thomas Arnold 17
  and *Essays and Reviews* 69, 84, 88–9
education 142–3:
  by repetition 8, 12, 170, 178, 240
  as conveying information 8, 46, 149, 239, 240
  of criminals 47–9
  as cultivation 39, 42–8, 63, 240, 293
  Darwinian views 168
  denominational schools 37–9, 115, 150–2, 241–6, 291–3
  and endowments and scholarships 40, 99, 117, 152–3, 206
  and *Essays and Reviews* 60–4, 69, 112–13
  and examinations board 41–2
  and government 28–32, 41, 49, 115–18, 258
  higher 237–9
  liberal views 33, 35–47, 51–3, 241, 244
  middle-class 40–2, 46, 49, 98, 114, 116, 170
  moral role 57
  national 37–41, 48–9, 150–4, 241–3, 246, 258, 291–3
  and payment by results 147–50
  reform 150–3, 242, 292, 293
  religious 151–2, 153, 246, 291, 293
  role of science 39–40, 42–3, 45–6, 54, 109–12, 170, 178
  secular 37–8, 241–2, 246

and Spencer 170, 178
and teacher training 26–8
technical 116
and Tractarians 29, 38
working-class 27–30, 39–41, 49
see also church schools; Clarendon Commission; classics; grammar schools; Rugby School; Sunday schools; Taunton Commission; universities
Education Act (1902) 291–4
Edward VI, King, and ritualism 277–8
Edward VII, King:
  coronation 1, 281, 282–90, 294
  as Prince of Wales 272, 289
Elementary Education Act (1870) 150–3, 242
Elgar, Sir Edward 288
Elizabeth I, Queen, and ritualism 278, 279
Ellicot, C. J., Bishop of Gloucester and Bristol 145–6, 245, 249–51
Endowed Schools Commission 206
English Church Union 220–1, 266
episcopacy:
  and constitutionalism 137
  High Church 295
  and loyalty to Church of England 136–7, 147
equality, religious 207, 242
Erle, Peter 115
Esher, Reginald Baliol Brett, 2nd Viscount 272, 285
Essays and Reviews 21, 58–60, 181–2, 239, 256
  and Clarendon Commission 93
  condemnation by bishops 70–4, 76, 78–81, 83–4, 87–9, 144, 157
  contributors 59–60, 65–7
  and Convocation of Canterbury 79–80, 89, 122, 125
  and Darwin 68
  and FT at Rugby School 58–65, 67–70, 72–89, 90–2, 113
  and FT as Bishop of Exeter 119, 121–7, 129–31, 133, 136–7, 144–6
  and FT as Bishop of London 195, 237, 248–51
  and liberalism 60, 65–73, 137, 192–3, 240
  opposition to 62–4, 67–89, 121–2, 191, 220
  and Rugby School 58–9, 74–6, 78, 80, 82–7, 92–3
  and Spencer 170
  and withdrawal of FT's essay 129–31, 145–6

Eusebius of Caesarea 257
Evangelicalism 13–14
  and episcopal appointments 196
  and *Essays and Reviews* 67
  and ritualism 217, 226
  and support for FT 124, 195
evolution:
  by natural selection 61, 167–9, 185
  and FT 184–8, 191–3, 256
  and Huxley 69, 176, 192
  as open-ended 167, 191
  and social Darwinism 168–9, 191–2
  and Spencer 171, 172–4, 176, 185–7, 191–2,
    256, 258
  and survival of the fittest 168–9, 173, 185,
    191–2
  see also Darwin, Charles
Exeter cathedral:
  chapter 156
  reredos 154, 219

Fairbairn, Andrew 291
Fitch, Joshua 150
Folland, Mrs, FT boards with 11
Ford, Prebendary 125
Forster, W. E.:
  and reform of elementary
    education 150–3, 242
  and Taunton Commission 115–17
France, war with 2–4, 6
Free Church of England 144
freedom:
  and determinism 184
  intellectual 60, 76, 79, 84, 137, 147, 175,
    190, 240
  religious 38–9
Freeman, Philip, Archdeacon of
  Exeter 123–5, 129, 130–1, 141, 145
Frere, Walter 277
Froude, James Anthony, and *Oxford
  Essays* 65
Froude, Richard Hurrell, *Remains* 21
Fry, T. C. 257

George II, King, coronation 284
George IV, King, coronation 281
Gladstone, W. E.:
  as Chancellor of the Exchequer 49,
    119
  and *Essays and Reviews* 67, 119, 126–7
  and FT's preferment 119–20, 131,
    195–7
  and Irish Home Rule 197, 239, 245

  and King's College, London 237, 241
  and liberalism 257
  as MP for Oxford University 34–5, 104,
    119
  and Rugby School 134
  and theological liberalism 33–4, 257
  and university reform 34–6
Goodwin, Charles, and *Essays and
  Reviews* 66, 68
Gore, Charles, and *Lux Mundi* 188
Goulburn, E. M.:
  and *Essays and Reviews* 81–2
  as Headmaster of Rugby School 53–5,
    57 n. 20, 100–1
grammar schools 40–2, 113–14, 116, 153
Granville, George Leveson-Gower, 2nd
  Earl:
  and Kneller Hall 49
  and Rugby School 55
  and Schools Inquiry Commission 115
Green, Simon 44 n. 78, 116 n. 83
Green, T. H. 115
Gregory, Robert 199, 213, 220, 227, 272
Guardian:
  and *Essays and Reviews* 68, 75
  and Rugby 53

Habgood, John 191
Halford, Sir Henry 83
Halifax, Sir Charles L. Wood, 1st
  Viscount 214, 266, 283, 285
Hamilton, Walter Kerr, Bishop of
  Salisbury 79
Hampden, Renn Dixon 34, 85
Harcourt, Sir William 275, 279
Harington, E. C., Chancellor of Exeter
  cathedral 125
Harris, Prebendary 125
Harrison, Frederic, and *Essays and
  Reviews* 68–9
Hawker, John Manley 141
Hayman, Henry, Headmaster of Rugby
  School 131–5
Hedgeland, Prebendary 125
Hegel, G. W. F. 26, 43, 179–80, 181
Hervey, Lord Arthur, Bishop of Bath and
  Wells 127
Hessey J. A., Archdeacon of Middlesex 198,
  203, 204, 215–16
High Churchmanship:
  and dogmatism 64–5, 66
  and episcopal appointments 196
  and *Essays and Reviews* 66, 89

High Churchmanship (*cont.*):
  and FT as Archbishop of
    Canterbury 257–8, 295–6
  and FT as Bishop of Exeter 136–7, 148,
    192–3
  and FT as Bishop of London 208–9, 214
  and FT at Kneller Hall 34, 38
  and Gladstone 35
  and Oxford Movement 16, 20–1
  and Phillpotts 123, 136
  and pre-Nicene Church 12–13
  and prosecution of King 222, 223, 226
  and ritualism 148, 214
  and Rugby School 55, 102
  and Temple family 13–14, 20–1
  see also Anglo-Catholicism
history:
  at Rugby School 112
  and human development 61–4
Hobhouse, Edmund 27
Holbech, C. 84
Holland, Henry Scott 220
Holy Communion:
  and ablutions 216, 220, 224, 226–7
  and coronation of Edward VII 286
  frequency of attendance 13
  position of celebrant 142, 224, 226–7
  and Real Presence 275
  and Reservation of the Sacrament 279
Home Rule, and Gladstone 197, 239, 245
homosexuality, views on 154
Hook, W. F. 114–15
Hope, St John 283, 286
Hornby, James John 25–6
Hort, Fenton J. A. 256
House of Lords:
  attendances 210–11
  and division of Exeter diocese 157
  and Education Bill (1902) 291–3, 295
  and payment by results 148–50
  and prayer for the dead 274–5
How, William Walsham:
  as Bishop of Bedford 198–9, 203
  as Bishop of Wakefield 198
Howe, Lord 83
Howley, William, Archbishop of
    Canterbury 89, 282
Huguenot congregation 247
humanity:
  and evolution 187–8
  religious development 61–3, 67, 69, 182
Humboldt, Friedrich Heinrich Alexander
    von 43

Hume, David 179–80
Huxley, T. H., and Darwin 69, 176, 192

imperialism, and trade 2
incarnation 130
incense, use of 216, 276–8
intercession, national 274
Ionian Islands, British administration 3–5,
  7
Ireland, Home Rule Bill 197, 239, 245
Iremonger, F. A. 159 n. 74
Irish Church, disestablishment 119–20, 207

Jackson, J. 204 n. 30
Jackson, John, Bishop of London
  and bishops' meetings 144 n. 31, 211 n. 51
  and diocesan organization 198, 199–200
  and FT's consecration 125–7
  and religious communities 228
  and ritualism 218
Jacobson, William 132
Jayne, F. J., Bishop of Chester 254
Jelf, Richard 72
Jenkins, Robert Charles 128–9
Jenkyns, Richard, Master of Balliol 15, 18,
  23
Jex Blake, T. W., Headmaster of Rugby
    School 134–5
Johnson, Samuel 14, 57
Jowett, Benjamin:
  and Civil Service 28
  commentaries on Pauline Epistles 35,
    52–3, 59
  and Darwin 169, 185
  and education 43–6, 150
  and *Essays and Reviews* 59–60, 65–7, 70,
    72–3, 80–2, 84, 87, 89, 131, 166
  friendship with FT 22, 72–3, 158–9,
    174–5, 252, 295
  and Hayman 131–2
  and Hegel 43–4, 180
  and Kantianism 180
  and liberalism 18, 26, 34–7, 52–3, 66, 119,
    131, 174–5, 190
  and mastership of Balliol 35–6, 44, 128,
    174
  and Netta Temple 158–9, 175
  and Oxford Movement 22
  and Tait 22

Kant, Immanuel 26, 167, 179–80, 181, 186,
  264
Kay-Shuttleworth, James 29, 38, 148–9

Keble, John, assize sermon 16
Kensit, John 276–7, 278
King, Edward, Bishop of Lincoln 196, 221–8, 245, 278
King's College, London 72, 237–9, 241
King's Somborne, experimental school 39–42
Kneller, Godfrey 30
Kneller Hall:
  FT as principal 28–51, 112, 122, 132
    closure 49–51, 74, 79
    and liberalism 33–6, 63
    pastoral care 139
    and practicality 46, 58, 139, 140
    and religious studies 29, 31, 49, 239
    and science 177
    and style of education 43–5
Knollys, Francis 285

Lachmann, C. C. F. W. 25
laity:
  and Anglo-Catholicism 216–17, 279
  and church schools 243
  and denominational education 243
  role 148, 208–9, 210, 212
Lake, W. C. 36, 53, 127–8, 132, 215
Lambeth Conference:
  (1867) 247
  (1878) 143
  (1888) 248–51
  (1897) 258–9, 267–70, 294, 295
Lambeth Opinions (1899–1900) 276–8, 295
Lang, Cosmo Gordon 175 n. 22, 189–90, 192
Lansdowne, Henry Petty-Fitzmaurice, 3rd Marquis 32, 55
Lascelles, Beatrice, *see* Temple, Beatrice
Lascelles, Lady Caroline (mother of Beatrice Temple) 159
Lascelles, William Sebright Saunders (father of Beatrice Temple) 159, 252
law, ecclesiastical:
  and Bishop King 222–3, 225, 228
  FT's support for 137, 223, 228, 236–7, 240, 257–8, 279–80
Lawlor, Colin R. 82 n. 71
lay readers 143
Lee, J. B. 129
Lee, Sackville Bolton 125, 141
Leigh, Lord 83
Leo XIII, Pope, *Apostolicae Curae* 265–7
Liberal Catholicism 257

liberalism, educational 33, 35–47, 63, 153–4, 241, 244, 257, 292
  and Rugby School 51–3, 58
liberalism, political 33, 150–4
  free-market assumptions 2, 41–2, 230–1, 244, 258, 293
  and FT 124, 152–3, 175, 197, 207–8, 242, 244, 257, 273, 293
  and Gladstone 34, 119, 197, 207
liberalism, theological:
  and Thomas Arnold 17, 53
  and Athanasian creed 146–7
  and *Essays and Reviews* 60, 65–73, 137, 192–3, 240
  and FT as Archbishop of Canterbury 257, 295
  and FT as Bishop of Exeter 119, 121–32, 145, 174–5, 190–1
  and Gladstone 33–4, 257
  and Jowett 18, 26, 34–7, 52–3, 65–6, 119, 131, 174–5, 190
  and Noetics 16
  and Stanley 52, 67, 119, 131
  and university reform 33
Liddell, Henry George 21, 196, 214
Liddon, H. P.:
  Bampton Lectures 62
  as chancellor of St Paul's 220
  and *Essays and Reviews* 62–4, 68, 220
Lightfoot, J. B. 196–7
lights, ceremonial 216–17, 276–8
Lingen, Robert:
  and appointment of FT as Bishop of Exeter 127
  and appointment of FT to Rugby 55
  and Committee of Council 28, 38, 47, 55
  as governor of Rugby School 134
  and Kneller Hall 33
literature, in education 109–13
logic, FT's lectures on 26
London Dock Strike (1889) 232–5
London University:
  and teaching of theology 239, 240–1
  as teaching university 238–9
  see also King's College, London
Lubbock, Sir John (later Lord Avebury) 233
Lucretius, FT's lectures on 25–6
Lusk, Sir Andrew 233
Lux Mundi 188, 220, 256
Lyne, Prebendary 125

Lyttleton, George William, 4th Baron:
and Clarendon Commission 92–3, 101,
103, 108, 110
and Taunton Commission 114, 116–17

Macaulay, Zachary, as governor of Sierra
Leone 6
McDonnell, Sir Schomberg 285
Mackarness, John Fielder 124–5, 130, 145
Maclagan, W. D., Archbishop of York 266,
276–8, 287, 293
Mallock, W. H. 169
Manning, H. E., Archbishop of
Westminster 233–5
Maronite Church 247
marriage, to deceased wife's sister 155
Martin, Dr G. C.(organist of St Paul's) 272
Marvin, F. S. 149 n. 47
masturbation, views on 154
mathematics:
in education 10, 42, 46, 96, 109, 111
FT's ability in 19, 23, 25, 175, 267
Mather, F. C. 13 n. 39
Maurice, F. D.:
and King's College, London 72
as theological liberal 119
Maynooth grant 34
Mayor, Robert B. 74–6
meritocracy, and education 44–5
Mews, Stuart 261 n. 27
Miall, Mr 284–5
middle class:
and education 40–2, 46, 49, 98, 114, 116,
170
and employment 2
and female emigration 232
and Rugby School 98
and social life 3
Milman, Henry Hart 89
miracle:
and agnosticism 147
and invariability of nature 66, 183–4, 188
mitre
and coronation of Edward VII 283–4
proposal to present to FT 259, 269
modern languages, at Rugby School 96,
111–12
Momerie, Alfred 237
monarchy, changes 2
Monro, 25
Moore, Aubrey Lackington 193
Moorhouse, James, Bishop of
Manchester 249–50, 254

morality:
and education 57, 240
in FT 180–1, 183, 188, 268
social 230–1
see also sexuality
Morant, Robert 291
Moseley, Henry 39, 116
Müller, Max 60, 69
Munro, H. A. J. 25

Nash, V. 233 n. 58
National Council of Evangelical Free
Churches 291
National Society 48, 115, 148
Neale, John Mason 130
Neligan, Bishop of Auckland 290
Nelson, Robert, *Companion for the Festivals
and Fasts of the Church of
England* 12–13
Newdegat, Charles Newdigate 83
Newman, J. H. 16, 18, 20, 220
and reason and morality 183
Tract XC 16, 18, 21, 59, 72
Noetics of Oriel 16
Nonconformity:
and churchyard burial 148
and education 37–8, 49–50, 150–2, 241,
245, 291–3
and FT 246–7
Norfolk, Henry Fitzalan-Howard, 15th
Duke 285
Northcote, Sir Stafford 104–5, 114, 116 n.
79, 122

Oakeley, Frederic 18, 21, 79
Oakley, J., Dean of Manchester 215
Old Catholics 247, 265, 276
Oxford and Cambridge Local
Examinations Board 42, 114
Oxford Essays (1856) 37–41, 46, 60, 64–5,
112–13, 117
Oxford Movement 16
and Athanasian creed 146
and FT 19–22, 26–7, 34
and liberalism 17
and reason and revelation 16–17
see also *Tract XC*; Tractarianism
Oxford University:
and grammar school examinations
41–2
and Oxford Movement 16–17
and religious tests 148, 241
see also universities

Paine, Thomas, *Age of Reason* 79
Paley, William, *Natural Theology* 66,
   184–6, 193
Palgrave, Francis Turner 31, 65
Palmerston, Henry John Temple, 3rd
   Viscount 49, 119
parents, and religious education 41–2, 116,
   244, 291
Parratt, Sir Walter 288
Parry (secretary to Balfour) 279
Parry, Sir Charles Hubert Hastings 288
parties, political 2, 231
patronage:
   ecclesiastical 140, 148, 206, 208
   and education 152
Pattison, Mark:
   and *Essays and Reviews* 59, 66–7, 84
   and liberalism 119
   and *Oxford Essays* 65
Pelham, John, Bishop of Norwich 147
pensions, FT's support for 230
Percival, John 132, 134, 141, 292
Percy, Charles Bertie 83
Perkins, Jocelyn 282
Perry, Bishop of Iowa 250–1
Phillips, Manderille (private secretary to
   Benson) 260
Phillpotts, Henry, Bishop of Exeter 125,
   136, 138–9, 141, 151–2, 156
Phillpotts, William John 141, 154
Philpott, Henry, Bishop of Worcester 85,
   87, 123, 127, 134
politics:
   changes 2
   and clergy 231
   Toryism of FT 19, 257–8
   see also liberalism, political
Ponsonby, Sir Henry 194–6
Portal, Abbé Fernand 266
poverty:
   of FT 19, 21, 24, 27, 155
   of Temple family 9, 16
   working-class 27, 230–2
Powell, Baden 16
   and *Essays and Reviews* 66, 72
prayer for the dead 274–5
Privy Council:
   Committee on Education 28–32, 41, 55,
      115–16, 148–9
   Coronation Committee 285, 286–7
   Judicial Committee 89, 154, 223, 226–7
processions, and carrying of lights 216,
   276–8

Protestant Truth Society 276–7
Prothero, Rowland 87 n. 90
Public Worship Regulation Act (1874)
   137
Pusey, E. B. 12, 14, 19–20, 23, 120–1, 124

Quarterly Review, and *Essays and
   Reviews* 69–70, 84

Raikes, Robert 151
Ram, Henry 277, 278
Real Presence 275
reason and revelation:
   and Noetics 16–17
   and Tractarians 16–17
Reformed Episcopal Church 144
religion:
   and human development 61–3, 67
   and science 16, 66, 166–7, 169, 171–2,
      174–84, 188–93, 239
   and university 16–17
remarriage, views on 155
Replies to 'Essays and Reviews' 81
Reservation of the Sacrament 279
revelation:
   and reason 16–17
   through Bible and Creation 176, 179–80,
      182–3, 236
Rhodes, Cecil 273
Richards, H. C. 277
Richards, Henry 204 n. 30
Ridding, George, Bishop of Southwell 243
Ridge, Ernest 260–3
Riley, Athelstan 277
ritualism:
   and FT 227–8, 230, 240, 245, 275–80, 281,
      294–5
   and imprisonment of clergy 143, 144,
      148, 218, 222
   and politics 291
   protests 216–20, 275
   support for 220–1
   and Tait 137
   see also ceremonial
Robertson (Rugby School tutor) 133–4
Robinson, Armytage 277, 283, 285–6
Roby, H. J. 114 n. 75, 117
Rolle, Lady L. B. 157
Roman Catholicism:
   and education 291
   and Maynooth grant 34
   and relationships with Church of
      England 265–6

Rosebery, Archibald Philip Primrose, 5th
    Earl 288
Rugby School:
    and academic standards 57, 94–5,
        103
    and Arnold 17, 21, 23, 36, 44, 52–5, 57–8,
        64, 99–103, 106
    and boarding-houses 58, 96, 105–8
    and boys' beer 105
    and chapel 53 n. 7, 55, 57–8, 101–3
    and Clarendon Commission 92–101,
        103–5, 107–13, 118, 178
    curriculum 96–8, 108–13
    discipline 103–4
    effects of Crimean War 53–4
    effects on FT 91–2
    and fellowships 96
    finances 93–6
    foundation 56–7
    foundationers and boarders 95, 97–9
    and FT as Headmaster 55–118, 158
    and games 100–2, 105
    governors 113, 131–2, 134–5, 164, 290
    and liberal education 45
    and liberalism and conservatism 52–5,
        112–13
    and private tutors 96, 107–8
    and successor to Temple 131–5
    and Tait 23, 30, 52–6, 58, 100
    trustees 54–5, 57, 73, 78, 82–7, 92–3,
        95–6, 113, 131–5
    see also *Essays and Reviews*; Goulburn,
        E. M.; Hayman, Henry; Jex Blake,
        T. W.
rural deaneries:
    in Exeter 140, 156
    in London 203, 204, 206, 210, 212–13,
        227–8
    restoration of rural deans 209–10
Russell, Lord John 39, 49, 56

Sabli, Namadalla 247
St Albans, diocese 198
St Augustine's College, Canterbury 291
St Cuthbert's, Philbeach Gardens 214–18,
    277, 284
St Johns, Norwich 277
St Paul's Cathedral, reredos 218–21
Salisbury, Robert A. T. G. Cecil, 3rd Marquis
    245, 254–6, 258, 281, 292, 294
Sanday, William 256
Sanders, Henry:
    as Archdeacon of Exeter 141

    as Headmaster of Blundell's
        School 14–15
    as Vicar of Sowton 125, 129
Sandford, E. G., *Memoirs of Archbishop
        Temple*
    and Benson 157
    and coronation of Edward VII 289
    and FT as Archbishop of
        Canterbury 257, 269–70, 273, 289,
        290
    and FT at Balliol 25–6, 82
    and FT as Bishop of Exeter 121 n. 8,
        138–40, 141, 155, 157–8, 174
    and FT as Bishop of London 198, 221,
        224, 230, 237–8, 244
    and FT as Chaplain-in-Ordinary 90
    and FT on education 45
    and FT's Bampton lectures 179–81, 188,
        190
    and FT's early life 4–5, 8
    and FT's health 51, 263
    and FT's ordination 29
    and Octavius Temple 7
    and Rugby School 54–5, 58, 75 n. 55, 97,
        99–100, 290
    sources 18 n. 52, 97, 99–100
Sandford, Francis 55
Sandford memoirs, *see* Sandford, E. G.,
        Memoirs of Archbishop Temple
Schools Inquiry Commission, *see* Taunton
        Commission
science:
    in education 39–40, 42–3, 45–6, 54,
        109–12, 170, 178
    and evolution 167–9, 171, 172–4
    and FT 61, 109–11, 128, 166, 175–93
    and theology 16, 66, 166–7, 169, 171–2,
        174–8, 179–84, 188–93, 239
Scott, George Gilbert 154
Scott, Robert:
    friendship with FT 20–1, 25, 37, 56, 73,
        76, 85
    and mastership of Balliol 35–6, 132
Scott (Rugby School tutor) 134
Selborne, Roundell Palmer, 1st Earl 238–9
sexuality, FT's views 154–5, 200–1
Shaftesbury, Anthony Ashley Cooper, 7th
        Earl 27, 119–21, 232
Shairp, J. C. 82–3
Sheepshanks, John, Bishop of
        Norwich 277
Sheriffe, Lawrence 55
Sidgwick, Arthur 92 n. 5, 97, 101, 104

Sierra Leone:
  Liberated Africans Department 7
  and Octavius Temple 6–7
Simpson, J. B. Hope 57 n. 18, 58
Sion College 238
Sisters of the Church, Kilburn 228–9,
  230
Sisters of the Faith, Stoke Newington
  229–30
Skipwith, Sir Thomas 83
slavery, abolition 7
Smith, Sir Herbert Llewellyn 233 n. 58
Smith, Prebendary 125
Snell, F. J., *The Early Associations of
  Archbishop Temple* 4–5
Social Science Association, and Schools
  Inquiry Commission 114
society, and education 61
Society of Antiquaries 283, 286
society, changes 2
Society of St Dunstan 284
South African War 273–5
  and day of intercession 274
  and prayer for the dead 274–5
  and war victims 273–4
Spencer, Herbert:
  *Education, Intellectual, Moral, and
    Physical* 169–70, 178
  and First Cause 173–4, 181–2, 186
  First Principles 170–4
  and FT 176–80, 183, 185–7, 191–2, 256,
    258
  and survival of the fittest 168, 173
Spurgeon, C. H. 232
Stanford, Sir Charles Villiers 288
Stanley, A. P. 7, 252–3, 295
  and Balliol 22
  and commentaries on Pauline
    Epistles 35, 52
  as Dean of Westminster 132
  and denominational education 241
  and *Edinburgh Review* 69, 84, 88–9
  and *Essays and Reviews* 60, 69–70, 73–4,
    78, 84–9, 131
  and FT's preferment 121
  and liberalism 52, 67, 119, 131
  and Rugby School 52–3
Stanley, Edward Henry Smith, Lord
  Alderley 86–7, 114, 116 n. 79
Stephenson, A. M. G. 251 n. 102
Stubbs, William, Bishop of Oxford 223,
  224–5, 265–6
succession, apostolic 208–9

Sumner, John Bird, Archbishop of
  Canterbury, and *Essays and
  Reviews* 70–1
Sunday schools 150–1, 153
Tait, Archibald Campbell:
  as Archbishop of Canterbury 120, 142,
    263, 294
  and Athanasian creed 146–7
  at Balliol 18, 21–2, 189
  as Bishop of London 50, 70–2, 119
  and bishops' meetings 142
  and clergy discipline 218
  and Convocation 145
  death 157, 194
  and *Essays and Reviews* 70–82, 84, 86–9,
    125, 137, 157
  and FT's preferment 119–21, 125, 128–9,
    131
  ill-health 125, 128, 144 n. 31
  influence on FT 22–5, 44, 49, 51, 296
  and Irish Church disestablishment
    119–20
  and Rugby 23, 30, 52–6, 58, 100
  and Schools Inquiry Commission 114
Talbot, Edward S., Bishop of Rochester
  254
Tate, Thomas 31
Tatham, Prebendary 125
Taunton Commission 114–18, 150, 152, 153,
  159, 258, 293
Taunton, Henry Labouchere, 1st
  Baron 114–17, 159
teacher, as role model 43–4, 45–6, 48, 63, 240
teacher training 27–32, 49–50, 244
  pupil-teachers 148–9
  see also Kneller Hall
teetotalism 19, 139, 155, 206, 232
temperance movement 155, 206, 230, 232,
  246
Temple, Beatrice Blanche (wife of FT):
  at Lambeth 261
  and coronation of Edward VII 288, 290
  courtship 158–61
  family background 3, 159, 196
  and family papers 18 n. 52
  and illness and death of FT 293–4
  marriage 161–2, 252, 258
  and social issues 232
Temple, Dorcas (mother of FT):
  and early education of FT 7–9, 63
  relationship with FT 10–12, 14, 18–19,
    90–1, 158
  and religion 5, 12–14, 21, 296

Temple, Frederick (*Cont.*):
  appearance 24, 197–8, 211, 251
  as Archbishop of Canterbury 254–80,
    281–96
    accusations of senility 261–4
    appointment 254–6, 266
    assessment 294–6
    at Windsor Castle 162, 258
    and Benson's staff 260
    and bishops' meetings 274, 290
    and Canterbury residence 265
    chaplains 260, 261, 263, 264, 284
    confirmation 256, 266
    and conservatism 256–8, 295–6
    and coronation of Edward VII 1,
      281–90, 294
    and Davidson 258–62, 264, 270, 290
    and death of Victoria 281
    as diocesan bishop 264–5
    enthronization 265
    final illness and death 293–4
    and House of Lords 274–5, 291–3, 295
    and Lambeth Conference 258–9,
      267–70, 294
    and Lambeth Palace 259, 271
    and letter-writing 262, 264, 270
    and provincial bishops 270
    and ritualism 275–80, 281, 294–5
    and Roman Catholic Church 266–7
    and South African War 273–5
    staff 260–2
    and Victoria's Diamond Jubilee 270–3
  as Bishop of Exeter 120–35, 136–65
    appointment 120–1
    as Bampton lecturer 174–6, 179–93,
      236, 264
    and bishops' meetings 141–5
    and cathedral reredos 154, 219
    and clergy 136, 137–41, 148, 156, 157–8,
      197
    consecration and confirmation 125–9,
      133, 141, 145, 222, 252, 295
    and Convocation 144–7
    courtship and marriage 159–62
    and diocesan reorganization 142, 143,
      155–7
    and educational reform 150, 152–3,
      292, 293
    election 122–5, 141
    enthronization 129–31, 166
    and *Essays and Reviews* 121–7, 129–31,
      133, 136–7, 140, 144–6
    and Hayman 131–5

    and House of Lords 148–50, 157
    and laity 148
    and loyalty to Church of
      England 136–7, 147, 240
    and Old Boys meetings 4–5
    opposition to 120–5, 129–31, 136,
      144–5, 156, 189, 191, 198, 252
    and ruridecanal conferences 140, 156
    support for 128, 130–1, 145
  as Bishop of London 194–213, 214–53
    and Anglican provinces 247–8
    and bishops' meetings 144, 211, 228,
      243, 248
    and church schools 205–6, 241–6, 257
    and City churches 203–4, 247
    and clergy 200–3, 204, 206–7, 208,
      227, 236–7
    and Convocation 211
    and Davidson 194–7
    and diocesan conferences 206–8, 210,
      212–13, 238
    and *Essays and Reviews* 196, 237,
      248–51
    and family life 163
    and House of Lords 211
    and London Dock Strike 233–5
    and London University 238–41
    and national education 241–6
    and new church building 203–4, 205
    and Nonconformists 246–7
    and prosecution of King 223–7
    and religious communities 228–30
    responsibilities and delegation
      198–200
    and ritualism and ceremonial 214–28,
      230, 240, 245, 258
    and rural deaneries 203, 204, 206–7,
      209, 210, 212–13, 227–8
    and social issues 230–5
  character:
    brusqueness 24, 113, 121, 138, 139, 189,
      197, 200, 259, 262, 264, 267–9, 294
    conscientiousness 9, 19, 23–4, 58, 99
    eccentricity 26
    emotionality 26, 50–1, 99, 289–90
    enthusiasm 58, 155–6
    generosity 230
    harshness 200–2
    independence 264
    insensitivity 231, 270
    kindness 25
    and masterly inaction 201, 229, 264,
      279

naïvety 66, 155, 228
obstinacy 145, 235–6
as private person 1, 259
self-confidence 49, 92, 113, 132
sense of duty 263, 269
sense of humour 25, 116, 139, 160–1, 263
sensitivity 32
seriousness 24
simplicity 66, 190
'uncourtly manners' 139, 140, 268, 295
unwillingness to compromise 138, 154
early career:
  and Committee of Council 28–9, 38, 41, 50, 55
  as fellow of Balliol 23–8
  as inspector of training colleges 50–1
  as principal of Kneller Hall 28–33, 35, 41, 44–6, 49–50, 58, 63, 74, 112, 122, 132
education:
  academic success 15
  at Balliol College 15–23, 82
  at Blundell's School 7, 9–14, 21, 24
  at home 7–9, 46, 63
  knowledge of Greek and Latin 5, 8, 10, 163, 267
and Evangelicalism 13–14
friendships:
  as Archbishop of Canterbury 258–61
  at Balliol 19–23, 27, 33, 35–7
  at Blundell's School 11
  as Bishop of Exeter 130–2, 141, 150, 157, 175
  as Bishop of London 196, 252–3
  and *Essays and Reviews* 72–3, 76–82, 87, 90–1, 121–3, 128, 130–2, 145, 191
  and Rugby School 54
as governor of Rugby School 113, 134, 164, 290
as Headmaster of Rugby 52–118
  and academic standards 94–5, 103
  appointment 55–6, 58
  and appointment of successor 131–5
  and boarding-houses 105–8
  and boys' beer 105
  as Chaplain-in-Ordinary 90
  and Clarendon Commission 92–101, 103–5, 107–14, 118, 178
  and curriculum 96–8, 109–13

  and discipline 103–4
  as Doctor of Divinity 90
  effects of Headship 91–2
  and *Essays and Reviews* 58–70, 72–93, 113, 178
  and games 100–1, 105
  and private tutors 107–8
  relationships with pupils 91, 99–101, 158
  relationships with staff 100, 105
  salary 96
  and school chapel 101–3
  and school finances 93–6
  and Tait 52, 55–6
  and Taunton Commission 114–18, 159, 258, 293
  and trustees 82–4
health 51, 74–6, 196, 251–22, 254, 261–3, 282–3, 289, 293–4
opinions:
  on apostolic succession 208–9
  as constitutionalist 137, 147, 155, 236–7
  on education, *see* education
  and educational liberalism 35–52, 257, 292
  on establishment 207–8, 236, 245
  on patronage 140, 148, 206, 208
  political 19, 124, 231–2, 257–8, 293
  and political liberalism 124, 152–3, 175, 197, 207–8, 242, 244, 257, 273, 293
  on sexual morality 154–5, 200–1
  and teetotalism 19, 139, 155, 206, 232
  and theological liberalism 121–5, 145, 174–5, 191–3, 241–2, 254, 257, 273, 292, 295; see also *Essays and Reviews*
  on wealth and poverty 27
private life:
  early years 5–9
  engagement 3, 158–9
  marriage 161–2, 252, 258
  mother 10–12, 14, 18–19, 90–1, 158
  poverty 9, 16, 19, 21, 24, 27, 155
  relationship with sons 91, 162–5
  sister 90–1, 122, 158
  sources 4–5, 10
religious life:
  confirmation 12–14, 102
  frequency of Communion 13
  and High Church tradition 12–13, 20–1, 34, 38, 102, 257, 295–6
  ordination 29, 140
  and Oxford Movement 19–20

Temple, Frederick (*cont.*):
    writings and sermons
        'The Education of the World' 60–4,
            67–9, 73–5, 80–4, 87, 124 n. 17, 125,
            181–2, 188, 239
        'National Education' 37–41, 46, 60,
            64, 112–14, 117, 242, 244, 292
        'The Relations between Religion and
            Science' 174–93
        Rugby Sermons 82, 85
Temple, Frederick (son of FT) 162–5,
    288–9
Temple, Netta (sister of FT) 8, 27, 90–1,
    122, 158–9, 175
Temple, Octavius (father of FT):
    army career 3–4
    character 7, 9
    in Ionian Islands 3–5, 7
    marriage 8
    religious views 14
    in Sierra Leone 6–7
Temple, William (paternal grandfather of
    FT) 14
Temple, William (son of FT) 162, 163–5,
    255, 264, 288–9
Tennyson, Alfred, *Becket* 196
Theistic Church 236
theology:
    liberalism, *see* liberalism, theological
    and London University 239–41
    and science 16, 66, 166–7, 169, 171–2,
        174–84, 188–93, 239
Thirlwall, Connop, Bishop of St
    David's 79, 85, 127
Thomson, William, Archbishop of
    York 249–50, 254, 256
Thorold, A. W.:
    as Bishop of Rochester 223
    and Schools Inquiry Commission 115
Thynne, Prebendary 125
Tilliard, James 31
Tilsit, Peace (1807) 4
Tract XC 16, 18, 21, 59, 72
Tractarianism:
    and education 29, 38
    and Gladstone 35
    and Lingen 127
trade, and imperialism 2
Trower, W. J., subdean of Exeter (later
    Bishop of Oxford) 123–5, 138,
    141
Truro diocese, creation 156–7
Tully, Col. 273

unemployment 230–1
universities:
    reform 17–18, 33–7, 128
    and religious tests 148, 241
    see also Cambridge University; King's
        College, London; London
        University; Oxford University

Vaughan, H. H., and Clarendon
    Commission 93–4, 96, 108–11
Victoria, Queen:
    coronation 282, 285
    death 281, 283
    and Diamond Jubilee 270–3
    and FT's preferment 194–7, 254–6, 258,
        294
    and South African War 273–4
Voysey, Charles 236–7

Wace, Henry 238
Wadham College, Oxford 14–15
Wallace, Arthur, and natural selection
    167
Walrond, Theodore 36, 55, 132, 161
war, changes 2, 273
Ward, W. G. 18, 20, 23, 53, 79
Warner, Henry Lee:
    and Clarendon Commission 97–8,
        104–5, 108
    and Irish Home Rule 197
Warwick, Lord G. G. 83
Welldon, James 288
Wellesley, Gerald 33, 122, 195
Wellington School 121, 158
Welsh Church, disestablishment 207–8
Wesleyans, and FT 20
Westall, Henry 214–18, 277–8, 284
Westcott, B. F., Bishop of Durham 243–4,
    245, 254, 256, 268
*Westminster and Foreign Quarterly
    Review*, and *Essays and
    Reviews* 68–9, 84
Whately, Richard 16
Whewell, William, *Astronomy and General
    Physics* 166–7, 169
Whipple, Henry B., Bishop of
    Minnesota 249–50
Whitehead, Sir James, Lord Mayor of
    London 233–4
Wilberforce, Samuel, Bishop of Oxford:
    and Darwin 69, 176
    and *Essays and Reviews* 67–70, 79, 121
    and FT as Bishop of Exeter 121–2

and Goulburn 53, 55
ordination of FT 29
William IV, King, coronation 281–2, 285, 286
Williams, Isaac 20
Williams, Rowland, and *Essays and Reviews* 59, 66, 72, 89
Wilson, H. B., and *Essays and Reviews* 59, 66, 72, 89
Wilson, J. M. 111–12, 147, 292
Winnington-Ingram, Arthur 251–2, 281, 293–4
Wood, C. L. (later Lord Halifax) 214, 266

Wooll, Dr 100, 103
Woollcombe, Archdeacon 125
Wordsworth, Christopher, Bishop of Lincoln 125–7, 222
Wordsworth, John, Bishop of Salisbury:
and church schools 244
and prosecution of King 223, 225
and Roman Catholicism 265–7
working class:
and education 27–30, 39–41, 49
FT's support for 230

Zaba, N. F. 32, 47